ROYAL HISTORICAL S

STUDIES IN HISTO

New Series

ELECTORAL REFORM AT WORK

ELECTORAL REFORM AT WORK

LOCAL POLITICS
AND NATIONAL PARTIES, 1832–1841

Philip Salmon

THE ROYAL HISTORICAL SOCIETY
THE BOYDELL PRESS

First published 2002
The Royal Historical Society, London
in association with
The Boydell Press, Woodbridge
Reprinted in paperback and transferred to digital printing 2011
The Boydell Press, Woodbridge

ISBN 97 0 86193 261 0 hardback
ISBN 978 1 84383 642 1 paperback

The Boydell Press is an imprint of Boydell & Brewer Ltd
PO Box 9, Woodbridge, Suffolk IP12 3DF, UK
and of Boydell & Brewer Inc,
668 Mt Hope Avenue, Rochester, NY 14620, USA
website: www.boydellandbrewer.com

A CIP catalogue record for this book is available
from the British Library

Library of Congress Catalog Card Number 2002066444

This publication is printed on acid-free paper

Contents

List of Illustrations

Frontispiece: Detail from the 'Bedford Town Election' of 1832, dated 1835, artist unknown

Plate Acknowledgements

The frontispiece/jacket illustration is reproduced by permission of Bedford Borough Council, England; plate 1 by permission of Suffolk County Council, Libraries and Heritage; plates 2 and 3 by permission of Nottingham City Council Leisure and Community Services, Local Studies Library; and plate 4 by permission of the Mansell Collection: Timepix/Rex Features.

List of Figures

List of Tables

Publication of this volume was aided by a grant from the Scouloudi Foundation, in association with the Institute of Historical Research. It was further assisted by a generous award from the Marc Fitch Fund.

Acknowledgements

This account of the workings of the first Reform Act started life as a University of Oxford doctorate, fashioned and completed under the direction of David Eastwood, and examined by Angus Hawkins and the late John Phillips in 1997. Its subsequent development owes a great deal to their advice and encouragement, and to the invaluable contribution of Peter Mandler during his two-year stint as my advisory editor. I am also grateful to John Prest for his punctilious reading of early drafts and generosity with ideas over many years, Michael Hart for his electoral expertise (and library), Miles Taylor for a very useful review at a critical stage and, my fellow doctoral student Joe Coohill for sharing his research on the early Liberal party. My former tutor William Thomas provided many useful transcripts, while Matthew Cragoe offered important advice and information relating to Wales. The extent to which I am indebted to the late John Phillips will be immediately apparent to those familiar with his work, especially in the final chapter on municipal reform. His assistance with an earlier article on this subject was invaluable and I am grateful to the editor of *Parliamentary History*, Clyve Jones, for allowing me to reproduce part of it here in a revised format.

My past and present colleagues at the 1820–32 section of the *History of Parliament* in the University of London deserve a special mention. Stephen Farrell painstakingly read the entire text, while Howard Spencer, David Fisher, Terry Jenkins and Margaret Escott have all assisted at various stages, especially on local constituency matters. Christine Linehan, the executive editor of this series, made many improvements while preparing the book for publication. Numerous archivists and librarians have also assisted me with this project, particularly those in the local record offices of England and Wales. Without their patience and expertise, not least in locating often uncatalogued solicitors' papers, there would have been little to write about.

My ultimate debt is to the Salmon and Ulmschneider families, who have borne the brunt of my obsession with this topic for almost a decade. My mother and sister, in particular, have willingly helped in local archives and with the counting of literally thousands of votes in pollbooks. Mark Shaffer and Noel Norris have provided much valued friendship and support. I can't promise that they won't be called on again, but I am assured that the first monograph is always the hardest. In finally completing it, as in everything else, I have been aided at every stage by my wife Katharina. I can only hope that her first book on Anglo-Saxon markets has benefited as much from me as this study owes to her.

Philip Salmon
Oxford, January 2001

Abbreviations

BeRO	Berkshire Record Office
BIHR	*Bulletin of the Institute of Historical Research*
BL	British Library
Bodl. Lib.	Bodleian Library, Oxford
BRO	Bedfordshire Record Office
BuRO	Buckinghamshire Record Office
CKS	Centre for Kentish Studies
CRO	Cornwall Record Office
CuRO	Cumbria Record Office
DRO	Devon Record Office
DuRO	Durham County Record Office
EHR	*English Historical Review*
ERO	Essex Record Office
GCRO	Glamorgan Courty Record Office
GRO	Gloucestershire Record Office
HeRO	Hertfordshire Record Office
HJ	*Historical Journal*
HMC	Royal Commission on Historical Manuscripts
HRO	Hampshire Record Office
HuntRO	Huntingdonshire Record Office
JBS	*Journal of British Studies*
LAD	Lambeth Archives Department
LAS	Lincolnshire Archives Service
LDA	Leeds District Archives
LRO	Lancashire Record Office
NAO	Nottinghamshire Archives Office
NLW	National Library of Wales
NRO	Northamptonshire Record Office
PH	*Parliamentary History*
PP	Parliamentary papers
PRO	Public Record Office
RCA	Reform Club archives
ShRO	Shropshire Record Office
SoRO	Somerset Record Office
SRO	Sheffield Record Office
StRO	Staffordshire Record Office
SufRO	Suffolk Record Office
SuRO	Surrey Record Office
UCL	University College London
VCH	Victoria County History
WRO	Wiltshire and Swindon Record Office
WSRO	West Sussex Record Office
WYAS	West Yorkshire Archive Service

Introduction

This book is about the political modernisation of Britain that resulted from the 'Great' Reform Act of 1832. It argues that this extensively debated parliamentary reform moved the nation far closer to a modern type of electoral system than has previously been supposed, and that this happened in two principal ways. First, this study explains how the Reform Act's curiously neglected practical provisions, far from being mere 'small print', as has often been assumed, transformed the business of obtaining the vote and led to the emergence of new forms of party organisation and voter partisanship after 1832. Second, it demonstrates how the Reform Act's long overlooked constitutional interaction with other institutions of early nineteenth-century government, most notably the parish vestry, the board of guardians and the municipal corporation, caused new types of nationally-oriented party structures to multiply through all levels of British politics, so laying the foundations for the representative democracy of the Victorian era.

Such a work is long overdue. Charles Seymour's classic account of the operation of the early Victorian representative system dates from 1915 and Norman Gash's rather different kind of study, which was primarily concerned with the persistence of electoral corruption and control, from 1953.[1] New archive collections and analytical techniques, including the rise of a whole new discipline of psephology, would alone make a fresh investigation of this subject necessary, but this book also has a further imperative behind it. Since the 1950s most scholarly attention in the field of nineteenth-century elections has centred on the study of voting behaviour, with little consideration for the constitutional context in which it actually took place. Using the information in pollbooks, numerous studies have examined how Victorians voted in terms of their class, occupation and religion. This is not the place to offer a detailed critique of this type of electoral sociology.[2] Neither, given the well-rehearsed difficulties of analysing pollbooks, is it entirely fair to point out that the only widespread conclusion to emerge from such work (beyond oddities, like the absurd fact that most butchers voted Tory) has been the strikingly close association of religious Nonconformity and the Liberal vote.[3]

---

1 Charles Seymour, *Electoral reform in England and Wales: the development and operation of the parliamentary franchise*, New Haven, Conn. 1915; Norman Gash, *Politics in the age of Peel: a study in the technique of parliamentary representation, 1830–1850*, London 1953.
2 For an excellent critical study of this type of electoral sociology see Jon Lawrence and Miles Taylor (eds), *Party, state and society: electoral behaviour in Britain since 1820*, Aldershot 1997.
3 See, for example, John Vincent, *Pollbooks: how Victorians voted*, Cambridge 1967, 16,

What is abundantly clear, however, is that this type of sociological analysis has now run its course, and that there still exists a need for a wider historical explanation of the processes governing electoral behaviour.[4] The most recent computer-assisted studies of borough pollbooks have convincingly demonstrated the rise of far more persistent forms of voter partisanship after 1832.[5] But the reasons behind that partisanship are still unclear. Many voters were not political ideologues, nor even perhaps ideologically aware. Indeed a significant minority of them, as this study reveals, remained remarkably indifferent to their new voting rights in the immediate aftermath of 1832. Precisely how they became attached to party and, in direct contrast to the voting habits of their predecessors, then began to exhibit increasingly persistent forms of partisan allegiance in successive elections, continue to be questions of major importance, which this book aims to answer.

The account that follows offers a startling new insight into the role of the representative system itself in shaping electoral behaviour. Its overarching argument is simply that the manner in which people acquired their vote had a powerful impact on how they perceived and used it. This is not to deny the importance of political principles and ideology in determining how voters behaved or how political parties fared in this period. Nor is it to downplay the role of cultural and constitutional idioms in shaping popular perceptions of party and state.[6] It simply brings to prominence those neglected aspects of the electoral system which helped to generate party attachments in the first place, by bringing individual voters face to face with political realities on a regular basis. These practical and technical mechanisms have been overshadowed by ideology, the cant of party and the rhetoric of Westminster in previous accounts of British political life. This book redresses the balance by showing how the operation of the reformed electoral system itself had a major impact upon individual political awareness and national party performance after 1832.

61–4; Richard W. Davis, *Political change and continuity, 1760–1885: a Buckinghamshire study*, Newton Abbot 1972, 103–97; T. J. Nossiter, *Influence, opinion and political idioms in reformed England: case studies from the north-east, 1832–74*, Hassocks 1975, 162–76; John A. Phillips, *The Great Reform Bill in the boroughs: English electoral behaviour, 1818–1841*, Oxford 1992, 239–94.

4   This point has been powerfully made by Miles Taylor, 'Interests, parties and the state: the urban electorate in England, c. 1820–72', in Lawrence and Taylor, *Party, state and society*, 50–78.

5   Phillips, *Boroughs*; John A. Phillips and Charles Wetherell, 'The Great Reform Bill of 1832 and the rise of partisanship', *Journal of Modern History* lxiii (1991), 621–46, and 'The Great Reform Act of 1832 and the political modernization of England', *American Historical Review* c (1995), 411–36.

6   See James Vernon, *Politics and the people: a study in English political culture c. 1815–1867*, Cambridge 1993.

Historiography

The Reform Act of 1832, with its extension of the franchise and re-distribution of English and Welsh constituency seats, occupies a central place in the
political and social history of modern Britain. The first of a series of major
electoral reforms – 1832, 1867, 1884 and 1918 – from which there evolved a
remarkably long-lasting voting system, its intentions and effects have
inspired a vast and complex debate, spanning some 150 years of historical
writing.[7] Few events in modern British history have so deeply divided not just
contemporaries, many of whom were moved either to apocalyptic
forebodings or to utopian prophecies during its stormy passage through parliament, but also subsequent generations of politicians and writers, whose
polemics have often echoed those of the original protagonists. Earlier
commentators included Karl Marx, who denounced its aristocratic trickery,
and George Macaulay Trevelyan, the last representative of a grand Victorian
tradition of so-called 'Whig' historians, for whom the Reform Act was synon-
ymous with liberal and democratic progress.[8] Reacting against the prevailing
'Whig' interpretation, a subsequent generation of mid twentieth-century
'conservative' revisionists, taking their cue from Sir Lewis Namier, then
questioned the Reform Act's popular political significance altogether.[9] Since
then, this Namierite revisionism has itself been revised by a younger generation of historians, who have opened up new lines of inquiry by rehabilitating
the role of party and principle in explanations of political life, especially in
terms of language and ideologies, and more recently by adopting 'post-
modernist' approaches.[10]

Before outlining the principal arguments of this enduring debate, it is
worth raising two of its most significant features straight away. First, although
some parts of the Reform Act have received a great deal of attention – abolition of 'rotten boroughs', re-distribution of parliamentary seats, extension of
the borough franchise to £10 householders and the county vote to £50

---

[7] The subsequent electoral reforms of the twentieth century were far less comprehensive
and controversial: David Butler, *The electoral system in Britain since 1918*, Oxford 1963, and
British general elections since 1945, Oxford 1989; Martin Pugh, *The evolution of the British electoral system, 1832–1987* (Historical Association pamphlet, 15), London 1990.

[8] Karl Marx, 'The elections in England, Tories and Whigs', and 'Lord John Russell', in *Karl
Marx and Frederick Engels on Britain*, Moscow 1953, 349–55, 426–45; G. M. Trevelyan, *Lord
Grey of the Reform Bill*, London 1920.

[9] Gash, *Politics in the age of Peel*; Donald Southgate, *The passing of the Whigs, 1832–1886*,
London 1962.

[10] For example Richard Brent, *Liberal Anglican politics: Whiggery, religion, and Reform,
1830–1841*, Oxford 1987; Frank O'Gorman, *Voters, patrons, and parties: the unreformed electorate of Hanoverian England, 1734–1832*, Oxford 1989; Peter Mandler, *Aristocratic government in the age of Reform: Whigs and Liberals, 1830–1852*, Oxford 1990; Phillips, *Boroughs*;
Joseph Coohill, 'Ideas of the Liberal party: perceptions, agendas, and Liberal politics in the
House of Commons', unpubl. DPhil. diss. Oxford 1998; Vernon, *Politics and the people*.

occupiers[11] – the same cannot be said of the remaining two-thirds of its provisions.[12] Many of these admittedly appear rather mundane – annual voter registration, shortened duration of polls, standardised election procedures – but, as this study demonstrates, at the time they represented fundamental innovations, whose 'knock-on' effects profoundly altered the legal and constitutional framework of political activity on the ground, sometimes in completely unforeseen ways. This leads to the second and more important point, which is that one of the striking peculiarities of the existing literature has been its tendency to gloss over the practical workings of the Reform Act and to lose sight of its operational details. The study of electoral behaviour has, in effect, become detached from the study of the representative system. Historians have not only assumed that the Reform Act functioned as it was supposed to, translating legislative intent into electoral reality, but they have also misconstrued some of its more basic provisions. Anyone reading the act itself, rather than the *English historical documents* abstract, for example, might be surprised to discover that it did not limit the post-1832 freeman franchise in boroughs to the existing voters only.[13] It did not stipulate 'that only those freemen who possessed the vote in 1832 could continue to exercise the vote during their lifetime', as one writer, in line with many previous accounts, has recently stated.[14] On the contrary, clause 32 of the Reform Act specifically allowed for the creation of new resident freemen after 1832, 'in respect of birth and servitude', and only abolished the electoral rights of the non-resident freemen and possible future 'honorary freemen' or 'freemen by marriage'.[15] Indeed, it was precisely because of this, that when the old municipal corporations were abolished in 1835, responsibility for all those who 'might hereafter have acquired, in respect of birth or servitude, as a burgess or freeman, the right of voting' had to be transferred to the new annually elected town councils.[16]

---

[11] For full details of the Reform Act's redistribution of seats and the voting qualifications in operation after 1832 see appendices 1 and 2.

[12] Of the Reform Act's eighty-two clauses, only twenty-eight dealt with these better known provisions and the related issue of boundaries: 2 Will. IV c. 45, 725–30, clauses 1–10, 12–25, 27–30.

[13] A. Aspinall and E. A. Smith (eds), *English historical documents*, XI: *1783–1832*, London 1971, 341–53.

[14] Taylor, 'Interests, parties and the state', 55. Similarly misleading statements can be found in H. J. Hanham, *The reformed electoral system in Great Britain, 1832–1914* (Historical Association pamphlet, 69), London 1968, 34, and Eric J. Evans, *The Great Reform Act of 1832*, London 1994, 68–9, and can be traced as far back as Charles R. Dod's *Electoral facts*, London 1853, which incorrectly stated that the franchise of many boroughs had been 'limited as usual in 1832 to the existing resident freemen'. The same errors were reproduced in the Harvester reprint, edited by H. J. Hanham, Brighton 1972. For further details of this aspect of the freeman franchise see ch. 6 below.

[15] 2 Will. IV c. 45, 730, clause 32; William Russell, *A treatise on the Reform Act . . .*, London 1832, 43; Seymour, *Electoral reform*, 28.

[16] 5 and 6 Will. IV c. 76, 1014, clause 4.

This book's emphasis on these kinds of practical details, far from being just an exercise in filling an historiographical gap, adds a much needed fresh perspective to the debate that has raged about the broader political significance of 1832. Most assessments of the Reform Act's long-term impact have concentrated on the manner in which it was passed, and have barely paused to consider its 'small print'. As John Cannon has remarked, 'the provisions of the bill were less important than the *fact* of the bill, and it is as a *political* action that it must, ultimately, be considered'.[17] Thus, in his reading, 1832 marked not just 'the beginning of the transformation from one political system to another but also the foundation achievement of modern conservatism'.[18] Much of this kind of political analysis has inevitably focused on the motives of those behind the Reform Act, a major theme being whether the Whigs were making a 'great concession' to popular pressure, in order to 'prevent the necessity for revolution' as their leader Lord Grey, the prime minister, told parliament,[19] or whether their actions instead amounted to some form of political ploy, 'extraordinary tricks, frauds, and juggles', as Marx put it.[20] In a bold, but much mauled, interpretation, D. C. Moore asserted that the Reform Act was less a 'concession' than a conservative 'cure', designed to consolidate the political power of its landed promoters by separating urban and rural constituencies.[21] The 'concessional' view has proved the more acceptable, but has also prompted another type of debate about whether the Reformers were motivated by fear or by foresight. In the first full-length study of the act, published by W. N. Molesworth in 1865, for example, the Whigs were seen as being pushed into Reform by 'great social and popular forces'.[22] This view was echoed some fifty years later by G. S. Veitch's survey of its longer-term causes, in which it was asserted that 'a first and necessary step in parliamentary reform' was ultimately 'carried because public opinion demanded it'.[23] More recently Nancy LoPatin's study of political unions has again given 'significant weight to the view that the people forced the issue of Reform in 1832'.[24] Earlier 'Whig' historians like J. R. M. Butler and G. M. Trevelyan, however, highlighted 'the existence in parliament of a party whose leaders had long prepared the minds of the aristocracy

---

17 John Cannon, *Parliamentary reform, 1640–1832*, Cambridge 1973, 262.
18 Ibid. Similar, though less explicit, themes can be found in Michael Brock, *The Great Reform Act*, London 1973, and E. A. Smith, *Lord Grey, 1764–1845*, Oxford 1990.
19 T. B. Macaulay, *The complete works of Lord Macaulay*, London 1898, xi. 489; *Hansard*, 3rd ser. i. 613.
20 Marx, 'Lord John Russell', 432.
21 D. C. Moore, 'Concession or cure: the sociological premises of the first Reform Act', *HJ* ix (1966), 39–59. Moore's contribution is examined in more detail in ch. 4 below.
22 W. N. Molesworth, *The history of the Reform Bill of 1832*, London 1865, 2.
23 G. S. Veitch, *The genesis of parliamentary reform*, London 1913, repr. 1964, 355.
24 Nancy D. LoPatin, *Political unions, popular politics and the Great Reform Act of 1832*, London 1999, 14.

for Reform'.[25] For them, parliamentary reform was not forced upon the Whigs, but represented a deliberate and wise concession to popular feeling by 'liberal-minded aristocrats, peculiar to the history of our island'. In their broader political teleology, it was the very existence of these liberal saviours that explained 'why the political traditions and instincts that the English have inherited differ so profoundly from those of Germany, of France, or even of America'. 'For it can hardly be believed', declared Butler, 'that had they not acted as they did, England could have survived the years between 1830 and 1848 without some violent rebellion'.[26]

As well as differing on the political motives of those behind the Reform Act, historians have conducted an equally confusing debate about its effects, even over the most basic changes wrought in the size and structure of the electorate.[27] Once again surprisingly little account has been taken of the practical workings of the electoral system itself. For many years, for instance, the most widely held view was that the number of voters had increased by almost a half, from approximately 435,000 in 1831 to 653,000 by 1833. John Cannon's drastic reduction of the former figure to 366,000, however, suggested an increase which was 'nearer to 80% than the 50% usually quoted', until it became clear that his calculations were based upon the number of electors who actually polled, rather than the number of electors who were entitled to vote.[28] The original figure has since been reinstated, most notably in the work of Frank O'Gorman, but more recently Derek Beales has emphasised a whole new raft of problems affecting calculations of the pre-Reform electorate.[29] The most significant of these is what Beales identifies as 'plural voting', meaning the existence of 'individuals with votes in more than one constituency', who may have swelled the number of persons possessing the vote under the unreformed system by roughly 10 per cent.[30]

Similar difficulties, however, also present themselves in dealing with the electoral registers after 1832. As this study shows, many of these were not only incomplete and subject to the influence of local party manipulation, they were also beset with double or triple entries created by voters possessing more than one type of franchise, or qualifying for property in more than one parish.[31] Moreover, although residence became the pre-condition of voter

25 J. R. M. Butler, *The passing of the Reform Bill*, London 1914, 426.
26 Trevelyan, *Lord Grey*, 368; Butler, *Reform Bill*, pp. vii, 426. The most recent view of Lord Grey's role in the passage of Reform, however, is that it 'was not so much the outcome of a lifetime's commitment to liberty or liberal principles, as the result of political accident and party interest': Smith, *Lord Grey*, 3.
27 See, in particular, D. E. D. Beales, 'The electorate before and after 1832: the right to vote, and the opportunity', *PH* xi (1992), 139–50; Frank O'Gorman, 'The electorate before and after 1832: a reply', ibid. xii (1993), 171–83.
28 Cannon, *Parliamentary reform*, 259.
29 O'Gorman, *Voters, patrons, and parties*, 178–80.
30 Beales, 'The electorate before and after 1832', 144–5.
31 See ch. 1 below. For the registration returns and numbers who polled in each constituency in this period see appendix 3.

qualification in borough constituencies after 1832, the problem of 'plural voting' in the counties remained, both in terms of non-resident voters and of the additional county votes which borough electors might acquire. Much has been made of the Reform Act's supposed restrictions on polling in counties by borough electors, most notably by D. C. Moore, who used the curtailment of a freeholder's right to vote in the county (when the same property qualified him for a vote in the borough) to buttress his argument that Reform was designed to separate urban and rural constituencies, and thereby to restore the electoral potency of 'deference communities'.[32] As this study shows, however, Moore's hypothesis not only overlooked the extent to which the county electorate included all urban 40s. freeholders who did not meet the new £10 household qualification in the boroughs; it also failed to recognise the growing phenomenon whereby an enfranchised borough householder, in possession of another separate freehold not 'occupied by himself', could also qualify for an additional county vote.[33] At the same time, it put forward a sociological premiss which was rather at odds with the detailed reports drawn up by the boundary commissioners, many of whom, as one of them said, had 'pledged . . . to die on the benches of the House of Commons sooner than allow town influence to be shut out of county elections'.[34]

By focusing on the process of enfranchisement itself, this book not only helps to clear up much of this confusion about the reformed electorate, but also adds an important dimension which has hitherto been missing. Most discussions of the impact of the Reform Act upon voters concentrate on their increased numbers, their enhanced 'opportunity' to vote and their new patterns of electoral behaviour. This emphasis on quantitative change, however, has obscured many of the qualitative shifts that occurred after 1832. By separating the business of claiming a vote from the business of casting it, for instance, the new annual registration system encouraged those who qualified each year to regard themselves as voters, irrespective of whether or not there was an actual election.[35] Instead of the franchise being a privilege conferred only at election time and then only in the event of contest, often on a highly localised basis, it now became a far more permanent and personal possession, which was defined on a national basis by law. In those constituencies where 'corporate bodies' had previously controlled electoral rights, this

---

[32] Moore, 'Concession or cure', 39–59; 'Political morality in mid-nineteenth century England: concepts, norms, violations', *Victorian Studies* xiii (1969–70), 5–36; and *The politics of deference: a study of the mid-nineteenth century English political system*, Hassocks 1976.
[33] 2 Will. IV. c. 45, 728, clause 24. See ch. 4 below for a full discussion.
[34] E. J. Littleton diary, 29 Feb. 1832, StRO, Hatherton MSS D260/M/7/5/26/7. Much confusion remains about the precise impact of the boundary changes and division of counties that accompanied the Reform Act, a potentially vast area of study which is in need of much fuller treatment than can be given here (and which, in any case, is already being researched by the *History of Parliament*, as part of their forthcoming volumes on the *House of Commons, 1820–32*.) For a useful overview see Gash, *Politics on the age of Peel*, 67–85.
[35] See ch. 1 below.

move to a franchise based overwhelmingly upon the votes of 'individuals' was especially pronounced.[36] Add to this the considerable financial outlay involved in claiming and retaining the reformed franchise (which in the boroughs included prompt payment of local taxes and a 1s. registration fee), not to mention the inconvenience of potentially having to defend electoral qualifications in person against challenges in a court of law, and it becomes clear that the Reform Act represented an important shift in the popular conception of the vote. This was particularly evident in the large number of cheap voter guides introduced in the aftermath of 1832, such as James Coppock's *Electors' manual; or plain directions by which every man may know his own rights, and preserve them*, which was published in 1835.[37] As well as explaining the operation of the new franchise in clear and accessible terminology, these manuals encouraged voters to think of themselves as individual, critical agents, stimulating their sense of self-importance and the notion of inviolate electoral rights, 'not inferior in importance to Magna Charta', as one guide opined.[38] These and similar elements of electoral standardisation traced in this study point to the emergence of a far more recognisably 'modern' representative system after 1832, which straightforward quantitative comparisons with its predecessor have failed to reveal.

Only a few historians have turned their attention to the practical operation of the reformed electoral system. Moisei Ostrogorski's pioneering study of British and American politics, which appeared in 1902, offered the first generalised account of Victorian electioneering processes and party organisation, but was primarily concerned with the rise of the caucus in the second half of the nineteenth century.[39] Seymour's *Electoral reform in England and Wales* provided a far more comprehensive analysis of the operation of the franchise between the first and third Reform Acts, and remains the only full-length survey of its kind.[40] Gash's *Politics in the age of Peel* took a rather different approach. This seminal account was based less on the provisions of the Reform Act as they affected individual voters, local activists and party organisations, and much more on electoral structures at the level of MPs, senior political figures and traditional landed elites. In a direct challenge to the then prevailing 'Whig' assumption that the reformed system was superior to its precursor, Gash stressed what he saw as the continuing dominance of earlier electoral idioms and techniques – pocket and rotten boroughs, venality, corruption and proprietorial influence – and concluded that 'there

---

36 On these constituencies see R. G. Thorne (ed.), *The House of Commons, 1790–1820*, London 1986, i. 34–6; O'Gorman, *Voters, patrons, and parties*, 38–43.

37 A list of similar publications can be found in the bibliography.

38 *The Reform Act with explanatory notes and an analysis by a barrister*, London 1832, 1.

39 M. Ostrogorski, *Democracy and the organisation of political parties*, London 1902.

40 The fact that this book was reprinted in its original form in 1970 speaks for itself.

was scarcely a feature of the old unreformed system that could not be found still in existence after 1832'.[41]

Gash's work has had a number of important and enduring legacies, two of which stand out as ripe for corrective treatment. First, it initiated a comparative trend by which the post-1832 world has been judged according to essentially pre-Reform criteria, overlooking the many technical differences between the two electoral systems. The vast body of the act itself, it needs to be recalled, was not concerned with the problems of lingering corruption or control which have dominated most post-Gash discussions of electoral politics, but with the entirely novel challenges posed by the mobilisation of a new and enlarged electorate. Second, although Gash positively invited 'the criticism and correction of local historians' and provided an important stimulus to this field,[42] his conclusion that the Reform Act had a minimal impact on constituency politics has left little to stand in the way of the Namierite obsession with the manoeuvres and machinations of political elites in explaining national political developments after 1832. A typical feature of the subsequent literature has been its tendency to concentrate either on 'high' politics or on local politics, with little work focusing on the interaction between these two different levels of political life.[43] The study of national party politics in the post-Reform decade has, in effect, become artificially separated from what has traditionally been seen as the less important, and perhaps less glamorous, study of provincial politics.

More recent research has done much to rehabilitate the role of local politics and to accord a central place to the constituencies in explanations of national political life. O'Gorman's magisterial study of the pre-1832 electoral system, in particular, has presented a far more positive picture of local activity, popular electoral participation and party-based voting in the century before the Reform Act.[44] His detailed reappraisal of Hanoverian politics has revealed the genuine vibrancy of local electoral culture, demonstrating that most electorates were not 'corrupt, narrow and servile', and that electoral activity, far from being 'closed', was 'public, participatory and partisan'.[45] Of even more profound significance for the post-Reform period, however, has been the pioneering work of the late John Phillips on electoral behaviour before and after 1832. In his detailed analysis of eight borough constituencies between 1818 and 1841, and in his broader statistical assessment of general election results, Phillips underlined the 'critical, indeed watershed, role of the Great Reform Act', by showing that voter partisanship not only increased

---

41 Gash, *Politics in the age of Peel*, p. x.
42 Ibid. p. xvii. Gash's innovative work included a chapter on the local politics of Berkshire.
43 Notable exceptions include Robert Stewart, *The foundation of the Conservative party, 1830–1867*, London 1978, and D. H. Close, 'The elections of 1835 and 1837 in England and Wales', unpubl. DPhil. diss. Oxford 1967.
44 O'Gorman, *Voters, patrons, and parties*.
45 Idem, 'The electorate before and after 1832', 171–2.

after 1832, but also became more persistent and less changeable. 'The "Great" Reform Act', he concluded, 'justified its epithet by altering England's political environment profoundly'.[46]

It is this marked contrast between what these recent electoral studies have argued and what older standard accounts portrayed, that makes a re-evaluation of the practical operation of the reformed electoral system so necessary. O'Gorman and Phillips, in their different ways, have helped to elevate the historical importance of the constituency and to demonstrate that extra-parliamentary politics in this period warrants serious attention. Important differences, however, have also emerged. Phillips's work on borough polls convincingly demonstrated the immense politicising effects of the Reform Act upon voting behaviour after 1832, but as O'Gorman noted, his emphasis on the 'outputs' of electoral activity rather neglected the 'very stuff of electoral politics', such as the campaigns, canvassing and other electioneering practices which preceded any borough or, for that matter, county contest. Building on his own knowledge of these campaign processes in the unreformed electoral system, O'Gorman has pointed to what he sees as the strength of 'electoral continuities' after 1832, and has suggested that it was not long before the 'newer impulses' identified by Phillips 'weakened themselves' and gave way to the 're-assertion of more traditional influence and practices'. At the same time, however, he readily acknowledges the need for a much 'firmer overall model of the post-1832 electoral system', so that 'we may with greater certainty synthesise innovative with traditional elements, ideological with material qualities and, not least, campaign processes with political considerations in order to attain a balanced perspective upon the whole question of the status of the Reform Act of 1832'.[47]

Responding to O'Gorman's prompt, this book offers a new generalised model of how the electoral system functioned in the post-Reform decade. Where it differs from previous accounts is in its insistence that the study of voting behaviour cannot be separated from the physical and constitutional context in which it took place. The key to the rapid electoral politicisation of reformed politics, it is shown, lay in the practical working of the representative system itself, particularly the legislative ambiguities of the new and imperfect voter registration process. Of greater long-term significance, however, is this study's contention that the Reform Act's 'knock-on' politicising effects were not just confined to the electorate, where most attention has traditionally been focused, but that they also helped to impose a far more nationally-oriented political system upon local parochial, municipal and administrative life. A decisive shift in the balance of electoral forces at

---

46 Phillips and Wetherell, 'The Great Reform Act of 1832', 411; Phillips, *Boroughs*, 300.
47 O'Gorman, *Voters, patrons, and parties*, 393, and 'The electorate before and after 1832', 181–3.

constituency level was initiated, as older political idioms and influences began to be outmoded by new types of party-based attachments and more permanent forms of party organisation across all levels of British politics. As the following pages of this work make clear, these developments created a post-1832 political world that was not only distinctly 'reformed', but also far more recognisably modern than has previously been supposed.

Structure

This book is divided into three parts. The first (chapters 1 to 3) examines the practical operation of the reformed electoral system and its management. Chapter 1 traces the intricate workings of the new voter registration clauses, from their place in the legislation to their practical outcome in the constituencies, and explains how the complexities and costs of registering a vote deterred many from taking up their new electoral rights. This slack take-up of the franchise, it is shown, provided the opportunity for one of the key developments separating the post-Reform world from its predecessor – the emergence of permanently established local party organisations, for attending to the registration, whose activities contributed to a process of rapid electoral politicisation and the rise of more modern forms of voting behaviour after 1832.

Precisely how the parties organised their registration campaigns, and who ultimately succeeded in the annual legal contests to enfranchise political supporters and disfranchise opponents, are the subjects of chapter 2. Considerable debate surrounds the extent to which the Reform Act triggered new developments in central election management and constituency organisation, with obvious implications for any assessment of its long-term political significance. Although the 1830s have been traditionally viewed as a 'golden age' of club government, in which the pre-Reform political centres of Brooks's and White's were supplanted by an entirely 'new type' of central party organisation based around the Carlton and Reform Clubs, the precise part played by these new London centres in the election and registration campaigns of this period remains unclear.[48] This chapter seeks to clear up much of this confusion by providing a detailed reassessment of how the parties managed their election and registration activities during the post-Reform decade. Party managers on both sides, it is shown, remained deeply suspicious of extra-parliamentary activity and eschewed any centralised or systematic management of elections and registration. Instead, it was in the constituencies, rather than at the centre, that major organisational differences emerged, which were to have a decisive impact on the parties' electoral performance and were to provide the basis of a remarkable national recovery by the Conservatives.

[48] Gash, *Politics in the age of Peel*, 393.

Countering this discussion of the way in which 1832 transformed the representative system, chapter 3 concentrates on the more traditional and colourful aspects of an election, particularly its canvassing and campaign rituals, and, not least, its financial costs. In these areas there were important similarities between the unreformed and reformed electoral systems, which have been widely noted by historians. At the same time, however, it reveals that many of these features became subtly differentiated from their past forms and were increasingly standardised, either through the statutory provisions of the Reform Act, or as a result of common developments on the ground. Polling procedures and even the official language and expenses of an election became nationally regulated, helping to create a far more uniform electoral culture. Railway development also had an important impact on election-eering in this period, so that despite elements of continuity, the holding of an election was none the less a much more modern event after 1832.

Part two (chapters 4 and 5) concentrates specifically on the Reform Act in county constituencies. Compared with the amount of sophisticated work that has recently been carried out on borough pollbooks, the paucity of research on electoral behaviour in the counties after 1832 is striking. No general survey of the rural electorate has appeared since the publication in 1976 of Moore's original but highly problematic study, which used county pollbooks to identify parishes where a majority of the electors voted the same way as their landlord as part of a 'deference community', and argued that the Reform Act actually increased, and was intended to increase, aristocratic control over the rural electorate.[49] Despite the criticism of many local historians, Moore's work has proved remarkably resilient, not least because it remains the only survey of its kind. And although alternative models of rural politics, challenging the concept of 'electoral deference', have been put forward, most cogently in the work of O'Gorman, most of the literature rebutting Moore either does not apply specifically to the county electorate of the post-Reform period, or does not extend beyond one particular locality.[50]

In an attempt to solve these problems, chapter 4 presents a new general-ised account of rural electoral processes after 1832. Backed by a series of quantitative investigations, including a detailed assessment of the electoral unanimity of over 50,000 county voters, it stresses the vitality of rural elec-toral life and sets out a new analysis of the roles of landed influence, voter independence and party organisation in determining the outcome of county contests. Rural elections, it is argued, have too readily been dismissed as the simple product of deference and dependence on the part of voters. Chapter 4

---

[49] Moore, *Deference*, passim.
[50] See, for example, Frank O'Gorman, 'Electoral deference in "unreformed" England: 1760–1832', *Journal of Modern History* lvi (1984), 391–429; J. R. Fisher, 'The limits of defer-ence: agricultural communities in a mid-nineteenth century election campaign', *JBS* xxi (1981), 90–105; Alan Heesom, ' "Legitimate" *versus* "illegitimate" influences: aristocratic electioneering in mid-Victorian Britain', *PH* vii (1988), 282–305.

demonstrates that they were far more complex than this, and were often just as genuinely participatory events as their borough counterparts. Balancing this generalised approach, chapter 5 offers a series of detailed local case studies. These explore the political dynamics of voter registration, party organisation and landed influence within the specific contexts of North Devon, South Lincolnshire, West Somerset, North Wiltshire and the West Riding of Yorkshire. Contrary to what has often been assumed, they demonstrate that registration politics was often just as critical in the counties as it was in the boroughs, and that, by its ability to settle electoral outcomes in advance, it provides a far more plausible explanation than 'deference politics' for many of the so-called 'missing contests' of the early Victorian period.[51]

In part three (chapters 6 and 7), which considers the Reform Act in the boroughs, the process of politicisation is examined from an institutional as well as from an electoral perspective. Why, it is asked, did poor law administration and municipal government become so heavily politicised during the reformed period? Why did local political parties, whose primary concern was winning parliamentary elections, become so heavily embroiled in parish politics and the elections of guardians and town councillors? These developments have been observed across a wide range of local studies, both published and unpublished, but the practical mechanisms behind these processes have never been sufficiently explained.

Chapter 6 investigates the crucial, but strangely neglected, link between taxation and voting rights in borough constituencies after 1832. Under clause 27 of the Reform Act voter registration in the boroughs became entirely dependent upon the prompt payment of assessed taxes. In both the reformed parliamentary and municipal franchises, there was effectively 'no representation without taxation' for the urban householder. This chapter shows how this formal link between rates and votes transformed the structure of local politics by providing vestries, parish officials, local rate collectors and the New Poor Law unions of 1834 with a powerful influence over borough registration. It also traces the 'knock-on' effects of these rating requirements upon the popularity of the less costly ancient-right qualifications, including the much misunderstood freeman franchise, and highlights their special implications for the Dissenting community.

Chapter 7, broadening this rating and registration theme further, explores the structural and technical relationship that existed between municipal and parliamentary elections. It explains why national party interests came to dominate not only the passage of municipal reform in the House of Commons, but also the operation of the electoral system introduced for electing town councillors in 1835. Contrary to the experience in other periods, the vast majority of England's new council voters appear to have

---

[51] Robert Stewart, *Party and politics, 1830–1852*, London 1989, 38; Evans, *Great Reform Act*, 62; D. C. Moore, 'The matter of the missing contests: towards a theory of the mid-19th century British political system', *Albion* vi (1974), 93–119.

behaved at a local level precisely as they did in parliamentary elections, investing their choice of local councillors with a nationally-oriented partisan perspective right from the outset. The practical mechanisms behind this development were not only a crucial component in the rapid process of local electoral politicisation, but, as this study reveals, they also had fundamental implications for national party performance during this period.

One final point needs to be made about how this study differs from previous accounts. The prevailing image of the reformed electoral system has in large part been shaped from a rather narrow range of sources. Earlier writers, in particular, drew almost exclusively on the papers of major political figures held in national repositories, supplemented by the London newspapers, *Hansard* and *Parliamentary papers*.[52] If nothing else, this book asserts the importance of trawling through local archives for more 'grass roots' election material. Indeed, much of the evidence on which the three different sections are based was previously assumed not to exist. Canvassing books and solicitors' correspondence, for example, were dismissed by one electoral historian of this period as 'working papers which were rarely kept beyond the time of their immediate usefulness'.[53] The emergence of more permanent forms of political activism after 1832, however, required the compilation and storage of ever-increasing quantities of just such records. The repetitive legal structure of voter registration, in particular, relied heavily upon the building up of a detailed knowledge of individual voters and local conditions in order to support claims and objections in the annual registration courts. The new constituency associations, with their permanent offices and paid officials, were an obvious repository for this type of data and although many of them failed to survive the partisan turmoil of the 1840s, some of their more sensitive papers did, especially those relating to party organisation and finance. The records of the professional election agents and local solicitors employed by these associations to execute the essential routines of electioneering are of particular value. Again the cumulative nature of registration activity, and a cultural propensity to file rather than to destroy legal documents, accounts for the survival of this material among the local archive deposits of solicitors' firms.[54] The fact that election bills were usually not settled for years after a contest, and were even sometimes disputed for decades, has also helped to ensure the preservation of original accounts and invoices among their papers.

Using these types of hitherto untapped sources, and bringing together the work of many other local historians for the first time, this study presents a new generalised account of how the reformed electoral system worked in the aftermath of 1832. It examines the practical and constitutional context in

[52] For example Gash, *Politics in the age of Peel*; Seymour, *Electoral reform*.
[53] Moore, *Deference*, 3.
[54] These can be identified by the inclusion of 'Messrs' in the manuscript collections cited in the footnotes and bibliography.

which local parties operated and the act of voting actually took place. Many previous accounts of constituency politics have, of course, highlighted the importance of regional idiosyncrasy and provincial abnormality in this period. Richard Davis's study of Buckinghamshire, for example, reminds us that 'no county, after all, is exactly like any other county', and just the same might be said of the boroughs.[55] By focusing on what was common, rather than what was unique, to each constituency, however, a new synthesis has been developed. This places particular emphasis on the political processes and electoral mechanisms which affected every voter in every constituency, irrespective of regional diversity. Tracing the annual routines and rhythms of electioneering from the perspective of those who worked the system – particularly the local political activists, party associations and professional election agents – the three separate sections of this study together construct a new account of electoral politics after 1832, appropriate to the nation as a whole. The uniting thread, linking it all together, is the practical operation of the new and complex voter registration system which was introduced in 1832. It is this which is examined in the first chapter.

[55] Davis, *Buckinghamshire*, 11.

PART I

THE REFORMED ELECTORAL SYSTEM

1

Voter Registration and the Reformed Electorate

Of the eighty-two clauses in the Reform Act of 1832, nearly a third dealt with the setting up of a system of voter registration, which was designed to settle who could and who could not vote in parliamentary elections, well in advance of any contest that might take place.[1] Despite frequent complaints, mainly by Tory MPs, that 'registration had nothing whatever to do with the principle of reform' and that the Whig government was 'acting unfairly towards the county in introducing, under the "halo" of the Reform Bill, such an innovation in the whole system of conducting elections', these clauses attracted remarkably little detailed discussion during the Reform Act's otherwise stormy passage through parliament.[2] Charles Wynn was one of many deeply frustrated critics who 'should have been glad if the whole subject of registration had been considered with greater attention'.[3] The legislators, however, were convinced that by separating the business of claiming the vote from the business of casting it, registration would reduce the length and cost of elections, and remove party passion and electoral interests from the process of scrutinising and verifying voters. An election, it was thought, would then no longer be a 'scene of delay, confusion and expense, all endless and intolerable'.[4] But while the time allowed for an election was drastically reduced, from a previous maximum of two weeks to just two days, the procedure for compiling the new electoral registers actually lasted for over four months.[5] It also occurred annually, regardless of whether or not an election was expected to take place during the ensuing year. Involving every voter in every constituency, the new registration system extended, rather than limited, both the regularity and the complexity of activity associated with electoral participation, and greatly intensified political awareness. This chapter examines the response to this system, and shows how its practical operation in the constituencies completely transformed the nature of local and national party politics after 1832.

---

[1] 2 Will. IV c. 45, 738–41, clauses 26, 37–60, 72. On earlier attempts to set up a system of voter registration see John Prest, *Politics in the age of Cobden*, London 1977, 2–9; Seymour, *Electoral reform*, 105–7; J. D. Chambers, *An examination into certain errors and anomalies in the principles and detail of the registration clauses of the Reform Act . . .*, London 1832, 13–15.

[2] Speeches of Sir Charles Wetherell and John Wilson Croker, *Mirror of Parliament* ii (1831), 1890–2.

[3] *Hansard*, 3rd ser. xiv. 1288.

[4] *Edinburgh Review* lvi (Oct. 1832), 247.

[5] Polling was limited to fifteen days in 1785, and to a single day in borough constituencies in 1835: O'Gorman, *Voters, patrons, and parties*, 135; 5 and 6 Will. IV c. 36.

The registration system

Beginning on 20 June each year, voters living in a county constituency were given a month to submit a claim for inclusion in a preliminary register.[6] In theory, if already on the previous year's register, there was no need to re-apply, provided that the county voter retained precisely the same qualification and lived in exactly the same house.[7] In practice, the large number of voters who changed residences, if only within a few miles of each other, made the process of having to make a fresh claim each year quite common. In borough constituencies, where initial lists of rate-payers were automatically prepared by the overseers – and lists of freemen and burgesses by the town clerks – there was less onus on the individual voter to ensure his own registration.[8] Borough voters, in effect, had their votes registered for them, but this did not necessarily make their claim to the franchise any easier to sustain. Unlike county voters, all borough electors were disqualified for receipt of parochial relief, and needed to have resided within seven miles of the borough for at least six months before the end of July.[9] In addition, the new £10 borough franchise depended upon prompt payment of poor rates and other assessed taxes. If the rates due by 6 April were not paid by 20 July, the £10 householder would find himself disfranchised for the entire year in which the register was in force.[10] This placed tremendous powers of enfranchisement and disfranchisement in the hands of those responsible for assessing, collecting and administering local taxation.[11]

Since parliament was keen to destroy the perceived corruption and venality of the unreformed electoral system, safeguards had also been introduced to help eliminate fraudulent claims or dubious entries from the register. Before publishing the county lists, the overseers were empowered to write 'objected to' against the name of any claimant whose qualification they doubted.[12] (In the boroughs, unqualified voters were automatically omitted from the initial lists prepared by local officials.) Both county and borough lists were then prominently displayed during the first two weeks of August, in the hope that any unqualified electors would be recognised and objected to

---

6   2 Will. IV c. 45, 731, clause 37.
7   Ibid. 748, schedule H; Anon, *The reform bill rendered plain, being the substance of every clause . . .*, London 1832, 12.
8   2 Will. IV c. 45, 734, clauses 44, 46. See also Anon, *The assembled Commons or parliamentary biographer with an abstract of the law of election . . .*, London 1838, 260.
9   2 Will. IV c. 45, 729–31, clauses 27, 32–3, 36.
10   Ibid. 729, clause 27. Seymour, *Electoral reform*, 119, is uncharacteristically wrong on this point, stating that 'a person must have paid all his rates and taxes up to the time of making his claim'. Others have followed his error: A. B. Erickson, *The public career of Sir James Graham*, Oxford 1952, 169.
11   This is explored in ch. 6 below.
12   2 Will. IV c. 45, 732, clause 38.

and that omissions in the borough lists would be spotted and rectified.[13] Crucially, any voter or claimant enjoyed the right to challenge any entry on the displayed lists, but without having to specify the grounds for their objection.[14] As was pointed out early on, this meant that 'no one can tell what objection he is to meet; the notice, in truth, only letting him know that his vote is objected to'.[15] Instead, it was the responsibility of the person claiming the vote, the claimant, to arrange for his qualification 'to be proved' before a revising barrister in an open court, held between 15 September and 28 October.[16] Although the objector, or an agent acting on his behalf, also had to attend the court in support of the objection, he was not required to provide proof. As a county electors' manual suggested, 'if the respondent appear, the objector is not required to state the nature of his objections, but it is incumbent on the respondent to prove his qualification'.[17]

The weight of the law, in these circumstances, clearly lay on the side of caution and restriction, facilitating the objector rather than the claimant. Failure to appear or arrange for proof of a qualification in the court of revision, often at only three days' notice, would automatically result in disqualification.[18] Because so many voters were either unable or unwilling to attend, a considerable proportion of objections, regardless of their validity, led to disfranchisement. At the first Newcastle-under-Lyme revision, for example, 'no fewer than 54 of the 235 objections sustained were the result of the voter not appearing to uphold his claim'.[19] Of the forty-three names objected to during the Lonsdale ward revision in 1837, thirty-six (84 per cent) were struck off the Westmorland county register for 'non-attendance', a further two were disqualified because they were 'dead' and only five turned up to successfully defend their qualification.[20] No provision existed for costs to be awarded to compensate an individual for the time and expense involved in defending his vote against a 'frivolous' or 'vexatious' objection.[21] As a result,

---

13 Ibid. 732–5, clauses 38, 44, 46, 47.
14 Ibid. clauses 39, 47. In all constituencies, the objector was required to give official notice of an objection to the overseers before 25 August. In county divisions only, or when challenging the vote of a London liveryman, the objector also had to notify the person objected to. All objectors had to state their identity and place of abode in full: ibid. clauses 31, 48.
15 *Edinburgh Review* lvi (Oct. 1832), 246.
16 Someone else, 'in possession of the facts', could appear on the voter's behalf, but all parties were prohibited from being attended by legal counsel, even without their 'wig and gown': 'County electors' manual', DuRO, Strathmore MSS D/St/C1/16/262, fos 17–22; *The Times*, 1 Oct. 1835; 2 Will. IV c. 45, 737, clause 52.
17 Anon, *The county voters' manual; or practical guide for the annual registration of voters . . .*, London 1842, 21.
18 2 Will. IV c. 45, 733–6, clauses 42, 50.
19 *Staffordshire Advertiser*, 3 Nov. 1832.
20 Minutes of revising barristers' court, 20 Sept. 1837, CuRO, Lonsdale MSS D/Lons/L, 'Misc. election pps, 1836–37'.
21 J. A. Thomas, 'The system of registration and the development of party organisation,

in the event of an objection, 'the voter lost his vote if he did not appear, and if he did appear he lost his costs'.[22] Regardless of whether a voter resided in a borough or a county, inclusion on the electoral registers, in force for a full year from 1 November, frequently involved a good deal of initiative and expense.[23] After the Reform Act the onus lay with the individual not only to ensure that he met all the requisite criteria, but also to provide adequate proof of entitlement in a court of law in the event of an objection. In effect, as the *Staffordshire Advertiser* lamented, 'any man before he can give his vote under the provisions of that measure must establish his right by a preliminary law suit, an English law suit too, which, as everybody knows is no trifle'.[24] How, it must be asked, did the electorate respond?

Voter response: the politics of indifference

The number of people registering at the first revision of 1832 was far below what had been expected. Lord John Russell, the minister who had been charged with carrying the Reform Bill through the House of Commons, had confidently predicted that the electorate would double.[25] In fact the increase was a little under a half (*see* table 1). Even this was an exaggeration, since early registration returns tended to count the number of qualifications rather than the number of individual electors. Double or even triple entries were common, inflating the size of many pre-1835 electoral registers by an estimated 10 to 20 per cent.[26] If the earlier registration returns are accordingly scaled down, and then compared with those for the later 1830s (when duplicate entries were specified separately), between one-quarter and three-eighths of all who met the necessary qualifications in 1832 neglected to register their entitlement at that time. O'Gorman has shown that the shortfall was even higher in places like Ipswich and Nottingham, where 48 and 40 per cent respectively failed to enrol.[27] Of course many were keen to register, but the subsequent growth in the size of the electorate in the 1830s suggests that for every five who did rush out to claim the franchise there were nearly three who held back.[28] Given the level and role of public interest in the Reform debates and the imminence of a general election, why did so many in possession of a suitable qualification fail to claim their new electoral rights?

1832–1870', *History* xxxv (1950), 81–98 at p. 88 is misleading on this point. The power to award costs against unwarranted objections was not introduced until 1843.

22 PP 1846 (451) viii. 175.

23 2 Will. IV c. 45, 737–8, clause 54.

24 *Staffordshire Advertiser*, 3 Nov. 1832.

25 Seymour, *Electoral reform*, 77–8.

26 Based upon PP 1833 (189) xxvii. 111–249; PP 1837–8 (329) xliv. 553–858.

27 O'Gorman, *Voters, patrons, and parties*, 183 n. 22.

28 Reducing the inflated 1832 return of 656,258 by 20% leaves 525,006 'actual' voters, which is 300,351 (36.4%) less than the adjusted 1839 return of 825,357 (*see* table 1).

Table 1
Estimated number of voters in 1831 and registration returns for England and Wales, 1832–9

	(1831)	1832	1833	1834	1835	1836	1837	1839
Counties	(247,000)[a]	369,830	382,596	385,491	470,954	479,065	480,729	490,038
Boroughs	(188,000)	286,428	286,790	289,941	318,058	322,061	330,328	335,319
Totals	(439,200)[b]	656,258	669,386	675,432	789,012	801,126	811,057	825,357

Sources: see appendix 3 (the 1838 returns are missing from the Home Office data).

[a] Based upon the estimates in Brock, *Great Reform Act*, 312.
[b] Based upon O'Gorman, *Voters, patrons, and parties*, 179.

A baffled and concerned parliament focused on problems of accessibility, blaming the complexity and novelty of the new registration system for the disappointing response. 'Many persons', declared an 1834 select committee, 'in the haste and under the novelty with which the registrations were made, had neglected to register in 1832'.[29] Yet many cases of 'ignorance and inadvertence' clearly arose from indifference rather than implementation.[30] For those who were interested and alert, there was no shortage of information about the new electoral procedures that had to be followed. Reminders to register appeared frequently in the provincial press, alongside simple and clear instructions that were occasionally supplemented by registration circulars sent out by local candidates.[31] For the more avid electoral aspirant the new system also spawned a vast array of voter guides, explanatory pamphlets and election manuals. These ranged from step by step summaries, such as the *County voters' manual* which aimed to provide 'all that is necessary to inform them of their qualification, and the mode of insuring their privileges at the ensuing registration',[32] to full scale tracts and treatises.[33] What chiefly impressed *The Times* was the general level of apathy demonstrated by potential voters towards the franchise, rather than the number of obstacles in the

---

29 PP 1834 (591) ix. 265.
30 *Edinburgh Review* lvi (Jan. 1833), 545.
31 SuRO, SC38/1/5; DRO, 59/7/4/28; BuRO, Fremantle MSS D/FR/144/2/1; Julia H. Andrews, 'Political issues in the county of Kent, 1820–1846', unpubl. MPhil diss. London 1967, 113.
32 Anon, *County voters' manual*, 1.
33 See, for example, Anon, *The Reform Act with explanatory notes*; William Carpenter, *The electors' manual*, London 1832; George Price, *Complete election guide*, London 1832; F. J. N. Rogers, *Parliamentary Reform Act with notes*, London 1832; William Rowe, *The act for the amendment of the representation of the people in England and Wales*, London 1832; Russell, *A treatise on the Reform Act*; Charles Wordsworth, *The law and practice of elections . . .*, London 1832.

way of enfranchisement.[34] This was not just a phenomenon confined to the counties, where registration was voluntary, but also one affecting many boroughs. In Preston, for example, where the voters qualifying as 'inhabitants at large' could not be determined until they had actually submitted a claim, the local paper complained bitterly of the 'few persons thinking it worthwhile to pay the courts a visit'.[35] This apathy and indifference often represented a deliberate and obstinate response, rather than a purely passive one.[36] Many of the yeomanry, alleged the *Edinburgh Review*, 'doggedly refused to register themselves, saying, "they had always voted without being registered, and did not see why they should have any thing of the kind done now" '.[37]

The absence of prospective candidates and the likelihood of an uncontested return also lowered the number of claims. Over a quarter of all English and Welsh constituencies were without a Tory or – as they were now being called – Conservative candidate at the 1832 general election, which left staunch Tory partisans little incentive to register.[38] In Cheltenham, where a Liberal candidate was returned without opposition, many Tory supporters deliberately spurned the franchise.[39] At Westminster, where the 1832 election was fought between two Radicals and a Whig, it was reported that 'there has been a very great deal of apathy and indifference with respect to registering their votes'.[40] In places where there was no real prospect of a contest in 1832, and with the next general election not expected until 1839, many potential voters simply saw no urgency in registering.[41] The irony here, as the *Edinburgh Review* remarked, was that 'unless the excitement of a pending contest operate at the moment, voters will not register themselves; and yet the main use of the registry is to have their claims decided when men's passions are not aroused'.[42] Even when there was an intense partisan contest, a complete and full registration was still unlikely. Some dependent voters declined registration in precisely these circumstances for fear 'of being

---

[34] See Close, 'The elections of 1835 and 1837', 192; *Edinburgh Review* lvi (Oct. 1832), 247.

[35] James Aldridge, 'The parliamentary franchise at Preston and the Reform Act of 1832', unpubl. BA diss. Manchester 1948, 68–71.

[36] Thomas, 'The system of registration', 87.

[37] *Edinburgh Review* lvi (Jan. 1833), 545.

[38] In 1832 the Conservatives fielded 247 candidates in England and Wales compared to the Liberals' 509: F. W. S. Craig (ed.), *British electoral facts, 1832–1980*, Chichester 1981, 1. Over a quarter (26.4%) of all English and Welsh constituencies had no Tory candidate in 1832, compared to only 7% which lacked a Liberal or Radical: George Crosby, *Crosby's parliamentary record*, York 1841, passim; Charles R. Dod, *Dod's electoral facts from 1832 to 1853*, ed. H. J. Hanham, Brighton 1972, passim.

[39] Adrian Courtenay, 'Parliamentary representation and general elections in Cheltenham Spa between 1832 and 1848: a study of a pocket borough', unpubl. MPhil diss. Open University 1990, 44.

[40] PP 1835 (547) viii. 44, minute 644.

[41] In 1832, 89 out of 284 English and Welsh constituencies were uncontested.

[42] *Edinburgh Review* lvi (Jan. 1833), 544. See also PP 1835 (547) viii. 44, minute 650.

pressed to vote contrary to their consciences'.[43] The *Essex Independent* commented that

> a very powerful argument in favour of the vote by ballot has been furnished within these few weeks in Essex, by the reluctance on the part of the new constituents to register their votes . . . There are many voters whose livelihood may depend on not disobliging the party which they would desire to oppose.[44]

The financial cost of electoral participation was another significant deterrent, especially in the borough constituencies where possession of the new £10 householder franchise depended upon the prompt and full payment of 'all the poor's rates and assessed taxes'.[45] In some boroughs the financial advantages of keeping the official value of a property below £10 *per annum* clearly outweighed any electoral dividends. In Leicester, for example, 'descriptions of houses are made as good as they can be to be worth only £8 or £9 a year, to avoid the window tax and the late house tax'.[46] A decision not to register also avoided payment of the 1s. registration fee, which in the counties was charged only when making a new claim, but which in the boroughs was levied every year and collected as part of the poor rate.[47] An 1834 select committee concluded that 'the payment of the shilling operates against registration, and at the same time creates discontent'. In Hertfordshire, for example, it was revealed that 'many neglected or avoided to be registered on account of the payment of the shilling'.[48] Borough registration was, of course, supposed to be automatic, but in practice this fee provided the householder with an important element of choice. Because the 1s. was usually listed separately on the overseer's bill as 'a distinct payment from the other rates', it might easily be ignored or refused.[49] In the Monmouth district revision of 1834, for example, fifty-five householders out of a total of 291 chose not to pay it.[50] To some it was simply too much. As the *Preston Chronicle* suggested, 'to the poor man who reckons his earnings by *pence* . . . a shilling is a very serious and important amount'.[51]

The level of registration which did occur in 1832 owed much to the work

---

43 PP 1835 (547) viii. 404, minute 6708.
44 Undated cutting from the *Essex Independent* enclosed with Dr Forster to Sir T. B. Lennard, 19 Aug. 1832, ERO, Lennard MSS D/DL 044/1. For a similar analysis see also *Hansard*, 3rd ser. xiv. 1288.
45 2 Will. IV c. 45, 729, clause 27.
46 PP 1835 (547) viii. 129, minute 2207.
47 2 Will. IV c. 45, 738, clause 56.
48 PP 1834 (591) ix. 278; PP 1835 (547) viii. 59, minute 982.
49 PP 1835 (547) viii. 84, minutes 1453–6.
50 NLW, Leonard Twiston Davis MSS 4479. The constituency of Monmouth comprised three districts: Monmouth, Newport and Usk.
51 *Preston Chronicle*, 19 Oct. 1833, cited in David Walsh, 'Working class political integration and the Conservative party: a study of class relations and party political development in the north-west, 1800–1870', unpubl. PhD diss. Salford 1991, 378.

of agents and landlords, rather than individual initiatives. Leading proprietors frequently played a key role in the mechanism of enfranchisement, and
some even considered it a 'custom of landlords to see that their tenants are
registered'.[52] In North Northamptonshire, for example, Lord Fitzwilliam's
agents looked 'after the new claimants in their respective villages'.[53] In South
Durham, John Bowes and his agent Thomas Wheldon positively promoted
registration from Barnard Castle, while the initiative in the northern division
was taken by Lord Durham and Lord Londonderry.[54] Some, like Lord Lonsdale in Westmorland, made a clear distinction between the politics of individual claimants, helping only their own supporters.[55] Others, like Gilbert
Heathcote in South Lincolnshire, took a less partisan and more pedagogic
interest, and actively supported the work of local electoral associations like
the one established at Holbeach.[56] The extent and effectiveness of these
initiatives were nevertheless limited. In Staffordshire a clearly frustrated E. J.
Littleton was unable to 'induce' Lord Anglesey to 'direct his agents to register
the voters' on his estates.[57] Writing to the Tory leader Peel in 1837, Sir
George Clerk observed that it had taken the landed elites a long time to
'come at last around to a view of the necessity of exertion with respect to the
registrations'.[58] Relying on the local agents and leading tenants of a landed
estate to ensure their neighbours' registration was also far from straightforward or satisfactory. 'Leading tenants' on the duke of Bedford's estates in
Bedfordshire, like John Walker of Eaton, categorically refused to 'help with
registration', prompting a clearly overburdened steward to wish that the 'electors would do it themselves'.[59]

The difficulty of maintaining interest and enthusiasm in voter registration
in the longer term was reflected in a decline of registered electors in almost
half of the borough constituencies (49 per cent) and over a quarter of county
constituencies (27 per cent) at the second revision, in 1833. In twenty-four
boroughs, as D. H. Close has demonstrated, the decrease was over 10 per
cent.[60] In the Staffordshire Potteries it was reported that 'indolence, and the
feelings of indifference' had 'operated to a considerable extent in the diminu-
tion of the lists' compiled in 1833, which fell by almost 17 per cent.[61] Poorer

---

52 PP 1835 (547) viii. 44, minute 647.
53 J. C. Gotch to Earl Fitzwilliam, 14 July 1834, SRO, Wentworth Woodhouse MSS
WWM. G83/206.
54 Strathmore MSS D/St/C1/16/63–249; Paula Kim Vandersluys Radice, 'Identification,
interests and influence: voting behaviour in four English constituencies in the decade after
the Great Reform Act', unpubl. PhD diss. Durham 1992, 289–313.
55 'Misc. election pps, 1834–5 (33)', Lonsdale MSS D/Lons/L.
56 LAS, Ancaster MSS 3 Anc 9/13/74/207–19.
57 Diary entry, 16 June 1835, Hatherton MSS D260M/F/5/26/9.
58 Sir George Clerk to Sir Robert Peel, 13 Aug. 1837, BL, Peel MS Add. 40424, fos 67v–8r.
59 T. Bennet to W. G. Adam, 16 Aug. 1832, 10 June 1835, BRO, Russell MSS R3/3738,
3877.
60 Close, 'The elections of 1835 and 1837', 531.
61 Staffordshire Mercury, 5 Oct. 1833. See also the Stoke-upon-Trent returns in appendix 3.

householders, in particular, probably quit the registers for financial reasons. As William Davis, returning officer for Frome, explained in 1833, 'some of them have since applied to have their names struck out, on the ground that their house-rent was not £10 per annum, to which they were surcharged immediately after the election'.[62] Since partisan objections had yet to become a significant factor, most of these 1833 losses represented either inadvertent or wilful disfranchisement.[63] An Essex agent explained that 'immediately after a contest great apathy exists as to their names being properly inserted on the register'.[64] Thus in both borough and county constituencies it is clear that the expected 'stampede' for the vote implicit in the cautionary wording of the registration clauses failed to occur. A multitude of good reasons for avoiding political participation, combined with a continuing level of apathy towards the franchise, produced a situation in which, as Lord Brougham put it, 'the voter did not care for his vote and if left to himself would not go to register it'.[65]

The parties take over

Voter indifference after the Reform Act has been stressed here for two reasons. First, the impact of Reform on levels of electoral participation is a central feature of much recent debate about the importance of 1832.[66] Studies of voter turnout rates have reinforced the notion of high levels of political interest and involvement in both the unreformed and reformed electoral systems, despite the potential deterrents of an open voting system.[67] What turnout rates cannot reveal, however, are the number of potential political participants who may have qualified for a vote, but who never claimed it. The uniform system of voter registration introduced in 1832 provides a useful insight into this phenomenon, suggesting a level of indifference towards voting rights which the Reform Act's authors could hardly have anticipated given the popular furore that had accompanied its passage through parliament.

Second, these widely criticised 'lazy voters', who 'neglected to secure their privileges', provided the opportunity for one of the key electoral developments of the 1830s: the emergence of local party organisations for attending

---

62 PP 1833 (189) xxvii. 153.
63 In 1833 the number of days spent adjudicating objections fell by 28%: PP 1836 (240) xliii. 361.
64 PP 1835 (547) viii. 44, minute 650.
65 Cited in Seymour, Electoral reform, 116.
66 Beales, 'The electorate before and after 1832'; O'Gorman, 'The electorate before and after 1832'; Phillips and Wetherell, 'The Great Reform Act of 1832'. For the view that 1832 'limited popular representation' and restricted popular political participation see Vernon, Politics and the people, 38–9.
67 See O'Gorman, Voters, patrons, and parties, 188.

to the registration.[68] It might seem odd to attribute the genesis of constituency parties to political apathy, but if all possible electors had claimed their franchise entitlement in 1832, subsequent recruitment and enfranchisement of the unregistered by local parties would not have been necessary. The need to maximise electoral support became acute after the dismissal of the Whig government by William IV in November 1834 and the totally unexpected general election of January 1835, which left the parties far more evenly matched in parliament, thereby dramatically increasing the prospect of another dissolution. Local Conservative associations were established, as *Blackwoods' Edinburgh Magazine* explained in its campaign of 1835, 'to obtain lists of all the voters on the Conservative interest who can be put on the roll in every borough and county'.[69] One of the first activities of the Buckingham Conservative Association, for example, was 'to make a return of the persons entitled to vote and not on the register'.[70] Liberal associations were also instituted in order, as the inaugural meeting of the North Staffordshire Reform Association put it, 'to support the claims of Liberal electors at the barristers' courts'.[71]

The impact of this activity, and the extent of previous voter indifference, can be gauged from the dramatic increases in the size of the registered electorate at the next revision, that of October 1835 (*see* figure 1). Since the time spent hearing objections also grew by over a third in this year, this expansion is all the more impressive.[72] Conventional accounts usually highlight the leap of 123,000 county voters occurring immediately after the Reform Act of 1832.[73] But in 1835 85,463 voters were added to the county registers, a jump of over 22 per cent on the previous year (*see* table 1). If all those coming on to the rolls in 1835 had been registered in 1832, the Reform Act would have almost doubled the county electorate, just as intended, rather than increasing it by only a half.[74] Coupled with the 10 per cent rise in the size of the borough electorate, the percentage increases of 1835 represent the largest expansion of the electorate in the nineteenth century to occur in a year in which there was no measure broadening the franchise.[75]

68 *Staffordshire Mercury*, 5 Oct. 1833.
69 *Blackwoods' Edinburgh Magazine* xxxviii (July 1835), 9. For a similar statement of the aims of Liberal associations see the *Edinburgh Review* lxii (Oct. 1835), 182–3.
70 'Buckingham District Conservative Association minute book, 1837–43', BuRO, Archdeacon MSS D/AR/81/75/15, fo. 27.
71 Sir Thomas Sheppard to duke of Sutherland, 31 Aug. 1837, StRO, Sutherland MSS D593/P/22/1/12. The development of constituency associations is explored in ch. 2 below.
72 PP 1836 (240) xliii. 361.
73 Brock, *Great Reform Act*, 312; Seymour, *Electoral reform*, 533.
74 The increase would have been 85% rather than 49%.
75 Based upon figures in Craig, *British electoral facts*, 79, and *British parliamentary election results, 1832–1885*, London 1977, 623.

Figure 1
Trend in the number of registered electors
in England and Wales, 1832–9

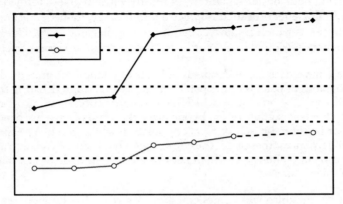

Sources: see appendix 3.

The scope for conflict: revisions and decisions

The capacity of local parties to engage in voter registration and to exploit the system was dramatically enhanced by the imprecise wording of the Reform Act and the conflicting interpretations that it allowed. The large number of registration manuals offering advice to electors, professional agents and revising barristers testify to intricacies and 'difficulties so perplexing and so notorious' that they have 'not only divided the revising barristers in opinion, but the bar in general'.[76] Even the more basic provisions of the act were prone to ambiguity, providing plenty of opportunity for the technically adept party agent to submit unusual claims and to lodge speculative objections against the votes of known opponents. The fortunes of local parties, in these circumstances, became heavily dependent upon the number of supporters who could be placed upon the registers each year, and the number of opponents who could be excluded. As the founder of the West Kent Conservative Association observed, 'the whole business of an election is now completely done in the barristers courts'.[77]

Even the most apparently uniform franchises came to embody a wide

---

76 Edward E. Deacon, *A letter to Sir James Graham on the bill . . . for the more effectual registration of voters . . .*, London 1837, 20.
77 Registration memo of Sir Edmund Filmer, 3 June 1836, CKS, Filmer MSS U120, C72/74.

variety of different qualifications in practice. Historians often refer to the £10 householders as a monolithic group, but under clause 27 of the Reform Act, occupation of 'any house, warehouse, counting-house, shop, or other building' being held 'either separately, or jointly with any land' formed an entitlement.[78] The effects of such imprecise terminology, framed 'most colloquially' and 'in terms which no lawyer can interpret', became immediately apparent at the first revision.[79] In Staffordshire, for example, it was reported that

> there have been some hundreds of hours of public time and, no doubt, some thousands of pounds of the public money consumed in debating the meaning of the word 'shop', a word which has no construction standing upon statutable or other legal authority. . . . In one place the sense of shop has been limited to describe those houses, or parts of houses, in which goods are exposed to sale publicly, in another place, the construction has been extended to all buildings or parts of buildings, in which persons engaged in trade or manufacture carry on their business.[80]

The £10 franchise was complicated even further by the fact that clause 27 appeared to allow the value of different buildings and land holdings to be added together, to form a cumulative qualification. Thus possession of land with a shed, a tool house, a goose house or other building worth £10 *per annum* was often considered 'sufficient' by informed legal opinion.[81] In Ripon, for example, John Brown successfully claimed a £10 borough franchise for a cow house and a dilapidated shed together worth £15 a year. Other voters were able to qualify by 'sheds for cattle' alone, which had been 'built with brick and covered with tiles'.[82] Critics might claim that clause 27 'could not mean to establish pig-sty tenements under the Reform Act', but the recorded rulings of revising barristers suggest that it frequently did.[83]

Other difficulties were caused by the continued existence of the ancient-right franchise holders. Many election petitions, or controverted returns, centred around the legitimacy of their claims. In Petersfield, for example, the revising barrister allowed shareholders in a cricket field to qualify, because they had polled at the previous contest of 1831. The subsequent election petition brought by the defeated candidate, Sir William Jolliffe, overturned this decision, and his opponent was unseated.[84] Diffi-

---

78 2 Will. IV c. 45, 729, clause 27.
79 *Staffordshire Advertiser*, 3 Nov. 1832.
80 Ibid.
81 See William M. Manning, *Proceedings in courts of revision . . .*, London 1836, 154–8.
82 W. F. A Delane, *A collection of decisions in the courts for revising the lists of electors*, London 1836, 37; PP 1835 (547) viii. 196, minutes 3236–8.
83 Deacon, *Effectual registration*, 20–1.
84 SoRO, Hylton MSS DD/HY box 17. The result of an election could be challenged or petitioned against in an 'election petition' or 'contested return'. Under clause 60 of the Reform Act, any electoral register could be scrutinised and, if necessary, amended by the committee of the House of Commons which was appointed to investigate.

culties over the rights of non-resident freemen were especially common. In Bedford, for example, the votes of the thirteen non-resident freemen who voted in the 1837 election were successfully challenged in a petition brought by the defeated Liberal candidate, which resulted in the Tory MP losing his seat.[85] In Worcester and Monmouth, however, similar challenges against the votes of non-resident freemen who resided outside the boroughs, but within seven miles of the polling booths, were unsuccessful.[86] Residence requirements were additionally complicated in 'cities and towns being counties of themselves'.[87] In Lichfield, for instance, considerable confusion arose over both the location and the duration of residence applicable to its freehold and annuitant voters, as well as its large number of freemen.[88] But it was the frequency of conflicting rulings over what constituted a 40s. freehold franchise that attracted the most publicity and concern.[89] As well as being held in land or property, which might include even a steam engine 'of the requisite value', a freehold tenure could also be derived from sources of income such as tithes, or tolls 'of markets, bridges and gates', rendering the permutations almost infinite.[90] One of the most celebrated cases related to apparently arbitrary decisions made on the electoral rights of shareholders in the New River Company.[91] As *The Spectator* explained:

> In Middlesex, the Barrister decides that a share in the New River Company is not a freehold; step across the line into Hertfordshire, and the New River votes are all good . . . go into Surrey and the proprietors of shares in the Thames Tunnel are not allowed to vote, although their title is not distinguishable from that of the New River Company.[92]

Compilation of the new electoral registers was entrusted to the parish overseers (except for lists of freemen and liverymen).[93] This greatly extended the potential sphere of partisan conflict and often helped to politicise the machinery of local administration. Critics of the system argued that it placed a tremendous onus on an unsalaried and impermanent official, often a small farmer or petty shopkeeper, who in any one year might have to compile as

---

[85] 1837 Bedford pollbook and 1838 election petition cuttings, BRO, Acc. 4002 Z 231/7/1 (c), 7/4 (b).

[86] Leonard Twiston Davis MSS 4412–14, 4546–50, 6025–6, 6159–62, 6777–86.

[87] 2 Will. IV c. 45, 730, clause 31. There were nineteen such cities or towns, out of which Bristol, Exeter, Haverfordwest, Lichfield, Norwich and Nottingham had a reformed franchise which included 40s. freeholders: *Dod's electoral facts*, passim.

[88] Edward Vaughan Williams to George Anson, 26 Sept. 1832, StRO, Anson MSS D615/P(P) 1/21.

[89] For a more detailed discussion see Prest, *Politics in the age of Cobden*, 32–4.

[90] *Manchester and Salford Advertiser*, 10 Oct. 1835; W. H. Cooke, *Plain instructions for overseers*, London 1835, 51.

[91] Delane, *Decisions in the courts* (1836), 294–316.

[92] Undated cutting from *The Spectator*, SoRO, Sanford MSS DD/SF/4547, fo. 48.

[93] 2 Will. IV c. 45, 731–2, 734–5, 738, clauses 37–8, 44–8, 56.

many as eleven separate electoral lists.[94] Instances of neglect, such as the unfortunate overseer of Hepscott in Morpeth who 'forgot' to compile the 1832 register, depriving the whole township of its franchise, or the unwitting overseers of Abingdon who failed to make out a list of £10 householders, heightened local party tensions and frequently led to accusations of partisan bias.[95] Accidental omissions had to be handled with extreme care, as a letter sent to the Nottinghamshire clerk of the peace revealed:

> I have seen Mr Wing this morning, and find from an examination of the revised list of Hucknall Torkard that all the names which were upon the register of 1836 were omitted. . . . I think I may safely now add that part to the register of this year. . . . As persons are always found ready to take advantage of any little irregularity and to raise objections, I recommend that nothing further be said about the matter.[96]

Local parties had good cause to be vigilant. In 1836, a Liberal overseer at St Pancras was found guilty of having 'wilfully contravened and disobeyed the provisions of the act, by placing fictitious voters on the list' and was promptly fined £50.[97] Corrupt officials faced a maximum penalty of £500, but an 1834 select committee believed that 'frauds of the grossest description were committed by interested agents and overseers of the poor, and by persons connected with them, in the management of the lists, which never came to the knowledge of the revising barristers'.[98] As a Conservative election agent suggested, 'overseers were men liable to frailties like all other men, and not more exempt from party feelings than others'.[99] The position of overseer, complained the *Manchester Guardian*, has become 'of late what it never used to be, a "political office" '.[100]

Tensions between the Established Church and the Dissenting community were easily exacerbated by aspects of the registration process. The practice of claiming a freehold vote in respect of seats or pews in a church worth 40s. a year, as a 'pew renter', helped to reinforce religious divisions, with claims for Established Churches far more likely to confer the vote than those in Dissenting chapels.[101] Sectarian grievances were further inflamed by the Reform Act's directions for displaying important registration notices on 'the

---

94 Chambers, *Errors and anomalies*, 35–6.
95 PP 1833 (189) xxvii. 189; W. F. A. Delane, *A collection of decisions in the courts for revising the lists of electors*, London 1834, 123–4; *The Times*, 3 Oct. 1835.
96 R. S. Fisher to E. S. Godfrey, 18 Oct. 1838, NAO, Edward Smith Godfrey papers QA CP 5/4/867.
97 *Annual Register*, 1836, appendix 267–70.
98 2 Will. IV c. 45, 742, clause 76; PP 1834 (591) ix. 279.
99 *The Times*, 2 Oct. 1835.
100 *Manchester Guardian*, 11 Oct. 1834.
101 See the breakdown of freehold qualifications in PP 1840 (579) xxxix. 188; Delane, *Decisions in the courts* (1836), 322–32.

doors of all the churches and chapels'.[102] In some places, like North Wiltshire, the lists were fixed on 'the Independent, Baptist, Wesleyan, Primitive and Allington Chapels', but many overseers insisted that it meant only Anglican buildings.[103] In Ripon, in another celebrated case, it was ruled by the court that posting notices on the doors of Established Churches alone was sufficient and within the meaning of the act.[104] An even greater grievance resulted from the provisions of the Reform Act requiring prompt payment of all 'assessed taxes'. This effectively made financial support for the Established Church a prerequisite of borough enfranchisement in parishes where the church rate was compounded with the poor rates.[105] The refusal of some Dissenters to pay their taxes on religious grounds often led to their electoral disqualification. In Manchester, for example, many anti-church rate Dissenters who' had refused to pay the most recent poor rate faced certain disfranchisement in the second revision of 1833.[106] This lent practical political urgency to the religious principle of Dissenting voluntaryism, and helped foster an image of religious partiality within the existing electoral system.

A more acute problem arose over clause 23 of the Reform Act, which enfranchised trustees or mortgagees in receipt of the profits and rents of an estate, and clause 26, which disfranchised any trustee not in receipt of rents and profits 'for his own use for six months at least'.[107] The original intention of clause 26 was to fix the time during which the voter must have been qualified, but the addition of the words 'for his own use' appeared to introduce an extra restriction.[108] The issue was whether a vote conferred under clause 23 might be cancelled three clauses later. It was a question with profound implications, particularly for the trustees of Dissenting chapels. During the heated partisan revision of 1835, their registration was systematically encouraged by Liberal registration societies and vociferously objected to by 'Anglican' Conservatives. The efforts of Dissenters 'to convert their places of worship into manufactories for votes' was firmly resisted by local Tory agents, who lodged wholesale objections against their claims.[109] What otherwise would have remained a minor legal matter therefore became a major issue of controversy, introducing an extra element of intense political and religious confrontation into the whole revision process. The initial rulings of revising barristers, as John Prest has shown, varied enormously, exposing the legal profession to charges of inconsistency, incompetence and even partisan and

---

102 2 Will. IV c. 45, 731, clause 37.
103 Parcel marked '1830–44', WRO, Messrs Keary, Stokes and White, box 415/432.
104 Delane, *Decisions in the courts* (1836), 127.
105 The relationship between rates and registration is discussed more fully in ch. 6 below.
106 J. P. Ellens, *Religious routes to Gladstonian Liberalism: the church rate conflict in England and Wales, 1832–1868*, University Park, Penn. 1994, 27–8.
107 2 Will. IV c. 45, 738–9, clauses 23, 26.
108 See Manning, *Courts of revision*, 163.
109 Deacon, *Effectual registration*, 24.

religious bias.[110] Faced with such acrimony, and in the absence of any coherent pattern of precedence, the legal profession increasingly erred on the side of caution and disfranchisement. The experience of Madeley parish, in South Shropshire, where all seven trustees 'in receipt of rents of freehold in [the] Wesleyan Methodist Chapel' vanished from the electoral register of 1836–7, was not uncommon.[111] By 1836 legal opinion on clause 26 had hardened. As the revising barrister for the Isle of Wight explained, 'it was considered that the period of enjoyment (six months) and not the mode of enjoyment formed the essential part of the enactment. We now think, however . . . that where a trustee has personally no beneficial interest in the trust estate he is not qualified to vote'.[112]

It was the system of objections which, above all else, fuelled party passion. Competition between the parties to enlist support was one thing, but objecting to the votes of known opponents introduced a far more confrontational element into the electoral process and affected the voter personally. At the 1835 revision, local party organisations, taking advantage of the fact that many voters were unable to attend in defence of their qualification, lodged an unprecedented number of 'frivolous' or 'vexatious' objections on a purely speculative basis.[113] Faced with so many completely unfounded objections, the revising barristers openly complained of 'their inability to order the voter's costs to be paid by the objector'.[114] At Salford, for example, after dismissing a 'purely vexatious objection' against the borough's Liberal MP, who had been forced to travel up from London, the barrister declared he was 'exceedingly sorry I have it not in my power to allow you costs against the objector'.[115] In subsequent revisions, such 'frivolous' or 'vexatious' objections became less effective as the parties themselves took on responsibility for defending the votes of their own supporters. This had two important effects. First, it tended to intensify a local party's hold over, and interaction with, the individual voter. Second, it helped to inject the process of adjudicating objections with an unintended level of complexity, as lawyers from both sides competed to argue increasingly intricate and detailed cases before the revising barristers. The result, as an agent for North Warwickshire suggested, was to 'throw the whole power of objection and defence into the hands of organised associations'.[116]

---

110 Prest, *Politics in the age of Cobden*, 36–41. The partisan provincial press, however, tended to exaggerate the political bias of revising barristers. Even in the intense West Somerset revision of 1835, for example, the Liberal agent was forced to concede privately that 'the barristers are both Tories but that upon the whole they have been courteous and impartial': White to Sanford, 27 Sept. 1835, Sanford MSS DD/SF/4551, fo. 52.
111 Electoral registers, ShRO, QE/6/2/2–3.
112 Manning, *Courts of revision*, 191–2.
113 See Prest, *Politics in the age of Cobden*, 26–7.
114 *The Times*, 3 Oct. 1835.
115 *Manchester Guardian*, 3 Oct. 1835.
116 PP 1846 (451) viii. 204, minute 200.

In Monmouth, the firm of solicitors retained on behalf of Lord Granville Somerset, the Conservative MP, divided their objections to Liberal voters into two categories: class I objections for 'those who had changed residence' and class II for 'technicalities'.[117] It was the latter which provided the most scope for the party agents. Insufficient descriptions of the voter or his property, inaccurate descriptions of the qualification, a discrepancy in the value of the property, an initial missing from a name; the list of obscure technical objections which could be brought against an opponent was almost endless. In Newport, for example, nine voters were 'objected to for having laid a bet or wager upon the *event* of an Election'.[118] In Westmorland, a Thomas Hindmore of Market Brough was struck off the register after an agent managed to prove he was 'an idiot in possession of property'.[119] The popularity and hereditary use of certain names, especially in Wales, and the fact that spelling had yet to settle into a modern standardised form, provided ample ground for objections based upon ambiguity or cases of confused identity. In Monmouth, where thirty-seven voters shared their name with another, there were five John Morgans and five John Williamses on the electoral register, all of whom needed to be clearly distinguished.[120]

Since it was possible to justify almost any objection on the basis of some obscure technicality, the work of resisting objections increasingly focused on issues of procedure, as well as entitlement, broadening the scope for litigation even further.[121] In Helston, for instance, the legality of the Radical notices of objection against Tory voters was successfully challenged on the ground that the description of the objector, William Pearse, was insufficient as 'there are several persons of the same name residing in the borough'.[122] Similarly in Bedford and Petersfield, partisan notices of objection were invalidated because they 'contained an insufficient description of place of abode'.[123] In South Hampshire, the overseers' objections to voters were rejected because the words 'objected to' had not been written directly 'opposite' the respondents' names, but in the margin instead. Yet in Middlesex an attempt by the Reform Association to invalidate overseers' 'objections' marked on the wrong side of the lists failed.[124] Intricate legal battles over procedural requirements distanced the individual voter even further from the mechanism of enfranchisement, injecting the whole revision process with an element of pettiness and unpredictability which was quickly picked up by the press. One newspaper reported how 'a whole string of objections in Devonshire was

---

117 Leonard Twiston Davis MSS 4608–9.
118 Ibid. 4589.
119 'Misc. election pps, 1834–5 (33)', Lonsdale MSS D/Lons/L.
120 Leonard Twiston Davis MSS 4593.
121 Under 2 Will. IV c. 45, 736–7, clause 50, the power of the revising barrister to rectify mistakes in the register was limited. See, for example, PP 1846 (451) viii. 192–206.
122 CRO, Messrs Rogers and Son DD/RO/8082.
123 Manning, *Courts of revision*, 216–18.
124 Ibid. 210; Delane, *Decisions in the courts* (1836), 244–5.

disallowed, because the overseers did not write the words "objected to" on the side of the page which the learned barrister fancied to be the right one; and the most trivial omission or mistake in the description of their qualifications has disfranchised thousands'.[125] It 'turns representation into a mockery', was another's damning verdict.[126]

The type of party conflict which registration encouraged at a local level ultimately found its way back into parliament, where electoral and party considerations increasingly thwarted legislative attempts to amend or overhaul the system. No significant proposal ever reached the statute book. Lord John Russell's bill of 1834, to restrict the number of objections and introduce fines for 'frivolous' objections made 'without probable cause', was initially well received, but its passage was interrupted by two changes of government, the 1835 general election and the passage of the municipal corporations bill, all of which intensified partisan interest in the role and utility of registration.[127] Russell's subsequent bill of 1836 was very similar, and despite it being 'emphatically a measure of government', even the Tory Lord Lyndhurst considered it 'an extremely good bill, which ought to have been adopted and been passed into a law'.[128] During its re-commitment, however, a number of alterations were made which 're-modelled most of its regulations'. The most substantial change involved replacing the existing 160 revising barristers with eight full-time itinerant ones, who instead of revising lists in October were to travel from one place to another and hold revisions all year round, coupled with the formation of a three-man court of appeal in London to ensure uniformity of decision.[129] Peel 'did not disapprove of the proposed registration court', but 'altogether dissented' from 'the nomination of the revising barristers by the home secretary', Russell himself.[130] As one revising barrister warned, it would give 'the ministry of the day an undue control over the registration of voters'.[131]

Another proposal with distinctly partisan implications was the enfranchisement of trustees in 'actual possession or receipt of the rents and profits of the same estate for charitable purposes'.[132] Alarmed Tories feared that this would 'give the Dissenters a chance of swamping the whole agricultural constituency'.[133] This tendency to view each alteration in a purely partisan light dogged negotiations. With an established Whig government and a

---

125 Undated cutting from the *Spectator*, Sanford MSS DD/SF/4547, fo. 48.

126 *Manchester and Salford Advertiser*, 10 Oct. 1835.

127 PP 1834 (368) ii. 163–203; PP 1835 (36, 577) ii. 583–667. On the link between municipal reform and registration see ch. 7 below, and Philip Salmon, 'Local politics and partisanship: the electoral impact of municipal reform, 1835', *PH* xix (2000), 357–76.

128 Speech of Lord Lyndhurst, 18 Aug. 1836, NRO, Cartwright (Aynho) MSS C(A) 8318.

129 PP 1836 (287) iii. 480–1.

130 Peel to Goulburn, 22 Aug. 1836, SuRO, Goulburn MSS Acc. 319, box 40.

131 Deacon, *Effectual registration*, 3. See also Prest, *Politics in the age of Cobden*, 48–9.

132 PP 1836 (287) iii. 505.

133 Deacon, *Effectual registration*, 24.

Tory-dominated House of Lords, the support of both parties was needed if any change was to be made. Public pressure to amend the system was considerable – in 1836, for example, the Bristol Liberal Association lobbied parliament for a simplification of the procedures – but partisan suspicion and acrimony increasingly doomed even the most basic attempts at modification.[134] Russell's 1837 bill to relax rate-paying requirements in the boroughs, for example, was cursorily dismissed by Peel as 'a shameful attempt at the end of a session to procure an electioneering advantage for the promoters of it'.[135]

Between 1834 and 1841, twenty-six bills concerning the registration system came before parliament.[136] Only one became law. Its object, however, was not to change or amend the system, but simply to clarify the confusion which had arisen as a result of the various registration bills of 1836, by legalising 'certain lists of voters', and allowing extra time for the submission of claims and objections at that year's revision.[137] This failure to implement even minor improvements to the system, or provide legislative clarification of even the most ambiguous issues, allowed litigious party conflict in the courts to run wholly unchecked and helped further to alienate the individual voter from the preliminary stage of electoral participation. Indeed, a complete overhaul of voter registration was one of the chief demands of the Chartists. Their detailed proposals for a new system occupied almost half the text of the *People's Charter*, and formed a central component of their radical extra-parliamentary campaign.[138] Conflict in parliament over the detailed provisions of various registration bills increasingly reproduced and even legitimised many of the legal dramas occurring at a local level in the revision courts. With extensive scrutiny from the press, it helped reinforce the primary perception of registration as an arena for party conflict rather than an impartial mechanism of enfranchisement.[139] Whether viewed from the perspective of voter indifference, or the ample 'scope for conflict' within the system, one of the unintended consequences of registration was clearly the additional boost given to the rise of party. Yet it was also the party struggle which prevented even the worst aspects of the system from being changed.[140]

---

134 *Bristol Gazette*, 4 Feb. 1836, cited in Peter Brett, 'The Liberal middle classes and politics in three provincial towns – Newcastle, Bristol, and York – c. 1812–1841', unpubl. PhD diss. Durham 1991, 298.

135 See PP 1837 (311) iii. 187; Peel to William Garnett, 11 July 1837, LRO, Garnett of Quernmore MSS DD/Q/box 9/47.

136 These are listed in the bibliography.

137 PP 1836 (563) iii. 755–6; 6 and 7 Will. IV c. 101.

138 Their proposals included the replacement of overseers by salaried registration clerks, new voter certificates and the introduction of substantial fines for 'frivolous objections': *The Chartist Circular*, 5 Oct. 1839. For an important recent discussion of this neglected aspect of Chartism see Miles Taylor, 'The six points: Chartism and the reform of parliament', in O. Ashton, R. Fyson and S. Roberts (eds), *The Chartist legacy*, Rendlesham 1999, 8–17.

139 See, for example, the *Lincoln Gazette*, 20 June 1837, and its report of a registration bill introduced by Elphinstone.

140 The registration system was not amended until 1843.

Registration as a mechanism of politicisation

With the length of an election in each constituency strictly limited to two days by the Reform Act, it was perhaps inevitable that some of the energy, excitement and entertainment of unreformed election campaigns should find expression in the new 'open courts' of revision.[141] Extant legal briefs used by the party agents usually testify to the more tedious aspects, page upon page of doodles, intermingled with phrases such as 'property belongs to wife' or 'not ten pounds value', filling their court papers.[142] But far from being a dry, rather mundane process, the annual courts of revision often became a popular public spectacle, with cases of individual personalities and local officials providing intense drama for the assembled inhabitants, in rooms sometimes 'crowded to suffocation'.[143] Oldham's 1835 revision was 'thronged, noisy and tumultuous'.[144] At Salford dozens of wives attended 'to support the claims of their husbands to vote . . . some of them bringing infants with them', while in neighbouring Manchester many voters were 'struck out for not appearing when they might be at the door and could not get into the room'.[145] Disturbances were frequent. On market day in Newport, for example, 'a progressive increase in the number and turbulence of the non-registered portion of the audience made it necessary to terminate the sitting'. Passions often ran high, particularly against those responsible for bringing objections. At Newport again one of the party agents 'was followed and hooted by the rabble and received a severe blow from a stone'.[146] Other revisions might be more good-humoured, but no less public and essentially theatrical occasions. In Bedford, for example, a hairdresser named Taylor was objected to because he had moved house. The revising barrister, playing to the crowd, determined that his vote 'must then, be shaved off the poll (laughter)'.[147]

The perception of registration as an annual political contest was enhanced by the frequent use of election-related buildings for revising the lists. In the parish of St Mary-Le-Bow, London, for example, the hustings structure left over from the 1835 general election was converted into a barristers court by the addition of 'two small tables'.[148] Agents were also under considerable pressure to use these public occasions to help foster local party awareness. The physical expansion of the electorate by 49 per cent in 1832, and by a further 17 per cent in 1835, meant that personal contact between elector and elected was often impractical and had to be increasingly supplemented, if not

---

141 See 2 Will. IV c. 45, 733, 736, clauses 16, 50.
142 Messrs Rogers and Son DD/RO/8048–59.
143 PP 1846 (451) viii. 213, minute 350.
144 *Manchester Guardian*, 3 Oct. 1835.
145 *Manchester and Salford Advertiser*, 26 Sept., 10 Oct. 1835.
146 Manning, *Courts of revision*, 71.
147 *Morning Herald*, 10 May 1838.
148 *The Times*, 2 Oct. 1835.

supplanted, by a more pronounced promotion of the party slate.[149] George Dashwood, for example, discovered that 'time may not allow a personal application to each individual elector' during the Buckinghamshire contest of 1835, and so promoted his status as 'a candidate on the Liberal side' far more intensely during ensuing revisions and the subsequent by-election.[150]

At the dramatic registration of 1835 the electorate not only became far more numerous, but also far more partisan. Trends in the levels of party-based voting after 1832 suggest a substantial hardening of party lines between 1835 and 1836, which has not received the attention it deserves. In an analysis of contests held between 1818 and 1910, for example, Gary Cox has calculated that at the 1835 general election, which was held following the relatively quiet registration of 1834, nearly a fifth of the voters (19 per cent) behaved in a non-partisan way, by 'splitting' their two votes between a Liberal and a Tory candidate.[151] At the subsequent general election of 1837, held after the intense registration battles of 1835 and 1836 had taken place, only 11 per cent of the voters demonstrated the same kind of non-partisan behaviour. According to Cox's figures, this 8 per cent decline in the level of non-partisan 'split' voting in 1837 was the largest single drop for any general election held between 1831 and 1910.[152] Alternative evaluations of partisan voting reveal the same basic feature. In T. J. Nossiter's survey of voting in northern boroughs, for example, the largest drop in the level of non-partisan 'split' voting (13 per cent) also occurred between 1835 and 1837.[153] More recent studies, while offering significant statistical refinements to the overall pattern, reveal the same basic trend of intense and rapid politicisation between the two elections of 1835 and 1837, on a scale unprecedented between the first and second Reform Acts.[154]

The 1841 general election furthers the impression of registration activity as an essential component in the process of politicisation. The level of non-partisan 'split' voting at this election was the lowest for any general election held under the terms of the Reform Act of 1832.[155] But with the partisan feeling of the electorate at its peak, the number of candidates from different parties contesting seats was, perhaps surprisingly, almost at its lowest.[156] This was because the same intense registration activity responsible for electoral politicisation increasingly provided one party with a clear majority of

---

[149] Gary W. Cox, The efficient secret: the cabinet and the development of political parties in Victorian England, Cambridge 1987, 128–9.
[150] Bodl. Lib., MS D.D. Dashwood C22, G1/3/6–4/2.
[151] A non-partisan 'split' refers to an elector's use of his two votes to support candidates from opposing parties.
[152] Cox, Efficient secret, 103–4.
[153] Nossiter, Influence, 178.
[154] See, for example, Phillips and Wetherell, 'The Great Reform Act of 1832', 416–24.
[155] Cox, Efficient secret, 93; Nossiter, Influence, 178.
[156] 51% of seats were uncontested in 1841 and 56% in 1847: W. O. Aydelotte (ed.), The history of parliamentary behavior, Princeton, NJ 1972, 237.

supporters on the electoral rolls, thus effectively pre-determining the result of an election and making a contest unnecessary. As *The Times* had remarked on one of the registration struggles which preceded the unopposed return of two Tory MPs for North Devon, 'come an election when it may, there is now no doubt whatever of the Conservatives securing a sure majority'.[157] Of the forty-nine English county divisions that were uncontested in 1841, as many as thirty-eight returned candidates exclusively from one party, the opposition having completely withdrawn from the field. In only eleven was the representation shared as part of a traditional 'compromise'.[158]

Party organisation of registration activity was fundamental to the process of politicisation, both at the parliamentary and municipal level. The introduction of annual town council elections in 1835 stimulated local party activity and affiliation further, but it was the close correlation between the municipal and parliamentary registration system which ensured the rapid politicisation of municipal electorates and provided a permanent mechanism for party gain.[159] Although the notion of the 'independent' elector remained central to the conception of electoral politics in the rhetoric of the period, the contested nature of registration politics heightened the importance of party attachments and lessened the space for the 'independent' voter in the political process. Neutral or 'floating' voters were often objected to by both political parties and effectively 'squeezed', in the hope that the voter would be forced to declare a party preference.[160] Each elector might be canvassed as many as three times by each party in the lead up to an annual registration revision. After an initial survey of partisan support, someone different would conduct a second canvass in order to ensure accuracy; then a cross-canvass would take place, which would involve posing as an agent of the opposition and attempting to solicit promises of support from 'suspect' voters.[161] These methods brought the agency of party into every elector's home and, by combining local issues with a national cause, brought the politics of Westminster much closer to the electorate.

Party organisation of registration ultimately contributed to what was probably the most distinctive feature of reformed electoral behaviour: the rise of far more persistent and permanent forms of partisanship. Longitudinal individual-level analyses of elections show that the probability, or 'hazard rate', of

---

[157] *The Times*, 30 Oct. 1839. For a case study of North Devon see ch. 5 below.

[158] Crosby, *Parliamentary record*, 227–38. The eleven uncontested seats with shared representation were West Cornwall, North Durham, West Gloucestershire, North Hampshire, Herefordshire, Middlesex, South Northumberland, East Somerset, South Staffordshire, West Surrey and the North Riding of Yorkshire.

[159] See ch. 7 below and Salmon, 'Local politics and partisanship', 363–76.

[160] PP 1835 (547) viii. 142; PP 1846 (451) viii. 192–206.

[161] See, for example, Ostrogorski, *Democracy*, i. 457–8; parcel marked '1830–44', Messrs Keary, Stokes and White, box 415/432; HeRO, Messrs Crawters of Hertford D/E Cr 105/5; 'Buckingham District Conservative Association minute book', Archdeacon MSS D/AR/81/75/15, fo. 41.

a partisan preference being repeated at a subsequent election increased enormously in the decade after 1832.[162] Two points, in particular, have emerged from studies of long-term partisan loyalties. First, many of those registered in 1834, who were then able to participate in the unexpected election of 1835, must already have been firm partisans. In Leicester, Durham, Bristol, Maidstone, Colchester, Northampton and Great Yarmouth, for example, over 70 per cent of the electorate simply repeated their 1832 mode of voting in the 1835 election.[163] This confirms that it was probably only the more informed and committed partisans who saw to their own individual registration in the immediate aftermath of 1832. Second, and more fundamentally, despite the enormous increase in the electorate at the revision of 1835, the propensity of voters to behave in a consistently partisan way continued to rise at both the 1837 and 1841 general elections. Recruitment of unregistered voters by local parties therefore encouraged a form of partisan allegiance that was not only rigid, but also substantially permanent. The intense politicisation of 1835–7 was clearly not ephemeral. Its legacy was that consistent partisanship rapidly became the norm throughout the 1830s. And, with the party allegiance of 'experienced' voters essentially fixed from one election to another, each party's ability continually to activate and recruit unregistered voters, through the medium of constant attention in the annual registration contests, increasingly determined party fortunes.

Three broad observations can be made about the structure of electoral politics after 1832. First, an initial pattern of voter indifference must be taken into account if a complete picture of the operation of the reformed electoral system is to be constructed. In the context of the 1830s, what voters neglected to do, rather than just what they did, constituted an equally essential and definitive component of many key political processes. It was the indifference of voters, rather than their enthusiasm, which provided such a powerful stimulus to the emergence of local party organisation after 1835, and which made the business of electoral recruitment at the annual registration revision so efficacious. Second, intense registration activity by local parties contributed to a substantial and sustained process of electoral politicisation. By objecting to the votes of known political opponents, defending the qualifications of friends and followers, and actively recruiting and enfranchising as many new supporters as possible, local registration societies polarised the reformed electorate along much more distinct party lines, and on a permanent long-term basis. Underpinning these party tensions, the system of voter registration exacerbated sectarian grievances. Conflicts over the electoral rights of Dissenting trustees, in particular, lent practical and public expression to key ideological differences between the parties on a

---

162 See Phillips and Wetherell, 'The Great Reform Act of 1832', 429–32.
163 Radice, 'Identification, interests and influence', 444–52; Phillips, *Boroughs*, 103, 138, 171, 204.

regular basis. Third, it is clear that the mechanism of voter registration introduced in 1832 proved intrinsically adversarial in its operation. It extended, rather than reduced, the frequency, length and complexity of activity associated with electoral participation. The very vocabulary of 'defendant', 'claimant' and 'objector', conceptualised the initial stage of the electoral process in terms of conflict and confrontation. Fuelled by the numerous ambiguities of the Reform Act, the 'litigious' instinct easily absorbed and then enhanced 'factious' rivalry in the courts of revision held every year. How the parties organised their registration activity, and which of them ultimately won the annual contests to enfranchise supporters and disfranchise opponents, are the subjects of the next chapter.

2

Conservative and Liberal
Electoral Organisation

Historians of the nineteenth century have long recognised the role of central election management and constituency organisation in shaping Britain's transition to a modern two-party political system. Considerable confusion, however, surrounds the extent to which the Reform Act triggered new developments in these areas, with obvious implications for any assessment of its long-term political significance. The 1830s, of course, have been traditionally viewed as a 'golden age' of club government, in which the pre-Reform political centres of Brooks's and White's were supplanted by an entirely 'new type' of central party organisation based around the Carlton and Reform Clubs.[1] But the precise part played by these new London centres in the election and registration campaigns of this period remains unclear. The Carlton, for instance, acquired a formidable reputation for the management of contests, costs and candidates after 1832, not least among Liberal journalists.[2] But to what extent did this image, neatly captured in accounts of its dealings with the young Benjamin Disraeli, reflect the reality?[3] And how comfortably did Sir Robert Peel's extensively cited exhortation to 'register, register, register!' fit with the broader attitudes and approaches to electoral management adopted by the leaders of both parties?

The commonly held belief that 'many aspects of modern party organisation date from the 1830s' has in recent decades been seriously challenged, most notably by O'Gorman who concluded his account of the unreformed electoral system by arguing that 'the new party clubs after 1832 were very like the old' and that 'even registration was little more than a streamlined means of locating voters'.[4] Some local studies too, while acknowledging that voter registration was 'new', have suggested that 'in practical terms' it 'made little difference' and that there was 'no great transformation in the operation of

---

1 Gash, *Politics in the age of Peel*, 393.
2 *Morning Chronicle*, 6 Jan. 1835; *Edinburgh Review* lxii (Jan. 1836), 172–8.
3 See, for example, the episodes concerning the Wycombe and Taunton elections of 1835: Robert Blake, *Disraeli*, London 1966, 120–4; R. E. Foster, 'Peel, Disraeli and the 1835 Taunton by-election', *Transactions of the Somerset Archaeological and Natural History Society* cxxvi (1982), 111–18.
4 Eric J. Evans, *Sir Robert Peel: statesmanship, power and party*, London 1991, 41; O'Gorman, *Voters, patrons, and parties*, 392.

electoral politics after 1832'.[5] This chapter seeks to clear up much of this confusion by providing a detailed re-assessment of how the parties managed their election and registration activities during the post-Reform decade. Most significantly, however, it also brings to prominence a number of fundamental differences between the parties in the development of their central institutions and constituency organisations, which were to have a decisive impact on their electoral performance in the localities and provide the basis of a remarkable national recovery by the Conservative party.

Central election management

The structure of control, 1832–5

The first of the new central party clubs to be established was the Carlton. Based at 2 Carlton House Terrace, which was to be its temporary home until the completion of more suitable premises in Pall Mall in 1835, its formation on 17 March 1832 was mainly the work of the so-called 'Charles Street Gang' of Tory activists, chief among them Joseph Planta, William Holmes, John Charles Herries and Charles Arbuthnot, who had informally managed the party's elections and press relations since the fall of the Wellington ministry in 1830.[6] Hopes that this club would promote new electioneering techniques and set up 'a permanent organising committee', with 'an ex-cabinet minister as chairman, to manage and superintend the elections from London', however, were quickly dispelled.[7] Indeed, the Conservative leaders remained extremely cautious about this type of activity after 1832. Both Peel and Wellington declined to act as the club's trustees, and although it acquired copies of county pollbooks, proposals for a centrally co-ordinated registration campaign were firmly rejected by the Tory managers in the summer of 1834. The setting up of an 'ad hoc' committee at the end of that year to manage the 1835 election campaign was therefore very much in line with previous practice. Other than the appointment of new personnel (Planta, Holmes and Arbuthnot had all retired) and its meeting daily at the 'top of the Carlton', by now an increasingly over-crowded social and dining centre, there was little to distinguish this body from its predecessors.[8] Headed by Lord Granville Somerset, its leading members were the chief whip Sir George Clerk, his two

---

5 Christopher J. Cooper, 'Electoral politics in Grimsby, 1818–35', unpubl. PhD diss. Open University 1987, 297–301; Sarah Richardson, 'Independence and deference: a study of the West Riding electorate, 1832–1841', unpubl. PhD diss. Leeds 1995, 42.

6 Gash, *Politics in the age of Peel*, 395–7; A. Aspinall (ed.), *Three early nineteenth century diaries*, London 1952, pp. xliv–lii.

7 Alfred Mallalieu to Lord Aberdeen, 4 July 1832, BL, Herries MS Add. 57421, fo. 104. Much has recently been made of this letter in Walsh, 'Working class political integration', 5, 149–51, but as Aspinall pointed out in 1952, 'it embodied ideas too revolutionary to suit the Tories of 1832': *Diaries*, pp. xliv–xlv.

8 Aspinall, *Diaries*, pp. lvi–lviii.

assistants Francis Bonham and Charles Ross, the whip in the upper house Lord Rosslyn, and the MP for Dublin University Frederick Shaw, who oversaw its Irish activities.[9]

Whig leaders were similarly circumspect in their approach to new types of electoral organisation. 'Radical Jack' Lord Durham's advice to Grey about the need to co-ordinate Liberal registration activity went unheeded at the first revision of August 1832, as did subsequent calls for 'more attention to electoral matters' and a campaign for a national Reform Association, which the new Radical secretary to the Municipal Corporations Commission, Joseph Parkes, tried 'in vain to raise' in 1834.[10] Although Parkes and a number of leading Radical MPs pressed ahead and established a Westminster Reform Club on 7 March 1834, there is no evidence to suggest that this club, which rented the first two floors of the home of Matthew Wood, Liberal MP for London, at 24 Great George Street, ever made any contribution to election or registration matters before it folded on 14 April 1836.[11] Indeed, when Parkes made 'a schism to introduce his clerk', the election attorney James Coppock, some of its more respectable members, including Wood himself, 'seceded from it altogether'.[12]

Like the Conservatives, the Reformers had developed no significant new electoral machinery by the time William IV dismissed the Whig ministry in November 1834, when they too assembled an impromptu election committee out of the few remaining activists in London. Meeting daily at 3 Cleveland Square, the residence of the former chief whip Edward Ellice, who was abroad, its leading members were the ex-cabinet ministers Lord Duncannon, Lord Mulgrave and Sir John Cam Hobhouse; the MP for Manchester, Charles Poulett Thomson; the private secretaries to Lord Althorp – Thomas Drummond – and to Lord Brougham – Denis Le Marchant; and Parkes, whose reports to Durham complained of overwork and a 'sore want of *men*' and 'money'.[13]

The result of this unexpected general election was to prove pivotal in stimulating new developments in electoral organisation on both sides. Early in May, for example, Bonham persuaded Peel that a 'very small committee'

9 Close, 'The elections of 1835 and 1837', 184–5.
10 Durham to Grey, 30 Aug. 1832, Durham University, Grey of Howick MSS; Coohill, 'Ideas of the Liberal party', 97–8; Parkes to Durham, 1 Mar. 1836, Lambton Estate Office, Chester-le-Street, Lambton MSS. For further details of Parkes's electoral activities see Philip Salmon, 'Joseph Parkes', *New dictionary of national biography*, forthcoming.
11 'Minute book of the Westminster Reform Club', RCA, shelf 3. Its leading members were Matthew Wood, Rigby Wason, John Wilks, Daniel O'Connell, Daniel Whittle Harvey and Parkes, of whom only the last was not an MP. See also Louis Alexander Fagan, *The Reform Club: its founders and architect, 1836–1886*, London 1887, 19, 31–2; W. Fraser Rae, 'Political clubs and party organisation', *Nineteenth Century* iii (1878), 911–15.
12 Letter from R. Sydney, 6 May 1873, RCA, shelf 3.
13 Close, 'The elections of 1835 and 1837', 177–9; Parkes to Durham, 13, 24 Dec. 1834, Lambton MSS.

consisting of no 'more than 7' should be permanently formed at the Carlton to 'obtain information and prepare' for elections.[14] There are no grounds, however, to suggest that its standing committee, which included Granville Somerset, Clerk and the future chief whip Sir Thomas Fremantle, played any part in the rapid spread of constituency associations or in the Tory registration drives of that year. Instead it was the ultra-Tories who initiated these developments. In the May 1835 issue of Blackwoods', for instance, a national campaign was launched, which was widely reported in the Tory press. It urged Conservatives to 'unite in associations in every city, borough and county' for 'the purpose of purging the election rolls' of Radicals and registering voters, 'on whose principles they can rely'.[15] 'It is in the registration courts', Blackwoods' emphatically declared, 'that the battle of the constitution is to be fought and won'.[16]

This, and a widespread belief that registration had been responsible for recent Tory electoral gains, was also the cue for a spate of activity by leading members of the Cleveland Square committee, who since the election had continued to sit and assist the chief whip Charles Wood in organising the parliamentary opposition.[17] Parkes, in particular, was convinced of the need for a 'National Club' to match the perceived advantages of the Carlton. 'We lose by our own neglect of registration', he wrote to Durham, adding, 'we must organize an association in London to work the reform bills, to point out to the country the facility and effect of organization' and 'to register Reformers and oppose foul registered Tories'.[18] To this end a 'considerable number of persons', among them the MPs Ellice, Lord Ebrington and Daniel Whittle Harvey, met under the chairmanship of Thomas Coke at the British Coffee House in Cockspur Street on 21 May 1835 to launch the Reform Association, in a bid to counteract the 'extensive formation of Tory Associations' and encourage 'all classes of Reformers' to organise and prepare for the approaching registration.[19] Initially without premises, it operated from Parkes's 'rooms upstairs' at his home in 21 Great George Street, which he found 'an intolerable nuisance', before eventually acquiring the lease on 3 Cleveland Row, 'opposite the palace' of St James.[20]

---

14 Stewart, Conservative party, 136–9; Close, 'The elections of 1835 and 1837', 429; Norman Gash, 'The organization of the Conservative party, 1832–1846, part II: the electoral organization', PH ii (1983), 132.
15 Blackwoods' Edinburgh Magazine xxxvii (May 1835), 796–814; Staffordshire Advertiser, 9 May 1835.
16 Blackwoods' Edinburgh Magazine xxxvii (May 1835), 813.
17 Close, 'The elections of 1835 and 1837', 180–1.
18 Parkes to Durham, 18, 26 Jan. 1835, Lambton MSS.
19 Founding address of the Reform Association, 20 May 1835, Strathmore MSS D/St/C1/16/263; The Times, 22, 25 May 1835. The association's launch is wrongly dated to 1834 in Jessie K. Buckley, Joseph Parkes of Birmingham, London 1926, 137; Gash, Politics in the age of Peel, 403; and G. B. A. M. Finlayson, 'Joseph Parkes of Birmingham, 1796–1865: a study in philosophic radicalism', BIHR xlvi (1973), 195.
20 Parkes to Durham, 1 June 1835, Lambton MSS.

As the summer deadline for submitting registration claims approached, the efforts of the 'ultra' groups within both parties to step up their activities intensified. In the July edition of *Blackwoods'*, the Tory historian and lawyer Archibald Alison issued detailed instructions for the formation of local Conservative committees, subscription funds for registration and the hiring of professional agents.[21] Warning his party that such exertions would be in vain 'if they are not aided by the general conduct of the Conservative leaders', he also called for the immediate formation of a central committee, 'aided by a few barristers and agents in the metropolis', to correspond with the provincial committees, calculate electoral prospects and select candidates in advance.[22] The Carlton committee established in May had clearly failed to meet these criteria, unlike the 'more enterprising and energetic' Reform Association with its unpaid activists such as Le Marchant, who reported to Mulgrave that he was running around the country visiting 'one political association a day'.[23] Indeed, the success of the Reform Association's summer campaign in the *Morning Chronicle* for subscriptions from 'all friends of the Liberal cause' enabled them to go much further than the Tories and to establish a central fund to help keep 'local districts properly registered'.[24] By September 1835 they had '£1,900 in hand', and 'more if necessary', to ensure 'the registration revision being duly done', and had appointed a permanent election agent, James Coppock, on a salary of £300 *per annum*.[25] These important new developments in central electoral organisation after the 1835 general election appeared to give the Reformers the upper hand. But how effectively would they be able to capitalise on these apparent advantages in the ensuing years? And to what extent would a new style of 'club government' really begin to emerge within either party by the end of the post-Reform decade?

The limits to central control: Bonham and Peel re-examined

Much has been made of the central election machinery developed by the Conservatives between 1832 and 1841.[26] Interference by the so-called 'party's London headquarters' in the constituencies, however, was unusual and unwelcome, as is attested by the failure of various attempts to co-ordinate

---

[21] *Blackwoods' Edinburgh Magazine* xxxviii (July 1835), 9–15.

[22] Ibid. 14.

[23] Le Marchant to Mulgrave, n.d., Mulgrave MSS M/411; Close, 'The elections of 1835 and 1837', 443. I am indebted to Peter Mandler for this reference to Le Marchant's activities.

[24] *Morning Chronicle*, 10 July 1835; *Edinburgh Review* lxii (Jan. 1836), 182–3; Parkes to Russell, 6 Oct. 1836, PRO, Russell MSS 30/22/2c, fo. 221.

[25] Parkes to Durham, 6 Sept. 1835, Lambton MSS.

[26] Most notably in the earlier work of Norman Gash, 'F. R. Bonham: Conservative "political secretary", 1832–47', EHR lxiii (1948), 502–22, and *Politics in the age of Peel*, 400, but also more recently by Walsh, 'Working class political integration', 5, 135–77.

local activities from the centre during this period. A typical example was the National Conservative Association, launched by Lord Sandon at the British Hotel in Cockspur Street on 25 April 1836 with a subscription fund at Coutts and Co., to direct the formation of local Conservative clubs 'amongst the trading and labouring classes'. Based in Pall Mall, its committee of thirty-nine members included Lord Salisbury and Lord Lincoln, the election managers Bonham and Holmes, and fifteen other Conservative MPs.[27] By January 1838, however, it had run into serious financial difficulties, exposing its committee to 'various threatened actions'.[28] Another abortive organisation was the 'Committee to *manage* the Registration of the Empire' started by Disraeli, Lord Strangford, Lord Exmouth, Lord de Lisle and Robert Scarlett early in 1838, for which a 'certain number of five pound subscriptions' were collected, despite Bonham warning of 'the inefficiency and utter absurdity of such a plan'.[29]

It would also be wrong to read too much into the role of leading party managers as presidents, vice-presidents or honorary members of the numerous constituency associations of the 1830s. High status figures lent them an essential element of prestige and dignity, and helped to legitimise the new kind of political activities in which they were engaged. But such men rarely took part in the work of local parties themselves. Lord Mahon, for example, was president of the Finsbury Conservative Association, chairman of the North Devon Conservative Association and vice-president of the London Conservative Association, but was more a figurehead than a leader or manager.[30] Indeed, his connection with the Finsbury Conservatives was simply the result of an unsolicited letter from the organisation's secretary, asking him to 'sanction the association by accepting the office of President' and thereby help 'inspire the association with confidence and energy'.[31] In a similar fashion Fremantle, the chief whip from 1837, agreed to attend annual dinners of the South Lancashire Conservative Association, was an 'honorary member' of the Banbury Conservative Association and acted as vice-president of the Buckingham Conservative Association, but his role was strictly benevolent rather than supervisory.[32] The contribution of these

[27] *Preston Pilot*, 26 June 1836, cited in Walsh, 'Working class political integration', 455, 580–2.
[28] Bonham to Peel, 9 Jan. 1838, Peel MS Add. 40424, fo. 277r.
[29] Ibid. fo. 277v; Stewart, *Conservative party*, 139; Gash, 'Electoral organization', 148.
[30] Thomas Edward Penfold to Mahon, 9 Nov. 1836; George Fursdon to Mahon, 9 Feb. 1838, CKS, Stanhope of Clevening MSS U1590, C381/1; Stewart, *Conservative party*, 135.
[31] Penfold to Mahon, 23 Nov. 1835, Stanhope MSS U1590, C381/1.
[32] *Preston Pilot*, 13 Sept. 1834; 'Banbury Conservative Association minute book, 1837–47', Oxfordshire County Archives Service, Acc. 1259, BCA I/1, entries 61, 128; 'Buckingham District Conservative Association minute book', Archdeacon MSS AR 81/75/15, fo. 1; Fremantle MSS D/FR 139/23/15, D/FR 110/18/1 fos 1–10.

leading figures to the success of constituency associations was one of polite endorsement rather than active involvement.

Gash's portrayal of Bonham as 'the permanent and indispensable official round whom the organization was built', and 'the cardinal figure in the extra-parliamentary management of the party', has been almost universally accepted, yet it is both empirically and intuitively questionable.[33] Would such an organisation, if it was really of importance to the party, have been entrusted to such a second-rate figure?[34] Unlike Parkes and Coppock at the Reform Association, in the crucial years of 1835 to 1837 Bonham had other duties, both as an MP and one of only two aides to the chief whip Clerk.[35] The loss of his seat in 1837 was a bitter blow and his subsequent attention to electoral organisation was always something of a palliative.[36] In reality, he could do little but monitor revision results submitted by local correspondents and constituency associations and, under the watchful eye of his chief Granville Somerset, calculate likely gains in the event of a dissolution.[37] Even in this relatively simple task, however, he was not without his critics or rivals. It is clear from the private correspondence between Peel and Henry Goulburn, for example, that the electoral calculations supplied by Holmes were still being heavily relied upon by the party leaders.[38] Charles Ross also provided Peel with a separate 'accurate account of the losses and gains' at the 1837 election. 'I know it is not as favourable as Bonham makes it,' he explained, 'but I think it is fairer.'[39]

Bonham was not without enemies in the party. Some of the perhaps less often consulted Peel correspondence at the British Library suggests that his relationship with other election managers and political leaders was awkward and, on occasion, even divisive. The very nature of his work inevitably aroused suspicion and hostility, especially among those aristocratic members who regarded their constituencies as personal fiefdoms. In one letter to Lord Ashley, for example, Lord Chandos was quick to accuse Bonham of 'utter incompetency' when arrangements went awry.[40] When in 1838 Sir James Graham complained to Bonham of 'serious divisions in our camp', and asked him to 'soften down asperities, to reconcile differences' and to help 'fuse the

---

33 Gash, 'Electoral organization', 133, and *Politics in the age of Peel*, 414. For a typical acceptance of his role see Cox, *Efficient secret*, 119, 125.

34 Significantly Parkes dismissed him as 'dirty old Bonham' and treated Holmes as a far more prominent figure: Parkes to Ellice, 24 Aug. 1837; Parkes to Durham, 14 Aug. 1835, 2 Oct. 1837, Lambton MSS; Parkes to Brougham, 2 Dec. 1837, UCL, Brougham MSS.

35 Granville Somerset to Peel, 9 Aug. 1837, Peel MS Add. 40424, fo. 47v.

36 See, for example, his emotional and at times almost illegible letter describing his defeat at Harwich: Bonham to Peel, 7 Aug. 1837, ibid. fos 23–4.

37 Hardinge to Peel, 6 Dec. 1836, Peel MS Add. 40314, fo. 159v; Close, 'The elections of 1835 and 1837', 185.

38 Peel to Goulburn, 21 Aug. 1837, Goulburn MSS Acc. 319, box 40.

39 Charles Ross to Peel, 22 Aug. 1837, Peel MS Add. 40424, fo. 97r.

40 Lord Chandos to Lord Ashley, 21 Sept. 1835, Peel MS Add. 40617, fo. 14.

party together', it was interpreted by Bonham personally, as a censure on his own conduct.[41] Although Graham later explained to Bonham that he had not meant 'to allude in an invidious sense in my former letter to any rising spirit of discontent as fostered by you', there was undoubtedly much more behind this than a simple misunderstanding.[42]

Bonham's notoriously uncomfortable relationship with the former chief whip Holmes would perhaps not have mattered had the latter not continued to play such an important role. Holmes not only actively managed a number of prominent and close-run by-elections, including Warwick in 1836 and Bridgwater in 1837,[43] but was also the party's advisor for Westmorland, Cumbria and Kendal, where he was 'very much looked up to by the Lowther set'.[44] He was a regular guest at Drayton Manor, particularly at election times or during a party crisis, such as the Conservative split over municipal reform in the summer of 1835, when Peel bolted to his country seat.[45] No love was lost between these two activists. On one occasion, when Holmes was described as being '*exceedingly* angry', it had to be rather euphemistically pointed out to Bonham that 'his anger may be directed against you'.[46] His close friendship with Peel meant that even as late as 1841, Bonham's superiors were actively warning him to 'keep Holmes in good humour'.[47]

Like his Liberal counterparts Parkes and Coppock, Bonham also had frequent occasion to feel that his services as an electoral manager were undervalued and frowned upon by the party leaders. By early 1841, for example, it is clear that communication between Bonham and Peel had become irregular.[48] In one revealing letter, Graham felt it necessary to reassure Bonham that 'as to what you say about yourself, I happen to know that Peel appreciates your work'.[49] Despite the personal loyalty that bound Bonham to Peel, important differences of style and approach inevitably arose from their respective preoccupations. In the summer of 1840, for example, Bonham became involved in negotiations to secure the *Courier* as an official newspaper of the Conservative party.[50] The chief whip, Fremantle, was initially prepared to indulge Bonham's plan, but as soon as it became clear that it might succeed, he and the whip in the upper house, Lord Redesdale, stepped in and firmly buried

---

41 Graham to Bonham, 16 Oct. 1838, Peel MS Add. 40616, fo. 20v.
42 Graham to Bonham, 21 Oct. 1838, ibid. fo. 21r.
43 W. M. Praed to Bonham, 22 Aug. 1836, Peel MS Add. 40617, fo. 23; PP 1870 (c. 11) xxx. 21.
44 Granville Somerset to Peel, 9 Aug. 1837, Peel MS Add. 40424, fo. 47v; Holmes to Peel, 1 Aug. 1837, ibid. fo. 1; Parkes to Durham, 2 Oct. 1837, Lambton MSS.
45 Parkes to Durham and Ellice, 14 Aug. 1835, Lambton MSS; R. W. Jeffery (ed.), *Dyott's diary, 1781–1845*, London 1907, ii. 347.
46 D. Lyon to Bonham, 'Thurs. afternoon' [1833], Peel MS Add. 40617, fo. 11.
47 Graham to Bonham, 1 Jan. 1841, Peel MS Add. 40616, fo. 188v.
48 Graham to Bonham, 6 Jan. 1841, ibid. fo. 193v.
49 Ibid. fo. 194.
50 Bonham to Fremantle, 12 Aug. 1840, Fremantle MSS D/FR/80/13.

it.[51] Like Parkes and Coppock, whose political perspective was also exclusively electoral, many of Bonham's ideas were simply too advanced for the party leaders.[52] Peel's comments on the scheme illustrate the fundamental difference in outlook between essentially progressive activists like Bonham, and a Conservative leadership that remained deeply suspicious of extra-parliamentary organisation. In direct contrast to Bonham's belief in 'the vast importance of *one* evening paper . . . on *which we can depend*',[53] Peel instead asked

> What language is this paper, the authorized organ of an opposition party to hold? And who is to suggest that language? . . . the case of an opposition is perfectly different from that of a government, yet even the government finds it no easy matter to have one recognized organ speaking the general collective voice of the Cabinet. . . . I individually will not have anything to do with the Courier, foreseeing nothing but embarrassment from the connection.[54]

Peel had serious concerns about the constitutional implications of extra-parliamentary political activity. Although he led a party whose electoral recovery was largely based upon the work of local constituency organisations, he played no part in their development and took remarkably little interest in their activities. Indeed, his well-noted disdain for party organisation and his 'executive style' once in office were just as apparent during his time as leader of the opposition.[55]

Peel's relationship with the new Conservative associations was always awkward and often hostile. He even refused to visit his local Staffordshire Conservative Club, prompting its secretary to write repeatedly to Lord Sandon to 'implore my lord that you will see Sir Robert Peel and see what can be done'.[56] Peel's dislike of public dinners and natural aversion to 'popular' politics were well known and provided his friends with frequent amusement.[57] In a typically dead pan account of a trip to Blackburn sent to Goulburn, for example, Peel complained that

> My efforts to escape unnoticed failed, but the only inconvenience I suffered was not from a Radical, but a Conservative assemblage (mob I must not call

51 Redesdale to Fremantle, 21 Nov., Fremantle to Redesdale, 27 Nov. 1840, ibid.
52 Joseph Parkes hatched a similarly abortive scheme to secure the support of the *Courier* for the Liberal party: Parkes to Cobden, 19 Feb. 1841, WSRO, Cobden MSS.
53 Bonham to Fremantle, 14 Oct. 1840, Fremantle MSS D/FR/80/13.
54 Peel to Fremantle, 25 Nov. 1840, ibid.
55 David Eastwood, 'Peel and the Tory party reconsidered', *History Today* (Mar. 1992), 27–33; Boyd Hilton, 'Peel: a reappraisal', *HJ* xxii (1979), 585–614.
56 John Smith to Lord Sandon, 11 Mar. 1836, 14 Apr. 1837, Harrowby MSS, cited in G. B. Kent, 'Party politics in the county of Staffordshire during the years 1830 to 1847', unpubl. MA diss. Birmingham 1959, ch. vii; 'Staffordshire Conservative Club minute book, 1835–43', StRO, Bill MSS D554/180.
57 Peel to J. S. Wortley, 14 Nov. [1835], SRO, Wharncliffe MSS WhM/526a/5 (1).

them) headed by pensioners who insisted for a long time in dragging me for about a mile into the town preceded by an enormous flag and a band of music. I escaped this infliction, but was pursued to the inn by my friends, who of course congregated half the town in front of the inn.[58]

Peel also declined any involvement with his own county's electoral arrangements, even in potentially damaging situations where he was the most obvious intermediary. In the Newcastle-under-Lyme election of 1835, for example, two Conservatives seeking re-election were joined by Peel's brother Edmund. In order to prevent the Conservative vote from being split, William Miller, who had sat since 1830, asked Peel to try to persuade Edmund to withdraw, but he refused to intervene, leaving his brother's 'decision to his own judgement'.[59] On another occasion, when Peel agreed publicly to propose the second Conservative candidate at South Staffordshire in 1837, he failed to turn up at the nomination, much to the astonishment of the Liberals.[60] When it came to filling Tamworth's second seat, Peel was also notoriously scrupulous about refusing to allow the Drayton Manor interest to be used with the borough's electors. In 1837, for example, the defeated Liberal candidate Captain Townsend publicly accused Peel of using his family's influence to help return a second Conservative MP, Captain A'Court. The fact that Peel actually challenged Townsend to a duel, even sending for his pistols, says a great deal about his extremely high standards of acceptable political conduct.[61] It was only through the furious backstairs negotiations of the two seconds, Sir Henry Hardinge and Rowland Alston, that the affair was finally settled with the publication of an apology stating that, 'whatever may have been the influence employed by any agent of Sir Robert Peel over his tenants', it was used without his 'sanction or knowledge'.[62]

Conservative initiatives in the registration courts similarly owed very little to Peel or the activities of Bonham. Even Peel's famous and frequently cited exhortation to 'register, register, register!' was not really what it appeared to be. This was no clarion call to emulate Daniel O'Connell's 'agitate, agitate, agitate!'[63] The Tory provincial press eagerly exploited the slogan, but in the main body of the 1837 speech from which it was taken Peel had in fact derided the whole process of registration as 'disagreeable', 'inconvenient' and,

58 Peel to Goulburn, 3 Sept. 1834, Goulburn MSS Acc. 319, box 40.
59 Peel to W. H. Miller, 26 Dec. 1834, Peel MS Add. 40407, fo. 279r; Philip Salmon, 'Newcastle-under-Lyme 1820–32', History of Parliament draft article.
60 George Anson to Lord Hatherton, July 1837, Hatherton MSS D260/M/F/5/27/12, fo. 114.
61 For a more detailed account of this episode see Norman Gash, Sir Robert Peel: the life of Sir Robert Peel after 1830, London 1972, 189–91.
62 Alston to Hardinge, 14 Sept. 1837, Peel MS Add. 40424, fo. 148; Standard, 16 Sept. 1837.
63 Ostrogorski, Democracy, i. 150; Close, 'The elections of 1835 and 1837', 456; Evans, Sir Robert Peel, 41.

above all, 'revolting'.[64] There was something inherently distasteful about a process denounced by his old friend, the Tory Jeremiah John Wilson Croker, as 'a constant canvass and an annual contest'.[65] Of course, for the more progressive election managers the very mention of registration represented something of a breakthrough over Peel's previous intransigence. At Conservative association dinners across the country, Peel's phrase lent important, if rather belated, official sanction to Tory registration campaigns.[66] Granville Somerset wrote to Peel to say that he was 'delighted to hear that you referred to the *registration* in your last Tamworth Speech', but the simple fact was that Peel was not really interested.[67] As late as 1837, for example, Bonham was still having to advise him of a basic provision whereby 'a change of residence is a positive disqualification under the third section'.[68] Always wary of extra-parliamentary power, Peel's attitude ultimately betrayed a deep concern about the constitutional implications of the whole voter registration system, as can be seen in the apposite complaint he made to Arbuthnot:

> The Reform Bill has made a change in the position of parties and in the practical working of public affairs, which the authors of it did not anticipate. There is a perfectly new element of political power, namely the registration of voters, a more powerful one than either the sovereign or the House of Commons. . . . Of what use is the prerogative of dissolution to the Crown, with an unfavourable registry, and the fact of its being known to all the world? . . . The registration will govern the disposal of offices and determine the policy of party attacks. . . . Where this is to end I know not, but substantial power will be in the registry courts, and there the contest will be determined.[69]

This striking analysis has been widely cited, but it is Arbuthnot's overlooked reply that reveals the general currency of these concerns among senior Tories. 'Your letter', he informed Peel, 'was so entirely in accordance with the Duke of Wellington's opinions, that I could not help sending it to him. . . . What you say of the registration is very true. It has become the governing power in the country'.[70]

---

64 'Address delivered at a Tamworth dinner, 7 Aug. 1837', Peel MS Add. 40424, fo. 172r.

65 Cited in William B. Gwyn, *Democracy and the cost of politics*, London 1962, 44.

66 For example 'Report of proceedings at South Lincolnshire Conservative Association dinner', *Lincolnshire Chronicle*, 13 Oct. 1837; 'Speech given at East Norfolk Conservative Association dinner, 1837', DRO, Bedford (London) MSS L1258 M/SS/C (DL) F 122.

67 Granville Somerset to Peel, 9 Aug. 1837, Peel MS Add. 40424, fo. 49v.

68 Bonham to Peel, [n.d.] 1837, ibid. fo. 263r.

69 Peel to Arbuthnot, 8 Nov. 1838, cited in C. S. Parker (ed.), *The life of Sir Robert Peel from his private papers*, London 1899, ii. 368. Peel's letter, however, should be dated 1839 (Aspinall, *Diaries*, p. lvii), and probably also refers to the initial registration campaigns of the Anti-Corn Law League.

70 Arbuthnot to Peel, 10 Nov. 1839, Peel MS Add. 40341, fo. 130.

The failure of central control: the Reform Association

Whig leaders were also circumspect about central election management during the 1830s, but probably to a lesser extent than their Conservative counterparts. Despite Professor Newbould's argument that the Whigs 'discouraged the efforts of agents like Joseph Parkes', and rejected central election management as 'an insidious democratic inroad on the aristocratic preserve' and 'a euphemism for Radicalism', the new Reform Association was initially extremely successful in its central management of local Liberal registration contests.[71] At their first revision of 1835, for example, 'the activity throughout the country excited through the agency of the Reform Association', was reported to have produced 'a great gain to the Liberal cause'.[72] Lord Melbourne, the prime minister, may have privately despaired of 'being able to manage or control' the activities 'at Cleveland Row',[73] but both he and the Whig leader in the Commons Lord John Russell received frank and regular reports from Parkes on electoral and political matters.[74] Whig disdain was clearly no insuperable obstacle either to the success or standing of the Reform Association. Indeed, in a far more positive reading of Whig dynamics, Professor Mandler has argued that 'Whig aristocrats were instrumental in establishing a Central Reform Association' and that far from viewing 'the Cleveland Square group' with suspicion, it was 'led by none other than those Foxite election organisers Mulgrave, Hobhouse and Duncannon'.[75] By focusing on the Whig leadership, however, neither account offers a sufficient explanation of why such an initially successful organisation, whose declared aim was to centralise and systematise the battle for the registration, fell into such quick decline.

The serious difficulties that affected the Reform Association's management of the 1836 revision, on which the 1837 general election was held, arose chiefly out of its organisational style and structure, rather than its relationship with the rest of the party. In direct contrast to the Conservative election managers, the Reform Association had adopted a highly centralised approach. Coppock, the association's secretary, later recalled that their 'object was to attend to the registration generally through England . . . in some instances by small grants of money, in others by advice'.[76] As a result, local Reform associations and their activists often lacked the same degree of local political assimilation, acceptance and autonomy as their Conservative

---

[71] Ian D. C. Newbould, *Whiggery and Reform, 1830–1841: the politics of government*, London 1990, 10, 32.

[72] Parkes to Durham, 23 Oct. 1835, Lambton MSS; Parkes to Charles Tennyson, 15 Oct. 1835, LAS, Tennyson D'Eynecourt MSS TdE H 31/11.

[73] W. T. McCullagh Torrens, *Memoirs of the rt. hon. William second viscount Melbourne*, London 1878, ii. 67.

[74] Parkes to Melbourne, 30 Aug. 1837, Royal Archives, Melbourne MSS box 79; Parkes to Russell, 6 Oct. 1836, PRO, Russell MSS 30/22/2c, fo. 221.

[75] Mandler, *Aristocratic government*, 164 n. 30.

[76] PP 1852 (1431) xxvii. 197–207, minutes 3506–99.

counterparts. 'I doubt some of the Reform Association correspondents being good for much', Parkes complained in the middle of the 1836 revision.[77] This more centralised structure placed a tremendous strain on one or two key individuals, especially Coppock, who, like Parkes, was over-burdened with charity commission work during much of 1836. The problem became acute during September, when Parkes informed the chief whip E. J. Stanley that 'Coppock has not put his best shoulder to the wheel'.[78] A month later Parkes was still complaining:

> Between you and I it has been hard work to keep Coppock up to scratch. . . . Now the registrations are on the eve of commencement, and he must be kept to the collar. . . . What with his salary, and what is better the *connection*, he ought in such times to give his best energies and attention to the cause.[79]

Another key development that impaired the work and standing of the Reform Association was the establishment of the Reform Club in February 1836, for which Parkes was largely responsible.[80] This ensured the gradual eclipse of 3 Cleveland Row as an election centre, with its pronounced emphasis upon registration activity, and the transfer of patronage, power and important pecuniary aid to the more illustrious setting of 104 Pall Mall, where the club was officially opened on 24 May 1836.[81] Both E. J. Stanley and Ellice, who strongly supported the work of the Reform Association, were vehemently opposed to another club precisely on these grounds.[82] As Ellice suggested to Parkes, 'we should rather endeavour by degrees to enlarge the foundations of our Reform Association, than risk the failure of a greater speculation'.[83] Parkes and other leading Radicals, however, effectively forced the Whigs to accept and adopt a new 'Liberal Union Club'.[84] While this ensured

---

[77] Parkes to Stanley, 9 Oct. 1836, UCL, Parkes MSS.

[78] Parkes to Stanley, 14 Sept. 1836, ibid.

[79] Parkes to Stanley, 9 Oct. 1836, ibid.

[80] For details of the club's formation see Stuart J. Reid, *Life and letters of the first earl of Durham, 1792–1840*, London 1906, ii. 74–80; Gash, *Politics in the age of Peel*, 406–10; Newbould, *Whiggery and Reform*, 194–6.

[81] It later moved to Gwydyr House, Whitehall (7 June 1838), thence to the Salopian Coffee House, 41 Charing Cross Road (29 Dec. 1840), before the completion of a new Pall Mall building on 1 Mar. 1841: Fagan, *Reform Club*, 35, 45, 70.

[82] Close, 'The elections of 1835 and 1837', 437; Parkes to Durham, 2 Feb. 1836, and 'memorandum by Molesworth on formation of Reform Club', 7 Feb. 1836, Lambton MSS.

[83] Ellice MSS, cited in Gash, *Politics in the age of Peel*, 405–6.

[84] Parkes to Brougham, 12 Feb. 1836, Brougham MSS. On Tuesday 2 Feb. 1836 Parkes, Molesworth, Hume, Grote and Ward had issued a circular announcing a new club, with a 'provisional committee' of fifty Radicals. Although Ellice and Stanley objected strongly, their hand had effectively been forced, since there were no Whigs in the proposed committee. On Sunday 7 February Parkes, Molesworth, Ellice and Stanley agreed to a new committee, with names acceptable to both sides, which was formally announced the next day at a meeting in Ellice's house: 'memorandum', 7 Feb. 1836, Lambton MSS; 'resolutions', 2, 8 Feb. 1836, RCA, box 75.

Whig support, and a membership of over 1,000, it also ensured Whig predominance. Only thirteen of the fifty original supporters of the club proposed by Parkes and Sir William Molesworth went on to join its first managment committee of thirty-five members.[85] Although the Radicals had achieved their goal of forming a central body to rival that of the Carlton, the Reform Club ultimately reflected and reinforced an essentially Whig outlook and agenda. Coppock, for example, was quickly replaced by Walter Scott as the club's secretary, receiving life membership in compensation.[86] More important, the Reform Club clearly failed to establish the registration committee that Parkes and Durham had envisaged. More than a year after its formation, Parkes was writing to Durham that 'we intend actively (thro' the Association) to attend to the next Registration'.[87]

The 1836 revision was therefore badly managed by the central Liberal organisers. By the middle of May 1836, £10,000 had been raised and 'invested in exchequer bills on account of the Reform Club' at Messrs Prescott, Grote and Co.[88] This substantial financial outlay by party members greatly diminished the income available to the Reform Association, producing, as Parkes complained, a 'great want' of 'funds for registration'.[89] It was not long before the authority of the Reform Association as an organisational centre was also challenged. In July 1836, for instance, Ellice's son overthrew its carefully laid arrangements for his return by the 'united Liberals' in the Newcastle-upon-Tyne by-election, destroying the party's hopes of success.[90] Parkes's enthusiasm, in many respects the driving force behind the Association, declined rapidly following the large number of Liberal defeats in the 1837 election, which effectively destroyed the Whigs' working majority. 'I am sure it is the *last* Liberal Parliament as the system now exists', he gloomily predicted to Stanley.[91] Thereafter Parkes became increasingly disillusioned with the Melbourne ministry and the chances of a Liberal revival, and took long trips abroad during both the 1838 and 1839 revisions.[92]

The Reform Association's gradual eclipse as an election centre was ultimately reflected in its capacity to fund candidates and contests. When the establishment of a central election fund was proposed in 1837, the objection raised by the Whigs was less one of principle, than the fact that the meeting was to be held at the Reform Association, with Coppock's name being on the

---

85 'List of members, 1836', RCA, box 75.
86 'Letter books, May 1836–Oct. 1848', RCA, shelf 17.
87 Parkes to Durham, 30 May 1837, Lambton MSS.
88 James Coppock to Messrs Prescott, Grote and Co., 16 May 1836, 'letter books', RCA, shelf 17.
89 Parkes to Durham, 19 July 1836, Lambton MSS.
90 Parkes to Durham, 26 July 1836, ibid.
91 Parkes to Stanley, 13 Aug. 1837, Parkes MSS.
92 Parkes to Durham, 16 Aug. 1838, Lambton MSS; Parkes to Ellice, 7 Nov. 1839, National Library of Scotland, Ellice MSS; William Thomas, *The philosophic radicals*, Oxford 1979, 300–1; 'Parkes', *New dictionary of national biography*, forthcoming.

list of originators.[93] A limited general election fund, similar in scope and function to the one in operation at the Carlton, was administered by the Reform Club at the 1841 election, with cheques being drawn at Messrs Ransom and Co.[94] But although Parkes and Coppock both continued to play some role in Liberal election management, the key organisational initiative had effectively passed to Pall Mall. By 1841 there was very little to choose between the two parties, either in terms of the style and structure of their central election management, or the level and intensity of their central organisational control.

'Club government' in context

The electoral performance of the parties in this period cannot simply be explained in terms of their different attitudes and approaches to central election management.[95] Leaders and moderates from both parties remained cautious about central control and, despite the initial successes of the Reform Association, both parties declined permanent organisation of local registration activity on a centralised and systematic basis. Peel's abhorrence of extra-parliamentary activity, in particular, suggests that the enormous growth of Conservative constituency organisations and partisan registration societies from 1835 onwards occurred almost in spite of the attitudes of political leaders. Where central initiatives for encouraging the growth and development of constituency organisations did develop, they were largely the preserve of 'ultra' elements within both parties, whose attempts to establish a more coherent and more systematic organisation of elections and registration were either rejected by the party leaders or, in the case of the Liberals, eventually marginalised and outmanoeuvred. In this context, the failings of so-called 'club government' clearly outweighed the successes.[96]

The discussion of the limited variations between the two parties in terms of central management has, however, hinted at greater differences in the origins and development of their respective constituency organisations. The system of claims and objections outlined in chapter 1 provided local activists with formidable opportunities for party conflict and the politicisation of the electorate on a far more permanent basis. Precisely how the parties adapted to the new operational realities of the reformed electoral system and approached the business of registration was to prove increasingly significant in determining their fortunes during the 1830s. As the remaining sections of this

---

93 Parkes to Stanley, 29 Dec. 1837, Parkes MSS; Brett, 'Liberal middle classes', 286.
94 Walsh, 'Working class political integration', 159–65; PP 1844 (538) xviii. 6, 8, 550, 557.
95 In his study of the Whig party, for example, Professor Newbould contrasted the 'singleness of purpose as existed between Bonham and Peel at the Carlton Club' with the attitude of the Whig leaders, who 'distrusted and neglected organisation': *Whiggery and Reform*, 14, 33.
96 Cf. Gash, *Politics in the age of Peel*, 393–427.

chapter show, it was at the local rather than the central level that the greatest differences were to emerge between the parties, and where the genesis for national party performance in this period needs to be firmly re-established.

Constituency organisation

Galvanised by electoral defeat and a desire to expedite a return to pre-Reform patterns of political allegiance, the Conservatives were initially far more active than the Liberals in the localities, and within two years of the Reform Act had established new constituency associations in at least fifteen boroughs and eleven county divisions.[97] By contrast, many of the embryonic Liberal organisations already in place fell into rapid decay and disunity after 1832. The network of Political Unions, in particular, which had played such a noisy part in the extra-parliamentary campaign for Reform, was to prove both structurally and temperamentally ill-suited to the permanent and mundane routines of electoral organisation. Many political unionists, after all, were non-electors, and largely indifferent to the registration and mobilisation of a reformed electorate from which they had been excluded.[98] The National Political Union, under the leadership of Francis Place, made an attempt to organise support for a co-ordinated Liberal registration campaign in 1832, but most Political Unions were pre-occupied with their own decline and deeply suspicious of any external interference, so the plan came to nothing.[99] By June 1834 even the famous Birmingham Political Union had collapsed, 'having been preceded to the grave by almost every Political Union in England'.[100]

The early lead in organisation taken by the Conservatives produced a small number of spectacular Tory victories at the unexpected general election of 1835, which were directly attributable to their superior registration activity. In Leeds, where the Tories had successfully objected to all the Liberal compounded rate-payers at the revision of 1834, they captured a Liberal

---

[97] Bath, Blackburn, Boston, Bristol, Bury St Edmunds, Halifax, Leeds, Leicester, Liverpool, Manchester, Newark, Nottingham, Rochdale, Stroud, and Yarmouth; Berkshire, Cumberland, South Devon, Durham, Essex, East Gloucestershire, South Lancashire, North Northamptonshire, West Suffolk, South Warwickshire, Worcestershire: Close, 'The elections of 1835 and 1837', 194–6; Walsh, 'Working class political integration', 195, 451; Stewart, Conservative party, 130–1; Gash, 'Electoral organization', 141–3; E. J. Burton to W. R. Cartwright, 16 June 1833, Cartwright (Aynho) MSS C(A) 8204.

[98] LoPatin, Political Unions, 3–4, 173; Carlos Flick, The Birmingham Political Union and the movements for reform in Britain, 1830–1839, Hamden, Conn. 1978, 100–1, 113; Close, 'The elections of 1835 and 1837', 195.

[99] The Examiner, 19 Aug. 1832.

[100] Flick, Birmingham Political Union, 109.

seat.[101] In Bristol, the Tory White Lion Club's policy of 'defending their own and attacking Whig registrants' helped ensure the return of two Conservatives.[102] Similar activities resulted in Tory gains in the boroughs of Halifax, Leicester, Rochdale, Ripon and Yarmouth,[103] and were recorded in the counties of Bedfordshire, Buckinghamshire, South Northamptonshire, South Warwickshire, West Suffolk,[104] Berkshire[105] and Westmorland.[106] However, it should be emphasised that these early activities were on a local rather than national scale, and inspired by circumstances peculiar to each constituency. The Tories were certainly better prepared, but in the years immediately after 1832 neither party possessed the necessary experience or the incentive to launch a full and systematic registration drive.[107] Nobody, after all, had anticipated a dissolution before 1839.

Liberal election managers and the Liberal press, however, eagerly seized upon registration as the principal factor explaining their losses in the 1835 general election. Parkes, for example, informed Charles Tennyson that 'the Tories crush us by registration. I am forming Warwickshire into Political Unions. I had a good defeat thro' the registration neglect, and I won't be beaten by *that* again'.[108] With the parties now so evenly matched in parliament, the key to any future election victory lay in establishing permanent associations and systematically attending to the registers. But in the ensuing rush to establish constituency organisations, subtle differences of stimulus, style and structure soon began to emerge between the parties. The Kettering Committee for the Registration of Liberal Voters was typical of the approach adopted by the Reformers. Established 'with a view of objecting to the claims of such as are not likely to vote in the liberal interest', one of its key aims was to keep in regular contact with Coppock, the secretary of the Reform Association.[109]

The formation of Conservative associations, by contrast, owed very little to the work of central election managers. Spurred on by well-publicised exhortations in *Blackwoods' Edinburgh Magazine*, most were set up with the

---

101 D. Fraser, *Urban politics in Victorian England: the structure of politics in Victorian cities*, Leicester 1976, 187; F. M. L. Thompson, 'Whigs and Liberals in the West Riding, 1830–1860', *EHR* lxxiv (1959), 220.

102 Phillips, *Boroughs*, 75.

103 Close, 'The elections of 1835 and 1837', 196.

104 E. J. Burton to William Grant, 30 June 1833, Cartwright (Aynho) MSS C(A) 8205.

105 *Hansard*, 3rd ser. xviii. 1277; BeRO, Bouverie-Pusey MSS D/E Bp/02/1/1a–j, 2b.

106 'Misc. election pps, 1834–5', Lonsdale MSS D/Lons/L; CuRO, Messrs Bleaymire and Sheppard D/BS/C, box 32.

107 Close, 'The elections of 1835 and 1837', 191–2.

108 Parkes to Tennyson, 31 Jan. 1835, Tennyson D'Eyncourt MSS H31/10; *Spectator*, 7 Feb. 1835.

109 'Whig committee books', NRO, Fitzwilliam (Milton) MSS Fitz. misc. vol. 503, Oct. 1835; Fitz. misc. vol. 502, 11 Dec. 1835; misc. acc. ZB 43, 27, 28 July 1837.

patronage and support of local Tory squires and MPs.[110] Instead of a central co-ordinating body like the Reform Association supplying inspiration and technical support, local Tory activists relied on the advice and experience of the small cadre of associations which were already well established. Sir Edmund Filmer's experience in setting up and helping to run the Bath Conservative Association, for example, was heavily drawn upon in the formation of the West Kent Conservative and Constitutional Association.[111] Sir Henry Mainwaring, along with many other local Tory activists, established the Cheshire Conservative Association expressly on the plans of the highly successful South Lancashire Conservative Association, which had been active since 1833.[112] Local Conservatives tended to be much more sensitive to charges of outside interference and central control than their Liberal counterparts, and they carefully cultivated an image of local autonomy and indigenous independent enthusiasm for their organisations. Because of Granville Somerset's prominent position as the Conservatives' election manager, for example, his name was deliberately kept out of the Monmouthshire Conservative Association.[113] As the local Tory agent recommended, in order to ensure success 'the society should *appear* to emanate from the Independent Country Gentlemen alone'.[114]

The marked tone of local autonomy among Conservative organisations found literary expression in their rules and regulations. The founding declaration of the Totnes Conservative Association, for example, made a point of proclaiming 'that this Association is entirely independent of any other association whatever'.[115] This contrasted strongly with the centrally affiliated status of many Reform associations. When the Denbighshire Reform Association was established, 'for attending to the registration of voters', it declared itself 'in connexion with the "British Reform Association in London" and as a branch thereof'.[116] Much of its inspiration came from one man, Robert Biddulph, who after his defeat there in 1835 had joined the staff at Cleveland Row.[117] The formation of its opposite number, the Denbighshire Conservative Association, could not have been more different. Developing gradually out of Tory meetings held in Ruthin, which were initially inspired by the issue of appropriation, its genesis was genuinely local, indigenous and popular.[118]

---

[110] *Blackwoods' Edinburgh Magazine* xxxvii (May 1835), 796–814; xxxviii (July 1835), 1–16.

[111] Filmer MSS U120, C72/74.

[112] *Oxford Conservative*, 7 Mar. 1835.

[113] Granville Somerset to Octavius Morgan, 1 Mar. 1841, NLW, Tredegar Park MSS 71/119.

[114] Rodney to Morgan, 7 Mar. 1841, ibid. 71/120.

[115] DRO, Totnes borough records 1579A/12/33.

[116] 'Founding address of Denbighshire Reform Association', 19 Sept. 1837, NLW, Chirk Castle MSS C89.

[117] Parkes to Stanley, 11 Oct. 1835, Parkes MSS.

[118] John Heaton to Sir Watkin Williams Wynn, 30 June 1834; John Roberts to Sir W. Williams Wynn, 10 Apr. 1835, NLW, Wynnstay MSS L919–20.

Despite Charles Wynn's very strong reservations about political associations, he felt obliged to accept a position as its vice-president because, as he explained to Peel, 'there is frequently utility in acquiescing in what one cannot prevent'.[119]

This Conservative suspicion of external interference meant that their constituency organisations became genuinely integrated into the various political milieux in which they were established. Conservative associations frequently tailored both their activities and their policies to suit local circumstances. In Brecknockshire, the Conservative Club deliberately kept their subscriptions very low because, as the local Tory MP put it, 'the Welsh Farmers never like to pay much'.[120] In deference to the large Dissenting community at Newport, no clergyman was allowed to serve on the Newport District Committee of the Monmouthshire Conservative Registration Association, despite a dearth of willing volunteers.[121] In East Sussex, the Hastings Rape Conservative Association even adopted a declaration in favour of tithe reform, because it was 'a subject which engages the peculiar attention of the yeomanry in this district whose co-operation it is desirable to have'.[122]

Conservative registration activity, especially in the counties, was also easily and efficiently assimilated into the existing patterns and rituals of local administration performed by Tory squires. Staffordshire's Conservative county association, for instance, held its meetings at assize time.[123] In Nottingham, the preliminary annual meeting of the county's Conservative registration committee was deliberately fixed for 2 p.m. on 8 July, 'as the visiting Governors of the Lunatic Asylum hold their quarterly meeting at noon on that day'.[124] The Conservatives appear to have been much better at both harmonising and legitimatising divergent electoral influences within the medium of a local constituency association. Indeed, those responsible for establishing their associations often went out of their way to overcome the suspicions of local Conservative leaders and enlist their full co-operation and support. When establishing the West Kent Conservative Association, for example, Filmer carefully courted Lord Marsham, the irascible leader of West Kent's Conservatives, recognising that his proposals would initially be unlikely to 'meet with your Lordship's full approbation'.[125] In East Sussex, Thomas Bellingham solicited and, after a lengthy and difficult negotiation,

---

[119] Charles Williams Wynn to Peel, 25 Apr. 1835, Peel MS Add. 40420, fo. 74r; Stewart, *Conservative party*, 135; Gash, 'Electoral organization', 150. The other vice-president was Charles's brother Watkin, Tory MP for Denbighshire.

[120] Col. T. Wood to John Jones, 3 Mar. 1836, NLW, Mayberry MSS 6679.

[121] H. J. Davis to Octavius Morgan, 6 May 1841, Tredegar Park MSS 91/134.

[122] T. C. Bellingham to Lord Ashburnham, 17 May 1835, East Sussex Record Office, Ashburnham MSS 3259.

[123] Jeffery, *Dyott's diary*, ii. 195–6.

[124] R. Milward to Burnell, 29 June 1836, NAO, Craven-Smith-Milnes of Hockerton (Winkburn) MSS DD/CW 7/19.

[125] Filmer to Marsham, 11 June 1836, Filmer MSS U120, C73/1, letterbook, fo. 20.

eventually obtained the backing of the earl of Ashburnham in establishing a local Tory association.[126]

Many Reform associations, by contrast, appear to have been set up in haste and lacked the same degree of local political assimilation, acceptance and enthusiasm. Some of them, such as the Newcastle Reform Association, never really got off the ground and had to be re-established.[127] Others became prey to internal divisions and the fragmentation of the Liberal alliance. By 1837 many of those established in 1835 had begun to disintegrate into their separate Whig, Liberal and Radical components. In the West Riding, for example, an important rift developed between the Whig controlled West Riding Reform and Registration Association and the increasingly progressive Liberal organisations of its various towns.[128] Borough Reform associations, in particular, had a tendency to split into Liberal and Radical factions. In Canterbury opposition to the New Poor Law led to the formation of a separate Radical association, while in Durham the registration revision of 1837 actually developed into a three-way contest between Tories, Whigs and Liberals.[129]

Even some of the initially most successful Reform associations eventually succumbed to these divisions. Bristol's Liberal Association, for example, achieved impressive gains of 349 voters at the 1835 revision (when they also objected to over 700 Tory freemen) and 156 in 1836.[130] Its heavy dependence on a small number of large subscriptions, however, meant that its activities were severely curtailed by the loss of two £500 subscribers later that year, one by death and the other from 'indisposition'.[131] Tory gains on the municipal council, and a fracturing of the Liberal alliance between the middle and working classes, accelerated its decline, and by 1839 the formation of a Liberal Protection Society and the emergence of Chartism had ensured an 'onset of apathy and a decline of party fervour'.[132] A similar picture emerges at Leicester, where the Reform association's superior registration activity in 1835 and 1836 helped to defeat the two Tory MPs in 1837, but a lack of cohesion and of willing volunteers brought about a decline thereafter.[133] Equivalent problems also affected the Reformers of Great Yarmouth, Bradford, North Durham and the West Riding.[134] As the chairman of the West Riding Reform and Registration Association complained to his counterpart at the Barnsley District Reform Association, soon after their crushing Liberal defeat

---

126 Bellingham to Ashburnham, 19 May 1835, Ashburnham MSS 3260.
127 Brett, 'Liberal middle classes', 250.
128 See the case study in ch. 5 below.
129 *Kent Herald*, 6 July 1837; Radice, 'Identification, interests and influence', 330.
130 Bush to Vyvyan, 29 Oct. 1835, 2 Nov. 1836, CRO, Vyvyan MSS DDV/BO/62/62, 77.
131 Bush to Vyvyan, 14 Aug. 1836, ibid. 75.
132 Brett, 'Liberal middle classes', 304–7, 353.
133 Radice, 'Identification, interests and influence', 255–8, 266–8.
134 J. Bayly to William Wilshere, 20 July 1841, HeRO, Wilshere MSS D/EX14/52; D. G. Wright, 'A radical borough: parliamentary politics in Bradford, 1832–41', *Northern History* iv (1969), 140–9; Radice, 'Identification, interests and influence', 332.

of 1841, 'there is no bond of union among us or we should not be now as we are *prostrate* before a *powerful* antagonist'.[135]

Local activists

All constituency associations ultimately depended on the genuine enthusiasm and support of local volunteers for their success and long-term survival. The patronage and financial assistance of landed elites was always important, but heavy-handed attempts to dictate policy, or to extend and consolidate landed control through the medium of party, invariably backfired. Lord Londonderry's hegemony over the Durham Conservative Association, for instance, increasingly undermined its influence, encouraging the fragmentation of Conservative support into independent factions, such as the Stockton Conservative Association, which was established in early 1838.[136] As a local paper later observed, there was a growing 'determination in the minds of the independent Conservatives no longer to submit to dictation'.[137] In Nottinghamshire, the formation of Conservative organisations also owed much to a powerful landed proprietor, the duke of Newcastle, but their subsequent strength and survival owed little to his patronage and much more to the inclusion, involvement and integration of local leaders and volunteers. The Pegge Burnells of Winkburn, near Newark, were typical of the unseen activists upon whom the county's Conservative association depended. The son, Edward, supervised local registration activity, assisted with candidate selection, and helped collect over £1,000 'ready for Conservative electioneering' at the 1837 election.[138] The father, Broughton Benjamin, meanwhile, took a keen interest in promoting Conservative operative societies and, for instance, in 1836 arranged for his son to send 'six hares and a brace of pheasants for the operative conservative dinner'.[139]

A comparison of different constituency organisations suggests that the Tories were much better at recruiting, resourcing and rewarding these local activists than the Liberals, who, by contrast, often complained about a lack of suitable volunteers willing to undertake the dull routines of registration and committee work between elections. Part of the reason for this stemmed from the centralised focus of many Reform associations, their frequent lack of genuine local assimilation and integration, and the increasingly disparate nature of the Whig–Liberal alliance. But a number of other factors also gave the Conservatives an important advantage in attracting local support. The lavish social functions held by many Conservative associations, for

---

135 F. H. Fawkes to Thomas Wilson, 31 Aug. 1841, LDA, Wilson MSS DB178/33.
136 Thomas R. Grey to Lord Londonderry, 14 Feb.; Londonderry to Stockton Conservative Association, 15 Feb.; John Cartwright to Londonderry, 16 Feb. 1838, DuRO, Londonderry MSS D/Lo/C447 (4)–(6); Stewart, *Conservative party*, 131.
137 *Durham Advertiser*, 2 July 1841, cited in Radice, 'Identification, interests and influence', 367.
138 Craven-Smith-Milnes of Hockerton (Winkburn) MSS, DD/CW 7/13–19, 8/17.
139 B. B. Pegge Burnell to Edward Pegge Burnell, 21 Dec. 1836, ibid. 7/20/b.

example, greatly broadened their popular appeal and membership. In Buckinghamshire, it was not the expense of registration or electioneering that put the county's Conservative association in the red every year, but the cost of its annual ball and dinner.[140] Drawing on the experience of Kent's Conservatives, the founders of Monmouthshire's new Conservative Association were told regularly to 'collect together the different classes of the constituency – mix with them, and sit with them at dinner', and 'to let them eat and drink as much as they will and be merry'. 'Do this', they were advised, 'and you need fear no opposition: every attempt to displace you will be impotent. The grand secret is sociability.'[141] As these recommendations suggest, leading Tory peers and personalities not only helped finance popular events, they also attended in person, providing 'a sort of magnet which draws the *vulgum pecus*'.[142] The South Lincolnshire Conservative dinner of 1837, for instance, was attended by forty-six leading peers and gentlemen, who footed the total bill of £642 6s. 6d. with subscriptions of between £5 and £40.[143] This Tory culture of sociability helped to gloss over potentially divisive political or religious debates within the party, and demonstrated an early awareness of the important interconnection between social amusement and continuous political activism. The methods perfected by the Tories in the Primrose League of the 1880s can, in effect, all be found operating at a local level in the 1830s.[144]

The large number of Conservative volunteers also resulted from the general inclusion of women and wives at festivals and balls, and their specific recruitment into additional organisations. In Canterbury, for example, a female Conservative club was established on 16 March 1836.[145] In Scotland, the Tories founded an autonomous association specifically for women.[146] Even where no separate organisation was set up, it is clear that the participation of women was usually welcomed rather than rebuffed. It was not unusual for their assistance to be publicly acknowledged in an association's published lists of subscribers and supporters, such as that circulated by the Monmouthshire Conservative Association in 1841.[147] Female Liberal activists, by contrast, are conspicuously absent from the record, suggesting, as one local study has recently observed, that 'in the cultural politics of gender at least the . . . Tories were light years ahead'.[148] The same might be said about

140 'Buckingham District Conservative Association minute book', Archdeacon MSS AR 81/75/15, fos 15–52.
141 Roberts to Morgan, 13 Feb. 1841, Tredegar Park MSS 71/29. I am indebted to Matthew Cragoe for this reference.
142 Ostrogorski, *Democracy*, i. 356.
143 LAS, Brownlow MSS 4 BNL/14; *Lincolnshire Chronicle*, 13 Oct. 1837.
144 Martin Pugh, *The Tories and the people, 1880–1935*, Oxford 1985, 41 passim.
145 Andrews, 'Political issues in the county of Kent', 122.
146 Walsh, 'Working class political integration', 203.
147 Circular letter, 16 Feb.1841, Tredegar Park MSS 71/114.
148 James Vernon, 'Politics and the people: a study in English political culture and communication, 1808–68', unpubl. PhD diss. Manchester 1991, 455.

the political recruitment and involvement of the young. Here the Tories again established a number of separate organisations, such as the Warrington Young Conservative Club, founded in 1835, and the Barnstaple Young Conservative Association, whose 'second annual dinner' in 1839 was attended by Sir Thomas Acland, MP for North Devon.[149]

The Reformers, by contrast, were 'not so well acquainted with the science of *eating* and *drinking* and *making speeches* as their Tory opponents', as one seasoned election agent put it.[150] Carlos Flick's conclusion that the Reformers of Birmingham 'were generally outeaten and outregistered' by their opponents captures an important linkage.[151] Social functions played an essential role in stimulating and sustaining partisan vigilance and enthusiasm for registration activity in the long lulls between elections. Many Reformers recognised this, but their own attempts to stage such festivities and functions repeatedly appear to have run into the twin problems of Liberal temperance and Whig aristocratic disdain.[152] After the highly publicised Middlesex Reform dinner of January 1837, for example, Parkes was furious that in spite of all the efforts of the county's two Liberal MPs, and its metropolitan location, there was 'no minister and no representative of a minister present even to acknowledge the toast of ministers'.[153] Edward Romilly's difficulties in organising a Liberal dinner at Ludlow, on the eve of the highly contested revision of 1835, are equally illustrative. He desperately tried to solicit the support of his close friend Edward Strutt, Liberal MP for Derby and a close ally of the duke of Devonshire.[154] 'I know that public dinners are no more to your taste than they are to mine', he pleaded, but

> your presence would do me more real survise [*sic.*] than you can suppose, not so much in making amusing speeches appropriate to such occasions, but in adding to the respectability of our party. If you, and John[155] and one or two of my friends would meet us, it would be easy then to get R. Slaney, Sir E. Smythe, A. Knight and others of the Whig Gentry to be present too, and in this way, the 'rag-tag and liberal tail' of Ludlow would gain respect and of course influence.[156]

---

[149] *Preston Pilot*, 14 Feb. 1835, cited in Walsh, 'Working class political integration', 203; William Bromklim-Daike to Acland, 22 Oct. 1839, DRO, Acland (BroadClyst) MSS 1148M/box 11(ii)/31.

[150] John Davis to Lord Mahon, 18 Sept. 1836, Stanhope MSS U1590 C382.

[151] Flick, *Birmingham Political Union*, 113.

[152] For a useful section contrasting Liberal temperance with Tory pub politics see (the book) Vernon, *Politics and the people*, 214–30.

[153] Parkes to Durham, 24 Jan. 1837, Lambton MSS.

[154] Edward Romilly to Edward Strutt, 24 Sept. 1835, NAO, Belper of Kingston MSS DD/BK/7/7/227; C. E. Hogarth, 'The Derbyshire parliamentary elections of 1832', *Derbyshire Archaeological Journal* lxxxix (1969), 73–4.

[155] John Strutt, Edward's brother.

[156] Romilly to Edward Strutt, 2 Oct. 1835, Belper of Kingston MSS DD/BK/7/7/228.

Working-class activists and operative societies

Another notable feature of the Conservative revival of the 1830s was their recruitment and mobilisation of working-class support.[157] In the forty-seven boroughs where artisanal workers formed over a third of the parliamentary electorate, the Conservatives captured 22 per cent of the seats in 1832, 51 per cent in 1835, 53 per cent in 1837 and 57 per cent in 1841.[158] The formation of Conservative operative societies, most notably in Yorkshire, Lancashire, Leicestershire, Staffordshire and Nottinghamshire, played an important part in this, providing the Tories with a popular partisan presence among the urban lower classes. As well as attracting working-class voters, these organisations recruited large numbers of unenfranchised urban activists to assist with the routines of registration.[159] In this 'noble object', declared the secretary of the Leeds Operative Conservative Society, was to be found 'the essence of Operative Conservative Societies'.[160] In Salford, where an operative organisation was established on 13 August 1835, it was reported that 'the first efforts of the Society were directed to the registration of voters and they succeeded in displacing about fifty bad votes'.[161] At Preston, the operative Conservative association paid 'a careful and vigilant attention to the parliamentary and municipal registration'.[162] For the same reason at the Bradford Operative Conservative Society

> the register for the Boro' . . . lay in the newsroom . . . for the purpose of recording the removal, disqualification or death of the Whig or Radical party in order to object, and the acquiring of a qualification or the removal of any of our own party in order to claim.[163]

In the close confines of a crowded urban community, these organisations ensured a core of partisan activity at the grass-roots level, which no amount of professional agents or financial resources could hope to rival. As the secretary of the Leeds operatives suggested, 'the humble Conservative possesses more real influence over his brother workmen than all the influence of the rich'.[164] Early Conservative operative associations, like those established in Bristol, Worcester and Leicester, amply demonstrated their utility in the

---

157 For an older, but still very useful, study of this aspect of 1830s Conservatism see R. L. Hill, *Toryism and the people, 1832–1846*, London 1929, passim.

158 Harold Bradford Raymond, 'English political parties and electoral organization, 1832–1867', PhD diss. Harvard 1952, 189.

159 Average membership was about 200–300 and comprised mainly factory workers, some employed by Tory manufacturers, and semi-skilled artisans.

160 William Paul, *A history of the origin and progress of operative Conservative societies*, Leeds 1839, 13–15.

161 Ibid. 26.

162 *Preston Pilot*, 16 July 1836.

163 'Bradford Operative Conservative Society minute book', WYAS, DB4 no. 3, fos 13v, 29v.

164 Paul, *Operative Conservative societies*, 28.

registration campaigns of 1834 and the subsequent election gains of 1835.[165] After Peel's brief ministry, hundreds more operative Conservative associations were formed, usually with the active financial assistance and patronage of upper-class leading Tories.[166] The forty honorary members of the Salford Operative Conservative Association, for example, included Lord Francis Egerton, Lord Maidstone, Sir Francis Burdett and Sir George Sinclair.[167] Staffordshire's operative societies, which by 1840 were firmly established in Walsall, Wolverhampton, West Bromich, Dudley, Bilston and Darlaston, enjoyed the support and patronage of Lords Ingestre, Sandon and Dartmouth.[168] In 1836 a National Conservative Association was also established in London, with the support of Lord Sandon, Lord Ashley and Lord Francis Egerton, in an attempt to recognise and legitimise the rapid spread of Conservative associations 'amongst the trading and labouring classes'.[169] Its central committee included both Bonham and Holmes, but there is no evidence to suggest that it interfered politically or financially with what was essentially a local and spontaneous movement.

In some places, such as Clitheroe, the Reformers established an operative society long before the Tories, but in most constituencies their organisations appear to have been hasty imitations, lacking the dynamism, financial and social patronage, and solidarity of their Conservative models.[170] As Derek Fraser concluded in his analysis of Joshua Walmsley's Liverpool Trademen's Reform Association, which attempted to emulate one established by the Conservatives in 1836, 'Liverpool Liberalism found it difficult to harness together élite Whiggism and retail and artisan radicalism'.[171] These divisions came to a head in 1841, when Walmsley put himself forward as a Liberal candidate for the borough and the old-fashioned Whigs of Liverpool refused to assist him.[172] The electoral impact of municipal reform also provided the Tories with a phalanx of rigid partisanship among alienated freemen voters, which was especially useful in creating genuine enthusiasm and active support in certain boroughs.[173] Their operative societies in Preston, Walsall, Bristol, Leeds and Leicester, for example, were especially concerned with organising the closely related annual municipal registration contests.[174] Of

---

[165] Radice, 'Identification, interests and influence', 235; William Betty (secretary of the Bristol Operative Conservative Association) to Sir Richard Vyvyan, 30 Jan. 1834, Vyvyan MSS DDV/BO/61/59; PP 1835 (547) viii. 379–421, minutes 6308–7186.

[166] *The Times*, 28 May 1835.

[167] Paul, *Operative Conservative societies*, 11; *Leeds Intelligencer*, 5 Mar. 1836.

[168] *Staffordshire Advertiser*, 1 Sept. 1838, 4 Jan. 1840.

[169] Walsh, 'Working class political integration', 580–2.

[170] Ibid. 294.

[171] Fraser, *Urban politics*, 190.

[172] Hugh M. Walmsley, *The life of Sir Joshua Walmsley*, London 1879, 128–35.

[173] See ch. 7 below, and Salmon, 'Local politics and partisanship', 372–4.

[174] *Preston Pilot*, 16 July 1836; *Staffordshire Advertiser*, 1 Feb. 1840; Vyvyan MSS DDV/BO/62/79; Paul, *Operative Conservative societies*, 14; *Leicester Chronicle*, 24 Sept. 1836.

course it needs to be stressed that lower-class membership was by no means restricted to these 'operative' societies alone. Wrexham Reform Association, for instance, consisted mainly of local tradesman, while at Bradford, where a surviving minute book provides rare details about the occupations of its members, the predominantly middle-class Reform society also included mechanics, shoemakers and machine makers.[175] Comparing the performance of the two parties is therefore rather problematic, but a number of additional factors do appear to have given the Tories organisational advantages.

In many towns and cities it is clear that the Conservatives benefited much more than the Liberals did from the work of Anglican activists in this new type of society, especially at the formative stages. In Lancaster, for example, the Revd T. Mackreth set up a new branch of the Tory Heart of Oak Club to cater exclusively 'for tradesmen'.[176] Two months after its formation the Bradford Operative Conservative Society recorded that 'the vicar of Horton paid a visit and invited a deputation to assist in the creation of a similar society in Horton township'.[177] The broad link between Anglicanism and Conservatism was clearly of importance here, but there is little evidence that Orange lodges provided the basis of any operative recruitment. Indeed, an investigation by the *Manchester Guardian* in 1836 revealed that only fourteen of the 380 members of the Salford Operative Conservative Association were former Orangemen.[178] Working-class Toryism appears to have relied on a far broader political and social platform than militant Protestantism alone, and issues such as opposition to the New Poor Law and factory reform were probably much more useful in capturing support.

The 'monarchical and military' obedience of the Tory operatives along with their public pledges to 'reverence the King and all in authority' contrasted strongly with the growing disunity and fragmentation of many Reform organisations.[179] Unlike Radical associations, whose leaders were usually working-class and whose politics became increasingly anathema to urban Liberalism, Conservative operative societies rarely developed their own political agenda, and remained strictly subservient to the authority of local Conservative leaders. They adopted and articulated values of traditional Toryism, in which 'the peer, the tradesman and the operative' respected their rank in society and became 'firmly united in the bonds of union and good fellowship'.[180] Their electoral activities, in particular, were closely supervised and co-ordinated by the agents of the local Conservative Associations. Even relatively autonomous organisations, such as the Bradford Operative Conser-

---

175 PP 1835 (547) viii. 187, minute 3100; Wright, 'Bradford', 151–2.
176 Walsh, 'Working class political integration', 319.
177 Wright, 'Bradford', 157.
178 *Manchester Courier*, 12 Mar. 1836, cited in Walsh, 'Working class political integration', 491.
179 Radice, 'Identification, interests and influence', 266; Paul, *Operative Conservative societies*, 8.
180 Hill, *Toryism and the people*, 47.

vative Association, for example, acted 'in conjunction with the Conservative Society' for electioneering and registration purposes.[181]

Conservative operative associations actively cultivated and courted sections of the working class that had not previously been politically active, and converted considerable numbers of those who had. In Dover, for example, it was reported that several 'lately decided Radicals have now Conservative handbills at their windows in token of their political conversion'.[182] Some Tory operatives were former members of Political Unions, disillusioned by Whig reforms and the exclusively middle-class agenda of the Liberals.[183] Others were fresh partisans, lured into political participation by the superior social and festive functions on offer. In contrast to the high moral tone often adopted by Radical and Liberal associations, Tory operatives invariably held their meetings in pubs, formed brass bands, organised regular balls, dances and dinners, and again welcomed the active participation of women.[184] Nine-tenths of the 3,000 people who attended the Salford Operative Conservative Society's third annual tea party and ball, for example, were female.[185] The activities of Oldham's Operative Conservative Association regularly involved 'a considerable number of females chiefly the wives of operative conservatives'.[186] In what was perhaps the most enterprising development of all, a small number of Conservative operative societies even began to perform a prudential function, offering, for example, sick care and burial clubs.[187] The Constitutional Pruning Society of Lewes, for example, acted as a 'benefit club' for lower-class Tory voters.[188] Preston's Operative Conservative Society, based at the Ship Inn, was even more innovative and not only established a 'sick and burial club' with subscriptions of between 2s. and 2s. 3d. per month, but also 'a building society for the benefit of its members'. On 4 July 1838 it was officially granted status as a Friendly Society.[189]

Anglican activists

It is important to recognise that, although Anglican clergymen tended to vote Tory and an important ideological relationship existed between Protestantism and Conservatism, in many elections candidates from both parties were able to call upon Anglican clerics to assist them in the work of

---

181 'Bradford Operative Conservative Society minute book', DB4 no. 3, fo. 38v.
182 Lord Mahon to Bonham, 30 Oct. 1838, Stanhope MSS U1590, C330/1.
183 Paul, *Operative Conservative societies*, 20, 32.
184 Warrington Operative Conservative Association, for example, established a brass band in 1838: *Manchester Guardian*, 26 May 1838, cited in Walsh, 'Working class political integration', 256–7.
185 Walsh, 'Working class political integration', 229.
186 Vernon, *Politics and the people*, 240–1.
187 Hill, *Toryism and the people*, 55–6.
188 PP 1842 (458) v. 185–6.
189 Walsh, 'Working class political integration', 230; PP 1842 (73) xxvi. 291.

canvassing and electoral mobilisation.[190] In the excitement of an election, there was no partisan monopoly over clerical assistance.[191] Between elections, however, Conservative organisation benefited much more from the permanent involvement and administrative assistance of the Anglican clergy, especially in the new but unglamorous routines of registration activity. A quarter of the founding committee-men of both the Monmouthshire Conservative Registration Association and the North Devon Conservative Registration Association, for example, were beneficed clergymen.[192] One fifth of the members of the standing committee of both the Staffordshire Conservative Club and the East Kent Conservative Association were Anglican clerics, while at Cheltenham, the long-term rallying and registration of Conservative voters 'owed as much to its clergy as to its election agents'.[193] By contrast, no Anglican clergyman appears on the lists of committee members, local assistants or subscribers to either the Denbighshire Reform Association or the South Devon Reform Association, despite the fact that in both these counties such figures prominently backed Liberal candidates in elections.[194] As Parkes complained, 'such parsons are as scarce as phoenixes'.[195]

Socially respectable, but politically unambitious, the lesser Anglican clergy became the unseen backbone of the numerous parochial subcommittees of many Conservative associations. They possessed the administrative ability, the ideological motivation and, above all, the necessary time to organise the routines of registration with vigour and energy. A quarter of those who attended the weekly committee meetings of the Buckingham District Conservative Association, for example, were clergymen.[196] Active clerical assistance also allowed the Tories to make superior use of the Church's parochial infrastructure for permanent but unobtrusive electioneering activity. In Hertfordshire, 10 per cent of the Conservative association's 170 district subcommittees, established 'for assisting the agents in watching over the registration', were managed by local clerics.[197] In Southwark, the Revd Dr Kenny of St Olave's played a leading role in supervising the registra-

---

190 Vincent, *Pollbooks*, 57–193; Phillips, *Boroughs*, 278–85; John Wolffe, *The Protestant crusade in Great Britain, 1829–1860*, Oxford 1991, 81–106, 198–246.

191 See ch. 3 below for a more detailed discussion.

192 Henry John Davis to Octavius Morgan, 18 May; James Birch to Morgan, 18 May 1841, Tredegar Park MSS 71/135, 57/280; Stanhope MSS U1590, C381/1.

193 Hatherton MSS D260/M/F/5/27/10, fo. 89; *Maidstone Gazette*, 21 Apr. 1835; Courtenay, 'Cheltenham', 71.

194 Chirk Castle MSS C89–90; Russell to W. G. Adam, 1 Sept. 1837, Bedford (London) MSS L1258M/SS/C(DL) F122, and 'expenses' E 79.

195 Parkes to Stanley, 11 Oct. 1835, Parkes MSS.

196 'Buckingham District Conservative Association minute book', Archdeacon MSS AR 81/75/15, fos 1–15.

197 'Resolutions of Hertfordshire Conservative Association', 27 May 1836, Messrs Crawters of Hertford D/E Cr 105/5; 'Committee minutes', 3 July 1837, HeRO, Messrs Longmore and Sworder D/EL/B562. Similarly, in the electoral district of Usk in

tion activity of the Brixton branch of the East Surrey Conservative Society, which he subdivided into nineteen parochial district committees. During its first year of existence, this branch alone increased the strength of the Conservative party by over 400 votes through their exertions before the revising barristers.[198] Like many Anglican clerics, Kenny was able to call upon the active assistance of minor ecclesiastical officers, particularly the parish clerks, whose appointment invariably lay in the gift of individual incumbents. 'We shall take our objections *very freely* to the Conservatives, particularly the *parish clerks*', commented one embittered Liberal agent in the run-up to the 1835 revision.[199]

Comparable documentary evidence for the involvement of the Nonconformist clergy in Liberal registration activity between elections is, unfortunately, singularly lacking. But it doubtless took place. The problem is that Dissenting chapels served more directly as local centres of electoral organisation, so that their preachers had no real need to become involved in the affairs of a separate Reform association, and have consequently left little record of their activities. Then there is the added difficulty of trying to identify who the Dissenting ministers were. Studies of Wales in later periods certainly leave no doubt about their ability to engage in the routines of canvassing and electioneering with equal aplomb, or of the fact that 'spread out across the county, often two or three to a parish, they formed a comprehensive local network' ideally suited to such activities.[200] But the extent to which they were really able to match their Anglican counterparts in terms of the time, financial resources and social connections required for year round registration activity must be questioned.

The prominence of local clergymen in Conservative associations became far more marked as the decade progressed. Even in a small borough like Banbury, nearly half of those who were invited to attend the Conservative association's annual dinner of 1841, held at the White Lion, were local clergymen.[201] As politico-religious tensions continued to develop, a growing number of parsons appeared willing to cast aside earlier reservations about open political activity, and to ignore the admonitions of those like the bishop of Gloucester, who declared that the clergy should not involve themselves in

Monmouthshire, 10% of the Conservatives' local parochial assistants were Anglican clergy: 'Minute book of Monmouthshire Conservative Registration Society', Tredegar Park MSS 71/710, fos 6–12.

[198] 'First annual report of the East Surrey Conservative Society for the hundred of Brixton, 1836', SuRO, Acc. 766, fos 5, 10–11.

[199] William Sowton to John Abel Smith, 3 Aug. 1835, WSRO, Add. MS 7171, fo. 31.

[200] Raymond, 'English political parties', 371–90; Matthew Cragoe, *An Anglican aristocracy: the moral economy of the landed estate in Carmarthenshire, 1832–1895*, Oxford 1996, 182–8.

[201] Of the 62 invited, 29 carried the title Reverend: 'Banbury Conservative Association minute book', Acc. 1259, BCA I/1, fo. 128.

politics.[202] Typical of the clerical speeches that found their way into the press of both sides, was this extract from a Hertford Conservative dinner in 1839:

> the Revd H. Demain returned thanks . . . there were those who said that the clergy had no right to pass an opinion on public men and affairs; but he need only apply to any well-directed mind for a confutation of the assertion; were not the Clergy citizens of the world? Had they not an interest in the safety and prosperity of the country?[203]

It was also not unusual for voters to be canvassed directly from the pulpit. In the course of the 1841 Ipswich contest, for instance, one Anglican priest declared in a sermon that to vote Liberal was to vote against God.[204] The Revd Francis Close, justifying his work for Cheltenham's Conservatives in an address to the Working Men's Association, developed a similar theme further:

> There is no distinction between politics and religion . . . in my humble opinion the Bible is Conservative, the Prayer book is Conservative, the Liturgy Conservative, the Church Conservative, and it is impossible for a minister to open his mouth without being Conservative.[205]

Such sentiments were, of course, hardly unique to the 1830s.[206] What distinguished their broader political implications from earlier periods, however, was the new and highly inflammatory way in which religious tensions were now accommodated and intensified by the whole voter registration process. The numerous technical disadvantages faced by Nonconformists, especially the trustees of Dissenting chapels, in the courts of revision, provided an annual source of politico-religious conflict at the formative stage of electoral participation.[207] The prominent part played by the lesser clergy not only in recruiting Conservative support, but also in objecting to the votes of their political opponents, was a far more permanent and brazen type of electioneering activity, which targeted and affected individual voters at a much more personal level. Representing a powerful link between registration and ideology, this type of activity helped to lend the association of Toryism with Anglicanism an increasingly provocative public face after 1832.

Despite regional variations in organisational style, structure and strategy, a number of fundamental differences clearly existed between the two parties at constituency level. In a wide range of localities Conservative activists came to terms with the post-1832 franchise far more quickly than the Liberals,

202 Courtney, 'Cheltenham', 70.
203 *County Press*, 6 Apr. 1839.
204 *Suffolk Chronicle*, 7 July 1841, cited in Keith Atton, 'Municipal and parliamentary politics in Ipswich, 1818–1847', unpubl. PhD diss. London 1979, 250.
205 Cited in Courtenay, 'Cheltenham', 96.
206 See, for example, O'Gorman, *Voters, patrons, and parties*, 359–68.
207 See chs 1, 6.

developing a more dynamic electoral infrastructure which was less centrally inspired and less susceptible to internal divisions and schism. Conservative constituency organisations were generally far more progressive and popular than those of the Reformers. In terms of their local integration and appeal, their social and festive functions, the active participation of women and youth, and the promotion of working-class Toryism as a viable alternative to working-class Radicalism, the Conservatives succeeded in establishing a politically homogeneous yet locally autonomous basis of support across many different types of constituency. Inevitably, their registration campaigns benefited considerably from these advantages, as well as the active assistance of the lesser Anglican clergy. Yet there was much more to each party's performance in the courts of revision than these factors alone. As the final section of this chapter makes clear, the increasing dominance of the Conservatives in the annual registration contests not only resulted from their adoption of different technical strategies, but also from the very nature and composition of the reformed electorate itself.

Registration and party performance

Funding, tactics and attitudes

No direct link between socio-economic status and party preference has emerged in numerous studies of occupational voting, although a small number of electors with above average wealth often exhibited a tendency to vote Tory.[208] In electoral terms such groups were numerically insignificant, accounting for a small proportion of most electorates, but in pre-electoral terms their financial support may have been important, perhaps even decisive. Extant registration accounts suggest that Tory registration campaigns were usually far better funded than those of the Liberals. The £2,970 17s. 3d. spent by the North Devon Conservative Association on the revisions of the period 1838–41, for example, greatly exceeded the expenditure of the North Devon Reform Association.[209] When the North Staffordshire Reform Association was established in 1837, it hoped to devote £300 to the annual registrations, depending on 'some assistance from the Whig Peers'.[210] The accounts of the Staffordshire Conservative Club, by contrast, show that at the previous two revisions they had quietly spent more than four times this amount.[211]

[208] Phillips, *Boroughs*, 267–70; Fraser, *Urban politics*, 217–22; Radice, 'Identification, interests and influence', 519–30; Wright, 'Bradford', 159–63; Nossiter, *Influence*, 170; Vincent, *Pollbooks*, 71–193.

[209] 'Expenses of registration', Acland (BroadClyst) MSS 1148M/box 8/17; DRO, Buller of Crediton MSS 2065M/SS2/5–9.

[210] Sir Thomas Sheppard to the duke of Sunderland, 17 Sept. 1837, Sutherland MSS D593/P/22/1/12.

[211] The Tories spent £946 4s. 2d. in 1835 and £362 6s. 4d. in 1836: Stewart, *Conservative*

Extra finance allowed the Tories to employ a number of expensive but highly successful strategies. Chief among these was their policy of alleviating the personal inconvenience suffered by electors after the Reform Act, by offering their supporters compensation for time spent hanging around the revising barrister's court. The West Kent Conservative and Constitutional Association, for example, established a special fund for 'supporting our friends when objected to by the opposite party'.[212] A North Devon registration contest of 1839 illustrated how effective such a strategy could be. While the number of objections made by both parties was roughly the same, the Conservatives' superior ability 'to make remuneration as well as for loss of time as for travelling and other expenses' meant that the number of Tory votes they successfully defended was over 36 per cent higher than their opponents.[213] Other advantages included paying for large print runs of prepared objection forms, often by the thousand, employing clerks to sign and send them, and the hiring of professional barristers and solicitors to help defend existing qualifications and establish new ones.[214]

Even when finance was lacking, the Tories appear to have been far more willing to run into arrears than to risk losing a revision. By May 1837, for example, the Staffordshire Conservative Association was over £1,000 in debt, mainly due to the payment of solicitors' fees which represented over half of its total expenditure.[215] Referring to Gloucestershire, Lord Ellenborough was informed by his agent of 'the shattered state of the finances of the Club: their debt having increased to between £200 and £300 this year owing to the very serious expense of the registration'.[216] The patronage of wealthy landed elites helped to solve many of these difficulties, but Conservative associations were also extremely innovative and resourceful in meeting their own costs. In some places, like Nottinghamshire, an annual registration fee of £100 or more was levied on each of the county's Tory representatives.[217] In Finsbury, the Conservative Association considered introducing 'a graduated scale of subscription according to the degree or rank of the members' in order to ease its borrowing.[218] Another common tactic involved charging newly-seated Tory candidates a share of all the previous revision costs. After his unopposed return for North Wiltshire in 1841, for example, the new Tory MP was presented with a bill for a third of all the registration expenses going

party, 380–1; 'Staffordshire Conservative Association minute book, 1835–43', Bill MSS D554/180.

212 'Memorandum', 20 June 1836, Filmer MSS U120, C72/74.

213 'North Devon registration' returns and circular, 1840, Acland (BroadClyst) MSS 1148M/box 8/17.

214 'Misc. election pps, 1840–1', Lonsdale MSS D/Lons.

215 Kent, 'Party politics in the county of Staffordshire', ch. vii.

216 H. L. Lawrence to Lord Ellenborough, 13 Nov. 1840, Peel MS Add. 40617, fo. 83v.

217 Thomas Moore to Edward Pegge Burnell, 3 Sept. 1837, Craven-Smith-Milnes of Hockerton (Winkburn) MSS DD/CW 7/13.

218 T. E. Penfold (secretary) to Lord Mahon, 9 Nov. 1836, Stanhope MSS U1590, C381/1.

back to 1836, which he felt bound to pay.[219] Rather than viewing registration debts as unnecessary or avoidable, the Tories fully embraced these financial burdens, accepting such costs as normal and routine. The first annual report of the East Surrey Conservative Society, for example, declared that it would be unacceptable 'if merely to save a few shillings of subscription the aim of the Society be shortened, and its energies checked'.[220] Commenting on the registration debts of the North Derbyshire Conservative Association, Henry Greaves observed that 'there are many districts in a similar situation . . . it is the case in several places in Yorkshire and may be considered a sort of annual blister or tax imposed upon us by the Reform Bill'.[221]

This pragmatic view of registration as an 'annual blister or tax' was far less apparent among the Reformers, whose registration campaigns frequently lacked the same degree of acceptance, financial support and funding possibilities. Liberal candidates were generally less willing to meet retrospective revision costs than their Tory opponents, and Liberal registration funds lacked the regular subscriptions of the Anglican clergy.[222] Both the Hertfordshire Conservative Association and the South Lincolnshire Conservative registration fund, which was set up 'to defray the expenses of a due registration', obtained more than 10 per cent of their entire annual income from clerical subscriptions.[223] Describing the role played by North Devon's Conservative clerics, a Liberal election agent claimed that 'their yearly subscriptions alone are more than sufficient to defray the costs of the examination of the voters at the registration'.[224] In addition, Liberal organisations failed to attract the same degree of upper-class interest and patronage as their Conservative rivals. Commenting on a general decline in local activists after the 1837 election, the *Edinburgh Review* noted that the resulting domination of registration by the wealthy few would increasingly benefit the Conservatives.[225] In his recent full-length study of the Liberal organisations of Newcastle, Bristol and York, Peter Brett came to the conclusion that they 'were not nurtured and financed in such a way as to ensure their continued support and existence', mainly due 'to an inherent distrust of popular participation on the part of the aristocratic whig leadership'.[226] Whig landed elites failed to embrace and encourage the politics of registration with the energy and enthusiasm of their

---

[219] £565 6s. 7d.: T. H. Sotheron to Walter Long, 1 Nov. 1841, WRO, Long MSS 947/1842/3.

[220] 'First annual report of the East Surrey Conservative Society', Acc. 766, fo. 3.

[221] H. M. Greaves to Bageshawe, 11 July 1836, SRO, Oakes of Norton MSS OD/1381.

[222] 'First annual report of the East Surrey Conservative Society', Acc. 766, fos 13–20.

[223] 'Hertfordshire Conservative Association cash book, 1836', Messrs Longmore and Sworder D/EL B563; 'South Lincolnshire registration subscriptions', 2 June 1835, Brownlow MSS 4 BNL/14.

[224] Partridge to Thomas Pring, 27 Mar. 1839, Buller of Crediton MSS 2065M/SS2/11.

[225] Cited in Close, 'The elections of 1835 and 1837', 450.

[226] Brett, 'Liberal middle classes', 353.

Tory opponents. As Parkes complained to Durham in 1836, 'our great want is of opulent landed proprietors to find funds for registration and contests'.[227]

There were a number of factors at work here, peculiar to Whiggery. Tensions existed within both parties over the effects and propriety of establishing constituency organisations, but some local Whig leaders were much more high-minded in their approach to registration than their Tory counterparts. Liberal registration activity was often severely compromised by a genuine Whig reluctance to restrict the franchise through the use of partisan objections. In Bedfordshire and South Devon, for example, Liberal registration activity was systematically undermined by the duke of Bedford's belief that only illegitimate voters should be objected to. His strategy of 'object to bad claims and support good', which was rigorously enforced by his Devon and Bedfordshire agents, failed to make any distinction between Whig and Tory voters, and gave the Conservatives an important electoral advantage in both divisions.[228] This intuitive Whig dislike of any artificial restriction of the franchise was reinforced by the high moral tone adopted by some Reformers towards the 'privilege of voting', which was felt by some to have arisen from 'an Act not inferior in importance to Magna Charta'.[229] In Ipswich, for example, a leading Liberal councillor, George Ridley, vehemently 'opposed attempts to disfranchise known opponents in the registration court' on constitutional grounds.[230] Another feature peculiar to the Liberals was a tendency to withdraw many of their objections to individual Tory voters during the course of a revision. The Preston Constitutional Reform Association, for example, deliberately withdrew 818 of its 900 objections during the 1835 registration.[231] Such public gestures of moral magnanimity highlighted the Liberals' ability, but also their disinclination, to wreak havoc with the franchise. Putting probity before party cost them both of these revisions, but allowed them to claim the moral high ground. Indeed, public exposure, rejection and repudiation of the Tories' 'unconstitutional' registration tactics was a regular feature of some campaigns, especially in Liberal strongholds. In Stroud, for example, the Liberals proudly boasted in 1838 that 'in the registration of this district . . . the advantage has been on the side of the Tories; and no wonder, for most objectionable and dishonourable means have been resorted to, to gain it, such as their opponents would scorn to enter into competition with'.[232]

Similar scruples compromised the registration activity of the West Somerset Reform Association at the crucial 1835 revision. The county's

---

227 Parkes to Durham, 19 July 1836, Lambton MSS.
228 T. Bennet to W. G. Adam, 10 June 1835, BRO, Russell MSS R3/3877.
229 *The Reform Act with explanatory notes*, 1.
230 Atton, 'Municipal and parliamentary politics', 355.
231 *Preston Pilot*, 17 Oct. 1835.
232 *Gloucester Journal*, 13 Oct. 1838, cited in Philip M. Walmsley, 'Political, religious and social aspects of Stroud parliamentary borough, 1832–52', unpubl. MLitt diss. Bristol 1990, 188.

Liberal MP Edward Sanford had grave misgivings about their plans to match the Tories' objections and expressed 'considerable doubt as to the propriety of the professional advisor of a sitting member endeavouring to substantiate objections to the claims of voters'.[233] He later warned his own agents that 'on no account whatsoever will I allow a single vote to be objected to; substantiate as many votes as you can'.[234] This provided the Tories with an obvious advantage, but it would be wrong to conclude that the increasing dominance of the Conservatives in the registration courts resulted from their use of objections alone. The Tories were not just better disfranchisers. Far more crucially, they also appear to have profited disproportionately from the widespread Liberal policy of enfranchising 'as many votes as you can'. As the last section of this chapter demonstrates, it was the recruitment of 'new' voters on to the registers that was ultimately to prove fundamental to the electoral performance of the parties after 1832.

The politics of the newly enfranchised
In recent years a number of pioneering studies have concentrated on assessing levels of partisanship over time, using computerised techniques of nominal record linkage. Instead of simply analysing levels of party voting at a single election, the partisan allegiance of individual voters is compared with their behaviour in subsequent contests, on a longitudinal basis. The risk, or probability, that the electoral behaviour of those voting in a certain way will change at the next election is usually supplied in the form of a 'hazard rate'. Two important conclusions have emerged from these new types of investigation. First, after 1832 those electors who cast a partisan vote at one election were increasingly likely to vote the same way in successive contests. In other words, 'experienced' voters quickly became a phalanx of rigid partisans. Second, Tory voters were generally less likely to change their colours in a subsequent election than Liberal ones, although the variation was often marginal.[235]

Both conclusions have important implications for the comparative performance of the parties in the registration courts. Since electors who had given a partisan vote were increasingly likely to cast the same type of vote in successive elections, it must have been the behaviour of the 'new' voters, and the conversion of previously 'non-partisan' voters, which accounted for the changing electoral fortunes of the parties. With the party allegiance of 'experienced' voters essentially fixed, as an electoral 'cohort', it was the newly

---

233 Sir T. B. Lethbridge to Sanford, with reply, 31 Aug. 1835, Sanford MSS DD/SF/4551, fo. 49.
234 Sanford to Thomas, 15 Sept. 1835, ibid. fo. 51.
235 Phillips and Wetherell, 'Great Reform Act of 1832', 411–36; Phillips, *Boroughs*, 7, 103, 138, 171, 190–5, 204, 221; Radice, 'Identification, interests and influence', 441–8, 452, 459; Salmon, 'Local politics and partisanship', 357–76.

registered who acted as the main catalyst for political change.[236] Put another way, swings in the electoral fortunes of both parties were heavily dependent upon either latent or induced partisanship among the newly enfranchised. It was each party's ability to activate unregistered partisans and recruit 'new' electoral participants, through the medium of registration, which increasingly determined the outcome of many elections during the 1830s.

One striking feature of the 1835 general election was the strong correlation between Conservative victories and earlier increases in the size of the registered electorate.[237] In a third of the contested English counties in which the Tories won seats in 1835, the registered electorate had increased by over 10 per cent from 1832 to 1834.[238] In South Hampshire, where the electorate had grown by 20.4 per cent, and in South Lancashire, where it had increased by 14.7 per cent, both Liberal members failed to get themselves re-elected. The same feature emerges in the subsequent by-elections of that year. In South Staffordshire, where local registration activity contributed to a 28.4 per cent increase in the size of the electorate from 1832 to 1834, the Liberals suffered a bitter defeat in May 1835.[239] Lord John Russell's humiliating loss of his South Devon seat also coincided with an increase of over 10 per cent in the county's electorate at the previous two revisions.[240] His principal election agent, James Terrell, offered this analysis:

> Since the election in 1832 the Conservatives have been very active in their registrations; they have been very vigilant; the other party certainly have not been; the difference between the registration of 1832 and the registration of 1834 amounts to 760, of whom I believe not less than 600 are of our opponents.[241]

These increases in the size of the electorate suggest that it must have been the larger number of fresh claims lodged by the Tories, rather than their use of objections alone, which accounted for the bulk of their registration gains. In the North Devon revision of 1838, for example, the Tories only made eight more successful objections than their Liberal rivals.[242] In this respect there

---

[236] The solidity of these 'cohorts' was often impressive. In the seven parliamentary elections held in Ipswich between 1832 and 1842, for example, nearly 80% of electors who voted more than three times *always* voted for the same party: Atton, 'Municipal and parliamentary politics', 362.

[237] See Close, 'The elections of 1835 and 1837', 197.

[238] The rates of increase were: Buckinghamshire (+1%), Cambridgeshire (+9%), South Derbyshire (−3%), South Essex (+4%), South Hampshire (+20%), Herefordshire (−1%), West Kent (+3%), South Lancashire (+15%), North Lincolnshire (−3%), East Norfolk (+3%), East Suffolk (+18%), West Suffolk (+12%), East Surrey (+12%), and West Surrey (+2%): appendix 3.

[239] See Kent, 'Party politics in the county of Staffordshire', ch. vii.

[240] See appendix 3.

[241] PP 1835 (547) viii. 167, minute 2821.

[242] The Tories successfully expunged 197 voters and the Liberals 189: registration returns, Acland (BroadClyst) MSS 1148M/box 8/17.

was little to distinguish between the parties. The Tories, however, also managed to enrol 595 more voters than the Liberals. In other words, over 98 per cent of the net Tory gain of 603 voters at this revision were 'new' recruits.[243] Westmorland's Tories also consistently registered more voters than their opponents. At the revision of 1835, for example, they enrolled seventy 'new' voters compared to the Liberals' twenty-eight, and in the following year, they registered thirty-six compared to a paltry four.[244] A similar pattern emerges from many borough revisions. The Buckingham District Conservative Association, for instance, enfranchised twice as many 'fresh' electors as their opponents at the revision of 1838.[245] Reporting on the 1837 revision in Harwich, the Conservative MP made a point of noting to Bonham that 'the new men admitted are rather in our favour'.[246]

Why were the Tories able to register more 'new' voters than their opponents? One obvious explanation was the absence of Tory candidates in many of the 1832 contests, which left many staunch Tory voters little incentive to register that year. Almost four times as many constituencies were lacking a Tory candidate, rather than a Liberal one, at the general election of 1832.[247] Indeed, in over a quarter (26.4 per cent) of all the 284 English and Welsh constituencies there was no Tory candidate in 1832. By contrast, only 7 per cent of constituencies had no Liberal candidate.[248] A 'positive' failure to register was, in these circumstances, likely to have been much more pronounced among Tory supporters. With the next election not expected until 1839, there was little reason for them to undergo the trouble and expense of registering in the years immediately after 1832. This perception, however, was fundamentally altered by the two changes of government in 1834, and the completely unexpected election of 1835. A significant proportion of those coming on to the registers for the first time after 1834–5 were probably erstwhile Tory supporters, who had previously spurned the franchise.

This is borne out in Cheltenham, where there was a strong correlation between Conservative prospects and the number of Conservative claims. Many of Cheltenham's Tories, 'lacking a feasible candidate in 1832, decided

---

243 Ibid.
244 'Misc. election pps, 1834–7', Lonsdale MSS D/Lons/L.
245 Archdeacon MSS D/AR/6/15/2.
246 J. C. Herries to Bonham, 4. Oct. 1837, Peel MS Add. 40617, fo. 37v.
247 In seventy-five English and Welsh constituencies there was no Tory candidate, compared to twenty constituencies with no Liberal or Radical candidate. In fifty of the seventy-five constituencies Liberal candidates were returned without opposition, while in the remaining twenty-five a contest was fought between Liberals and Radicals. In eighteen constituencies Tory candidates were returned without opposition, while in two, Newcastle-under-Lyme and St Ives, a contest was fought between three Tory candidates: Crosby, *Parliamentary record*; *Dod's electoral facts*, passim.
248 Based on the above figures. There were 203 borough constituencies and eighty-one county divisions in England and Wales: appendix 3.

Table 2
Party affiliation of 'experienced' and 'new' voters
on the Cheltenham register of 1838

	Number of voters	% Non-partisan	% Liberal	% Conservative
Experienced voters	766	–	60.5	39.5
New voters	597	–	29.6	70.4

Sources: Peel MS Add. 40617, fo. 51v; Messrs Ticehurst Wyatt D2025 box 137.

not even to register their vote'.[249] Subsequent events also gave them little incentive. The election of 1835 was fought between a Radical and a Whig, and although a Tory candidate contested the 1837 election, he came forward at the last minute, far too late for unregistered Tory partisans to enlist. At the following revisions many inactive Tory supporters therefore came on to the registers for the first time. In 1838, for example, 101 'new' Tory voters were added to the register compared with only forty-eight 'new' Liberals.[250] The effects of such an increase in the franchise were clearly revealed in a canvass of that year carried out by the Tory agents, who determined the partisan affiliation of 1,363 (87 per cent) of the 1,561 registered voters. (Of the remainder, 172 were described as being politically 'neutral' or 'unknown', and twenty-six were discovered to be 'double entries').[251] Table 2 compares the 'known' party allegiance of the 766 'experienced' electors, all of whom had voted in the 1837 election, with that of the 597 who were enfranchised subsequently. The 'new' electors, it can be seen, were decidedly more Tory than the 'experienced' ones.

Of course, not all newly registered voters were erstwhile Tory supporters who had previously chosen not to register. Some coming on to the registers for the first time were also newly qualified and had only recently attained the requisite age or property qualification.[252] Although both parties actively sought to enlist the support of these genuinely 'new' electoral participants, the superior financial organisation of the Tories, their specific promotion of partisanship among the young, and their army of local activists, again gave them a strategic advantage. In North Wiltshire, for example, the Tory agents hired horses to travel around 'obtaining signatures of new claimants for registration' and 'paid overseers for those claimants who would not pay their 1 shilling'.[253] Parochial canvassers of the Buckingham District Conservative Association made an annual 'return of the persons entitled to vote and not on

249 Courtenay, 'Cheltenham', 44.
250 H. Lawrence to Lord Ellenborough, 3 Nov. 1838, Peel MS Add. 40617, fos 51–2.
251 Ibid.
252 All voters had to be over 21: 2 Will. IV c. 45, 728, clause 20.
253 Parcel marked '1830–1844', Messrs Keary, Stokes and White, box 415/432.

Table 3
Votes cast by 'experienced' and 'new' voters
in the Leicester election of 1835

	Number of voters	% Non-partisan	% Liberal	% Conservative
Experienced voters	2,177	1.4	48.7	49.9
New voters	653	1.3	39.8	58.9

Source: Radice, 'Identification, interests and influence', 413–14, 449; Crosby, *Parliamentary record*, 80. This type of analysis assumes that non-partisan voters either 'split' their two votes between the parties or 'plumped' for just one Liberal or Conservative candidate when there was also another in the field.

the register'.[254] In Hertfordshire, the declared aim of the county Conservative association, established on 13 June 1835, was to note 'all changes of property . . . with the view of procuring the registration of new proprietors or tenants at the annual registrations, if the same are friendly to the Conservative cause, and of objecting to their registration, if not so'.[255]

A previous failure to register, however, was not only due to the lack of suitable candidates or requisite qualifications. As chapter 1 noted, the failure to claim the franchise could also result from indifference and the cost and inconvenience of electoral participation. Examining the political behaviour of what the provincial press often called 'lazy voters', who were not motivated enough to see to their own registration, is far more difficult.[256] But in constituencies where both parties put up candidates in 1832 and thereafter established associations to assist 'lazy voters' on to the register, the Tories still appear to have gained a disproportionate share of the votes cast by the 'new' electorate at subsequent polls. Contrary to what might have been expected, the allegiance of these 'lazy voters' was not evenly split between the parties. In Leicester, as Paula Radice has shown, both parties established highly effective constituency associations in 1832, and continued to recruit 'new' electors in subsequent revisions, making regular rate payments on behalf of electors to ensure and maintain their qualifications.[257] As a result, nearly a quarter (23.1 per cent) of the 2,830 electors who voted in the 1835 election were 'new' participants. Table 3, which compares the votes cast by the 'experienced' and 'new' electors at this contest, shows that the newly registered were approximately 10 percentage points more likely to vote Tory than those who had turned out in 1832. Put into perspective, without the 385 votes cast

---

[254] 'Buckingham District Conservative Association minute book', Archdeacon MSS AR 81/75/15, fo. 41.
[255] Messrs Crawters of Hertford D/E Cr 105/5.
[256] *Staffordshire Mercury*, 5 Oct. 1833.
[257] Radice, 'Identification, interests and influence', 220–8.

for the two Tory candidates by 'new' voters, the second Tory, Thomas Gladstone, would have polled slightly less than his nearest rival, William Evans. At this election, the Toryism of the newly registered was decisive in ensuring the defeat of both the sitting Liberal MPs.

A similar picture emerges from North Durham where, following the defeat of the Conservative candidate in 1832, both parties were extremely active in promoting the formation of associations and attending to the registration.[258] Because the 1835 election was uncontested – the Liberals enjoying a clear majority on the 1834 registers on which it was held – the number of 'new voters' at the subsequent 1837 contest was especially large. Nearly one-third of the voters at this election (32.7 per cent) were fresh electoral participants who had come on to the registers after the contest of 1832. Table 4, comparing the votes cast by the 'experienced' and 'new' electors, again illustrates that the newly registered exhibited a greater propensity to vote Tory than the seasoned electors. Here again the Tory candidate's lead among first-time voters was sufficient to make an important difference in what was otherwise an extremely close contest.[259]

Of course, this Tory bias among 'new' voters was neither a universal phenomenon, nor necessarily so conspicuous. In Guildford, for example, there was no discernible difference between the votes cast by the 'new' and 'experienced' electors in the elections of 1835 and 1837.[260] At the East Sussex contest of 1837, the difference between the partisan behaviour of 'new' and 'experienced' voters was far less pronounced than in North Durham. Here 46 per cent of the 'new' voters polled for both Tory candidates, compared with 42 per cent of the 'experienced' voters, while 33 per cent of the 'new' voters polled for the two Liberals, compared with 36 per cent of the 'experienced' voters.[261] In this contest the Tory bias of the newly enfranchised was insufficient to alter the overall result. But the general pattern of partisan behaviour among first-time voters was none the less distinct. If this election had been decided on the votes cast by the 'new' electorate alone, for example, both Tories would have been returned rather than just one.[262]

Indeed, the importance of even a very small lead among first-time voters should not be underestimated, as it might have proved decisive. In the Brighton election of 1837, for example, 17.7 per cent of the 'new' voters plumped for the single Tory candidate, compared with 15.5 per cent of the 'experienced' electors, while 35.2 per cent of the 'new' electors split their votes between the Tory and one other candidate, compared with 32.5 per

---

258 Nossiter, Influence, 70–5; Radice, 'Identification, interests and influence', 290–314.
259 See Radice, 'Identification, interests and influence', 458–9.
260 Ibid. 461.
261 1832 and 1837 East Sussex pollbooks and registers. With no contest in 1835, 1,501 (39%) of the 3,867 voters who polled in 1837 were 'new' or first-time voters, who had not polled or registered in 1832.
262 The result would have placed the two Tories at the top of the poll with 916 and 706 votes respectively, and the two Liberals at the bottom with 651 and 603.

Table 4
Votes cast by 'experienced' and 'new' voters
in the North Durham election of 1837

	Number of voters	% Non-partisan	% Liberal	% Conservative
Experienced voters	2,895	17.9	46.3	35.8
New voters	1,406	15.8	40.3	43.9

Sources: Radice, 'Identification, interests and influence', 459; Crosby, *Parliamentary record*, 54.

cent of the 'experienced' voters.[263] Viewed from this perspective the partisanship of both groups was almost identical. Yet, if this election had been decided on the votes cast by the 'experienced' electors alone, the single Tory candidate would have been defeated.[264] It was the slight lead among the 'new' voters which provided the Tory candidate with the slim majority of eighteen votes over his nearest rival. The work of the Brighton Conservative Association in identifying, recruiting and registering 'lazy voters' had played a major role in this, and after the election Bonham informed Peel that their victory was 'achieved solely by the good management of the Conservative Association'.[265]

More evidence of this Tory bias among those who had previously been indifferent to their electoral rights can be found among the surviving papers of the agents who actually worked the system. In West Somerset, where the registration campaigns of the local Tories and the Reform association had contributed to an impressive 15.6 per cent increase in the size of the electorate from 1835 to 1836, there was no equivalent increase in the number of Liberal voters polling in 1837 compared with 1835.[266] On the contrary, the number of Liberal partisans remained fairly static, while the Tory vote increased by roughly the same amount as the number of newly enfranchised electors.[267] The local Whig agent, James Waldron, was convinced that helping unregistered electors to obtain their franchise had proved

[263] 1835 and 1837 Brighton pollbooks. Both of these contests were fought between one Tory, two Liberals and one Radical candidate: Gash, *Politics in the age of Peel*, 384–90; Crosby, *Parliamentary record*, 35.

[264] The result would have put the Tory in third place with 481 votes, whereas in the actual election he came second with 819.

[265] Bonham to Peel, 23 Aug. 1837, Peel MS Add. 40424, fo. 141.

[266] For a more detailed analysis see the case study in ch. 5 below.

[267] 3,254 voters split their votes between the two Liberal candidates in 1835, and 3,410 in 1837. Almost 1,200 'new' voters were brought on to the registers in 1835, and an extra 1,189 electors cast clear Tory votes in 1837: Sanford MSS DD/SF/4548/26; SoRO, Dickinson MSS DD/DN/293.

counter-productive. Putting his case to the county's Liberal MP, he offered this striking analysis of the electoral dynamics of this period:

> I do not quite agree with your quotation from Sir Robert Peel 'Register, Register, Register!' I think it well for him, but bad for us, for I believe we have done injury to our cause by calculating that an elector who does not value the right of voting sufficiently to take care of his own interest would be for us and not against us.[268]

This Whig notion of an inherent Tory bias among those indifferent to their electoral rights suggests two important conclusions about the broader performance of the parties in this period. First, Liberal partisanship may have involved greater political interest, positive enthusiasm and ideological awareness than Tory affiliation. Key Whig–Liberal issues, such as the removal of religious disabilities, Irish Church appropriation, abolition of colonial slavery, adoption of the secret ballot and, eventually, free trade, essentially amounted to a cause, which required a cerebral understanding of complicated issues and a degree of personal credence and commitment. The Tory agenda, by contrast, was far less complex. To the politically ignorant and ideologically uninitiated it was potentially more accessible. Despite the Tamworth manifesto, the issues aired by most Conservative candidates rarely seem to have extended beyond a basic Church-and-Field Toryism, occasionally coloured by condemnation of the New Poor Law. Those electors who had previously been too politically or religiously apathetic to claim the franchise on their own were probably far less likely to embrace Liberal principles, at least without some active assistance. Again the evidence of election agents and activists amply bears out this analysis. The chairman of the Barnsley District Reform Association, for example, could hardly have made the point better when he warned his leaders at the West Riding Reform and Registration Association that

> It does not seem to be generally borne in mind that the Reform Bill has shown the electoral franchise to parties that have no idea of political duties or political principles: and that these feelings must be created or awakened in them, if they are to be enlisted in the ranks of Reform.[269]

Second, it is clear that substantial increases in the size of the electorate benefited the Tories far more than the Liberals, even in constituencies where both parties sought to enlist the support of the politically inactive at the annual registration. Perhaps the most extreme example of this occurred in South Staffordshire, where the electorate increased by an astonishing 89 per cent at the 1835 revision. To their surprise and delight, this produced 'a decided

---

[268] James Waldron to Sanford, 12 Aug. 1837, Sanford MSS DD/SF/4551, fo. 93.
[269] Thomas Wilson to Earl Fitzwilliam, 12 Aug. 1841, LDA, Wilson MSS DB178/33.

available majority of from 800 to 1,100 in favour of the Conservatives'.[270] The expanding electorate of the 1830s, it would appear, made future Tory election gains almost inevitable. And this crucial correlation between increases in the size of the electorate and Tory victories was certainly not lost on the Liberal election managers. After the 1837 contests, for example, Parkes reported to Durham that

> I had some curious tables of electoral numbers and increased constituencies in the counties to show you. In almost all the counties we lost in 1834–5 and lately, the constituencies have been *doubled* since 1833. Further, in those counties *we* have *best* registered the Tories beat us, their activity (excited by ours) having more *matériel* . . . to practise on.[271]

The appalling realisation that the Tories had 'more matériel' to work with provided clear proof to Parkes and other Radical activists that 'the next "go" must and will be for a re-construction of the whole representative system'.[272] The 'entire system is humbug', Parkes complained to Francis Place in 1838, 'and must be wholly reorganised'.[273] It was these Radicals' insistence upon the iniquity of 'the existing representative system and registration nuisance' that made Russell's 'finality' declaration of November 1837 so unacceptable, and their disaffection with the Whig–Liberal alliance so inevitable.[274] Indeed, total overhaul of the registration system was an increasingly conspicuous component of Radical discourse during this period and took up almost half of the 'People's Charter', with which both Parkes and Place initially flirted.[275] Thereafter Parkes, who knew little about Corn Law issues, lent his full expertise and support to the Anti-Corn Law League as a vehicle for attacking 'the Finality Men'.[276] 'You see how the Anti Corn Law agitation has smashed the Reform Bill's Finality Doctrine', he explained to Richard Cobden, 'the crush against the Representative system must come'.[277] Through his activities at the Reform Association, his official work on municipal corporation and charity commissions, and his wide experience of local and national election management, Parkes acquired a knowledge and understanding of the reformed electoral system probably unsurpassed by any of his contemporaries. 'Perhaps no man was better acquainted than he with the secret history of

---

270 John Smith to Lord Sandon, 11 Mar. 1836, Harrowby MSS, cited in Kent, 'Party politics in the county of Staffordshire', ch. vii.
271 Parkes to Durham, 15 Oct. 1837, Lambton MSS.
272 Parkes to Place, 18 Aug. 1837, BL, Place MS Add. 35150, fos 291–3.
273 Parkes to Place, 14 Dec. 1838, Place MS Add. 35151, fos 114–15.
274 Parkes to Melbourne, 30 Aug. 1837, Melbourne MSS, box 79.
275 *The Chartist Circular*, 5 Oct. 1839; Taylor, 'The six points', 8–13; Dorothy Thompson, *The Chartists: popular politics in the industrial revolution*, Aldershot 1984, 59.
276 Parkes to Cobden, 31 Jan. 1839, Manchester Central Library Wilson MSS; Parkes to Cobden, 30 Mar. 1839, Cobden MSS.
277 Parkes to Cobden, 23 Mar. 1839, Cobden MSS.

politics', commented *The Times* at his death.[278] By 1837 his verdict was clear. Writing to the Liberal chief whip in the middle of the 1837 election, Parkes was one of the first to warn that 'the *Representative System*, as at present constituted, cannot but pass annually more and more into the hands of the Tories. I have long foreseen it'.[279]

Party performance in the registration courts, and ultimately in elections, clearly had very little to do with central party management and much more to do with the structure and nature of party support as it developed at constituency level. It was here that the most pronounced differences emerged between the parties, especially in terms of organisational dynamism, unity and the recruitment of local activists. In the constituencies, significant tactical and temperamental dissimilarities developed between the parties over registration activity, particularly regarding the use of partisan objections and any 'artificial' restriction of the franchise. More important, however, party performance in the 1830s also depended upon subtle divergences in the accessibility and appeal of Toryism and Liberalism among first-time voters, including those who had previously failed to take up their electoral rights. With the partisanship of the 'experienced' voters increasingly fixed after 1832, it was the successful recruitment and mobilisation of large numbers of unregistered voters, which acted as the primary catalyst for political change. And it was here that the Conservatives gained their crucial advantage. This chapter has shown that party performance and electoral politicisation during this period need to be recontextualised, not only in terms of local rather than parliamentary politics, but also in terms of the composition and character of the reformed electorate itself.

---

[278] *The Times*, 12 Aug. 1865.
[279] Parkes to Stanley, 3 Aug. 1837, Parkes MSS.

3

The Election after 1832:
Tradition and Transformation

The previous two chapters have demonstrated how the annual registration system introduced by the Reform Act transformed the business of acquiring the vote and encouraged the development of far more modern types of party organisation and electoral behaviour after 1832. Alongside these dramatic developments, however, there were obviously elements of continuity, especially in terms of the established traditions of electioneering, that also need to be taken into account. O'Gorman, in particular, has written of how 'the carnival, the ritual, the processional and festive aspects of a campaign' were 'largely unhindered' by Reform, and has argued that 'the men, the institutions, the values, and the practices are remarkably similar each side of 1832'.[1] Local studies, too, have drawn attention to the widespread 'survival of pre-1832 electoral traditions', while the continuation of bribery and corruption (of which the Reform Act itself made no specific mention), featured prominently in many earlier accounts of reformed electoral politics.[2] As Gash's highly influential exemplar in this genre put it, 'there was scarcely a feature of the old unreformed system that could not be found in existence after 1832'.[3]

This chapter seeks to clarify the extent of these widely observed electoral continuities and to consider their significance after 1832. It demonstrates that even the most traditional aspects of an election were not entirely immune from the impact of Reform. Polling procedures, canvassing and campaign rituals, and, not least, the financial costs associated with electioneering became subtly differentiated from their past forms and were increasingly standardised, either through the statutory provisions of the Reform Act, or as a result of common developments on the ground. The business of claiming the vote became distinct from the business of casting it, enabling the duration of a contested election to be limited to two days, and to one day in the boroughs after 1835.[4] Even the official language and expenses of an election became nationally regulated, helping to diminish local

---

1   O'Gorman, 'The electorate before and after 1832', 182, and Voters, patrons, and parties, 392.
2   Edwin Jaggard, Cornwall politics in the age of reform, 1790–1885, Woodbridge 1999, 123; Seymour, Electoral reform, 165–97; Gywn, Democracy and the cost of politics, 61–92.
3   Gash, Politics in the age of Peel, p. x.
4   5 and 6 Will. IV c. 36.

idiosyncracies and create a far more uniform electoral culture. Railway development also had an important impact on electioneering in this period, so that despite the existence of elements of continuity, the holding of an election was none the less a much more recognisably 'modern' event after 1832.

The conduct of the poll

The impact of the 1832 Reform Act on the formalities of an election has often been overlooked. Under its provisions many practices which had previously been regulated by a mixture of local custom and ancient statutes were standardised for the first time. As well as defining on a national basis how the vote was to be acquired and by whom, the Reform Act also prescribed the times, location, and precise manner of taking, keeping and then declaring a poll, along with the official costs that could be charged to the candidates. These included 'by the day' payments of two guineas for each deputy appointed by the returning officer, and a further guinea for each of the clerks employed to record the votes in the polling booths.[5] Seven hours were permitted for voting on the first day, and eight on the second, when the polls had to close by 4 p.m. Declarations of the return, which in the counties were scheduled to take place two days later, had to be made 'not later than 2 p.m. in the afternoon'.[6] Even the official language of the poll became standardised, with the questions and oath that could be used to verify a voter's identity being strictly confined to the words contained in the act, 'any law or statute, local or general, to the contrary notwithstanding'.[7]

There were physical differences too, and not just in terms of the vastly expanded electorate of many constituencies.[8] The practice of holding an election 'in any church, chapel or other place or worship', which had been common in New Shoreham, for example, was now prohibited.[9] Of more widespread importance was the Reform Act's stipulation that 'a reasonable number' of polling booths be provided and that there be a limit of 'six hundred voting at one compartment' in the boroughs. This encouraged the traditional wooden hustings used for the nomination speeches and declaration of the poll to become increasingly elaborate in structure after 1832.[10] The height of this central and symbolic feature of the electoral landscape

[5] As well as a 'poll clerk', each polling booth invariably had a check (or 'cheque') clerk, whose duty it was to write down the vote of 'each man at the same time as the poll clerk, so that the cheque book be in every respect a facsimile copy of the poll': 'Instructions to managers of booths, Radnorshire election 1835', Mayberry MSS 6761.
[6] 2 Will. IV c. 45, 739–41, clauses 62–71.
[7] Ibid. 738–9, clause 58.
[8] Because of the Reform Act's disfranchisement of non-resident voters, not all borough constituencies had larger electorates after 1832.
[9] 'New Shoreham, 1820–32', History of Parliament draft article; 2 Will. IV c. 45, 741, clause 68.
[10] 2 Will. IV c. 45, 740–1, clauses 64, 68.

Plate 1. The hustings at Bury St Edmunds outside the Angel Hotel, July 1865

grew considerably, with polling areas and barriers usually being constructed on the ground floor, beneath an enclosed (and increasingly roofed) platform for the various officials, the candidates and their key supporters.

Plate 1 shows the typical layout of a hustings in a medium-sized borough, Bury St Edmunds, which was photographed a few years before the second Reform Act of 1867. With the elevation of the proceedings above and away from the crowd, special provision had to be made for an ever growing number of press reporters, who, in this instance, were provided with a makeshift rostrum below the speakers, complete with chairs. In larger constituencies, journalists were increasingly provided with accommodation within the hustings itself, which enhanced its size even further. The vast structure shown in plate 2, for example, which was photographed at Nottingham during one of the last elections to be held under the terms of the first Reform Act, was some fourteen metres (46 feet) in height. The fact that the extremely imposing town hall, in front of which it was erected, was not itself used for conducting the proceedings is also significant. Even though the Reform Act permitted 'any houses or other buildings' to be hired for polling, in contrast to many of the quite literally 'closed' borough returns of the unreformed period, elections after 1832 were distinctly outdoor events. The ever present threat of violence no doubt played a part in this – plate 3, for example, shows the ransacked Liberal committee rooms after the Nottingham election riots of 1865 – but another reason was that under clause 71 of the Reform Act, all

Plate 2. The hustings at Nottingham outside the Town Hall, May 1866

temporary polling structures had to be 'erected at the joint and equal expense of the several candidates'.[11] Although the cost per booth was limited to £40 in the counties and £25 in the boroughs, the new stipulations for multiple booths and the practice of charging for separate compartments provided ample and welcome opportunity for money to be made. At the 1841 Newark election, for example, the 'mayor's bill for hustings booths' came to £107 8s.[12] In the East Surrey by-election of that year, Edmund Antrobus was charged £156 3s. 3d. for his 'share of expenses of the several polling booths', while at Staffordshire in 1835, the cost of just one half of the hustings, polling booths and 'rent of ground' came to £232.[13]

Stricter polling regulations ended the almost completely free hand that had previously been exercised over the proceedings by the returning officers.[14] Abuses of their authority had been widespread before 1832, but under the Reform Act their discretion was limited and their powers were more clearly defined.[15] Their conduct was also more susceptible to challenge,

---

[11] Ibid. 741, clause 71.
[12] Messrs Hodgkinson and Beevor DDH/51/25.
[13] 'Abstract of expenses', SuRO, Acc 3033, fo. 42; Kent, 'Party politics in the county of Staffordshire', ch. vii.
[14] O'Gorman, *Voters, patrons, and parties*, 127–8.
[15] See, for example, 2 Will. IV c. 45, 741–3, clauses 70, 72, 79.

Plate 3. The Liberal committee rooms after the Nottingham
election riots of July 1865

either in the form of a traditional election petition against the return, or in
the courts of record at Westminster, where a maximum penalty of £500 was
introduced for any official found guilty by a jury of breaching the terms of the
Reform Act.[16] Add to this the host of popular election manuals, registration
guidelines and treatises on election law that were published in the wake of
1832, and it is clear that the Reform Act marks an important step in the

---

16 Ibid. 742, clause 76. The subject of election petitions unfortunately lies outside the scope
of this study, but it was undoubtedly another area of political life where significant legal and
organisational developments occurred after 1832: Close, 'Elections of 1835 and 1837',
444–8; Raymond, 'English political parties', 82–9.

move towards a more uniform and officially regulated national system of representation.[17]

Canvassing and the ritual of a campaign

One particularly striking development of the 1830s, as the two previous chapters demonstrated, was the way in which local activists in the constituencies seized upon the new voter registration system as a means of surveying and recruiting electoral support. In the unreformed system the only way of doing this had been via the canvass. It was upon the basis of this 'central feature of electioneering' that candidates and their organisations had decided whether or not to stand a poll.[18] The preliminary stages of an election campaign were, therefore, subtly different after 1832. Candidates were potentially relieved of the necessity of identifying voters and supporters via a canvass, the expense and exertion of which was only undertaken if the state of the registers initially seemed favourable. This was especially significant in large county constituencies, where canvassing could be especially exhausting and expensive.[19] When, for instance, Edward Richard Littleton declined to stand for South Staffordshire in 1837, refusing to follow in his father's footsteps, it was 'from disinclination to encounter the vexations, violence, and multifarious annoyances of a canvass'.[20] In the 1837 South Lancashire election, Liberal tactics forced Lord Francis Egerton to start canvassing at 5 a.m. every morning. His opponents, as he complained bitterly to Peel, 'violated all precedent by perambulating many minor districts through which I was obliged to follow them, for which I hope God may forgive them but I never will'.[21] Little wonder then, that by 1841 the decision to campaign was, wherever possible, effectively being made on the basis of the registry.[22] As a prospective Liberal candidate for North Devon put it in 1837, 'I wait for the registration before I pass the Rubicon'.[23]

It would be entirely wrong, however, to assume that because of this development the canvass was any less significant an electioneering institution

---

17 For example A. E. Cockburn, *Questions on election law arising from the Reform Act . . .*, London 1834; J. D. Chambers, *A complete dictionary of the law and practice of elections*, London 1837; T. Paynter, *The practice at elections being plain instructions*, London 1837; A. J. Stephens, *A practical treatise on the law of elections, with directions for candidates, electors, agents, returning officers, overseers, claimants, and objectors*, London 1840. See ch. 1 above, and the bibliography for similar publications.

18 O'Gorman, *Voters, patrons, and parties*, 91.

19 The impact of registration on county electioneering is discussed in chs 4 and 5 below.

20 Election diary, 24 July 1837, Hatherton MSS D1178/1.

21 Lord Francis Egerton to Peel, 6 Aug. 1837, Peel MS Add. 40424, fo. 17v; Egerton to duke of Sutherland, 26 July 1837, Sutherland MSS D593 P/22/1/5.

22 For more details see ch. 1 above and the case studies in ch. 5 below.

23 James Buller to Sir Thomas Dyke Acland, 22 Dec. 1837, Acland (Broadclyst) MSS 1148M/box 8/17.

after 1832. There was much more to the canvass than just measuring party strength. As a highly ritualised custom, providing an almost ceremonial form of contact between voter and candidate, canvassing even took place when there was no likelihood of an actual poll. Even in constituencies where there was simply no prospect of a contest, candidates were still expected to carry out a full and often costly campaign. That undertaken by Gilbert Heathcote in the uncontested South Lincolnshire election of 1837, for example, cost him £657 12s. 4d., while in Denbighshire in the same year the two unopposed Conservative candidates spent £1,495 5s. 6d.[24] Octavius Morgan's well documented canvass of Monmouthshire in 1841 was no less extensive or gruelling for knowing that his election was absolutely certain.[25] Most of the county was covered in his two-week tour of the constituency. With his principal agent accompanying him in his horse-drawn carriage, Morgan took four days to canvass Newport, Abersychan, Pontypool and Abergavenny, before arriving in Monmouth late on 23 June, in time to dine with the Conservative agents of the duke of Beaufort, Messrs Powles and Tyler.[26] The electoral importance of the county town was more than just symbolic. Like most parliamentary boroughs, Monmouth also contained a large number of county voters. Some 200 freeholders, thirty £50 occupiers, and fifteen copyholders and leaseholders resided within its limits.[27] Canvassing of this district therefore took Morgan and his escort of Powles, Tyler, Captain Powel, R. William and A. Ralls the best part of a day and a half, not because they needed to secure votes, but because with no rival candidates his campaign had become social and festive rather than overtly partisan. As Morgan noted in his diary: 'met with a very favourable and courteous reception from every one, even the bitter Radicals. Old Mr Lucas and Mr Hardwicke remember the contest in 1771 between Maurice and Morgan'. Indeed, even the former Liberal MP, William Addams Williams, joined Morgan's escort and accompanied him through the town.[28] After leaving Monmouth, Morgan travelled through Trelleck and Newchurch and then on to Chepstow, where he canvassed for three hours with the help of a local clergyman. His speed of travel was often painfully slow. On Saturday 26 June, for example, it took Morgan nine hours to cover the twenty odd miles from Chepstow to his family seat at Tredegar

---

24 Ancaster MSS 3 Anc 9/14/278–95; Wynnstay MSS L1091.
25 By the time of the 1841 general election, the Whigs had given up all hope of breaking the Conservatives' hegemony over Monmouthshire. This election, like every other since 1790, was uncontested. There had almost been a contested by-election in February 1841, when the sitting Liberal, W. A. Williams, vacated his seat due to illness, but the new Liberal candidate retired before the poll: Crosby, *Parliamentary record*, 155; *Monmouthshire Beacon*, 13 Feb. 1841; Tredegar Park MSS 1493.
26 Leonard Twiston Davis MSS 6370.
27 'Minutes of Monmouth Conservative Registration Society', Tredegar Park MSS 71/710, fo. 49.
28 The following account is based upon Morgan's 'Journal of canvass of county of Monmouth, June 1841', Tredegar Park MSS 1503.

Plate 4. The chairing ceremony, dated 1817, artist unknown
By permission of the Mansell Collection: Timepix/Rex Features

Park. Finally, after a week spent mostly in Usk, Llangibly and Caerleon, Morgan proceeded, as he described it, 'to the hills', where

> 60 freeholders on horseback met me and escorted me to Blackwood, where the horses were taken from the carriage and I was dragged through Blackwood in triumph, arriving at Tredegar the horses were again taken off, and the mob dragged me right through the town.[29]

These triumphal processions reached their peak on the actual day of election. Having canvassed Tredegar and Nantyglo over the weekend of 3 and 4 July, Morgan left Raglan early on Monday morning, and headed towards Troy, preceded, as he put it, 'by about 250 horsemen and a car (brake) full of banners and bearers from among the Tredegar labourers, with a train of about 24 carriages'. At 9 a.m. this enormous cavalcade was joined by that of Lord Granville Somerset and his supporters, with whom they advanced into Monmouth for the declaration of the return and the chairing ceremony.

This often rowdy custom of parading the successful candidates through the town in sumptuously decorated chairs, which is illustrated in plate 4, remained a popular electoral tradition with electors and non-electors alike, until its costs were declared illegal under the Corrupt Practices Act of 1854.[30]

---

[29] Ibid. 2 July 1841.
[30] 17 and 18 Vict. c. 102, 218, clause 7. In places where the chairing ceremony continued after 1854 it was in a muted form and 'free of all expense'.

Always something of an ordeal for the candidate and liable to get out of control, it probably became less common after 1832, although declining the honour in the pre-Reform constituencies had to be very carefully managed if the intended recipient was not to incur hostility or actual reprisals. When the Liberal MP Henry Warburton refused the chairing ceremony after his return for Bridport in 1835, for example, he was quick to issue a printed explanation of his political reasons, and to trumpet his concerns about the 'discomfort' to his supporters of 'trudging through muddy roads and streets, and exposing themselves to inclement weather, dressed as they would be, in their holiday garments'.[31]

The main function of the chairing ceremony, for all its potential symbolism, was to distribute money. Costs included paying for the gilding, silk and other materials used in the chair's construction, as well as exaggerated labour charges. 'Chair dressers' at the 1835 South Staffordshire election, for instance, received £20, while the one constructed for Heathcote in 1837 cost him £38. Added to this was the small change traditionally thrown from the chair. At the North Staffordshire contest of 1837, for example, the new Conservative MP spent £10 on 'silver for distribution on chairing day'.[32] Perhaps inevitably, these ceremonies often ended in scuffles and outbursts of violence, and Morgan's was to be no exception. 'After the return', he noted,

> a fight ensued to destroy my chair because, as I afterwards learned, I had brought some banner bearers from Tredegar. However, we mounted our chairs and ere we quitted the square a mob was made, not mine, the platform wrecked, the canopy torn down [and] to prevent myself falling amidst the blows, I was obliged to jump off and [take refuge] in the Beaufort Arms.[33]

Canvassing, as Morgan's journal amply demonstrates, was extremely punishing, even when there were no votes at stake. The strains of this type of ritualised campaigning were further increased by the inevitable host of local well-wishers anxiously pressing their advice on the candidate and desperately tying to ingratiate themselves with his election committee, usually in the hope of some financial reward. This type of activity could range from simple offers of help with canvassing to the sending of reams of unsolicited advice, such as the twenty-three page handwritten memorandum on election management addressed to Charles Tennyson a week before his re-election for Lambeth in 1835.[34]

The canvass was even more cumbersome in the event of an actual contest, when a number of tacit and customary conventions came into play. The

[31] 'To the electors of Bridport, 13 Jan. 1835', Bodl. Lib., MS Don. d. 95, fos 264–6.
[32] Kent, 'Party politics in the county of Staffordshire', ch. vii; Ancaster MSS 3 Anc 9/14/278.
[33] Tredegar Park MSS 1503, 5 July 1841.
[34] 'Memorandum of matters requisite to be done for an *efficient* and *economical* management of the election of a member for the borough of Lambeth', LAD iv/3/88.

permission of landlords, for example, usually had to be sought prior to the canvassing of tenants.[35] Being the first in the field, in the hope of securing promises from undecided voters, required particular care and discretion. Too early a canvass could easily backfire and incur greater expense and unpopularity for having disturbed the peace of the constituency. Too assertive or assuming an approach, by the same token, often led to accusations of presumption or dictation. Rival candidates and their agents, therefore, usually had some form of arrangement in operation about when to commence the canvass. The Whig candidate at Hertford, for example, made a point of writing to a rival's agent to inform him that

> I am going to a meeting of *my friends* at an inn tonight. But as it is merely to make them a speech, and to assure them that whatever may have been said, that I will go to the poll, I do not consider that canvassing and I write this to set your mind at ease. I intend to be in town tomorrow afternoon.[36]

This loading of the canvass with all sorts of local protocols and pitfalls compromised its effectiveness as a straightforward measure of support. Lord Francis Egerton's proud boast to Peel after the 1837 general election, that in 'Manchester we had 1,935 promises and polled 1,930 votes', suggests that his canvass of South Lancashire was extremely accurate.[37] But matching the number of promises with the total votes cast, as O'Gorman has shown, hardly proves that electors voted the way in which they had previously indicated.[38] Many votes in the final poll would have been cast by unanticipated supporters, those who had refused to pledge and some who had given false promises of support, either out of malice, or in a mercenary attempt to make a contest, and its associated expenditure, more likely. Despite the normative concept of a pledge as contractual and binding, therefore, even firm promises of support could never be wholly relied upon.[39] In the North Devon by-election of 1839, for example, 235 voters who had 'promised' to support the Liberal candidate failed to vote for him.[40] The loss of Lord Ingestre's seat at Hertford in 1835 was completely unforeseen given that 'he had on the canvass books a majority of more than fifty promises'.[41] Indeed, many a defeat, like that of Charles Morgan in Brecknock borough, was later discovered to be 'the result of bad votes'.[42] Clearly the candidate who relied upon such pledges did so at his peril. As Egerton put it to his brother while

---

35 The role of landlord influence is examined in ch. 4 below.
36 William Cowper to unidentified agent, undated, Stanhope MSS U1590, C382.
37 Peel MS Add. 40424, fo. 17v.
38 O'Gorman, *Voters, patrons, and parties*, 103–4.
39 Ibid. 95
40 Canvassing and polling returns, Buller of Crediton MSS 2065M/SS2/11. See ch. 5 below for a more detailed analysis of this contest.
41 'Lord Mahon's address to the electors of Hertford', 6 Jan. 1835, Stanhope MSS U1590, C384.
42 Col. Wood to J. Jones, 10 Jan. 1833, Mayberry MSS 6603.

canvassing South Lancashire in 1835, 'I have a clear majority of promises, but I put no implicit faith in such'.[43]

The unreliability of the traditional canvass was further enhanced by voters being absent when called upon, although comments such as 'wife says he will vote', 'wife favourable to be seen again' or even 'wife promised' also testify to the importance of women in determining and exercising the elective franchise.[44] As the Disraelis suggested in *The Election* (1834), 'if the men have the votes, the women have the influence'.[45] In addition, there were always a number of electors who quite unexpectedly turned out to be unable to poll. Out of a total of 1,324 voters on the 1836 register for Cheltenham, for example, an 1837 canvass by the Conservative agents revealed that twenty had died since the last revision, 197 had left the borough, two were in prison, and five were 'ill' and 'unable to get out of bed'.[46] Another common problem was that in the heat of an election, voters were sometimes persuaded to withhold or even to withdraw their promises on the understanding that another candidate would enter the field, however unlikely this might be. In the preparations for the Sandwich by-election of 1839, for example, numerous placards were issued 'calling upon the electors to suspend their promises as a candidate of Conservative principles will undoubtedly come forward in due time'.[47] In the event, however, no Conservative actually stood. These threatened candidatures undermined the authority of the traditional canvass even further, and again help to explain why the new form of registration-based electioneering activity was so useful and eagerly embraced.

Canvassers

All parliamentary candidates were expected to undertake a personal canvass, irrespective of the likelihood of an actual poll. Indeed, in small constituencies it was considered quite feasible for a candidate to call on every voter. This personal contact, as much a ritual as a necessity, could usually only be avoided if the candidate was ill, incapacitated, or had recently suffered a bereavement. Thus J. G. Boss's absence from the Northallerton contest of 1832, to be with his dying wife, did not prejudice his return, despite another Liberal candidate attempting to take his place.[48] In any other circumstances, however, neglecting to call upon voters in person was, as one agent put it,

---

[43] Egerton to duke of Sutherland, 17 Jan. 1835, Sutherland MSS D593 P/22/1/5.
[44] 1841 Newark canvass book, Messrs Hodgkinson and Beevor DDH/51/19, fos 34–49. A woman's 'interest' might also be sought over an estate: Mary Thorold to Heathcote, 22 July 1839, Ancaster MSS 3 Anc 9/14/355.
[45] Benjamin Disraeli and Sarah Disraeli, *A year at Hartlebury or the election*, London 1983, 135.
[46] Messrs Ticehurst Wyatt D2025, box 136.
[47] Mahon to Bonham, 27 Nov. 1838, Stanhope MSS U1590, C330/1.
[48] Leeds District Archives, Battie-Wrightson MSS BW/P16.

'short-sighted and impolitic'.[49] Sir James Hamlyn Williams's failure to canvass Carmarthenshire personally, for example, was thought by his agents to have played a large part in the loss of his seat at the 1837 general election.[50]

One significant development after 1832, however, was that, with more voters, contact between electors and elected often became less practicable. In constituencies with substantially enlarged electorates it became far more difficult for the candidate to visit every voter in person, although some tried. George Dawson, for example, boasted to Bonham that during a 'most arduous' tour of Devonport in 1839 he had 'actually visited 2,000 houses', the number of registered voters being 2,121.[51] But such zeal was exceptional, and in most of the larger constituencies supplementary arrangements had to be made. A common tactic involved dividing the constituency into separate canvassing districts or 'stations', which were usually overseen by a district chairman, and into further subdistricts each managed by a local assistant.[52] The adoption of this type of arrangement was by itself nothing new – there were plenty of large constituencies before 1832 – but the extent to which it was used and the number of party activists who could be called upon to assist in such work undoubtedly was unprecedented. The rapid spread of constituency associations, with their armies of aspirant supporters, created a whole new breed of election busy-bodies, whose appetite for advice was eagerly fed by enterprising publishers. One effect of this was that printed pre-election canvassing books, containing step-by-step instructions and blank response columns (such as that sold by W. H. Clark, stationer, of 59 Charing Cross Road, London), became increasingly common after 1832, an innovation which again helped to standardise electioneering procedure.[53]

The status and local standing of the principal canvassers was paramount. In most county constituencies, for example, it was the respectable yeomen and their sons, rather than local attorneys or their clerks, who made the best impression.[54] Close friends of the candidate, even if highly respected, were also not necessarily suited for such work because, as one Liberal agent put it, 'they are too apt to make their returns of promises too favourable', which 'turn out quite incorrect at the day of election'.[55] In addition, there was a fine line to be drawn between neglecting voters and swamping them with incessant house calls. The number of canvassers therefore had to be carefully controlled, with neither too many nor too few being employed. In his memo-

49 Charles Smith to Horace Twiss, 18 Aug. 1841, Bodl. Lib., MS Don. d. 95, fos 158–9.
50 D. Samuel Davis to John Johnes, undated, NLW, Dolaucothi MSS L2087.
51 Dawson to Bonham, 30 Dec. 1839, Peel MS Add. 40617, fo. 79r.
52 Messrs Longmore and Sworder B562; Tredegar Park MSS 71/710; Messrs Hodgkinson and Beevor DDH/50/7.
53 WRO, Messrs Creswick and Co. 137/97/27. Earlier types of canvass books were usually based upon annotated registers and, before 1832, on old pollbooks and tax records.
54 Shield to Heathcote, 15 Dec. 1834, 9 May 1835, Ancaster MSS 3 Anc 9/14/262, 274.
55 Hawkins to Heathcote, 3 July 1839, ibid. 14/378.

randum on Liberal election management, J. M. Cape even outlined the type of personality required and the right type of approach:

> The qualities of a good canvasser are patience, perseverance, courtesy united with firmness, and an earnest zeal controlled by a sound discretion. A canvasser on behalf of a Liberal candidate ought never to forget that if on the one hand a favor be solicited, yet on the other there is a duty to be discharged. While asking, therefore, the support of an elector, he should bear in mind that he is, at the same time, affording to that elector an opportunity to fulfil a social obligation.[56]

Anglican clergymen, with their often unique knowledge and standing in the community, made particularly good canvassers, especially in the counties. Indeed, in his study of electioneering, the late E. A. Smith concluded that the 'resident political parson was in many ways the perfect election agent', and much the same might be said of most Dissenting ministers. In Carmarthenshire, for example, it has been suggested that the Nonconformist priests provided 'a comprehensive network ideal for canvassing' on behalf of Liberal candidates.[57] Joseph Parkes's description of the Anglican clergy as 'an organised and influential band of canvassers, ready in every parish to start at a minute's notice' was not mere polemic.[58] However, his insistence that they were, by definition, all Tory undoubtedly was. The tie between denomination and party was far looser on the Anglican side than it was among Nonconformists. Anglican clergymen can be found canvassing for the Reformers in the Radnorshire and South Staffordshire contests of 1835, in the North Northamptonshire and Carmarthenshire elections of 1837, and in the North Devon by-election of 1839.[59] Religious issues were certainly an essential electoral determinant in many contests, but in practice the link between Conservatism and Anglicanism could be undermined by private relationships, localised political perceptions, and individual patterns of parochial benefaction or patronage.[60] Even Lord John Russell, despite his highly inflammatory stance on Irish Church appropriation, enjoyed the active assistance of over a

---

[56] LAD iv/3/88, fo. 11.

[57] E. A. Smith, 'The election agent in English politics, 1734–1832', EHR lxxxiv (1969), 14; Cragoe, Anglican aristocracy, 182.

[58] Parkes to Durham, 19 July 1836, Lambton MSS.

[59] E. J. Littleton to Sir Harford Brydges, 17 Dec. 1834; Revd Jones to J. Morgan, 26 Dec. 1834, Mayberry MSS 6631, 6644; 'Whig election committee minute book', 17 July 1837, NRO, Misc. Acc. ZB 43; Revd David Herries to Sir James Williams, 4 Aug. 1837, Dolaucothi MSS L2281; Revd John Kingdon to Buller, 5 Mar. 1839, Buller of Crediton MSS 2065M/SS2/10.

[60] Church livings were often distributed on a purely partisan basis by Whig and Tory benefactors according to local political needs: M. T. Bass to Lord Lichfield, 4 Jan. 1840, Anson MSS D615/P(P)/3/11; duke of Rutland to Edward Burnell, 22 Jan. 1837, Craven-Smith-Milnes of Hockerton (Winkburn) MSS DD/CW/7/13; Parkes to Durham, 18 Jan. 1835, Lambton MSS.

dozen Liberally-minded Anglican clerics in the South Devon by-election of 1835.[61]

A closer look at canvassing arrangements in South Lincolnshire reveals the extent to which two Reformers, Gilbert Heathcote and Henry Handley, relied upon the active assistance of the Anglican clergy.[62] Fifteen of Heathcote's principal canvassers in Kesteven were incumbent clergymen, who between them covered some twenty-seven different parishes at the uncontested election of 1835.[63] Two parsons, in particular, were especially active on his and Handley's behalf in the 1830s. The first was the Revd William Brocklebank, rector of Norton Disney since 1799, who in 1837 informed Heathcote that he had 'commenced a canvass immediately on the death of the King on behalf of Mr Handley and yourself in the 3 parishes of Carlton le Moorland, Norton Disney and Stapleford'.[64] The second was the Revd Charles Tomblin, vicar of Walcot and Langtoft, who played an important role in south Kesteven and south-east Holland. During a canvass of 1839, for example, made necessary by the prospect of an imminent dissolution, Tomblin informed Heathcote that 'the result of my canvass in your favour at Barholm in the evening and the day was attended with very flattering results', adding that 'if you could lend me lists of electors for Baston, Thurlby and the district between Deeping and Spalding, I would feel much obliged' since 'I have arranged with Fountain to take the district' and he 'is coming to my church tomorrow'.[65]

Clergymen and priests ultimately enjoyed one crucial advantage over any other class of canvasser, including even the candidate himself. Their spiritual or moral authority placed them in a much stronger position to 'release' or 'absolve' voters from any previous pledges of support.[66] This could be especially useful in contests where an early canvass had given one side an advantage. In the 1832 Brecknock borough election, for example, it was alleged that the completely unanticipated defeat of the Tory candidate, Charles Morgan, was entirely 'due to tradesmen breaking their pledges as a result of pressure from Dissenting ministers'.[67] In the North Devon by-election of 1839, it was the Anglican clergy who released voters from their earlier promises to James Buller, thereby helping to ensure the totally

---

61 At least 13 clergymen subscribed towards his election fund, including one archdeacon and one prebendary of Canterbury Cathedral: Bedford (London) MSS L1258/M/SS/C (DL) E 79.

62 *Dod's parliamentary companion*, London 1833, 120, 123.

63 Ancaster MSS 3 Anc 9/14/276–7.

64 Brocklebank to Heathcote, 14 July 1837, ibid. 14/323.

65 Tomblin to Heathcote, 6 July 1839, ibid. 14/369.

66 For a useful survey of the type of spiritual authority exercised by the Dissenting ministers of Carmarthenshire see Cragoe, *Anglican aristocracy*, 182–8.

67 Elizabeth Mayberry to Edward Mayberry, 4 Jan. 1833, Mayberry MSS 6601.

unexpected triumph of the Conservatives.[68] In these circumstances, the role of the clerical canvasser served to undermine the reliability of the traditional canvass further, making the alternative pre-electoral framework provided by registration activity even more attractive as a preliminary measure of party support.

Treating and election expenses

The huge cost of electioneering remains one of the most vivid images of politics in the nineteenth century. Every aspect of an election campaign – from canvassing right through to the poll and beyond – involved a substantial financial outlay, some aspects of which have already been touched on. Although there were activists, such as the president of the North Staffordshire Reform Association, who believed that 'thanks to the Reform Bill the horrid expenses of a county contest are vastly curtailed', there is not much evidence to suggest that the cost of an election declined significantly after 1832, although there were areas where developments did occur, as the last section of this chapter demonstrates.[69] Nevertheless, local associations and party committees were rarely in a position to take over full responsibility for the funding of campaigns, which on the whole remained an expense that the candidate himself was expected to bear, usually with the help of large donations from a few wealthy patrons and interested benefactors. There is also little support for the Liberals' claim that a large Conservative election fund was administered by the Carlton Club.[70] Of the two parties, it was generally the Liberals who were more active in providing assistance from the centre, both in terms of financial support for candidates and by helping to direct and fund local registration activity. The Reform Club's 'general fund', for example, was used far more widely than was the Carlton's in the limited number of contests that took place in 1841.[71] Local Conservative leaders, as chapter 2 revealed, jealously guarded their local autonomy, and probably expected their candidates to fund their own election costs to a much greater extent than did their Liberal or Radical counterparts. When William Baring, for example, refused to contribute towards the cost of his return for North Staffordshire in 1837, despite his being heir to a fortune, many Conservatives

---

68 Charles Buller to Miss Georgy Buller, Mar. 1839, Buller of Crediton MSS 2065M/SS2/11. See ch. 5 below for a more detailed account of this contest.
69 Sir Thomas Cotton Sheppard to the duke of Sutherland, 17 Sept. 1837, Sutherland MSS D593/P/22/1/12. For a useful discussion see Gywn, *Democracy and the cost of politics*, 21–92.
70 See ch. 2 above.
71 PP 1844 (538) xviii. 550–7. A fairly typical arrangement existed at Southampton, where the finance committee donated an initial £1,000 towards the return of the two Liberal candidates, Edward Hutchins and Captain Mangles: 'Coppock's memorandum', 19 Jan. 1841, GCRO, Dowlais Iron Company records D/D G, vol. 1841 (i), fo. 243.

cancelled their subscriptions to the Staffordshire Conservative Association in protest.[72]

The venality of the reformed electoral system has been well demonstrated by historians, most of whom have drawn extensively upon the mass of evidence brought before the parliamentary bribery committees of this period.[73] Whether or not bribery actually increased after 1832, however, is very difficult to assess.[74] The new financial burdens of voter registration and the rating requirements of the Reform Act doubtless provided new opportunities and incentives for electoral corruption.[75] But it was only in 1842, with the passage of the Bribery Act, that what actually constituted an illegal payment to an elector, either in the form of 'head money' or 'corrupt treating at elections', became properly defined, and only in 1854 that the 'first exact and complete definition of bribery' was placed on the statute book.[76] Focusing too much on bribery also risks neglecting an essential point, which is that many of the costs charged to candidates were actually unauthorised. One of the most striking features of original election accounts is the almost total lack of control that the candidate himself exercised over his expenditure. For many publicans, tradesmen and electors, an election was the perfect opportunity to try to extract as much as possible, in what amounted to a ritualised process that was widely regarded as legitimate and routine.[77] It was not unusual, for example, for public houses to act 'in concert in making out their claims'.[78] Venality, in these circumstances, was not so much foisted upon the constituency by the candidate, as intrinsic to the ritual and occasion of the election process itself.

Mahon's career as MP for Hertford provides a useful insight into this phenomenon. When he and Lord Ingestre were successfully petitioned against by their Liberal opponents in April 1833, they lost their seats because of the excessive 'treating' that had been sanctioned by their election committee without their knowledge.[79] Their refusal to pay these unauthor-

---

72 Kent, 'Party politics in the county of Staffordshire', ch. vii.

73 See, for example, Seymour, *Electoral reform*, 165–233; Gash, *Politics in the age of Peel*, 105–202.

74 For the view that corruption became 'more broadcast and open than it had been before' see K. Theodore Hoppen, 'Roads to democracy: electioneering and corruption in nineteenth-century England and Ireland', *History* lxxxi (1996), 553–71 at p. 559.

75 See ch. 6 below.

76 5 and 6 Vict. c. 102, 463, clauses 20–2; 17 and 18 Vict. c. 102, 217–20, clauses 2–23; Seymour, *Electoral reform*, 227. Earlier Bribery Acts, such as those of 1839 and 1841 were concerned with improving the way in which parliament investigated election petitions: 2 and 3 Vict. c. 38; 4 and 5 Vict. c. 57, 58.

77 O'Gorman, *Voters, patrons, and parties*, 142.

78 John Vivian [sic.] to Sir Richard Vyvyan, 30 Sept.1841, Vyvyan MSS DDV/BO/45/3.

79 Mahon to J. M. Carter, mayor of Hertford, 10 Jan. 1837, Stanhope MSS U1590, C382. For a useful discussion of the Hertford petition and its consequences see Violet Rowe, 'The Hertford borough bill of 1834', *PH* xi (1992), 88–107.

ised bills, however, was to plague both candidates for many years to come.[80] Indeed, the combined costs of the 1832 election, and the expenses of fighting the subsequent petition, left both men in severe financial difficulties. As Mahon later reminded Lord Salisbury, his sponsor in the 1835 election, 'in my present circumstances and having within the last five years spent between seven and eight thousand pounds in electioneering, I could devote only a few hundred pounds to the present object'.[81] Because of the unpaid election expenses of 1832, the bill for Mahon's return in 1835 was astronomic. It was common knowledge that Salisbury would be paying and at least £2,500 of the £6,000 charged related to previous debts to creditors.[82] Although it was by no means unusual for outstanding bills to be carried over in this way, Mahon had clearly not anticipated that this would include previous 'unauthorised expenditure' as well. As he complained to a clearly disgruntled Salisbury:

> I had strictly forbidden and I thought effectively prevented any treating at public houses or any other sources of expense. I felt persuaded that we were keeping our purse-strings as tight as possible. . . .The demands of the publicans after the solemn and public warning previously given both by Ingestre and myself for entertainment during the elections . . . are as you truly observe a mere extortion.[83]

A rare collection of original receipts sent to Messrs Ticehurst Wyatt, the solicitors who handled the 1841 Cheltenham election for the Conservatives, provides a useful insight into the way such large, unauthorised bills could quite easily accumulate.[84] A total of eleven canvassing agents were engaged before the election on the standard retaining fee of five guineas each.[85] Canvassing itself, which commenced two weeks before the election, was paid at the rate of two guineas per day. This increased to three guineas on both the nomination day and the borough's single polling day. Messengers were also employed at all of the polling booths for a fee of 5s. per day. These bills alone came to a total of £342 16s. 8d.[86] In addition, a host of lesser officials required payment. Writing clerks, whose work included 'letters to absent voters, circulars, copying district polling books and copying registers of voters' were paid a

---

80 The Globe, 12 Apr. 1836; Edward Lawrence to Mahon, 5 Dec. 1836, Stanhope MSS U1590, C382. These debts began to be settled on an individual basis from 1838: Messrs Longmore and Sworder D/EL 4001/1–49.

81 Mahon to Salisbury, 1 Dec. 1834, Stanhope MSS U1590, C382.

82 Salisbury to Mahon, 1 Aug. 1835, ibid.

83 Mahon to Salisbury, 2 Aug. 1835, ibid.

84 Although final election accounts are common, it is the original bills that demonstrate the difference between what was charged and what was eventually settled upon by the committee. See, for example, the similar collections of original bills in Buller of Crediton MSS 2065M/SS2/5–9 and Leonard Twiston Davis MSS 4495–539.

85 Bills 105–16, Messrs Ticehurst Wyatt D2025/ misc. box 136; David Eastwood, 'Contesting the politics of deference: the rural electorate, 1820–60', in Lawrence and Taylor, Party, state and society, 32; O'Gorman, Voters, patrons, and parties, 88.

86 Sum of bills 105–16, Messrs Ticehurst Wyatt D2025/ misc. box 136.

fee of 10s. per day, but even these relatively small sums could easily mount up. One William Coombs, for example, received £8 10s. for seventeen days of such work.[87] The ceremonial ritual of the election was also reflected in the large set of bills for decorations. Some £208 19s. 7d. was spent on 'hand flags, union jacks, bunting, ensigns, poles, banners' and the labour involved in putting them up.[88] The cost of printing election bills and 'addresses, adverts, cards, pamphlets and letters' amounted to a further £164 15s. 10d.[89] An additional £154 6s. ½d. was spent on 'bows, ribbon, silk, satin, rosettes' and the hire of furniture for the committee rooms, making the total expenditure on materials greater than the cost of hiring all the election agents.[90] In fact, agents' fees represented less than a fifth of the total bill.

By far the largest set of submitted invoices, however, related to the catering charges incurred in each of the seven polling districts. Although beer was only 2s. a gallon, it was not uncommon for fifty or sometimes 100 gallons to be given away by a single public house on both nomination and polling days.[91] Large quantities of wine, ginger ale and soda water were also charged for, along with the cost of supplying tobacco and providing free breakfasts, luncheons and dinners.[92] The annotated notes accompanying these invoices reveal that they were very carefully scrutinised by the solicitors, the demands of many publicans clearly being extremely high. The Shipton Beer House, for instance, in district 7, submitted a claim for £34 6s. which was deemed 'exorbitant; 1/6th would be ample'.[93] Even though many of the publicans' bills were scaled down in this way, the total amount settled in catering costs for all of the seven districts still came to £876 19s. 4d.

In addition, there were a large number of miscellaneous claims, amounting to some £86 6s., which covered items like newspapers for the committee rooms, candles, bill posting, biscuits and buns, and the cost of hiring and then replacing damaged hats. Included in these was a bill for £5 submitted by one John Emery, for 'neglect of business and loss of income', against which an agent had written 'this won't do'.[94] The same agent also claimed for expenses

---

[87] Bill 128, ibid.
[88] Bills 55–64, ibid.
[89] Bills 92–102, ibid.
[90] Bills 65–71, ibid.
[91] This seems to have been the going rate: 12 quarts of ale (3 gallons) cost Newark's Conservative committee 6s. in 1841 (Messrs Hodgkinson and Beevor DDH/51/26), while 4 barrels of ale cost William Scourfield £4 4s. in the Haverfordwest contest of 1837 (NLW, Lucas MSS 44–98).
[92] The practice of providing free breakfasts on the day(s) of the poll was especially common, though the value of such 'refreshment tickets' could vary. Liberal tickets in the North Northamptonshire contest of 1837, for example, were worth 10s. each, 'split' voters being given 'half tickets', but those issued in Carmarthenshire in 1835 were worth half these amounts: NRO, Misc. Acc. ZB 43; Dolaucothi MSS L4134.
[93] Bill 41, Messrs Ticehurst Wyatt D2025/ misc. box 136.
[94] Bills 140–54, ibid.

incurred in protecting supporters and temporarily waylaying opponents, explaining that

> Turner's bill . . . was for 6 men watching one night at 2s. per head. This was resorted to in order to prevent the voters being carried off. I omitted Lawrence's bill, which was promised him, he took off Joseph Bunting and Joseph Davies, the latter of whom always polled for Berkeley [the Liberal candidate] to prevent him voting.[95]

Almost every aspect of this contest appears to have attracted a host of fortune-hunters assiduously pressing their claims on the committee and their solicitors. Even the work of canvassing, for which carefully selected election agents had been specifically retained, was not immune from its fair share of hopeful claimants. The following note from James Woollett, soliciting the sum of £5, was typical:

> I believe I have a claim on the Conservative Committee for 3 weeks canvassing had I have been in a situation I should not have made any claim I should a given my survises with a great deel of pleasure but as I am not of a situation and a family to maintain, I am bound to do so. Therefore gentlemen I leave it with yourselves.[96]

One final election expense not covered in this particular set of invoices was for music and bell ringing. Ringers were usually hired at the rate of two or three guineas per day for peals at the start of the canvass and on nomination and polling days.[97] Choristers were also commonly employed, along with the type of marching band that can be seen performing at the chairing ceremony depicted in plate 4.[98] In the Newark election of 1841, for example, more than £135 was spent on a band of twenty men and four boys with five drummers and pipers.[99] In the East Surrey elections of 1837 and 1841, the band cost the Conservatives £105 10s. and £99 4s. respectively.[100] Like the canvass, a band was an essential part of the ritual of a campaign, even when there was no actual contest.[101] The proceedings at the uncontested Launceston election of 1837, for example, were held to the accompaniment of three.[102]

---

95 Bills 140–54; letter from H. Stiles, 13 July 1841, ibid.
96 Bills 140–54, ibid.
97 Ancaster MSS 3 Anc 9/14/278–95; 1837 election bills, Lonsdale MSS D/Lons/L; Messrs Hodgkinson and Beevor DD/1440/83/1–3. These were often hand bells rather than church bells.
98 See, for example, C. E. Hogarth, 'The 1835 elections in Derbyshire', *Derbyshire Archaeological Journal* xciv (1974), 50.
99 Messrs Hodgkinson and Beevor DDH/51/25.
100 'Abstract of expenses', SuRO, Acc 3033, fos 39, 44.
101 See, for instance, the bills for a band in the uncontested North Wiltshire election of 1841: Long MSS 947/1842/3.
102 Thomas to J. C. Adams, 17 Aug. 1837, CRO, Adams of Laneast and Egloskerry MSS DD/AM/534.

Figure 2
South Hampshire Conservative election round, 1835

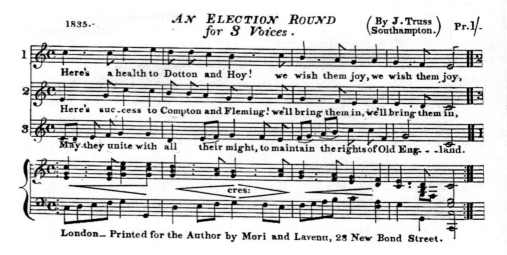

Source: HRO, Compton MSS 12M60/91.

The music performed was usually adapted especially for the occasion. Just as local parties often had special colours and cockades, so too they also acquired their own particular tunes and jingles set to popular melodies by aspiring local composers and authors.[103] The lesser Anglican clergy were again prominent on the Conservative side in this activity, and invariably injected an important inflammatory note into their political burlesques. The refrain of a Radnorshire Conservative ballad penned by the Revd Morgan Evans, for instance, began with the lines 'all the Dissenters can never destroy, our good constitution, which all now enjoy'.[104] In an age where the only music was live, and the only record was written, selling song sheets as election mementos also provided a popular way of boosting circulation and defraying printing costs. Rounds and part writing were a particularly economical method of eulogising a number of different candidates at the same time. The round shown in figure 2, for example, for which supporters were charged 1s., was distributed by the Conservatives at both the South Hampshire and the Southampton elections of 1835.

The financial costs of a seat in parliament did not end with the return. Historians have made much of the large sums often involved, but elections,

---

[103] For a brief survey of the idiom see Roy Palmer, *The sound of history: songs and social comment*, Oxford 1988, 246–56.
[104] 1832 election song, NLW, Harpton Court MSS 2628.

for all their notoriety, were isolated and ephemeral events.[105] Attempts to limit election expenses, whatever their success, did nothing to reduce the continuing day-to-day costs of political representation. These included contributions to local charities, patronage of clubs and societies, and providing assistance to poorer constituents. Since this work was part of an MP's essential public duty, it was important to ensure that it received maximum publicity. As a Conservative agent for Newark reprimanded W. E. Gladstone after he had given a donation privately in 1837, 'I want the people of the town to know'.[106] Similarly, when Mahon mentioned his intention of donating some money at a ball held to raise funds for the Hertford infirmary, his agent was quick to 'recommend the money not be given at the ball as it will then be known only as the proceeds of the ball and neither your lordship or the Conservative interest will gain any credit, but if given afterwards in the proper quarter as a donation it will have the effect it ought to have'.[107]

Another common practice was to distribute coals during cold weather and provisions of food. The recipients would preferably be voters and steps would usually be taken to ensure that no confusion took place with any other charitable work. In the winter of 1838, for instance, another agent wrote to inform Mahon that his gift 'was not distributed in coals as a fund exists here out of which all the poor are supplied at half price, it was given away in provisions and 200 partook of it, all voters for your lordship'.[108] Alongside this kind of prominent charitable work, there also existed the considerable financial commitment of subscriptions to schools, infirmaries, local literary societies, bible societies, libraries and mechanics institutes. Coming as this did on top of the annual registration expenses and, after 1835, the cost of helping to fight the municipal elections, the constant financial outlay involved in successfully representing a constituency was clearly high. In 1839, when rumours of a dissolution were rife, Mahon's annual maintenance costs at Hertford amounted to nearly £400, in spite of his very 'limited fortune'.[109] A breakdown of his expenditure during this non-election year is reproduced in figure 3.

The ultimate problem for most candidates was that wealth was often regarded as a *sine qua non* of a candidate's fitness for the representation. Controlling expenditure was therefore a fine balancing act between public expectations on the one hand and financial expediency on the other. As Cape's election memorandum rather euphemistically put it, 'economy however must not be allowed to entrench on the efficient management'.[110] Over-zealous retrenchment, in particular, could very easily backfire. Shortly

---

[105] Gash, *Politics in the age of Peel*, 113–33; Gwyn, *Democracy and the cost of politics*, 21–48.
[106] Caparn to Gladstone, 9 Dec. 1837, NAO, Glynne-Gladstone MSS DD/449/27/1.
[107] Lawrence to Mahon, 21 Feb. 1837, Stanhope MSS U1590, C382.
[108] Longmore to Mahon, 29 Jan. 1838, ibid.
[109] Mahon to Longmore, 17 Jan. 1840, ibid.
[110] LAD iv/3/88, fo. 4.

Figure 3
Expenses of Viscount Mahon, MP for Hertford, in 1839

		£	s	d
January	Cash paid coal fund subscription	2	2	–
	Dr Mathias Gilbertson, by your order.	40	–	–
April	Paid for dinner ticket (Mr Longmore's dinner)	–	12	6
May	Paid arrears of medical club subscriptions to			
	Mr Thomas (1837 and 1838)	2	2	–
June	Paid subscription to National School	2	2	–
	Paid for dinner ticket (Mr Ryder's dinner)	–	12	6
	Paid towards borough elections (Sir M.F.)[a]	25	–	–
July	Paid Brown School subscription	1	1	–
	Paid subscription to races	20	–	–
October	Paid donation to Green School sermon	1	–	–
	Paid subscription to new organ at All Saints Church	10	–	–
	Paid Herts. Literary Soc. June 1839 to Xmas 1840	2	2	–
November	Paid subscription (municipal election)[b]	10	–	–
	Paid Dr to lying-in Charity.	1	1	–
	County Press (extra editor)[c]	25	–	–
December	Paid Medical Benevolent Society 1839 and 1840	2	2	–
	Paid Girls' Green School	1	1	–
	Paid further at lying-in gift on Lady	3	7	6
	Mahon's safe confinement			
	Paid Haslam Lawrence and Co. for distributions	55	17	5
	to the poor at Christmas and subsequently			
	Paid Mr Haslam small payments made by him	7	1	–
	during the year to persons in distress			
	Penny Club subscription	1	–	–
		213	3	11
	Various payments throughout the year to persons			
	ill and in distress, and registration expenses 1839	160	5	6
		£373	9s.	5d.

Source: Longmore to Mahon, 15 Jan. 1840, Stanhope MSS U1590, C382.

[a] This refers to Sir Minto Farquhar's unsuccessful candidacy in the May 1839 Hertford by-election.
[b] This was to help fight the borough's municipal elections.
[c] The local Conservative newspaper.

before the loss of Sir James Hamlyn Williams's Carmarthenshire seat in 1837, for example, one of his principal agents had warned that

> if we attempt to starve the cause it will go against us, and in saving our member's pocket we may lose the election. Whether it costs Sir James one or two thousand is a thing I cannot understand he can care about. A man as he is, rolling in riches and with a clear income of at least 12,000 per annum . . . were I in his situation I should think the seat cheaply got at twice two thousand.[111]

The difficulties of trying to control expenditure also meant that in constituencies where the strength of parties was fairly evenly balanced, agreements were sometimes reached between the parties about sharing the representation and avoiding the expense of a contest. This inevitably involved candidates in a good deal of negotiation, not only at constituency level but also with the central election managers, whose plans might be entirely different.[112] In such cases, like that of the well-documented disagreement between Staffordshire's leading Conservatives and the party managers about whether to contest the county's southern division in 1841, it was invariably the wishes of the local leaders that prevailed.[113] As Kent noted in his study of this election, 'the Staffordshire Conservative gentry, in holding the purse strings of the election, could hold both local and national leaders up to ransom'.[114] As long as election costs remained high, therefore, the real power, the financial power, tended to remain in the hands of the traditional elites within each constituency.

There was one other traditional aspect of election expenditure, however, where a significant reduction did begin to emerge after 1832, which has still to be explored. This had nothing to do with the Reform Act, or even with later attempts to prohibit bribery and treating. Instead, as the final section of this chapter makes clear, this development arose out of a much broader nineteenth-century revolution, which was to have a far reaching impact on all aspects of politics and society.

Carriage and conveyance

Getting voters to the polling booth had always been essential, and the practice of transporting or 'conveying' electors at the expense of the candidate and his committee remained a central feature of electioneering after 1832.[115]

---

111 Major Herbert Evans to John Johnes, 1 Aug. 1837, Dolaucothi MSS L2164.
112 See, for example, Mahon's draft letter to Bonham about sharing the representation at Hertford and avoiding the expense of a contest: Mahon to Bonham, Jan. 1837, Stanhope MSS U1590, C382.
113 Gash, *Politics in the age of Peel*, 257; Patrick J. Doyle, 'The general election of 1841: the representation of south Staffordshire', *Transactions of the South Staffordshire Archaeological and Historical Society* xii (1971), 57–61.
114 Kent, 'Party politics in the county of Staffordshire', ch. v.
115 See, for example, Gwyn, *Democracy and the cost of politics*, 48–51.

Even in borough constituencies, where the voters had little distance to travel, considerable numbers expected to be taken to the poll in a horse-driven carriage provided by one of the candidates. Many, of course, were elderly or infirm electors, such as the man 'with a diseased knee' who applied to the Liberal committee for 'two places in a coach' in order that he could lie 'in a horizontal position' when he went to poll at the 1839 North Devon by-election.[116] For others, however, a free carriage ride was regarded as an essential part of the election ritual itself, especially during bad weather. Even in the geographically compact borough of Cheltenham, for example, the Tory candidate's 1841 bill for the hire of 'carriages, flys and phaetons', came to £105 17s. 6d. With most carriages being let by the livery stables at the rate of £1 6s. per day (including a driver), about eighty of these must have been deployed by the Conservatives alone on polling day.[117] Similarly at Newark in 1841, Gladstone and Lord John Manners spent a total of £120 17s. 8d. on 'fetching voters', which amounted to nearly a fifth of their total bill.[118]

In the larger county divisions, the provision of transport was far more important, and could even prove decisive. As an experienced agent in North Lincolnshire noted, 'very few indeed of the smaller voters would go any great distance to give their votes without being conveyed'.[119] Some voters even demanded that they travel with their families.[120] Helping to bring voters in from remote parts of a county division was particularly expensive – so much so that rival candidates usually came to some form of agreement about sharing costs.[121] In the preparations for an abortive South Lincolnshire contest in 1835, for example, the rates of reimbursement for voters were agreed by the parties as follows:

Distances of less than 1 stage or equal to	1s. 5d.
more than 1 stage, less than 2	1s. 10d.
greater than 2	15 shillings

Only applies to plumpers, split voters = shared cost with other party.[122]

The main difference, however, between mobilising the electorate of a borough and a county division was not just cost, but the existence of a large number of county outvoters. In most county divisions, somewhere between 12 and 25 per cent of the total registered electorate was non-resident.[123] It

---

116 Spence to Davy, 5 Mar. 1839, Buller of Crediton MSS 2065M/SS2/10.

117 Bills 75–90, Messrs Ticehurst Wyatt D2025/ misc. box 136.

118 1841 election expenses, Messrs Hodgkinson and Beevor DDH/51/25.

119 Ancaster MSS 3 Anc 9/14/272.

120 See, for example, 'Conservative election committee minute book', 3 June 1841, Messrs Longmore and Sworder D/EL/B562.

121 See, for instance, the travel arrangements for the West Somerset election of 1832: Sanford MSS DD/SF/2810.

122 Ancaster MSS 3 Anc 9/14/272.

123 *Hansard*, 3rd ser. lxxxv. 863. See ch. 4 below for a discussion of what made non-resident voting possible.

was this group that required the greatest organisation and assistance with travel. In the East Surrey contest of 1837, for example, the Conservatives spent an astonishing £1,117 11s. 10d. on 'travelling expenses to outvoters', including 'coaches, cabs, flys and horses'. This sum alone was commensurate with the entire cost of a medium-sized borough return. Moreover, the number of county outvoters grew rapidly after 1832. In East Surrey, this was reflected in a disproportionate rise in the amount spent by the Conservatives on bringing them in at the 1841 by-election. While the total expenditure in both contests remained almost the same, at about £7,500, the cost of conveying outvoters rose by almost 40 per cent between 1837 and 1841.[124]

The development of new forms of transportation in the 1830s therefore had a significant impact on electioneering. Railways revolutionised the organisation of many county contests, facilitating much easier and cheaper electoral participation by outvoters and resident electors alike. The London and Birmingham Railway, for example, which was opened fully in 1838, not only passed through the county constituencies of Middlesex, Hertfordshire, Bedfordshire, South Northamptonshire, and North Warwickshire, but also the major parliamentary boroughs of Marylebone, Coventry and Birmingham. The Grand Junction Railway, which linked Birmingham with Liverpool and Manchester, traversed six county divisions and six boroughs.[125] Political leaders and election managers were quick to appreciate their potential, and took an acute interest in promoting their development. Indeed, it was upon the basis of his apparently improper dealings with a number of early railway companies that Francis Bonham was eventually forced to resign from the Conservative government in 1845.[126]

In many places a complex web of agreements and negotiations often sprang up between local political interests and the new railway companies. The provisional committee of the Eastern Counties Railway, for example, included two MPs and a Conservative candidate.[127] Its principal agent in Suffolk was a local Conservative leader and a prominent Ipswich councillor.[128] In York, the railway tycoon George Hudson used his considerable influence to assist the return of a Tory candidate, J. H. Lowther, in the 1835, 1837 and 1841 general elections. Lowther, in return, sponsored the York and North Midlands Railway Bill through parliament in 1836. When the Tories

[124] 'Abstract of expenses', SuRO, Acc 3033, fos 38–44.
[125] North and South Cheshire, South Lancashire, North and South Staffordshire, North Warwickshire, Birmingham, Liverpool, Manchester, Stafford, Warrington and Wolverhampton.
[126] Gash, 'Bonham', 507–8.
[127] John Francis, A history of the English railway: its social relations and revelations, 1820–1845, London 1851, i. 26; Jack Simmons, The railways of Britain, New York 1968, 8; PP 1840 (474) xiii. 533.
[128] John Chevallier Cobbold: Atton, 'Municipal and parliamentary politics', 57, 166, 415. Cobbold became chairman of the Eastern Union and Bury and Ipswich Railway in 1838, and was MP for Ipswich 1847–68.

won control of York city council the following year, they nominated Hudson as the new mayor.[129] With local political interests playing such a prominent part in the development of the railways, it is hardly surprising that they were quickly incorporated into future election strategy. In Bedfordshire, for instance, a local Liberal election agent pointed out the impact of the new London and Birmingham line on his party's polling arrangements:

> in future the voters for Leighton or Ampthill ought to be forwarded to Leighton and those for Bedford and Sharnbrook to Stony Stratford by the railroad, having persons at Leighton and Stony Stratford to take charge of them and forward them to their places of polling and having carriages or means of conveyance provided there for the purpose. In this way they might go and return in a day, being carried to the poll, polled and brought back in time to return by the evening train.[130]

The 1837 general election was the first in which local election managers became acutely aware of the potential of the growing railway network. Accounts from all over the country testify to its importance. In South Lancashire, for example, the Liberal election committee of Edward Stanley and Charles Townley distributed 'cards for the railroad' to all their principal supporters, enabling voters to use not only the celebrated Liverpool and Manchester Railway, at the opening of which the former cabinet minister William Huskisson had been killed by a train in 1830, but also the more recent lines of the Manchester, Bolton and Selby Railway, the Bolton and Leigh Railway and the North Union Railway.[131] Travelling by train was not only cheaper. It was also about three times quicker than even the fastest express coach. During the North Northamptonshire election of 1837, for example, the special messengers travelling by road took one hour to travel the six or seven miles from Wellingborough to Kettering with the latest state of the poll.[132] The average speed of travel on the London and Birmingham Railway, by contrast, was twenty-two miles per hour.[133] More important, the electoral impact of the railways was not just confined to the counties. Access to a borough election also became much easier for those with multiple residences. Lord Hatherton, for example, recounted with some astonishment how a man was able to vote 'both at Stafford and Liverpool before 12 'o'clock' on 26 July 1837, by using the Grand Junction Railway.[134]

Of course not all voters were happy to travel by train. Early English railways were surprisingly free from fatal accidents, but the frequency of minor

---

129 Brett, 'Liberal middle classes', 320, 334.
130 'Mode of conveying London voters, 1837', BRO, Russell MSS R/Box 768. In the event, however, there was no Bedfordshire contest in 1837 nor 1841.
131 Robert E. Harvey to Robert Statter, 1837, LRO, Knowsley MSS DDK/1740/4.
132 NRO, Misc. Acc. ZB 43.
133 PP 1839 (517) x. 494–500.
134 Election diary, 26 July 1837, Hatherton MSS D1178/1.

and localised incidents helped fuel fear and suspicion. When Hatherton and his son took the first public trip on the London and Birmingham Railway in the middle of the 1837 general election, for example, their train crashed into Euston Grove station on the way back.[135] Some voters inevitably preferred to make their own travel arrangements, rejecting the obligation to an election committee that usually, but not automatically, accompanied receipt of expenses. As the duke of Bedford's steward reminded one over-enthusiastic Liberal election agent, 'there is also to be considered that many persons may have a prejudice against railway travelling, more particularly when at the expense of another'.[136]

The largest group to benefit from the railways were the London outvoters, who were usually canvassed and then conveyed into their respective counties by the large London-based central election committees. The North Northamptonshire Reform Association, for example, used 'Mr Coppock of the Reform Association' to organise their London outvoters and to call 'them at the proper time and send them to the poll'.[137] An increasingly significant electoral group in most county divisions, these London outvoters helped to inject an important metropolitan ingredient into many local contests, providing a physical connection with a Westminster-orientated political agenda. In the Midlands county of Bedfordshire, roughly 10 per cent of the registered electorate lived in the capital.[138] Even in more distant counties a considerable proportion of outvoters were from London. Over a third of East Norfolk's non-resident electorate in 1837 resided either in London, or at a 'great distance'.[139] In East Sussex, 37 per cent of the registered outvoters came from London in 1832, and 39 per cent in 1837. Even more tellingly, an additional 8 per cent of the London outvoters participated at the 1837 contest in comparison with 1832.[140]

During the two parliamentary sessions of 1836–7, an additional 1,500 miles of railway network was authorised for construction through private legislation.[141] By the time of the 1841 general election, some 1,650 miles of track were open for public use.[142] Electioneering reports from all over the country suggest that, where a contest did occur in 1841 (registration having settled many outcomes in advance), the new railways were heavily used by

135 Ibid. 13 July 1837.
136 T. Bennett to Christian Stacey, 19 Dec. 1837, BRO, Russell MSS R/Box 768.
137 Whig committee minute books, 11 Dec. 1835, Fitzwilliam MSS Fitz. Misc. vol. 502; 27–8 July 1837, NRO, Misc. Acc. ZB 43.
138 BRO, Russell MSS R/Box 768.
139 322 voters came from 'London and distant' out of a total non-resident electorate of approximately 949: 1837 East Norfolk pollbook, 197–208.
140 The turnout rate for registered London outvoters was 39% in 1832 and 47% in 1837: 1832 East Sussex pollbook, 80–90; 1837 East Sussex pollbook, 91–105. There was no contest in 1835.
141 Simmons, Railways, 6.
142 W. M. Acworth, The railways of England, London 1889, 3.

local committees and their agents. In the West Riding, for example, the Liberal election committee for Sheffield relied upon the Leeds railway to bring in voters, to transport election agents and to communicate with other committees.[143] Even where there was no contest, as in South Staffordshire, it is clear that the business of canvassing and general election management still benefited from the new railway network and the related development of the electric telegraph.[144] In some county contests, election committees even tried to gain an advantage over their rivals by booking special 'voter trains' in advance. The minute book of the Hertfordshire Conservative Association, for example, suggests that it secured exclusive use of the Broxborne Railway for conveying voters in the Tory interest to Hertford, Bishop's Stortford, Hoddesdon and Buntingford.[145] Special 'railway conductors' were employed to escort the Tory voters on and off the carriages and to the correct polling places. Their payment of one guinea per day by the Hertfordshire Conservative Association, which was substantially more than the messengers or local clerks received, suggests the real electoral importance attached to their work.[146] Even greater use of the railway system was made by the association's London committee, based at 36 Lincoln's Inn Fields, which managed all the Tory electors 'residing within 6 miles of London'. In an attempt to muster their supporters more effectively and reduce costs, they arranged 'that voters from London who are to poll at Watford, Hemel Hemstead and Birkhamstead be conveyed by the Birmingham Railway to those places, and those to poll at St Albans be conveyed by the same railway as far as Watford'.[147]

The fact that county electors, whether resident or non-resident, could get to the poll more easily and cheaply is one of the less well-researched psephological developments of the 1830s. In many counties the outvoters, residing beyond the county boundaries, actually outnumbered the £50 tenants-at-will, as will be seen in the next chapter. Moreover, continuing development of the railway network encouraged increasing levels of outvoter participation, helping to dilute and even diminish the electoral potency of resident influences and exclusively local concerns.[148] Subsequently, in the mid-1840s, railways became especially important in facilitating the wholesale mobilisation of the new class of county voter created by the registration campaigns of the Anti-Corn Law League. Swamping the county registers with thousands of manufactured 40s. freehold voters was one thing, but getting them to a poll was quite another. Without access to the quick and inexpensive transportation of the League's non-resident urban freeholders, Cobden's registration

---

143 Matthew Hobson to G. Hall, 1 July 1841, SRO, MD/2695/39–46
144 Hatherton diary, 6 July 1841, Hatherton MSS D260M/F/5/26/22.
145 'Conservative election committee minute book', 3 June 1841, Messrs Longmore and Sworder D/EL/B562.
146 Ibid. 15 Oct. 1841.
147 Ibid.
148 This is discussed more fully in ch. 4 below.

crusade would have been a hollow threat.[149] One enduring legacy of railway development, in these circumstances, was to help bring about the political demise of the county interest.

Assessments of the Reform Act, no less than any other historical event, are complicated by elements of change and continuity. Alongside the dramatic transformations to the electoral system outlined in chapters 1 and 2, there was much that appeared familiar, especially in terms of the campaign rituals and treating of voters traditionally associated with pre-Reform election-eering. These ongoing theatrical and ceremonial features of an election were important for two reasons. First, they helped to ensure that most candidate's costs remained high after Reform, despite the duration of the poll being reduced and the emergence of cheaper forms of voter transportation. Second, despite the impact of registration and the emergence of more permanent forms of partisanship, these campaign rituals helped to keep alive a persistent tension between the electorate and the elected, which was perhaps best enshrined in the chairing ceremony, an ordeal that left the candidate at the mercy of his constituents. Candidates were clearly less the originators of such rituals, than the hapless recipients. Custom and convention, it would seem, continued to provide an important counterpoint to partisanship by offering an alternative way of viewing a candidate's performance and fitness for repre-sentation, and by allowing plenty of space for voter choice, local independ-ence and the politics of negotiation within the electoral process.

The cultural similarities between the unreformed and reformed systems, however, should not be allowed to obscure the very substantial operational changes that took place after 1832. Indeed, even the most central traditions of electioneering were not immune to the impact of Reform. The type of registration activity outlined in chapters 1 and 2, for instance, provided a far more effective means of assessing and recruiting support than the highly ritu-alised canvass, which was extremely cumbersome and unreliable. The prelim-inary stages of a post-1832 election campaign therefore became subtly differentiated from their past forms, with registration being eagerly seized upon as the best means of identifying voters and supporters, and the canvass itself becoming more about mobilisation, ritual and cajolery, and ceremonial exchanges between constituents and candidates. Far more significantly, this chapter has demonstrated that many key components of an election were subject to a process of standardisation after 1832, either through the statutory provisions of the Reform Act, or as a result of common developments on the ground. Registration and polling procedures, the location and number of booths, and even the official language and expenses of an election were now formally prescribed on a national basis by law, added to which there emerged a whole new corpus of election guides providing technical advice on every-

---

[149] See Prest, *Politics in the age of Cobden*, 85–8.

thing from voting qualifications to the management of a full-scale contest. This move to a more uniform electoral culture coincided with important modifications to traditional forms of political influence and control (which will be examined in chapters 4 and 5) and the rise of more permanent and nationally-oriented patterns of partisanship in both parliamentary and local elections (*see* chapters 6 and 7). All these elements helped to produce an electoral system that was distinctly 'reformed' and more 'modern' after 1832.

PART II
THE COUNTIES

4

Electoral Behaviour in the Counties: Influence and Independence

Much attention has recently been focused on re-examining the electoral dynamics of borough constituencies, both before and after 1832.[1] By contrast, there has been a marked absence of similar revisionist work on the reformed rural electorate. This is surprising given that the existing literature is so sharply divided into two schools of thought. First, there are the detailed local studies which tend to stress the importance of issues and the active political agency of individual voters in determining patterns of rural voting after 1832.[2] The variety and particularism of these political issues, however, has made it difficult to draw any general conclusions about the nature and operation of the county electoral system as a whole. Indeed, most of these local studies have been at pains to point out regional idiosyncrasy and abnormality. Richard Olney, for example, warned that Lincolnshire was not 'typical of the majority of English counties; nor was it, perhaps, typical even of the rural counties'.[3] Tom Nossiter came to a similar conclusion about County Durham, insisting that 'the north-east was isolated from the rest of the country; it diverged from the national pattern in both the structure of landownership and the nature of agriculture'.[4] Likewise Edwin Jaggard's recent analysis of Cornwall politics portrayed 'a political culture different in some ways from the remainder of England'.[5] As Richard Davis suggested in his study of Buckinghamshire, 'no county, after all, is exactly like any other county'.[6]

Thus while issues were an essential ingredient of most county contests, they are not very useful for constructing any broad analysis of the county electorate as a whole. Even the most commonly voiced political concerns of the

[1] Phillips, *Boroughs*; Phillips and Wetherell, 'Great Reform Act of 1832', and 'The Great Reform Bill of 1832'; O'Gorman, *Voters, patrons, and parties*; Taylor, 'Interests, parties and the state'; Vernon, *Politics and the people*.
[2] Davis, *Buckinghamshire*; Jaggard, *Cornwall politics*; Olney, *Lincolnshire*; David Eastwood, 'Toryism, Reform, and political culture in Oxfordshire, 1826–1837', *PH* vii (1988), 98–121; D. Foster, 'The politics of uncontested elections: north Lancashire 1832–1865', *Northern History* xiii (1977), 232–47; J. R. Fisher, 'Issues and influence: two by-elections in south Nottinghamshire in the mid-nineteenth century', *HJ* xxiv (1981), 155–65; Thompson, 'Whigs and Liberals in the West Riding'.
[3] Richard J. Olney, *Lincolnshire politics, 1832–1885*, Oxford 1973, pp. vii–viii.
[4] Nossiter, *Influence*, 2.
[5] Jaggard, *Cornwall politics*, 214.
[6] Davis, *Buckinghamshire*, 11.

1830s, over religion, the New Poor Law and agricultural protection, were subject to very different regional interpretations and impact, over and above which most candidates then had to address a range of highly localised matters. The composition of county electorates also varied widely in terms of religion, class and employment, ensuring divergent patterns of reception and response. And while it is true that the policies pushed by Liberal candidates throughout the 1830s were usually more specific and well defined than those of their opponents – especially on religious issues, such the removal of Dissenters' disabilities – there was no fixed party agenda here, advocated in any systematic or coherent way. Local realities were frequently far removed from the rhetoric of national politics. Without clear direction from the leadership in Westminster for much of the decade, party lines on particular issues were often blurred and specific policy pledges were very much left to individual MPs. The diverse blend of national and local issues, around which most county elections revolved, defies easy summary, still less synthesis, on any national scale.

This helps to explain the remarkable resilience of the second school of far more generalised models of rural electoral life, put forward most strikingly in the works of Norman Gash and D. C. Moore. In direct contrast to the local studies, these accounts contextualise rural elections primarily in terms of the pervasive authority exercised by landed, proprietorial elites. According to Gash, for example, 'the great territorial magnates, both whig and tory' were able 'to maintain their influence, and in favourable conditions to exercise a preponderant power' after 1832, and 'thus only the positions of the duke of Buckingham and the duke of Bedford explain why Buckinghamshire was mainly a tory and Bedfordshire mainly a whig county'.[7] Similar views were voiced by some contemporary observers. According to the Conservative Lord Stanley, for example, 'it was known that when any man attempted to estimate the probable result of a county election, it was ascertained by calculating the number of great landed proprietors in the county, and weighing the number of occupiers under them'.[8] County pollbooks, asserted Joseph Parkes, were 'almost a topography of the estates'.[9]

This view was taken to its apotheosis in the work of Moore, who argued that Reform actually increased, and was intended to increase, aristocratic control over the rural electorate. Adding a quantitative base to his investigations, Moore used county pollbooks to identify parishes where a majority of the electors voted the same way as their landlord, as part of a 'deference community'.[10] Both Moore's methods and his powerful paradigm about deference voting have attracted substantial and sustained criticism ever since. Yet

7 Gash, *Politics in the age of Peel*, 185. It is only to fair to add that Gash included a local study of Berkshire in his otherwise generalised account of the reformed electoral system.
8 *Hansard*, 3rd ser. lvi. 809.
9 PP 1835 (547) viii. 105.
10 Moore, *Deference*, 30–133, 137–242.

there is no denying that twenty-five years after it was published, his *Politics of deference* remains an influential work, technically flawed but impossible to ignore as the only full-length survey of its kind.

Two points, in particular, stand out about this rather curious state of research into county politics after 1832. The first is that although many alternative models of rural politics challenging the concept of 'electoral deference' have been advanced for the unreformed electoral system, most cogently in the work of O'Gorman, their transferability to the post-Reform period remains problematic.[11] County constituencies after 1832 were very different from their predecessors, both in terms of their geographical layout and their electoral composition. As many as twenty-seven of the forty English counties were divided into two (or, in the case of Yorkshire, three) separate divisions by the Reform Act.[12] In addition, many of the towns and boroughs located within these divisions either acquired or lost representatives, altering the political dynamics of counties in ways which remain largely unresolved.[13] The right of voting was also extended to £10 copyholders and leaseholders, and to £50 tenants-at-will, creating a whole new body of voters who were registered and polled differently. Models of unreformed 'electoral deference' therefore need to be applied with care, and contextualised within these altered political parameters, if they are adequately to capture the workings of the post-1832 system. David Eastwood's broad reappraisal of deference politics has done much here.[14] But the bulk of the existing literature on the county electorate does not apply specifically to the post-Reform period, nor does it usually extend beyond one particular locality. Even Alan Heesom's compelling account of the 'legitimate' forms of electoral influence accepted and articulated at Westminster was only tested against the experience of North Durham, between 1819 and 1852.[15] Many of the crucial political developments which were common to all localities after 1832, especially with regard to the impact of new forms of political activism on county politics, have yet to be fully teased out and given the attention they deserve.

The second striking feature of the existing literature is the paucity of quantitative work on county pollbooks. This is particularly surprising given the sophistication of much recent quantitative research on borough polls and the

---

11 O'Gorman, *Voters, patrons, and parties*, 224–44, 334–42, and 'Electoral deference in "unreformed" England', 391–429. O'Gorman himself has readily acknowledged the need for post-1832 'modifications' to be made to his 'model of the pre-1832 electoral system': 'The electorate before and after 1832', 181.
12 2 Will. IV c. 45, 727, clauses 12–14.
13 Cf. Gash, *Politics in the age of Peel*, 65–101; Seymour, *Electoral reform*, 12–76; Moore, 'Concession or cure', 39–59, and 'The other face of Reform', *Victorian Studies* v (1961), 7–34. The forthcoming *History of Parliament* volumes on the *House of Commons, 1820–1832* will offer much-needed information on the impact of boundary changes at constituency level, especially their effect on local political interests.
14 Eastwood, 'Contesting the politics of deference', 27–49.
15 Heesom, ' "Legitimate" *versus* "illegitimate" influences', 282–305.

centrality of statistics to Moore's highly contested, yet remarkably resilient, theory of 'deference communities'. Moore used the total number of votes received by each candidate, rather than the amount of split votes or plumpers cast by the voters, to try to identify parishes where 'all or significant majorities' of the voters polled the same way, 'as members of geographically definable blocs'.[16] Looking simply at these final tallies, however, led Moore to make generalisations about individual voting behaviour which were totally at odds with the evidence of the pollbooks. In certain Northamptonshire parishes, for example, Moore concluded that 'majorities of the voters' behaved identically and 'split their votes between Cartwright and Althorp (group 9)'.[17] But in half the parishes he listed in this group this was not the case. In the parish of Geddington, for example, only three of the sixteen voters cast their votes in this way. At Great Oxenden only two out of the twenty voters split their votes between Cartwright and Althorp. These simply cannot be described as 'majorities of the voters', especially when, as at Great Oxenden, nine voters behaved in a completely different way by splitting their votes between Althorp and Milton, and a further eight split them between Cartwright and Knightley.[18] An assessment of voting behaviour based on the total number of votes received by each candidate, rather than the individual choices made by each voter, led Moore to draw a number of unsustainable conclusions about the nature of the reformed rural electorate.[19]

The problems and pitfalls of analysing county pollbooks are, to be fair, real and acute. But to conclude, as the late John Phillips did, that the 'potential rewards of a study of the county electorate would not be sufficient to justify the effort', seems unduly negative.[20] Phillips suggested that 'impossible obstacles bar the way of a quantitative assessment of county elections', a view evidently endorsed by O'Gorman in an important review.[21] But the techniques of nominal record linkage that Phillips so effectively applied to borough elections, which permit a longitudinal analysis of partisan voting over time, have been successfully transplanted to county contests as well.[22]

[16] Moore, *Deference*, 8–9, 29.

[17] Ibid. 113.

[18] 1831 Northants pollbook, 36, 49, 50. In the 3 parishes of Marson Thrussell, Geddington and Great Oxenden far larger numbers in fact split their votes between Althorp and Milton, and between Cartwright and Knightley, than Moore claims.

[19] For a more detailed critique of Moore's methodology see Philip Salmon, 'Electoral reform at work: local politics and national parties, 1832–41', unpubl. DPhil. diss. Oxford 1997, 161–7.

[20] Phillips, *Boroughs*, 40.

[21] Ibid. 39; O'Gorman, 'The electorate before and after 1832', 172. Others have also protested against this dismissal of the county pollbook: S. Baskerville, P. Ademan and K. Beedham, 'Manuscript poll books and English county elections in the first age of party: a reconsideration of their provenance and purpose', *Archives* xix (1991), 385.

[22] See, for example, the longitudinal analysis of North Durham's voters in Radice, 'Identification, interests and influence', 458–9. Many of the technical problems of individual identification associated with longitudinal studies of voting behaviour – shared

Indeed, it was the application of exactly these methods that allowed the behaviour of 'new' and 'experienced' voters at the East Sussex and North Durham contests of 1837 to be compared as part of the discussion in chapter 2.

Phillips's additional assertion, that 'both before and after 1832 most electoral activity occurred in the parliamentary boroughs', is altogether more contentious.[23] County elections may have been contested far less frequently than in the boroughs, but this was precisely because electoral activity in the counties was often so intense that political struggles were actually settled in advance of an election, obviating the need for an official poll. Much has been made of these so-called 'missing contests', including, more recently, their implications for the 'political participation' of voters 'who had the theoretical right to vote, but who lacked the practical opportunity to exercise it'.[24] Looking at electoral activity only in terms of voting, however, entirely neglects what O'Gorman has called 'the very stuff of electoral politics' – the requisitions and rallies, public speeches and preliminary skirmishes – which were the inevitable precursors to any county, or indeed borough, contest.[25] Many county campaigns petered out at these early stages, through lack of support and poor prospects. Others proceeded to the rituals of the nomination and the theatre of the canvass, on the basis of which unpopular candidates usually retired from the field. In both cases the sphere of electoral activity could be just as overtly public and potentially participatory as the final mechanism of the poll.

Above all, focusing only on polling overlooks the pre-electoral activity of voter registration. Contrary to what has been assumed by many historians, this was just as critical in the counties as it was in the boroughs after 1832.[26] Moore, in a memorable essay underpinning his theory of 'deference communities', attributed the 'missing contests' of English counties to 'political decisions' made by the leaders of 'definable groups and networks' of voters and their shifting 'exigencies of cohesion'.[27] After 1832, however, it was registra-

---

names, unknown occupations, moving populations – are tackled by local genealogical societies on a regular basis. The increasing number of publications aimed at this popular field of historical inquiry are potentially of great use to electoral historians.

23 Phillips, *Boroughs*, 40.

24 Beales, 'The electorate before and after 1832', 150. The classification of elections into 'contested' or 'uncontested' is far less indicative of political activity than has been previously supposed. The volumes of the *History of Parliament* shed much-needed light on the type of activity which this terminology obscures, including unendorsed or phantom nominations, token or purely vexatious oppositions, and undeclared or abortive polls on the ground.

25 O'Gorman, 'The electorate before and after 1832', 181. For the view that electoral historians have generally given too much 'explanatory weight' to 'the longitudinal analysis of pollbooks' see Taylor, 'Interests, parties and the state', 52–3, 67–71.

26 Stewart, *Party and politics*, 38; Evans, *Great Reform Act*, 62.

27 Moore, 'The matter of the missing contests', 109, 116–17.

tion which increasingly provided an alternative and authoritative basis upon which to choose either an electoral compromise or, as was more often the case, to force a complete withdrawal by one side altogether. It was in the annual registration courts that many elections were effectively being pre-determined.[28] Registration politics not only offers a more plausible alternative to 'deference politics' for explaining the 'missing contests' of this period, but it also reveals much about the effects of local political struggles on the ground *between* elections, as well as opening up new and much needed quantitative perspectives for the study of county politics as a whole. Despite all the literature on local politics after 1832, the impact of registration and party organisation on the electoral dynamics of county constituencies has yet to be fully explored.

The following two chapters aim to fill some of these gaps. This chapter re-visits the most debated and familiar aspects of rural electoral life – landed influence and voter independence – but, for the first time, with specific reference to the post-1832 period and evidence from a wide range of different localities. As well as using traditional types of written sources, the account employs new quantitative techniques to assess patterns of rural voting over time, based upon the votes of over 50,000 individuals. The behaviour of different franchise groups and the resident and non-resident electorate is also compared, and a new interpretative framework for understanding county politics is developed, which stresses the limits to landlord influence and the genuine vibrancy of rural electoral life. Countering this generalised approach, chapter 5 presents a series of far more detailed case studies. These explore the political dynamics of voter registration, landed influence and electoral politicisation within the specific contexts of North Devon, South Lincolnshire, Bedfordshire, West Somerset, North Wiltshire and the West Riding of Yorkshire. Taken together, and by focusing on what was common rather than unique to each constituency in this period, these chapters aim to present an alternative generalised account of rural elections after Reform, appropriate to the nation as a whole.

The nature of landed influence

In many respects the use of landed influence in elections after 1832 functioned along similar lines to that advanced by O'Gorman in his recent study of the unreformed electorate.[29] Much the same type of evidence that he drew upon from a period of almost a hundred years can be produced for the post-Reform decade alone, although there were some important developments in this period, as the following sections of this chapter make clear.

---

28 The proportion of contested county elections was 70% in 1832, 46% in 1835, 52% in 1837 and 24% in 1841: Raymond, 'English political parties', 267.
29 O'Gorman, *Voters, patrons, and parties*, 224–44, 334–42.

Adhering to tacit conventions that rewarded restraint rather than coercion, the exercise of landed control remained subject to constant public scrutiny and practical limitations. Rival landowners kept a close watch on each other and heavy-handed landlords often found themselves pilloried and chastised by the local press.[30] Indeed, the extensive publicity given to cases of 'undue influence' says much about commonly held notions of acceptable electoral conduct.[31] When the young Lord Ward flouted convention during the general election of 1837, for example, by intimidating the tenants of a Staffordshire estate that was being held in trust for him, he was accused by the Whigs of 'using most unconstitutional influence'.[32] Even then the principal Whig trustee of the estate, Lord Hatherton, refused to intervene to guarantee the tenantry 'the free exercise of their political opinions'. As he explained to his chief agent, 'to influence Lord Ward's tenants against him, would I fear, be considered by all who were not actually engaged in the contest as an extraordinary act on my part'.[33] Significantly, Hatherton's restraint paid off. Despite the 'extraordinary exertions' of Ward's agents, the election swung in favour of the Liberals. Hatherton believed that the young Lord Ward and his Tory henchmen had been taught a harsh lesson, noting in his diary that 'the licking has certainly done them good, made them civil, unpresuming, even apologetic'.[34]

Acres, it must be stressed, conferred responsibility first and influence only second. It was the exercise and execution of that responsibility – the duties of which were increasingly being formally encoded in publications such as the Revd S. G. Osborne's *Hints to the charitable* (London 1838) – which might, under favourable circumstances, elicit widespread electoral influence. Good landlords would usually command genuine feelings of respect and loyalty among their tenants and neighbours, which would be reinforced by a shared sense of community and an open awareness of their mutual interdependence and common interest. In these circumstances, it was not so much the land-lord who deliberately sought to direct votes, as the voters themselves who actively sought guidance. In the North Northumberland election of 1835, for example, the opinion of Sir Charles Monck was consulted rather than openly canvassed. As he replied to one correspondent:

> Mr Walters, my steward, informs me that your sons, who are electors of the north division of this county enquired of him yesterday for whom I intended to vote and declared that they wished to know it before they formed their own

30 Salisbury to Mahon, 31 Mar. 1835, Stanhope MSS U1590, C382; *Wiltshire Independent*, 20 July 1837.
31 See, for example, the anonymous handbill entitled 'Les Jours Viendra' sent to William Battie Wrightson, [1832], Battie-Wrightson MSS BW/P16.
32 John Barker to Hatherton, 12 July 1837, Hatherton MSS D260 M/F/5/19/9. Lord Ward was not due to inherit these Dudley estates until he was 21.
33 Hatherton to John Barker, 14 July 1837, ibid.
34 Election diary, 3 Aug. 1837, Hatherton MSS D1178/1.

determination. I feel much flattered by this testimony of confidence from your family, and have no hesitation in declaring [my] . . . wish that Lord Ossulston and Mr Liddell may be chosen.[35]

Such courteous and consultative exchanges drew little contemporary comment, precisely because they were routine rather than irregular. 'Illegitimate' influence, by contrast, was unconventional and conspicuous, and formed a powerful weapon with which to harangue political opponents. In the rhetoric of this period, it became the universal scapegoat and a highly effective polemical device.[36] Unsuccessful candidates, in particular, were far more likely to blame their defeat on intimidation or foul play, than to acknowledge their genuine unpopularity. Contemporary accounts of heavy-handed influence therefore need to be treated with caution. Indeed, even when pique was not an obvious factor, the use of landlord influence might still be grossly exaggerated. Despite Lord Francis Egerton's large majority of 1,246 votes in the 1837 South Lancashire contest, for example, he still complained to Peel that 'Lord Derby, Lord Gifford and Sir Hesketh Fleetwood all gave the last turn of the screw to a reluctant tenantry'. 'Without such exertion on their part', he alleged, 'I should have stood at least 300 higher on the poll.'[37]

The surviving election correspondence between Derby and the Liberal committee, however, presents a rather different picture. Considerable confusion had existed among Derby's tenants regarding his wishes, especially in the area around Pilkington where Tory canvassers, aided by the presence of a local Conservative operative society, had been particularly active.[38] Indeed, the deputy chairman of the Liberal committee had repeatedly asked Derby to clarify his position for the benefit of his tenants.[39] His reply, however, which was intended for use as a circular, demonstrated great propriety. Even such a powerful magnate, it would seem, could not afford to appear too assertive or assuming when soliciting support:

> If any of my tenants entertain any doubt as to their vote in the approaching contest, they will perhaps be not displeased that I should at once say that the way in which they can, if they desire it, both please me and meet my own wishes, would be by voting for *both* the candidates who are proposed in opposition to the late members, viz. *Messrs Stanley and Townley* . . . though of course it is not for me to dictate *to anyone* to act against his conscientious opinion.[40]

35 Monck to Creighton, 11 Dec. 1834, Northumberland Record Office, Middleton (Belsay) MSS ZM1/B16/XI.
36 See, for instance, its use against Lord Londonderry in North Durham: Radice, 'Identification, interests and influence', 346–51.
37 Lord Francis Egerton to Peel, 6 Aug. 1837, Peel MS Add. 40424, fo. 17r.
38 See *The Times*, 29, 30 Nov. 1836.
39 Robert Harvey to Robert Statter, [undated], Knowsley MSS DDK 1740/4.
40 Lord Derby to Robert Statter, [undated], ibid.

The chairman of the Liberal committee, Thomas Tynen, expressed 'great alarm' at Derby's caution, and his disappointment was by no means atypical.[41] Despite all the efforts of election agents, it was often extremely difficult to persuade landed proprietors to overcome such scruples, even when their influence might prove decisive. Soliciting private support was one thing, but securing public endorsement was quite another. In the pre-electoral negotiations that preceded the South Nottinghamshire election of 1837, for example, a clearly frustrated Conservative agent was informed that although the head of an influential local family was 'a *staunch Conservative* and hopes to see Lord Lincoln and Colonel Rolleston returned for South Notts, his lordship at the same time does not wish actively to interfere though he trusts his tenantry in that part of the county will . . . unite for the Conservatives'.[42]

Peers, as these last two examples suggest, could be particularly circumspect, not least because under a standing order of the House of Commons passed in 1701, members of the Lords were forbidden to interfere in elections. While it is true that this was never strictly enforced, it nevertheless inhibited both the expression and exercise of a peer's electoral influence.[43] Moreover, in the wake of parliamentary reform electoral interference by the peerage was subject to increased scrutiny. Some peers even felt obliged to decline roles as presidents of the newly formed constituency associations, fearing that acceptance would compromise both their public standing and the spirit, if not the letter, of the constitution. When the duke of Sutherland was asked to become president of the North Staffordshire Reform Association, for example, he was worried by its implications: 'I am quite convinced of the necessity of attention to the registration', he wrote, 'but I am not sure how far it is right for a Peer's name to appear in the association, however he may approve of the object.'[44] Similar perceptions were shared and articulated by leading local activists. When establishing the East Sussex Conservative Association, for example, Thomas Turner was quick to remind the earl of Ashburnham that 'as a peer of the realm you are precluded from taking any active part in such an association'.[45]

Landed elites also found their electoral influence restricted economically. The size, composition and economic circumstances of an estate often precluded any wholesale interference with the votes of tenants, who in many regions enjoyed considerable security of tenure, either as long or life leaseholders or as copyholders.[46] Even where eviction of a recalcitrant tenant was legally possible, it might not be financially feasible. Farms without tenants

---

41 Thomas Tynen to Lord Derby, [undated], ibid.
42 C. Chondlers to Mr Tollington, 24 June 1837, Craven-Smith-Milnes of Hockerton (Winkburn) MSS DD/CW 7/13.
43 O'Gorman, *Voters, patrons, and parties*, 262; Heesom, ' "Legitimate" *versus* "illegitimate" influences', 282–3.
44 Sutherland to T. C. Sheppard, [1837], Sutherland MSS D593/P/22/1/12.
45 Turner to Ashburnham, 18 Apr. 1835, Ashburnham MSS 3257.
46 O'Gorman, *Voters, patrons, and parties*, 241–3.

decayed rapidly and in some parts of the country, as the Whig agent for South Devon observed, finding a replacement £50 tenant-at-will was extremely difficult.[47] In these circumstances, landlords simply could not afford to be too heavy-handed, nor too choosy when it came to filling vacant tenancies. 'Landowners', as Cragoe concluded in his study of rural Carmarthenshire, 'were never, in fact, completely free agents', and 'very few would have been prepared to run the gauntlet of communal hostility and public censure that might follow a series of capricious evictions'.[48] Extensive landownership, therefore, did not automatically confer widespread electoral influence. Even in the most favourable conditions proprietorial influence would rarely extend beyond the number of immediately dependent tenants and traders, many of whom might not even possess the vote. As the prominent landowner Lord Shrewsbury explained to the earl of Lichfield on the eve of a North Staffordshire contest:

> Do not however think that my interest will have any considerable influence in the election. Though my property here extends over nearly 10,000 acres, with upwards of 300 tenants, yet there are only twenty-nine who rent to the amount of £50 a year and upwards. At least half of the estate is on life leases.[49]

Quantifying landed influence: voter unanimity

So how many county voters were actually affected by landed influence after 1832? Some measure of the possible extent of 'deference voting' can be obtained by examining the tendency of parishes to vote in a uniform manner, in agreement with a local landlord. Because of the way most county pollbooks were compiled, parishes with extremely high rates of unanimity, where nearly all the electors voted the same way, can be easily identified by inspection. Obviously such parishes are only one highly conspicuous manifestation of landed influence, especially in view of the fact that some parishes may have had several landlords. Nevertheless, by allowing for a certain rate of disagreement, or 'dissidence', within each parish this problem can be minimised. Building on the type of techniques that have been used by O'Gorman and Eastwood, the number of parishes with unanimity rates of 85 per cent or above has been analysed for consecutive contests held in West Kent, East and West Norfolk, East Sussex and North Northamptonshire during the 1830s.[50] Table 5 presents the results of this extensive analysis, which is based upon an examination of the votes of 53,241 individuals at eleven different county polls.

---

47 PP 1835 (547) viii. 173, minute 2917.
48 Cragoe, *Anglican aristocracy*, 171–2.
49 Shrewsbury to Lichfield, 12 June 1832, Anson MSS D615/P(P) 1/19.
50 O'Gorman, 'Electoral deference', 413–24; Eastwood, 'Oxfordshire', 112–13.

Table 5
Parishes with voter unanimity of 85 per cent or more
in eleven county contests

1	2	3	4	5	6	7
Contest		Number of voters	% parishes with >85% unanimity	% electorate polling with unanimity	Average no. voters per parish	Average no. voters per parish with unanimity
West Kent	1835	4,549	29	9	25	9
	1837	6,641	11	3	36	10
East Norfolk	1832	6,229	31	16	17	9
	1835	6,385	25	13	18	10
	1837	6,744	24	10	19	9
West Norfolk	1835	3,944	34	14	12	6
	1837	5,900	28	9	18	6
East Sussex	1832	2,753	33	17	18	10
	1837	3,869	21	4	25	6
N. Northants.	1832	3,063	28	11	18	8
	1837	3,164	43	20	18	9

Source: pollbooks.

A number of features are immediately apparent. It is clear, for example, that although the parishes with this high level of political agreement usually accounted for somewhere between a quarter to a third of the total number of parishes (*see* column 4), the proportion of the electorate actually involved in such behaviour was far lower (*see* column 5). At the 1835 West Kent election, for instance, the proportion of parishes exhibiting 85 per cent uniformity or above was 29 per cent.[51] However, the number of electors who actually voted together in these unanimous parishes was only 419, or a mere 9 per cent of the total turnout of 4,549. Only two of the parishes where unanimity occurred had more votes than the average of twenty-five (*see* column 6), a further eleven contained between ten and twenty-five electors, while forty had less than ten.[52] Indeed, taken together, the average number of voters in the unanimous parishes was just nine (*see* column 7). Similar features can be seen in all the other elections analysed in this table.[53] Parishes with more than 85 per cent voter unanimity were on the whole much smaller than the norm, suggesting that there were substantial limits to the influence of landed elites.

[51] 53 parishes out of a total of 185: 1835 West Kent pollbook.
[52] The average size of the parish has been determined by dividing the total number of electors (4,549) by the total number of parishes (185).
[53] See also the similar analysis of county contests in South Lincolnshire and Rutlandshire in ch. 5 below.

By far the most interesting conclusions, however, concern the development of electoral unanimity over time. In all but one of the counties analysed, the number of parishes exhibiting this level of political agreement declined significantly at the next election.[54] The fall in the proportion of the electorate actually involved in unanimous voting was even more pronounced, indicating that influence over the larger parishes was difficult to maintain. This is confirmed by looking at the individual parishes themselves. In West Kent, for example, there were thirteen parishes with more than ten voters where the level of uniformity was above 85 per cent at the 1835 election. The largest was Benenden, where forty-nine electors out of a total of fifty-five (89 per cent) voted for both the Liberal candidates, followed by Eltham, where thirty-five out of a total of forty-one (85 per cent) plumped for the single Conservative.[55] At the subsequent election of 1837, however, just two of these thirteen parishes continued to poll with such unanimity. The largest was again Benenden, where a spectacular fifty-five electors out of an increased figure of sixty-three (87 per cent) plumped for the single Liberal candidate, while the other was Chelsfield, where seventeen out of twenty (85 per cent) voted for the two Conservatives.[56] In all of the remaining previously uniform parishes, however, the level of unanimity now dropped to below 85 per cent, and in six of them to less than 65 per cent.[57] In contrast to the thirteen large parishes that had voted with unanimity at the election of 1835, there were now just five.[58] Whatever influences were at work in 1835 appear to have been far less effective in 1837.

The same trend can be observed in the other county divisions. In West Norfolk, for instance, nine of the fourteen parishes with above ten electors that had exhibited uniformity in 1835 failed to do so again in 1837.[59] One of them was Northwold, where twenty-six out of thirty voters (86 per cent) polled identically in 1835.[60] Two years later, however, the number of electors polling in this parish had increased to forty-four, while the number polling the same way had only risen to thirty (68 per cent).[61] This tendency for

54 Significantly the exception, Northamptonshire, was one of the three county constituencies (the others were Cambridgeshire and Huntingdonshire) from which Moore drew his conclusions: *Deference*, 103–33.
55 1835 West Kent pollbook, 10–11, 44–6.
56 1837 West Kent pollbook, 4–5, 42–3.
57 Kingsdown, Mereworth, Meopham, Snodland, Southfleet and Wilmington: ibid. 65, 71, 73, 97–8, 128, 156.
58 Benenden, Chelsfield, Chiddingstone, Smarden and West Farleigh: ibid. 4–5, 42–3, 81, 144–5, 153.
59 1835 and 1837 West Norfolk pollbooks, passim. The five that retained their unanimity were Elmham North, Kenninghall, Letheringsett, Marham and Wighton: 1837 West Norfolk pollbook, 14–15, 87–8, 109–10, 122, 128–9.
60 1835 West Norfolk pollbook, 67–8.
61 1837 West Norfolk pollbook, 102–3.

unanimity to decline as the number of voters expanded was also evident in East Sussex, where the electorate grew by almost 40 per cent between 1832 and the next contest of 1837.[62] Just one of the parishes with more than ten voters that had exhibited a level of political agreement of 85 per cent or above in 1832 did so again in 1837.[63] The unanimity that had earlier been demonstrated by 370 electors failed to re-materialise when the number of voters increased to 491.

Even the smaller uniform parishes, of ten or fewer voters, were not entirely immune from this type of political splintering as they expanded in size electorally, although they tended to be more resilient. Of the forty such parishes at the 1835 West Kent election, no less than twenty-six failed to deliver another uniform vote in 1837, and in eleven of them the level of unanimity actually dropped to below 65 per cent. In Bredhurst, for example, all four electors polled identically in 1835, but only five out of an expanded electorate of eleven (45 per cent) did so again in 1837. At Kemsing, nine voters out of ten (90 per cent) polled the same way in 1835, but only nine out of fourteen (64 per cent) two years later.[64]

Two broad conclusions can be drawn from this analysis. First, and perhaps not surprisingly, as parishes grew in size electorally they became less easy to control. Many new voters, especially those coming on to the registers for the first time in 1835 or 1836, appear to have rejected any earlier parochial consensus. Second, as turnout rates increased, levels of agreement were further undermined. Those who had previously chosen not to exercise their franchise had a marked tendency to poll independently of their neighbours when they did vote. A strong correlation therefore existed between increasing levels of electoral participation and greater levels of voter independence. In the face of an expanding rural electorate and enhanced electoral participation, the use of landed influence appears to have been increasingly limited after 1832. In all but one of the county divisions analysed in table 5, the proportion of the electorate affected by this particular indicator of landed control declined quite dramatically at the next election.[65]

Clearly there are other ways in which landed influence might be quantified, as the next two sections of this chapter indicate. Based on the criteria used to compile table 5, however, it is possible to provide a combined estimate of the proportion of electors involved in 'deference voting' at all eleven

---

62 See appendix 3.
63 1832 and 1837 East Sussex pollbooks, passim. The parish was Horsted Keynes: 1837 East Sussex pollbook, 48–9.
64 1835 West Kent pollbook, 96, 138; 1837 West Kent pollbook, 78, 128.
65 Obviously the level of political agreement which has been employed in this analysis is only one possible measure of 'deference voting'. Lowering the level of unanimity, however, and allowing up to one-fifth of the voters to behave freely in each parish, does not necessarily alter the overall picture. In West Kent, for example, the proportion of the electorate demonstrating this lower level of unanimity (80%) was 12 per cent in 1835 and 6 per cent in 1837, while in East Sussex in 1837 it was 7 per cent: 1835 and 1837 West Kent pollbooks, passim; 1837 East Sussex pollbook, passim.

of these contests. The total number of electors who voted in this sample of contests was 53,241, while in the parishes with unanimity rates of 85 per cent or above, there were a total of 5,847 uniform voters. Viewed from the perspective of this analysis, therefore, almost 11 per cent of the electorate polled in a manner that was compatible with the existence of a local electoral interest.[66] Put differently, the votes of 89 per cent of these county electors appear to have been relatively free from any discernible forms of landed control.

Quantifying county voters: franchise groups

Of all the different types of county voters, it is the £50 tenants-at-will who have traditionally been considered the most susceptible to landlord influence.[67] Created under the notorious 'Chandos clause', which was added to the Reform Bill by the marquess of Chandos, this qualification comprised occupiers of lands or tenements liable to a 'yearly rent of not less than fifty pounds', most of whom, but not necessarily all, were tenant farmers.[68] By 1837, when it was becoming obvious that the Conservatives were gaining the upper hand in the county registration battles, Liberal election agents like Joseph Parkes increasingly sought solace in the belief that the county registers were being swamped by the tenants of Tory landlords. 'The tenant at will clause and open voting ruin [us] and will lose us more county seats' he complained to Durham after the 1837 revision.[69] This general Liberal diagnosis was also shared by many Tories, including even the original author of the clause who, following his spectacular victory in the Buckinghamshire contest of 1835, proclaimed that 'the fifty-pound renter's clause in the Reform Bill has been found efficient'.[70]

These perceptions have been widely accepted, but they sit rather awkwardly with electoral realities on the ground. Although no official breakdown of the county electorate was prepared prior to the dramatic revision of 1835, it is clear from individual county registers that there was no disproportionate growth in the number of £50 occupiers at this, or any other revision. On the contrary, throughout the 1830s there was a very slight decline in the proportion of £50 occupiers. In South Essex, for example, 28 per cent of the registered electorate qualified as £50 tenants-at-will in 1832, but in 1839 this proportion had dropped by 2 percentage points.[71] Such decreases were often

66 Weighting the average by the number of voters in each division makes little difference to this calculation, the result being 10.87% rather than 10.98%.
67 Seymour, Electoral reform, 21, 79.
68 2 Will. IV c. 45, 728, clause 20; Radice, 'Identification, interests and influence', 182–3; Prest, Politics in the age of Cobden, 30.
69 Parkes to Durham, 15 Oct. 1837, Lambton MSS.
70 T. L. Crosby, English farmers and the politics of protection, 1815–1852, Hassocks 1977, 93.
71 South Essex registers, ERO, cupboard 2.

more marked in counties where they had initially been most numerous. In South Shropshire, for example, the £50 occupiers constituted 36 per cent of the electorate in 1833–4, but 30 per cent three years later.[72] The breakdown of county electorates compiled by the Home Office between 1835–40 confirms this general trend.[73] In the thirty-six English county divisions for which unambiguous figures are provided (there were sixty-nine in total), the proportion of £50 occupiers remained stable, dropping from an average of 23.1 per cent at the revision of 1835 to 22.6 per cent in 1839. At the same time, the proportion of 40s. freehold voters marginally increased, from 63.4 per cent of the county electorate in 1835 to 64 per cent in 1839.[74] A similar pattern emerges from Wales, where the £50 occupiers comprised 26.6 per cent of the electorate in 1835 and 24.1 per cent in 1839, and the 40s. free-holders 53.1 per cent and 56.3 per cent respectively.[75] Liberal apprehensions about the increasing dominance of the £50 tenants-at-will, it would seem, were largely unfounded. If anything, their electoral significance declined slightly throughout the 1830s and instead it was the 40s. freeholders who grew in importance.

Moreover, although it is true that £50 tenants-at-will were more likely to turn out to vote than other classes of voter, this should not be over-emphasised. In many counties variations between the turnout rates of different franchise groups were negligible. In the North Northamptonshire contest of 1837, for example, 1,777 of the 2,144 registered freeholders (83 per cent) polled compared with 822 of the 962 occupiers (85 per cent).[76] In the seventeen county divisions for which Home Office returns were compiled in an unequivocal way, £50 occupiers were only marginally (4.3 percentage points) more likely to poll than the 40s. freeholders, as can be seen from table 6.[77] One reason for the small variation in turnout may have been that free-holders sometimes owned a small village business. Although keen to enjoy a degree of social prestige through inclusion on the county registers, some

---

[72] South Shropshire electoral registers, ShRO, QE/6/2/2, 3.

[73] PP 1837–8 (329) xliv. 553–79; PP 1840 (579) xxxix. 187–200.

[74] Based on the returns for North and South Cheshire, East and West Cornwall, North and South Devon, Dorset, North and South Essex, East and West Gloucestershire, Herefordshire, Hertfordshire, Huntingdonshire, East and West Kent, North and South Leicestershire, Monmouthshire, North and South Northumberland, North and South Nottinghamshire, Oxfordshire, Rutland, East and West Suffolk, East and West Sussex, North and South Warwickshire, North and South Wiltshire, East and West Worcestershire and the East Riding of Yorkshire.

[75] Based upon the returns for Anglesey, Brecknockshire, Cardiganshire, Carmarthenshire, Carnarvonshire, Flintshire, Glamorganshire, Merionethshire, Montgomeryshire, Pembrokeshire and Radnorshire.

[76] 1837 North Northamptonshire pollbook, 96.

[77] Many of the Home Office returns failed to differentiate sufficiently between the various franchise qualifications and provided the total number of qualifications, rather than the actual number of electors. It is also not always clear whether the returns relate to the revisions of 1835, 1836 or 1837: PP 1837–8 (329) xliv. 566, 620–88.

Table 6
Turnout rates for £50 occupiers and freeholders in seventeen county contests in the election of 1837

	Number on the registers	Number who polled	% Turnout rate
£50 occupiers	22,297	18,530	83.1
Freeholders	76,982	60,620	78.8

Source: PP 1837–8 (329) xliv. 553–79. Based on the figures for Buckinghamshire, South Chester, North Derbyshire, South Devon, South Essex, Huntingdonshire, East and West Kent, Middlesex, East and West Norfolk, North Nottinghamshire, Oxfordshire, West Suffolk, North Warwickshire, North Wiltshire and East Worcestershire.

probably preferred not to exercise their voting rights for fear of losing customers from among the opposite party.[78] Local influences may have worked in two different ways here, cajoling some while deterring others.

Urban or town-dwelling 40s. freeholders, by contrast, were not only more likely to vote than their rural counterparts, they were also on the increase after 1832.[79] County electorates, of course, had always included voters living in unenfranchised towns and cities. After Reform, however, they not only included freeholders in the parliamentary boroughs who failed to meet the new £10 householder qualification, but also enfranchised £10 householders who possessed a separate 40s. freehold qualification which was not 'occupied by himself', such as an office, workshop or a plot of land.[80] Much has been made of the Reform Act's supposed intention to reinforce distinctions between urban and rural constituencies, but this is simply not borne out by an analysis of their electoral composition on the ground.[81] Even in a highly agricultural division such as East Norfolk, for example, voters residing within Norwich represented approximately 10 per cent of the resident county electorate who went to the poll in 1837.[82] Divisions which were less agricultural in character often had a far higher proportion of urban freeholders. Over 60 per cent of those who voted in the 1832 North Durham contest, for example, resided in a parliamentary borough.[83] In the West Riding, a quarter of the electorate qualified in respect of property within a borough, while a further 45 per cent lived in the densely populated, but unrepresented, towns of the Aire and Calder valleys.[84] Nearly two thousand of the 7,822 votes for the Tories in

78 PP 1835 (547) viii. 183.
79 For useful discussions of urban freeholders see Taylor, 'Interest, parties and the state', 55–6; Prest, *Politics in the age of Cobden*, 31–4, 80, 132; Gash, *Politics in the age of Peel*, 91–4.
80 2 Will. IV c. 45, 728, clause 24.
81 Moore, 'Concession or cure', 39–59, and 'Political morality in mid nineteenth-century England', 5–36.
82 1837 East Norfolk pollbook, 169–81.
83 Radice, 'Identification, interests and influence', 508.
84 PP 1857–8 (108) xlvi. 577; Thompson, 'West Riding', 215–17.

the South Lancashire contest of 1837 were cast by Manchester residents.[85] In 1852 a Home Office enquiry finally ascertained that nearly one-fifth of the county electorate in England, and approximately one-sixth in Wales, qualified in respect of a property situated within a parliamentary borough.[86] Although it was not as high as this in the 1830s, some measure of the likely growth of urban penetration after 1832 can be gauged from individual pollbooks. In the East Sussex election of 1832, for example, approximately 9 per cent of the votes were cast by the urban freeholders of Brighton. By 1837, however, this had increased to 12 per cent.[87] Moreover, at both these elections the turnout rate of the Brighton voters was some 5 percentage points higher than all the other electors, perhaps reflecting the ease with which they were able to get to the polling stations erected in the town.[88]

Finally, although there was usually some variation in the voting tendencies of those with different electoral qualifications, the choice of candidate exhibited by one group of voters was rarely at odds with that of another. While the £50 occupiers might demonstrate a slightly different degree of support in comparison with the freeholders, the polling by each group would invariably return the same two candidates. This was true of both the agricultural constituencies and the more industrialised county divisions. In her study of North Durham, for example, Radice found that 'neither in 1832 or 1837 did the voting of the freeholders as a whole differ from that of the £50 tenants'.[89] The same feature applies even in those counties where a particularly high level of parochial unanimity suggests a strong degree of landed control. In the 1837 North Northamptonshire contest, for example, 43 per cent of the parishes exhibited unanimity levels of 85 per cent or above (see table 5). The £50 occupiers and freeholders, however, still reached the same electoral verdict, with 51 per cent of the freeholders and 64 per cent of the £50 occupiers voting for both of the Conservative candidates. (The single Liberal, by contrast, was supported by 42 per cent of the freeholders and 31 per cent of the £50 occupiers).[90] And while it is true that the occupiers exhibited a higher degree of Conservative support than the freeholders, it should be stressed that this extra proportion of occupiers over freeholders translated into a mere 3 per cent of the voters who polled in this contest as a whole.[91]

---

[85] Egerton to Peel, 6 Aug. 1837, Peel MS Add. 40424, fo. 17v.
[86] PP 1852 (4) xlii. 303.
[87] 1832 and 1837 East Sussex pollbooks.
[88] In 1832, 257 out of 299 Brighton voters polled, giving a turnout rate of 86%. By contrast, 2,496 of the remaining 3,083 voters polled, giving a turnout rate of 81%.
[89] Radice, 'Identification, interests and influence', 510.
[90] 1837 North Northamptonshire pollbook.
[91] The 13 percentage point difference between the freeholders and the 822 £50 occupiers who polled in this contest translates into 107 voters, or 3.4% of the total turnout of 3,164: ibid.

Quantifying county voters: resident and non-resident behaviour

As this chapter suggests, far too much has been read into the electoral role of landlords and tenants in explaining the essential dynamics of rural political life. Significant technical, customary and economic restrictions governed landed influence, and the £50 tenants-at-will were neither the distinctly partisan, nor the rapidly expanding, electoral group that has often been portrayed. The role of non-resident electors, who lived outside the counties where they had a vote, has by contrast been largely overlooked. This is surprising given that in many constituencies they actually outnumbered the £50 occupiers. This was not just true of non-agricultural divisions like South Durham, where there were a mere 490 £50 occupiers compared with 723 outvoters on the 1840–1 register.[92] Even in the Huntingdonshire election of 1837, for example, only 461 £50 occupiers polled compared with 536 outvoters. At this contest, non-resident voters constituted nearly one-fifth of the total, the vast majority of them residing in the adjacent counties of Cambridgeshire, Northamptonshire and Bedfordshire.[93]

This level of non-resident voting was possible because the provisions of the 1832 Reform Act only demanded 'bona fide occupation' of lands or tenements for certain less wealthy categories of county elector.[94] These included the sublessees or assignees of the newly qualified leaseholders, and all freeholders with estates valued at under £10 annual value which were held for life, rather than by outright possession, except where such estates had been acquired through marriage, devise (i.e. by a will) or promotion to a benefice or office.[95] To these must be added the £50 occupiers or tenants of land, for whom non-residence was usually impractical and, therefore, extremely rare. County pollbooks provide very few examples of non-resident occupiers. The man who lived at 14 Wilson Street, Finsbury, London, and rented a silk mill at Braintree, for example, was one of only three non-resident £50 occupiers who polled in the North Essex election of 1832.[96]

After 1832 the vast majority of outvoters were either the outright possessors of freehold estates worth at least 40s. per year, or freeholders with a life interest in property which had either been inherited or was valued at above £10 annual value.[97] The exact proportion of outvoters varied widely, but in most counties they comprised somewhere between 12 and 25 per cent of the total registered electorate. Their numbers also increased throughout

---

92 1841 registers and lists of outvoters, Strathmore MSS D/ST/C1/16/298, 304–6.
93 PP 1837–8 (329), xliv. 560; 1837 Huntingdonshire pollbook, 67–71.
94 For a detailed breakdown of voting qualifications after 1832 see appendix 2.
95 2 Will. IV c. 45, 727–8, clauses 18–20; Rogers, *Parliamentary Reform Act*, 19; 'County electors' manual', Strathmore MSS D/ST/C1/16/262; 'An analysis of the qualifications for the southern division of Devon', DRO, 59/7/4/28; Seymour, *Electoral reform*, 12–13.
96 1832 North Essex pollbook, 36, 123, 134.
97 In addition, there was also a small number of non-resident £10 copyholders and leaseholders, as well as a few mortgage lenders and proprietors of tithes and glebe lands.

the 1830s, despite the additional difficulties that they may have encountered in attending the annual registration contests.[98] In East Sussex, for example, 12 per cent of the registered electorate were non-resident in 1832. By 1837, however, this had risen to 14 per cent.[99] Despite their non-residence, the turnout rate of outvoters was usually quite high. Indeed, in some counties a trip from an adjacent county to the main polling place might prove easier than making a journey across remote and inaccessible parts of the county division. In Westmorland, for example, one-sixth of those who voted in the 1832 election were non-resident, most of them travelling in from Cumberland, Lancashire and the North Riding.[100] As the decade progressed the expansion of the railway network, especially the completion of the Grand Junction and London–Birmingham lines, also helped facilitate increasing levels of outvoter participation, particularly among the London-based voters.[101] Outvoters therefore accounted for a significant proportion of the active electorate in many county constituencies.

Outvoters have been highlighted because, as property holders who were unaffected by the type of restrictions described above, they were probably less susceptible to the local pressures underpinning deference and landed control, and were able to exercise their political conscience relatively freely, with little fear of intimidation or reprisal. Although the large number of uncontested elections has helped to obscure the degree of correlation between the votes cast by the resident and non-resident electorate, original canvassing records can fill in some of the gaps. In the uncontested Westmorland election of 1835, for example, fifteen Tory agents conducted a canvass on behalf of the Lowther family. A number of important observations can be drawn from their survey of almost 2,000 voters, which amounted to 43 per cent of the registered electorate.[102] First, and most important, while there was some regional variation in the degree of support exhibited by the resident voters, the overall voting intention of the non-resident and resident electorate was, nevertheless, almost identical. Both groups overwhelmingly favoured the two Tory candidates. The combined canvassing results of the East and West wards indicate that 64 per cent of the 1,323 resident voters surveyed supported the Tories, compared with 66 per cent of the 539 outvoters, while 28 per cent of the resident voters were Liberal, compared with 29 per cent of the outvoters. A quite remarkable degree of correlation therefore existed between the voting intentions of non-resident and resident electors for the county as a whole.

---

98 *Hansard*, 3rd ser. lxxxv. 863; PP 1846 (451) viii. 266, minute 1382; PP 1864 (203) x. 425, minute 89.
99 1832 and 1837 East Sussex pollbooks.
100 'List of non-resident voters', Lonsdale MSS, D/Lons/L; polling returns, Messrs Bleaymire and Shephard D/BS/C, box 32.
101 See ch. 3 above.
102 The following analysis is based upon Lonsdale MSS D/Lons/L, 'Westmorland elections, 1835', bundles 23, 33.

Table 7
Votes cast by resident and non-resident electors in the East Sussex election of 1837

	Number of voters	% Non-partisan	% Liberal	% Conservative
Residents	3,512	23.1	34.9	42
Non-residents	357	9.6	34.4	56

Source: 1837 East Sussex pollbook. This type of analysis assumes that non-partisan voters either 'split' their two votes between the parties or 'plumped' for just one Liberal or Conservative candidate when there was also another in the field.

Regional variations in the voting intentions of both groups can also help to quantify the possible extent of any proprietorial influence at work within the constituency. In the East ward, for example, the resident electors were 13 percentage points less likely to vote Tory than the outvoters, and roughly 9 percentage points more likely to vote Liberal. By contrast, in the West ward exactly the opposite was true. Voters living in this half of the county, which was dominated by the Lowther Castle estates of the earl of Lonsdale, were 10 percentage points more likely to vote Tory, and 11 percentage points less likely to vote Liberal, than the non-resident voters. These regional idiosyncrasies suggest that proprietorial influence, even at its most effective, probably only affected about 12 per cent of the resident electors, or approximately one in ten of the entire electorate. Put the other way, roughly 90 per cent of Westmorland's electors seem to have exercised their franchise relatively freely. How else can the striking similarity between the voting intentions of the non-resident and resident voters be explained?

The inferences drawn from these canvassing returns are supported by an analysis of the few county pollbooks that provide details of the voters' actual place of residence, rather than just their place of qualification, thereby allowing a direct comparison between resident and non-resident voting behaviour to be made. Two such pollbooks exist for the East Norfolk and East Sussex elections of 1837, both of which were straight party contests between two Liberal and two Tory candidates. An analysis of the votes cast by the 10,613 electors who polled at these two elections is presented in tables 7 and 8. In East Sussex it can be seen that the two Liberal candidates received support from almost identical proportions of the outvoters (34 per cent) and resident voters (35 per cent). The major difference in the behaviour of the two groups lay in the resident electorate's much greater propensity to cast a non-partisan vote, rather than to vote for the two Tories (*see* table 7). While approximately 8 per cent of both groups cast non-partisan plumps, by voting for just one of the two party candidates, nearly 15 per cent of the resident electorate split their votes between the parties, compared with only 1.7 per

Table 8
Votes cast by resident and non-resident electors in the East Norfolk election of 1837

	Number of voters	% Non-partisan	% Liberal	% Conservative
Residents	6,074	6.4	43	50.6
Non-residents	670	3.1	47.1	49.8

Source: 1837 East Norfolk pollbook.

cent of the outvoters.[103] It was this high level of split votes among the resident electors that ensured the re-election of one of the Liberal candidates, Charles Cavendish.[104] His popularity among the resident voters, and the correspondingly different levels of split votes cast by resident and non-resident electors, may well have resulted from the substantial landed influence wielded by the Cavendish family in East Sussex.[105] As in their native Derbyshire, the Cavendishes sought to influence one of their tenant's votes, but allowed the second vote to be cast entirely freely.[106] This, and the fact that the Cavendish interest found itself increasingly at odds with some of the more advanced aspects of Liberalism, may explain why Cavendish–Tory split votes accounted for 9.5 per cent of the total votes cast by the resident electorate, compared with a mere 0.3 per cent of the votes cast by non-residents. Taken together, these differences suggest that landed influence, even at its most pervasive, probably affected about 13 per cent of the resident voters, or about one in nine of the entire electorate. Again, some 89 per cent of the East Sussex electorate would appear to have exercised their franchise relatively freely.

Differences in voting behaviour by residence, however, were far less apparent among the 6,744 electors who polled in the East Norfolk contest of 1837 (*see* table 8). Indeed, in this election a quite remarkable correlation can be seen to have existed between the resident and non-resident communities, despite the influence allegedly 'much possessed' by Baron Wodehouse, the earl of Orford and the marquess of Cholmondeley within this predominantly agricultural division.[107] The influences that were brought to bear at this election appear to have produced no distinguishable pattern of resident polling, other than a slightly reduced propensity to cast two Liberal votes by compar-

---

103 1837 East Sussex pollbook, 91–105.
104 Split votes cast by the resident electors accounted for almost one-fifth of all the 1,793 votes that he received.
105 *Dod's electoral facts*, 304.
106 *Derby and Chesterfield Reporter*, 15 Jan. 1835.
107 *Dod's electoral facts*, 227; B. D. Hayes, 'Politics in Norfolk, 1750–1832', unpubl. PhD diss. Cambridge 1957.

ison with the outvoters. Both electoral groups overwhelmingly favoured the two Tory candidates, and both placed the same Liberal candidates in third and fourth position. Such rare glimpses into the voting behaviour of the resident and outvoters of Westmorland, East Sussex and East Norfolk provide further quantitative evidence for the existence of a rural electorate that was relatively free of landed controls. These close correlations between the behaviour of resident voters and those coming from different parts of the country, who often commanded more votes than the much maligned £50 occupiers, suggest that local landed influences had little discernible impact on the behaviour of the rural electorate as a whole. The neglected county outvoters, who were on the increase both in terms of numbers and turnout after 1832, helped to ensure that county politics never became a local community cabal.

County representation: tensions and transformations

The genuinely open and participatory nature of rural politics was ultimately reflected in the relationship that existed between the county and its representatives. Knights of the shire, no less than their borough counterparts, were expected to look after local interests in parliament and to carry out essential prescriptive functions within the constituency. Their performance as both parliamentarians and as local dignitaries received close scrutiny from the provincial press and the electoral bodies that had backed their return, and they were never above censure or reproach. In the run-up to the 1837 Hertfordshire election, for example, the Conservative committee held meetings to ensure 'that the parliamentary conduct of our two respected members, Lord Grimston and Mr Abel Smith, has merited our confidence and gratitude', before approving their re-selection.[108] In North Devon, Sir Thomas Acland received numerous resolutions warning him that his lukewarm stance on Protestantism and protection had 'been such as to forfeit the confidence formerly reposed in him by the electors of this district' at the time of the rumoured dissolution of 1839.[109] The correspondence between local agents and MPs, in particular, testifies to the ease with which support could quickly turn to resentment and disquiet.[110] Failure to pay sufficient attention to issues of local concern could have profound consequences and, as one Tory agent pointed out, 'when a connexion is, as it were, broken off it requires very great exertion and expenditure (as many thousands as it ought to do hundreds) to renew it'.[111]

108 Conservative minute book, 1837 election, Messrs Longmore and Sworder D/EL/B562.
109 Resolutions 1839, Acland (BroadClyst) MSS 1148M/box 8/17.
110 See, for example, the letterbook of John Smith, WSRO, Smith MSS Add. 7171, fos 3–10
111 Lawrence to Mahon, 5 Dec. 1836, Stanhope MSS U1590, C382.

Voters made their discontent clear at county meetings and through the public medium of petitions and requisitions to popular leading figures, all of which received extensive coverage in the provincial press. This close scrutiny was encouraged and formally encoded in the re-election process, during which sitting members invariably appealed to, and were expected to justify, their parliamentary record. There was far more to this than just ritual self-deprecation and displays of humility before the electorate. An election, as Sir James Graham reminded his East Cumberland constituents shortly before they turned him out in 1837, 'will give you an opportunity of exercising your judgement on my public conduct'.[112] Outright rejection was especially common in cases of absenteeism or neglect. When Sir George Clerk lost his Midlothian seat in 1837, for example, Bonham confided to Peel that it was 'very much from his own want of personal attention to his constituents'.[113] The cardinal sin of neglecting a seat was a particularly powerful weapon with which to harangue political opponents. The Conservative contender in the South Durham election of 1841, for example, dedicated much of his election address to reminding voters that the Liberal MP 'spent but little of his time in the neighbourhood . . . being fond of spending his time abroad and half- frenchified'.[114]

The support of a voter was not only dependent upon an MP's conduct, it frequently became almost contractual. Voters solicited favours, pushed local issues, expressed individual political concerns, and generally made their support highly conditional, even to the point of seeking a pledge from a candidate. In the South Lincolnshire election of 1835, for example, one of Gilbert Heathcote's more prominent tenants requested his continued support for the agricultural interest and the campaign to move London's cattle market from Smithfield to Islington in return for his own and his son's support.[115] Alongside these political demands there were many that were personal. The following note to the Conservative MP for Hertfordshire from Henry Cole, a paper-hanger from Cheshunt, was typical:

> I should be so very much obliged to you to get my son in the India Warehouses on London Docks as a labourer he is 5ft 8in high, if the election comes to a poll, I shall be shure to give you a plumper.[116]

Underscoring this type of bargaining process, registration and the rhetoric of the reformed period increasingly encouraged voters to think of themselves as individual, critical agents. Popular county electors' manuals explained the operation of the new electoral system in clear and accessible terminology, stimulating a sense of self-importance, and the concept of inviolate voting

---

112 Crosby, *Parliamentary record*, 49.
113 Bonham to Peel, 5 Aug. 1837, Peel MS Add. 40424, fo. 10v.
114 Election speech of James Farrar, 23 June 1841, Strathmore MSS D/ST/C1/16/281.
115 John Tatum to Heathcote, 21 Dec. 1834, Ancaster MSS 3 Anc 9/14/258.
116 Cole to Lord Grimston, 1835, Messrs Crawters of Hertford D/E Cr 105/2, fo. 815.

rights.[117] And instead of the franchise being a privilege conferred only at election time, and then only in the event of a contest, voters were now qualified separately and on a national basis by law. In the annual revision courts, individual voters were frequently forced to defend their qualifications in person, sometimes at considerable inconvenience and financial cost to themselves. In these circumstances the franchise became more of a personal possession, which had been fought for and was jealously guarded.

Other tensions between the representatives and the represented resulted from the exaggerated popular expectations arising out of Reform, and its longer-term partisan aftermath on the ground. Well beyond the anomaly of 1830–2, local loyalties and political ties continued to be disturbed by MPs changing sides or returning to their pre-Reform party allegiance. In his account of the 'desertions from Whiggery', Robert Stewart has estimated that at least forty-one 'moderate' Whigs had made their way into the Conservative party by 1837.[118] These defections created considerable tension at constituency level, as traditional proprietorial and personal bonds became strained. The 'Netherby turncoat' Sir James Graham, for instance, despite his extensive estates at Netherby being considered 'the pride of Cumberland', suffered the humiliating loss of his seat for East Cumberland in 1837.[119] Before his defeat, an 'anti-Graham paper' had been signed by 2,255 electors, nearly half the division's total.[120] As Bonham sarcastically explained to Peel, this 'very precious loss' was 'between ourselves rather a striking retribution for the very skilful manner in which Graham contrived to put the county divided for the Whig party'.[121] As late as 1839, when assessing Conservative prospects of filling a vacant East Cumberland seat, Graham was still experiencing 'some difficulty in persuading some of my tenants and old adherents'.[122] Even where voters did choose to follow their representatives and switch parties, as in Oxfordshire, it was usually less out of blind obedience to their authority, as in agreement with their politics.[123] In this sense many landed desertions from Whiggery anticipated, rather than activated, a genuine swing in rural public opinion towards the Conservative party.

Interactions between MPs and the represented were also disrupted in organisational terms, as more formal party-based structures increasingly took over responsibility for electoral management and control. The operational

117 *The Reform Act with explanatory notes*; 'The county elector's manual', Strathmore MSS D/ST/C1/16/262; 'North Derbyshire elector's manual', 1839, SRO, Bagshawe MSS Bag C 762(2).

118 Stewart, *Conservative party*, 108–9, 374.

119 Erickson, *Graham*, 46, 136–8.

120 John Parker to Edward Burnell, [1837], Craven-Smith-Milnes of Hockerton (Winkburn) MSS DD/CW 7/14.

121 Bonham to Peel, 9 Aug. 1837, Peel MS Add. 40424, fo. 43v.

122 Graham to Bonham, 23 Dec. 1839, Peel MS Add. 40616, fo. 139v.

123 Eastwood, 'Oxfordshire', 109.

demands of voter registration, in particular, required new and more permanent types of routine political activism, for which managers of large landed
estates were often ill suited or just too busy. The duke of Bedford's steward, for
example, was well aware in 1832 that 'a good deal has to be done as to proper
registration of the new constituency', but three years later the 'present registration' was still found to be 'imperfect'.[124] Similarly in East Sussex, Lord De
La Warr, Lord Camden, Lord Ashburnham and other leading Tories reluc-
tantly came round to the necessity of forming a Conservative association for
'seeing to the registration', after their estate managers had proved unequal to
the task.[125] Recognition of such electoral impotence was often coloured by a
sense of astonishment at the changes that seemed to be taking place. As
Camden put it to Ashburnham, 'it is extraordinary that so large a majority of
Conservative landlords should not be able to dispossess either of the present
members for East Sussex of the[ir] seat'.[126]

The emergence of these constituency associations transformed the style
and structure of county politics in subtle yet significant ways. Although most
organisations relied heavily on the patronage and financial support of traditional landed elites, their status was far from subservient. Heavy-handed
attempts to dictate policy or extend landed control invariably backfired.
Instead, as chapter 2 demonstrated, constituency organisations owed their
effectiveness to the genuine inclusion and integration of local party activists
and volunteers, willing to perform the dull routines of registration with
energy and enthusiasm. The primacy of such work inevitably brought about a
shift in political control. When Lord Londonderry resisted the establishment
of a Conservative registration association at Stockton in 1838, for example, it
was precisely out of fear that it would make the 'large landed proprietors' sub-
ordinate to the 'gentlemen of the town'.[127] His suspicions were well founded.
Some of the more detailed local studies have pointed to an important transfer
in electoral power that was taking place at constituency level. In his account
of Cornwall politics, for example, Jaggard discovered that the new registration committees established by the two major parties led to 'various gentry
families who had once been their chief political managers' being 'elbowed
aside by attorneys, farmers, "plodding shopkeepers" and others eager to assist
their party'.[128] Historians of West Riding politics have also observed that
registration 'had a profound effect on the balance of power' and 'reduced the
importance of the influential gentleman in politics'.[129] Similar developments

[124] Bennet to Adam, 8 July 1832, 10 June 1835, BRO, Russell MSS R3/3731, 3877.
[125] Ashburnham MSS 3256–60.
[126] Camden to Ashburnham, 10 Jan. 1837, ibid. 3256.
[127] Londonderry to Stockton Conservative Association, 15 Feb. 1838, Londonderry MSS
D/Lo/C447 (5); Radice, 'Identification, interests and influence', 357–8.
[128] Jaggard, *Cornwall politics*, 101–2.
[129] Thompson, 'West Riding', 222; D. Fraser, 'The fruits of Reform: Leeds politics in the
eighteen-thirties', *Northern History* vii (1972), 89–111 at p. 102.

were detected in Staffordshire by G. B. Kent, who concluded that the county's new Conservative and Reform associations made great territorial magnates, such as 'the Ansons and Gowers if not redundant, a somewhat antiquated form of electioneering influence'.[130]

Rather paradoxically, the decision of South Staffordshire's leading Tories to avoid a contest in 1841, against the wishes of both the Conservative association and Francis Bonham, has often been cited as evidence of the ultimate electoral control still exercised by traditional landed elites in the reformed period.[131] However the contest of 1837, of which the events of 1841 were only the corollary, offers exactly the opposite view. At this election, the Staffordshire Conservative Association put forward two Conservative candidates to run in the southern division, expressly against the wishes of many leading Tories who deemed it 'imprudent to incur the expense of a contested election (and the hazard of a defeat)'.[132] On the advice of Messrs Briscoe, Horden and Smith, the firm of solicitors handling the registration, the Conservative association overruled its critics and forced an expensive contest on the county, but it only succeeded in returning one of its candidates. Writing to Lord Hatherton after the election, the new Liberal MP Colonel Anson was incredulous as to why such an unnecessary contest had been forced on the constituency by the Conservative association and its activists, and was astounded that 'Lords Talbot, Dartmouth, Stamford etc. could not have prevented it'. Like Lord Camden in East Sussex, he appeared genuinely dumbfounded at the alterations taking place in county politics: 'in what a position do the landed aristocracy acknowledge themselves to be in', he declared, 'if they are forced to submit to Briscoe and Co.? This is much worse than Dan's tail'.[133]

This chapter has challenged the remarkably resilient view that voting behaviour in county elections was mainly the product of landed influences and does not merit detailed investigation. Widely considered to be unsuitable for quantitative analysis, the vibrancy and vitality of rural electoral life has been obscured and the study of county pollbooks has even been dismissed as otiose.[134] Taken individually, the various quantitative techniques that have been employed in this chapter do not match the sophistication of recent work on the boroughs, but cumulatively they are, none the less, telling. The vast majority of county voters were far from politically deferential or

---

130 The earl of Lichfield and the duke of Sutherland, respectively: Kent, 'Party politics in the county of Staffordshire', ch. vii.
131 Gash, Politics in the age of Peel, 254–7; Stewart, Conservative party, 133; Kent, 'Party politics in the county of Staffordshire', ch. v.
132 G. D. Simpson to Sandon, 7 July 1837, Sandon Hall, Harrowby MSS.
133 Anson to Hatherton, 8 Aug. 1837, Hatherton MSS D260/M/F/5/27/12, fo. 119. 'Dan's tail' refers to the group of Irish Radical MPs, led by Daniel O'Connell, upon which the Whig government depended for its majority between 1835 and 1841.
134 Phillips, Boroughs, 39–40.

dependent when it came to exercising their franchise. Indeed, in many county constituencies only between 10 and 15 per cent of the electorate appears to have exhibited behaviour consistent with the existence of a local landed interest. Contextualising rural elections primarily in terms of proprietorial influence and control is, in these circumstances, clearly unsatisfactory. Whether viewed from the perspective of voter unanimity, electoral participation by qualification, or through the comparative polling of the resident and non-resident communities, it simply fails to account for the political behaviour of the vast majority of county electors. It also tends to presuppose a freedom of action that most landed elites in reality did not possess, especially in the face of the new political tensions and expectations aroused by the Reform Act. Where proprietorial influence did operate, it was within well-defined social and political conditions that were contractual, rather than coercive, and which were reinforced by important economic constraints.

Above all, explanations of reformed rural politics grounded in landed influence sit uneasily with many of the post-1832 organisational developments discussed in chapters 1 and 2. The post-Reform recognition that local parties had to become more organised was, of itself, indicative of the weakness and ineffectiveness of landed control, but as the last section of this chapter has argued, it also reconfigured the structure of rural politics in additional ways. In some counties the developments of the 1830s appear to have brought about an important shift in the balance of power, as new forms of political activity increasingly supplemented, if not supplanted, older political idioms and agencies of electoral control. The next chapter explores these themes in more detail for six different localities, each of which is the subject of a separate case study. By examining the interplay of organised registration, landed control and voter politicisation, much-needed light is shed on the impact of the political alterations taking place in county constituencies after 1832, irrespective of their regional diversity.

5

County Politics and Registration: Case Studies

It has long been recognised that national political history can only really be written 'on an established basis of local history'.[1] Countering the thematic approach adopted elsewhere in this book, this chapter presents a detailed analysis of six county divisions during the post-Reform decade. Although each study is firmly rooted within its local context, particular attention has been paid to the role of landed influence and the impact of registration activity, the former because it has hogged so much of the historiographical debate and the latter because it continues to be widely regarded as mainly a borough phenomenon.[2] The following surveys of North Devon, South Lincolnshire, Bedfordshire, West Somerset, North Wiltshire and the West Riding of Yorkshire demonstrate that in these county divisions, at least, partisan registration activity became decisive in determining the outcome of elections and the fortunes of political parties.

The choice of these constituencies was largely determined by the need to avoid an over-reliance on newspaper accounts, with their highly partisan reports of local registration activity, and the availability of suitable archive material relating to the work of local agents and activists on the ground. But the counties selected also differ markedly in terms of their electoral size and structure, and in their patterns of landownership and political control. By focusing on those electoral processes which were at work in all county divisions, however, these regional variations have not prevented the creation of an overall synthesis appropriate to the reformed county electorate as a whole. The conclusion reached by recent historians of borough politics, that 'the Reform Act could scarcely have caused a more drastic alteration in England's political fabric', is ultimately just as valid for the counties as it is for the towns.[3]

North Devon

The newly created county division of North Devon was not contested at any general election between 1832 and 1841, but its political skirmishes and struggles were no less vibrant or dramatic. Developments in the registration

---

[1] Gash, *Politics in the age of Peel*, p. xvii.
[2] Stewart, *Party and politics*, 38; Evans, *Great Reform Act*, 62.
[3] Phillips and Wetherell, 'Great Reform Act of 1832', 412.

courts, in particular, meant that the two seats which were held without opposition by the Whigs in 1832 and 1835 were soon lost, the first as part of a well-mannered concession in 1837, the second as a result of a bitterly contested by-election two years later. Much of the inspiration for the resurgence of Tory activity in North Devon came from the humiliating defeat of Lord John Russell at the May 1835 by-election in South Devon. Here, as Russell's election agent explained, the Conservatives had 'been very active in their registrations' and 'very vigilant'.[4] Adopting similar tactics, North Devon's Tories launched their own registration drive at the subsequent 1835 revision, helping to bring an impressive 1,653 electors on to the electoral rolls and increasing the size of North Devon's electorate by a remarkable 27 per cent.[5] By the time of the revision of the following year, at which objections were made to hundreds of Liberal voters, the secretary of the newly established North Devon Conservative Association felt confident enough to write to the former MP, Sir Thomas Acland,[6] to request that he 'accede to their wishes and take his seat in the House of Commons should the best endeavours of the division be successful in returning him at the next election'.[7] Acland accepted and a preliminary canvass early in 1837 indicated that his electoral prospects were extremely good. According to Lewis Buck,[8] the former MP for Exeter who chaired the Tory election committee, the canvass showed 'a large majority of the electors being determined to return the worthy Baronet to Parliament [at] the first opportunity that may present itself'.[9]

The strength of Acland's support, however, was not put to the test in the 1837 election, much to the chagrin of his more ardent supporters. Instead, a traditional compromise agreement was hatched between the division's leading political families about sharing the representation between the two parties and avoiding a contest. Although this arrangement enabled Acland and the senior of the two Whig members, Lord Ebrington,[10] to be returned at very little cost, it was deeply unpopular with many Conservative activists on the ground, who felt that the second seat had been within their grasp. Their chance to capture it came just eighteen months later when Ebrington's long rumoured vacation of his seat, based on the declining health of his father, finally occurred.[11] On the strength of yet more Tory gains at the 1838

4   PP 1835 (547) viii. 167, minute 2821.
5   See appendix 3.
6   Sir Thomas Dyke Acland (1787–1871), of Killerton, Exeter, MP for Devon 1812–18, 1820–31, and North Devon 1837–57.
7   C. Palmer to Sir Thomas Dyke Acland, 14 Sept. 1836, Acland (BroadClyst) MSS 1148M/add/36/477.
8   Lewis William Buck (1784–1858), MP for Exeter 1826–32, and North Devon 1839–57.
9   Buck to R. Ilbert, 19 Jan. 1837, DRO, Ilbert of West Alvington MSS 316 add/3M/04/59.
10   Hugh Fortescue, Viscount Ebrington (1783–1861) of Castle Hill, Barnstaple, MP for Devon 1818–20, 1830–2, Tavistock 1820–30, and North Devon 1832–9.
11   This was due to Ebrington's appointment as Irish Lord Lieutenant rather than, as Dod

registration, and with the full backing of the North Devon Conservative Association, Buck put himself forward for the vacancy, overthrowing the county's carefully laid compromise arrangements. This infuriated the Whigs and placed Acland in an extremely awkward position.

It had long been assumed that James Wentworth Buller,[12] also a former MP for Exeter, would simply replace Ebrington as the Liberal MP for North Devon, enabling the compromise to continue as before. This assumption was reinforced by the close family ties and personal friendship between Acland and Buller, and their mutual recognition that the Whigs could not be expected to relinquish the second seat without a fight.[13] Significantly, Buller only agreed to become Ebrington's successor once he had assured himself of the strength of local Whig support. His unexpected defeat at Exeter in 1835, where his family possessed considerable influence, had made him especially sensitive to the importance of effective registration. In a typically candid letter to Acland he made his position clear:

> It cannot be expected that the party which recently returned two members will tamely surrender both seats. I have not yet received the registration, which has been promised, and therefore I am not able to express an opinion on the relative strength of parties in North Devon. I wait for the registration before I pass the Rubicon and I shall not commit myself by becoming a candidate unless I am satisfied that I stand on firm ground.[14]

The ensuing canvass undertaken by Buller's solicitor, Isaac Davy of Crediton, and the North Devon Reform Association during January 1838 left little doubt as to the Whigs' entitlement to return one of North Devon's representatives. Buller secured firm pledges of support from 3,854 voters, an impressive 49 per cent of the division's total registered electorate, over and above which many more unpledged voters were considered to be 'favourable'.[15]

One month after Buller committed himself, however, an important development occurred which substantially altered the balance of parties in North Devon. On 9 February 1838, at the Old London Inn in Exeter, thirty-one 'influential Conservative electors' met 'to extend and bring more fully into operation' the registration activities of the North Devon Conservative Association.[16] A special committee was established under the chairmanship of Sir

recorded, his succeeding as 2nd earl Fortescue, which did not occur until 1841: *Dod's electoral facts*, 85; Thorne, *The House of Commons, 1790–1820*, iii. 791. The ongoing rumours about Ebrington's likely vacation of his seat were, however, based upon the declining health of his father.

[12] James Wentworth Buller (1798–1865), MP for Exeter 1830–5, and North Devon 1857–65.

[13] See, for example, Buller to Acland, 27 Oct. 1837, Acland (BroadClyst) MSS 1148M/box 8/4. Acland and Buller had neighbouring estates a few miles north of Exeter.

[14] Buller to Acland, 22 Dec. 1837, ibid. box 8/17.

[15] 1838 canvassing returns, Buller of Crediton MSS 2065M/SS2/11.

[16] 'Meeting of influential Conservative electors', Stanhope MSS U1590, C381/1.

Thomas Wheler, in order to establish 'a proper and organised system of watching and working out the registration'.[17] It was the spectacular results that they achieved at the 1838 revision which not only prompted Buck to contest the vacancy, but also forced the Reformers to fundamentally reassess their whole electioneering strategy. Buller, in particular, became especially keen for a complete review of registration activity to be undertaken and wrote to Ebrington for support. Ebrington's reply, however, was less than sanguine:

> I ought long since to have answered that part of your letter relating to a pro-posed reform in our registration arrangements. That some change in them is necessary I am quite sensible, for though I have no doubt but that the Tories have greatly exaggerated their gains on the last registry (having I believe taken to themselves the whole of the newly added voters), yet I have as little doubt but that by their superior organisation they have had considerably the advantage of us. The powerful aid of the Clergy which very generally gives the gratuitous services of an active and intelligent agent in each parish is difficult for us fully to counteract by any means within our reach.[18]

Ebrington's claims about the role of the Anglican clergy were well founded. A quarter of those present at the inaugural meeting of the Conservative regis-tration committee, for instance, were clergymen, including two who were archdeacons.[19] His despondency, however, failed to deter Buller. Despite the obvious gains made by the Tories in the 1838 registration revision, he was determined to defend what he considered to be the Whigs' natural right to one of the county seats.[20] Writing to J. H. Tremayne,[21] shortly before the election, he made his position clear:

> I do not believe that I should have consented to offer myself as a candidate, if I had not felt that the Ultra Tories are not entitled to one seat for North Devon and it is quite clear they only hoped to obtain it by canvassing in Acland's name and fighting under his colours. My returns, if they be realised, assure me a certain victory, but you and I know from experience that overwhelming strength on paper affords an uncertain guarantee for success.[22]

The North Devon by-election of 1839 was therefore an extremely bitter contest, not just between two parties, but between different approaches to county representation. Acland, whose relationship with the North Devon Conservative Association was already showing signs of strain, was left with

---

17 Ibid.
18 Ebrington to Buller, 14 Dec. 1838, Buller of Crediton MSS 2065M/SS2/11.
19 Stanhope MSS U1590, C381/1.
20 Buller to Sir Humphrey Davis, 15 Dec. 1838, Buller of Crediton MSS 2065M/SS2/11.
21 John Hearle Tremayne (1780–1851), of Heligan, MP for Cornwall 1806–26.
22 Buller to Tremayne, 27 Feb. 1839, CRO, Tremayne of Heligan MSS DDT 2823.

Table 9
Canvassing returns and actual votes, North Devon, 1838–9

Name of electoral district	Buller's canvass (1838)	Buller's canvass (1839)	Polled by Buller (1839)	Pledges for Buck (1839)	Polled by Buck (1839)
South Molton	332	402	398	171	225
Barnstaple	429	408	369	376	483
Holsworthy	361	250	228	300	316
Torrington	220	173	146	262	294
Crediton	443	441	425	168	213
Cullompton	400	314	287	519	610
Tiverton	360	417	358	377	453
Chulmleigh	407	379	361	94	130
Ilfracombe	300	219	238	196	243
Bideford	302	176	146	395	477
Hatherleigh	302	296	284	225	275
Totals	**3,856**	**3,475**	**3,240**	**3,083**	**3,719**

Source: Buller of Crediton MSS 2065M/SS2/11.

little option but to support Buck publicly. As Buller's cousin Charles,[23] the Liberal MP for Liskeard, explained to his sister Georgiana, 'Sir Thos Acland could not do otherwise than vote and act for Buck, the chairman of Sir T's committee. I am happy to say that no unkindness is or will be felt in that quarter.'[24] As if to reinforce their break with the past, Buck's supporters broke many of the tacit conventions governing electoral conduct. The most important of these related to Buller's pre-election pledges, on the strength of which he had considered that his prospects were reasonably good.[25] Canvassing undertaken by Richard Gould, the secretary of the North Devon Reform Association, and George Colis, the chairman of the Tiverton Reform Association, indicated that although Buller had lost 459 supporters at the registration revision of 1838, he still had a majority of 392 firm pledges over his rival.[26] A breakdown of these canvassing returns and the number of votes cast

23 Charles Buller (1806–48), of Polvellan, MP for West Looe 1830–1, and Liskeard 1832–48.
24 Charles Buller to Miss Georgy Buller, Mar. 1839, Buller of Crediton MSS 2065M/SS2/11.
25 Buller to Tremayne, 27 Feb. 1839, Tremayne of Heligan MSS DDT 2823.
26 'Voters actually engaged to vote for J. Wentworth Buller', 24 Jan. 1838, Buller of Crediton MSS 2065M/SS2/11; George Colis to Buller, 7 Mar. 1839, ibid. SS2/10.

in each district, however, revealed that many of Buller's firmly pledged supporters failed to poll for him on the day, while his rival fared far better than had been anticipated (*see* table 9). As one of the Liberal canvassing agents observed, 'we polled 235 less than our return' and 'our adversary 636 more'.[27]

Such a large number of broken pledges was not sufficient on its own to account for Buck's victory, but it was unusual. Charles Buller was convinced that the Anglican clergy had been responsible, morally 'releasing' voters by telling them that 'their word given six months ago to Mr Buller is not binding on them', and raising the 'cry of Popery because Mr Buller has married a Papist'. 'Whatever may be the faults of the Whigs', he declared, 'they do not tell the falsehoods nor canvass with the bitterness of the Tories'.[28] In this respect at least, the role of the clergy in this by-election was not that dissimilar to the personal campaign that they had helped wage against Lord John Russell in the South Devon by-election, four years earlier.[29]

Other factors, however, also contributed to Buller's defeat. Table 9 clearly shows that between 1838 and 1839, the most dramatic Liberal losses took place in two neighbouring electoral districts, Holsworthy and Bideford, which were situated in the north-west of the county. In fact, the losses in these two districts alone accounted for over half of the aggregate.[30] Because no pollbooks survive for Devon in this period, canvassing records provide the only insight into voting patterns on a parish-by-parish basis.[31] The surviving returns for 1838 suggest that these two electoral districts contained a number of parishes where all the resident voters had pledged support for the Whigs, possibly as a result of proprietorial influence. In Holsworthy, for example, uniform voting ought to have occurred in at least three of the twenty-three parishes it contained. In the parish of Luffincott, all five voters had pledged themselves to support Buller, in Tetcott all seventeen, while in North Petherwin, all sixty voters had promised to vote Whig. In total, nearly 17 per cent of Holsworthy's electorate resided in parishes which had given uniform pledges of support.[32] Although this is not sufficient to suggest that proprietorial influence was decisive in determining voter behaviour, it is enough to suggest that in certain electoral districts the Reformers were relying heavily on the operation of influence to secure their majority. This is important for two reasons. First, the Tory registration campaign of 1838 appears to have

27 Canvass and poll, ibid. SS2/11.
28 Charles Buller to Miss Georgy Buller, Mar. 1839, ibid.
29 The Anglican clergy played a prominent role in the South Devon by-election of May 1835: PP 1835 (547) viii. 169–83, minutes 2842–3073; E. Romilly to E. Strutt, 27 Apr. 1835, Belper of Kingston MSS DD/BK/7/7, fo. 223.
30 A total of 379 Liberal voters were 'lost' between the canvasses of 1838 and that of 1839. Of these, 237 (63%) came from Holsworthy and Bideford.
31 Pollbooks of the 1839 by-election were in circulation at the time: R. Bremridge to Acland, 24 Oct. 1839, Acland (BroadClyst) MSS 1148M/box 11(ii)/31.
32 Canvassing returns of Isaac Davy, Buller of Crediton MSS 2065M/SS2/11.

made significant inroads into these pockets of Whig proprietorial control, through the use of carefully targeted objections. Secondly, what influence remained appears to have been poorly managed by Buller's committee during the actual election itself. The duke of Bedford's interest, for example, was simply overlooked and not officially secured until the very last minute.[33] On his agent's instructions alone depended nearly 100 votes.[34]

Buck's agents also had no qualms about breaching convention by canvassing their opponent's tenants. Their judicious circulation of parish petitions in support of agricultural protection assisted them greatly here. As the chairman of Buller's committee observed, 'in a short period the yeomanry were pleased with such attention, and not being habited to examine any proposition beyond the plough in their own fields many were led away from us to the other side'.[35] One of the few clergymen to support Buller actively wrote to warn him that his election would depend heavily upon a 'declaration *respecting the support of the existing Corn Law*'.[36] The Tories were also acutely aware of the importance and influence of the local publicans. As well as securing their own inns, they again flouted custom by attempting to take over all those engaged by the opposition. As William Callon explained to Thomas Pring, one of Buller's principal agents:

> When your first letter arrived, I desired my friend Mr Walker to secure inns; he did so and thereby secured eleven votes. Buck's party have since been doing all in their power to get them away, offering to send more horses and voters to them, but in order to keep them Mr Sloley has been obliged to rent their stables for the two days, and to pay for hay and corn according to a scale and to guarantee so many dinners to each.[37]

The widespread realisation that the Tories were fighting a new type of campaign, however, did nothing to lessen the blow of Buller's defeat. Numerous letters of condolence bear testimony to a widespread sense of disbelief in the Liberal camp. 'It appears to me a dream', wrote one well-wisher.[38] The contest was also expensive. Buller's total costs amounted to almost £5,000, of which only £100 appears to have been defrayed by a subscription raised at the Reform Club in London.[39] James Coppock's role at 3 Cleveland Row was limited to the co-ordination and financing of advertisements in the press, rather than any direct participation.[40] The only really

---

33 Lord John Russell to Buller, 5 Mar. 1839, ibid. SS2/10.
34 Thomas Pring to Buller, undated, ibid. SS2/11.
35 Partridge to T. Pring, 27 Mar. 1839, ibid.
36 Revd John King to Buller, 5 Mar. 1839, ibid.
37 William Callon to Pring, 9 Mar. 1839, ibid. The bill for this alone came to £130, excluding any professional charges.
38 R. S. Hillett to Buller, 19 Mar. 1839, ibid.
39 'North Devon election, Mar. 1839', ibid. SS2/2, fo. 20. The total cost was £4,969 14s. 6d.: ibid. SS2/5–9.
40 Coppock to Davy, 30 Jan. 1840, ibid. SS2/11.

substantial contribution towards Buller's expenses, £500, was donated privately by Ebrington a few days before the election, once the scale of the contest had become apparent.[41] In the inevitable post-mortem which followed, both the role of agricultural protection and the superior electoral management of the Tories were singled out by the chairman of Buller's election committee as having been significant. However, it was his future instructions to the Liberal agents which went to the crux of the matter. To Pring, for instance, he wrote:

> Pray cease to abuse the clergy as a body of men, where individuals neglect their office prove it in another place. Their yearly subscriptions alone are more than sufficient to defray the costs of the examination of the voters at the registration.[42]

This recognition of the enormous damage that had been caused by well-funded Tory registration activity prompted a thoroughgoing reappraisal of Liberal strategy. Buller himself had been pushing for a review of registration activity for nearly a year, a review that was eventually promised for January 1839 and then postponed as a result of preparing for the by-election.[43] Once the Reformers had come to terms with Buller's defeat, one of the first actions of the North Devon Reform Association was to establish a special Liberal registration fund. This, at least initially, was quite successful in soliciting large donations, even from normally circumspect ministers of the crown. Ebrington, for example, rather unimaginatively subscribed in his son's name.[44] A similar re-examination of strategy was undertaken by Buck's ever assiduous Tory election committee and the North Devon Conservative Association. Unlike the Reformers, however, the Tories identified registration not just as an important factor, but as the decisive factor explaining their victory. Sir Thomas Wheler, for instance, claimed that:

> to the registration of 1838 was the success of Mr Buck's cause solely and entirely attributable, for without such registration it is quite clear that the Conservatives were and would have continued in a minority, they having increased their strength by at least 600 and won their subsequent election by *only* 480.[45]

With both sides now fully cognizant of the impact of registration, and organised accordingly, the contested revision of 1839 was every bit as bitter and vehement as the by-election. The North Devon Reform Association lodged nearly a thousand objections to Conservative voters and entered 843 Liberal

---

41 Ebrington to Sir Humphrey Davis, 13 Mar. 1839, ibid.
42 Partridge to Pring, 27 Mar. 1839, ibid.
43 Ebrington to Buller, 14 Dec.; Buller to Davis, 15 Dec. 1838, ibid.
44 Ebrington to Buller, 4 Jan. 1840, ibid.
45 'North Devon registration', Acland (BroadClyst) MSS 1148M/box 8/17.

Table 10
Summary of the North Devon registration revisions, 1838–40

	1838	1839	1840
Number of Tory claims	710	995	608
Number of Liberal claims	115	843	386
Number of Tory objections	287	940	482
Number of Liberal objections	412	956	777
Number expunged by Tories	197	597	286
Number expunged by Liberals	189	489	380
Total net gain for Tories	**+603**	**+260**	**+128**

Source: Registration returns, Acland (BroadClyst) MSS 1148M/box 8/17.

claims, seven times more than in the previous year.[46] The response of the Tories was to defend vigorously the votes of their own supporters, while lodging an equally large number of objections to Liberal voters and an even greater number of Tory claims. No effort was spared on either side, though the Tories were undoubtedly the more ingenious and resourceful of the two protagonists, even assessing the future impact of property changes on the electoral composition of each district.[47]

A breakdown of this crucial 1839 registration, along with those of the previous and subsequent years, is provided in table 10. Over half (152) of the gains made by the Tories in 1839 can be seen to have resulted from lodging more fresh claims than their rivals. However, their superior ability to defend the votes of their supporters was also extremely important, accounting for 108 (42 per cent) of their 260 gains. Although the number of Tory and Liberal objections was roughly the same, 467 Tory voters were successfully defended compared with only 343 Liberals.[48] The reason for this crucial difference lay in the deliberate strategy adopted by Wheler, the chairman of the North Devon Conservative Registration Committee, who insisted that 'objections could only be met by bringing up Conservatives to substantiate their claims, to a large majority of whom it was found in practice necessary to make remuneration as well for loss of time as for travelling and other expenses'.[49]

This Tory willingness to compensate their supporters financially for time spent hanging around the revising barrister's court was greatly facilitated by

[46] 'Registration returns', ibid.
[47] These included the purchase of an estate at Stoodleigh by a leading Tory of Bristol, Alderman Daniel: R. Bremridge to Acland, 24 Oct. 1839, ibid. box 11(ii)/31.
[48] *The Times*, 30 Oct. 1839.
[49] 'North Devon registration', Acland (BroadClyst) MSS 1148M/box 8/17.

the substantial registration fund at their disposal. Their income from annual subscriptions alone amounted to about £620. Despite spending £510 6s. 8d. on registration in 1838, they still had a balance of £755 4s. 8d. to hand the following year. However, even this was not sufficient to cover the large expense involved in remunerating individual voters, and by the end of the 1839 revision they were running a total deficit of £260.[50] After conferring with the leading members of the Conservative association, Wheler decided to carry this debt forward and add it to the expenses of the following revision which came to a further £790. The Tories then split the outstanding balance of £1,050: £685 14s. 2d. was defrayed by the subscriptions of 1840, and, in a move that was becoming increasingly common in other constituencies, Acland was presented with a registration bill for £500, which he duly paid.[51]

In addition, the Tories raised a further £148 10s. 2d. by mounting a campaign to collect uncollected subscriptions accumulated during the previous three years. This attention to finance contrasted sharply with the rather lackadaisical approach of the Reformers. During 1840, for example, many Liberal subscriptions remained unpaid, the treasurer failing to chase them up and allowing them to lapse.[52] Indeed, during 1840, various efforts to improve the Liberals' registration machinery all appear to have come to nothing.[53] Thus although table 10 shows that the Reformers were still active at the revision of 1840, in reality they had already begun to lose heart. At this revision, the Tories successfully defended 397 (51 per cent) of the 777 Tory voters who were objected to by the Liberals, while lodging 222 more fresh claims than their rivals. As a result, by the time of the 1841 election, the Tories were able to claim a clear majority of at least 868 on North Devon's electoral registers.[54]

In these circumstances there was simply no point in the Reformers contesting the 1841 general election. The real battle had already been fought and won. As *The Times* commented on this county division, 'come an election when it may, there is now no doubt whatever of the Conservatives securing a sure majority'.[55] A constant attention to the registers in subsequent years enabled both Buck and Acland to ride out the partisan turmoil of the 1840s with ease, and to sit uncontested until 1857.[56] This Tory ascendancy, however, was not just about the inevitable return of two Tory candidates as a result of superior registration activity. It also represented the emergence of a new style of county electioneering, which overthrew the compromise arrangements of the division's leading political families and initiated a particularly ruthless by-election in which the accepted principles

---

50 'Expenses of registration', ibid.
51 Ibid.
52 Ebrington to Buller, 4 Jan. 1840, Buller of Crediton MSS 2065M/SS2/11.
53 Ebrington to Buller, 14 July 1840, ibid.
54 'North Devon registration', Acland (BroadClyst) MSS 1148M/box 8/17.
55 *The Times*, 30 Oct. 1839.
56 Acland (BroadClyst) MSS 1148M/box 8/5.

and protocols of electioneering were cast aside. The Tory victory of 1839 confirmed the primacy of registration, and all those associated with it, as the defining electoral dynamic within North Devon. It also necessitated a realignment of political forces among the division's leading Conservative activists. With Buck in parliament, the agent for Barnstaple, Richard Bremridge, took over management of the Tory election committee and responsibility for registration in the electoral districts of Chulmleigh and Tiverton.[57] With at least three of the division's eleven electoral districts under his control, and having served as an agent since 1824, Bremridge now emerged as one of North Devon's leading election attorneys. In July 1847, in what was fast becoming a characteristic career path for the successful election attorney, Bremridge was elected MP for his home town of Barnstaple.[58] The verdict of the *Westminster Review* on the elections of that year was clear: 'Under the present constitution', it concluded, 'the electioneering agents are all-powerful'.[59]

South Lincolnshire

The extent to which an examination of registration activity and party organisation can offer new perspectives on county politics, even in a thoroughly documented constituency, is well illustrated by South Lincolnshire.[60] Although only contested in 1841, this predominantly agricultural division was also far from quiescent. The career of Gilbert Heathcote,[61] the constituency's MP from 1832 to 1841, is especially illustrative of the important political developments that were taking place on the ground. Heathcote had 'the weight of family tradition, political connection, and a numerous tenantry to support his claims' to represent the division.[62] His family were by far the largest proprietors in Kesteven with about 17,500 acres. A marriage connection with the barony of Willoughby de Eresby also meant that they could rely on an extra 13,500 acres at Grimsthorpe. Heathcote claimed to have successfully 'kept aloof from all political unions . . . both on the one side and on the other', but he was generally considered to be a moderate Reformer.[63] He

57 Bremridge to Acland, 24 Oct. 1839, ibid. box 11(ii)/31.
58 PP 1852-3 (382) viii. 174, minutes 2986-7; Charles R. Dod, *Dod's parliamentary companion*, London 1847, 135. For a useful discussion of the growing influx of election agents into parliament see Raymond, 'English political parties and electoral organization', 298-304.
59 *Westminster and Foreign Quarterly Review* xlviii (1847), 346.
60 See Olney, *Lincolnshire*.
61 Gilbert John Heathcote (1795-1867), 1st baron Aveland, MP for Boston 1820-32, South Lincolnshire 1832-41, and Rutland 1841-56.
62 Olney, *Lincolnshire*, 100; *Dod's electoral facts*, 188.
63 Charles R. Dod, *Dod's parliamentary companion*, London 1833, 123; *Lincolnshire Chronicle*, 3 Oct. 1837.

sometimes shared canvassing arrangements with the division's other member Henry Handley, who was a radical Reformer, but during the 1835 election Heathcote also received the tacit backing of many prominent Tories.[64] Their acknowledged leader, the highly influential Lord Brownlow,[65] explained why:

> although you are not exactly the *man after my own heart* in political matters, yet as I am inclined to believe that you entertain Conservative principles to a greater extent than either of the other three late representatives of this county, you are the only one of them, towards whom I can honestly manifest any indication of good will upon the present occasion.[66]

The 1835 election was uncontested, but it was no less formative. With a dissolution not expected until 1839, neither side had been prepared for a contest. The unexpected election exposed important organisational deficiencies on both sides. Heathcote, for example, was warned by one of his agents that 'the registry of the votes being well attended to is a *great object* and their canvassing being *done well* is another matter of *great consequence*'.[67] The Tories, in particular, were galvanised into far more rigorous activity, and on 2 June 1835 'a subscription' was 'entered into to defray the expenses of a due registration of voters by the employment of professional men . . . previous to the formation of a general association'. This raised £273 for contesting the Southern registration, and £230 for the Northern.[68] Agents were then hired to attend to the 1835 revision and the results carefully monitored in what was initially something of an experiment. The following letter sent to Brownlow by one of his treasurers outlined the Conservatives' strategy:

> Agents should be requested to make out three returns as soon as the revising barristers have done their rounds which I have numbered as follows:
> No. 1 The number of *new voters* on the Conservative side whose claims are admitted
> No. 2 The number ditto on the Radical side
> No. 3 The number of Radical votes, if any, which they have been able to get struck off the list.
> This will enable us to see at once what ground we are likely to gain by attending to the registration.[69]

The following year Tory registration activity was put on a more secure footing with the formation of a county Conservative association based at Sleaford.

---

[64] W. Dolby to Heathcote, 26 Dec. 1834, Ancaster MSS 3 Anc 9/14/245; Olney, *Lincolnshire*, 100–3.

[65] John Cust, 1st earl Brownlow (1779–1853), MP for Clitheroe 1802–7.

[66] Brownlow to Heathcote, 3 Jan. 1835, Ancaster MSS 3 Anc 9/14/228. The 'other three late representatives' referred to were Henry Handley, and the two Liberal members for the Northern division, Charles Pelham and Sir William Ingilby.

[67] Unidentified agent to Heathcote, 9 May 1835, ibid. 14/274.

[68] Notes of meetings, 2, 15 June 1835, Brownlow MSS 4 BNL/14.

[69] Richard Ellison to Brownlow, 15 Aug. 1835, ibid.

The 1837 general election was again uncontested, but further Tory successes in the registration courts helped to ensure that partisan loyalties were now becoming far more rigid and electorally well-defined. One manifestation of this was Heathcote's growing difficulty in justifying his 'independent' position, despite being Kesteven's largest proprietor. An increasingly party-dominated agenda on a whole range of concerns, including Dissenters' grievances, Irish Church appropriation, and protection, sat uneasily with his personal rather than partisan approach to individual issues. His opposition to the abolition of church-rates, for example, infuriated many Liberal Dissenters, and even assured him of the active political support of some of Kesteven's Anglican clergymen.[70] But at the same time his ongoing support for the Whig's Irish Church policy alienated many important Conservative sympathisers, including Sir Culling Smith and Lord Saye and Sele, who as a result felt that they could no longer give their support 'consistently with our political opinions'. In a similar vein his stance as a friend of the 'agricultural interest' was undermined by the inconsistency of his votes on the malt tax repeal.[71]

These matters were pushed to a head by the South Lincolnshire Conservative Association at a special dinner in Sleaford, held to celebrate the registration of 1837, to which Heathcote was invited 'with a view of ascertaining *what* his politics really were'.[72] His letter of refusal, in which he reiterated his intention to keep 'aloof from all political unions', produced an extremely angry response. The chairman's attack on Heathcote, which was reported extensively in the provincial press, suggests a dramatic hardening of political attitudes at constituency level:

> Mr Heathcote has of late so worded his speeches that they were completely undecided in point of political tendency . . . if Mr Heathcote by such milk-and-water policy as this expects to conciliate the Conservatives and gain their support, he grossly deceives himself . . . I must say that I infinitely prefer the honest downright Radicalism of Mr Handley than this milk-and-water of Mr Heathcote! (Cries of 'So do we!')[73]

The increasing difficulties of maintaining a moderate, non-partisan position were further illustrated in 1839, during a canvass made necessary by the imminent prospect of a dissolution. Outraged by Heathcote's independence, and emboldened by their successes in the registration courts, the Conservatives for the first time decided to contest the division and brought forward Christopher Turnor, who was immediately accused of being presented 'pur-

---

70 Stranger to Heathcote, 27 June 1837; Brocklebank to Heathcote, 14 July 1837, Ancaster MSS 3 Anc 9/14/306, 14/323.
71 Smith to Heathcote, 1 Jan. 1835; Collin to Heathcote, 21 Dec. 1834, ibid. 14/231, 14/242.
72 *Lincolnshire Chronicle*, 13 Oct. 1837.
73 Ibid.

suant to a recent decision of the Carlton Club'.[74] This he vociferously denied.[75] His connection by marriage to the earl of Winchilsea, the Conservative association's president, was the real reason for his selection. Turnor was not necessarily a popular choice, but the very presence of a Conservative candidate served to test old loyalties and fashion new ones. Henry Nevile and his small estate at Stubton, for example, had always supported Heathcote, but he now wrote to explain that

> I consider it an object of such importance to secure the return of Mr Turnor for South Lincolnshire that I am unwilling to weaken the effect of my vote by dividing it. Supposing his election certain, I need not say that the same Conservative feelings would prompt me to support you in preference to Mr Handley.[76]

By 1839, with his partisanship still unclear, Heathcote's personal and proprietorial influence as the largest landowner lacked the necessary political foundation to make it really effective. His canvassing correspondence reveals that most electors either pledged or declined their support on the basis of party lines, rather than proprietorial or personal sympathies. Heathcote's political conduct was judged according to well-defined normative concepts of party and agenda. John Phillips, for example, wrote to explain that

> Your vote . . . on the Irish question approving of the general policy of ministers . . . has declared you to be a dreaded Ministerialist and we cannot understand how a friend of the agricultural interest can consistently support men whose great object seems to be the annihilation of that interest.[77]

The Tories also benefited from 'employing the leading Attorneys (a powerful knowing body) on their behalf'.[78] Even Heathcote's former agent at Grantham, for example, declared in favour of Turnor and took his influence with him.[79] Another agent informed him that it had become 'the general talk at market tables . . . that you will lose your election'.[80] In these circumstances, the support of his fiercely protectionist father-in-law, Lord Willoughby, was decisive, not just for the weight of his 13,500 acres but also for the vital message of confidence that it sent to the agricultural interest.[81]

It was with the issue of protection in mind that Heathcote was finally forced to retire at the 1841 general election. His approval of the Whig budget made the continued support of his father-in-law extremely unlikely;

---

74 1841 South Lincolnshire pollbook, 5.
75 Ibid. 8.
76 H. Nevile to Heathcote, 23 July 1839, Ancaster MSS 3 Anc 9/14/359.
77 J. Phillips to Heathcote, 28 June 1839, ibid. 14/382.
78 Revd Brocklebank to Heathcote, 28 June 1839, ibid. 14/419.
79 Hawkins to Heathcote, 3 July 1839, ibid. 14/378.
80 J. M. Andrews to Heathcote, 18 June 1839, ibid. 14/427.
81 Willoughby to Heathcote, 2 July 1839, ibid. 14/363.

Willoughby lost no time in transferring his substantial interest to the two Conservative candidates, Turnor and Trollope, both of whom were fiercely protectionist.[82] Handley's position was equally fraught, despite a 'personal' commitment to protection. Although Sir William Ingilby eventually persuaded him not to retire, strong party-based perceptions also undermined his position. As Handley himself put it:

> I cannot divest myself of the conviction that so long as the Corn Laws form the badge of Party, and the important interests involved in them are prostituted to the purposes of Party struggles for the attainment of political power, frequent cases might and would occur, involving Reform Principles on the one hand, and Agricultural Protection on the other.[83]

If by 1841 Handley's position had become precarious, Heathcote's had become untenable. The decline of his family influence, unattached as it was to a clear party line and ideology, suggests important limits to proprietorial control at work in this large county division.[84] Much was made by Olney of the role of landed influence at the ensuing election, but an examination of the surviving pollbook shows that although there were eighty-two parishes out of a total of 240 (34 per cent) in which 85 per cent or more of the voters polled identically, most of them were comparatively small.[85] Only four of these parishes were larger than the average parish size of twenty-nine voters, a further twenty-two contained between ten and twenty-nine electors, while fifty-six had less than ten participants. Indeed, almost a third of the parishes exhibiting this level of unanimity fielded four voters or less.[86] As a result, the number of electors who actually voted as part of a unanimous group at this election was only 792, or a mere 11 per cent of the total turnout of 7,020.[87]

By 1841, proprietorial influence in South Lincolnshire was limited. A combination of partisan registration activity and issues such as protection had helped to polarise the electorate along clear party, rather than proprietorial, lines. Significantly, over 80 per cent of the electors cast straight party votes in the general election, either by plumping for Handley or by splitting their votes between the two Tory candidates, Trollope and Turner.[88] This contest was also important in breaking a long succession of uncontested elec-

---

82 *Stamford Mercury*, 18 June 1841.
83 1841 South Lincolnshire pollbook, 12–13.
84 By 1839 there were 8,729 registered electors: PP 1840 (579) xxxix. 187–201.
85 Olney, *Lincolnshire*, 32–4; 1841 South Lincolnshire pollbook, 48–218. For a more detailed discussion of this type of county pollbook analysis see ch. 4 above.
86 The four largest unanimous parishes were Fulbeck (where 32 out of 36 voters polled identically), Heighington (35 out of 37), Martin (33 out of 35) and Metheringham (53 out of 57). The average number of voters per parish has been obtained by dividing the total number of voters (7,020) by the total number of parishes (240).
87 An identical proportion to the 'average' which was calculated in ch. 4 above: 1841 South Lincolnshire pollbook, 48–218.
88 Ibid.

tions, which had provided electors with important opportunities for exercising unrestrained political independence during routine but otiose pre-electoral canvasses.[89] In the uncontested 1835 election, for example, many landlords, such as the duke of St Albans, Lord Middleton, Sir Richard Sutton, Sir Robert Flexon and Sir John Thorold, had given their tenants the 'free exercise of their elective franchise, without any interference' in the certain knowledge that there would be no poll.[90] Heathcote's canvassing correspondence suggests that this helped to foster an important degree of independence and conditional support, even among tenants whose compliance was never automatic and sometimes highly contractual.[91] One tenant, for example, informed Heathcote that 'you certainly will have a vote from me should it be required as also from my son Henry, trusting you will continue to support the agricultural interest and allow me to request your aid to do away with Smithfield Market and to have the cattle market held at Islington'.[92]

Heathcote's assumption of his father's seat in the neighbouring county of Rutland in 1841 lessened the blow of his retirement from Lincolnshire, but even here his return was not as straightforward as he might have hoped, and again suggestive of important political developments on the ground. With a population of only 19,000 (compared to South Lincolnshire's 145,000), Rutland was by far the smallest English county.[93] The greater degree of control exercised by the family was reflected in the fact that Heathcote's father, Sir George, had sat unchallenged since 1812.[94] For the first time since 1761, however, arrangements between the county's leading families now failed to prevent a contest, leaving Heathcote to engage in a fierce party conflict in which he and the sitting Liberal were backed by 45 per cent of the voters, and the single Tory candidate by 40 per cent. Again local landed influence appears to have had a limited effect on electoral behaviour. Although nineteen of the county's fifty-four parishes (35 per cent) exhibited voter unanimity levels of 85 per cent or above, all of these parishes were small, even by Rutland's standards. Just one, Empingham, was equal in size to the average parish of twenty-five voters, eight contained between ten and twenty electors, while ten polled fewer than ten voters. Put into context, of the 1,337 voters who participated at this contest, only 171 (13 per cent) polled as part of a unanimous group in agreement with their neighbours.[95] By 1841 even a

---

89 The last contested election was 1823.
90 Ancaster MSS 3 Anc 9/14/221–4, 244–5.
91 Annotated canvass book, ibid. 14/216.
92 John Tatum to Heathcote, 21 Dec. 1834, ibid. 14/258.
93 *Dod's electoral facts*, 188, 268.
94 Sir Gilbert Heathcote (1773–1851), of Normanton, MP for Lincolnshire 1796–1807, and Rutland 1812–41. Contests in Rutland had been avoided through careful negotiations between the leading proprietors: Ancaster MSS Anc 13B/11/a–gg.
95 Analysis based on 1841 Rutland pollbook, 3–34. The average number of voters per parish has been obtained by dividing the total number of voters (1,337) by the total number of parishes (54). At Empingham 22 of the 25 voters polled identically: ibid. 10–11.

minute county such as Rutland was showing signs of a new political vibrancy and exhibiting extremely diverse and highly partisan patterns of voting. For all his family's vast acres and numerous tenantry, Heathcote's return here was far from automatic, and poor recompense for the loss of his South Lincolnshire seat.

Bedfordshire

A brief survey of Bedfordshire provides further insights into landed influence, the development of partisanship and the impact of protectionism during the 1830s. Bedfordshire stands out for two reasons. First, it has traditionally been viewed as a predominantly proprietorial constituency in which 'only the position' of the duke of Bedford explained why it was 'mainly a whig county'.[96] Secondly, unlike most counties it was not divided after 1832 or affected by boundary changes or the acquisition of extra MPs. The developments which occurred in this county were therefore entirely voter or issue related, rather than the product of territorial re-configurations on the ground. Although the Bedford family owned almost a third of the county and enjoyed an additional alliance with the Whitbread interest, their 'preponderant' political influence was far from guaranteed.[97] During the 1830s the ties binding the Bedford estates together were weakening and a significant degree of independence began to emerge among their tenants. The duke's own idiosyncrasies played a key part in this. His promotion of modern high farming techniques, for example, led to the establishment of an ostensibly apolitical county agricultural society which by the late 1830s provided farmers with a significant, independent forum of their own. This was reinforced by the duke's image of benevolence which respected and gave expression to a tenant's independence, both as a farmer and an elector. The duke publicly contrasted his own behaviour with that of his Tory neighbours, such as Lord St John,[98] who had no qualms about discharging tenants who supported both Whig candidates in the 1832 election, despite his declaration of 'non-interference'.[99] Although this earned the duke genuine respect, in the longer term it increasingly restricted and prescribed his own political behaviour. As Eve Cottingham found in her study of the Bedford estates, 'far from being deferential the Bedford estate farmers were anxious to be represented fully, not caring to

[96] Gash, *Politics in the age of Peel*, 185.
[97] Ibid. Bedford owned about 87,000 acres out of a total of 296,000, while the Whitbread interest controlled approximately 14,000 acres, chiefly at Southill, Cardington and Elstow: J. Bateman, *Great landowners of Great Britain and Ireland*, London, 1883, 3.
[98] Lord St John of Melchbourne and Bletsoe, who owned about 8,000 acres.
[99] T. Bennet to W. G. Adam, 18 Apr. 1833, BRO, Russell MSS R3/3752.

adopt the complacent attitude of their landlord, nor taking at face value the promises of the county MPs'.[100]

Developments in the registration courts also undermined the duke's political position. Like many leading proprietors, Bedford was keen to assist his tenants and their neighbours on to the new electoral rolls. Indeed, no sooner had the Reform Act been passed than his steward wrote to inform W. G. Adam that

> a good deal has to be done as to proper registration of the new constituency. . . . I suggest we get our leading tenants in respective districts to see that their neighbours are properly registered. . . . Elections will not be what they have been, but will still require some attention. Won't take steps without your sanction but the great exertions of the opposite party make me anxious about Tavistock.[101]

The steward had good cause to be worried. According to the Conservative agent in neighbouring South Northamptonshire, the Tories spent over £3,000 on 'the registry' at the first Bedfordshire revision, and had large subscriptions ready for the next.[102] By the time of the heavily contested revision of 1835 it is clear that both his enthusiasm and confidence were waning. Leading tenants such as John Eaton had refused to 'help with registration', forcing the steward 'to do it' himself.[103] One of his comments on the 1835 revision simply stated, 'wish the electors would do it themselves', the returns themselves being described as 'imperfect from non-attention Whigs paid last year'.[104] The estate's management of registration was further hampered by its high-minded policy of 'object to bad claims and support good', which failed to discriminate effectively between Whig and Tory claimants.[105] Like many other Reformers, the duke had strong reservations about restricting the franchise and subverting the constitution through the use of factious objections. Thus despite the family's early and extensive promotion of registration activity in Bedfordshire and South Devon, in both counties the Tories slowly but inexorably gained the upper hand.[106] Throughout the 1830s the comfortable coexistence of Bedfordshire's Whig and Tory MPs served to obscure, rather than highlight, these developments and helped to foster complacency in the Bedford camp. Local Tory agents, for example, frequently commented

[100] Eve Cottingham, 'The Bedford estates and agricultural politics in early Victorian England', unpubl. BA diss. Oxford 1981, 10.
[101] Bennet to Adam, 8 July 1832, BRO, Russell MSS R3/3731.
[102] E. J. Burton to William Grant, 30 June 1833, Cartwright (Aynho) MSS C(A) 8205.
[103] Bennet to Adam, 16 Aug. 1832, BRO, Russell MSS R3/3738.
[104] Bennet to Adam, 10 June 1835, ibid. R3/3877.
[105] Ibid.
[106] Bedford's promotion of registration activity in South Devon worked principally through his patronage of the South Devon Reform Association. Superior registration activity by the Tories helped the Conservatives to win both seats in 1837: George Stanley Carey to Bedford, 11 Aug. 1837, Bedford (London) MSS L1258M/SS/C (DL) F122.

on the ease with which they were able to share the division.[107] The events of 1839 increased their confidence and by June 1840 Tory registration activity was put on a permanent and professional footing with the establishment of the Bedfordshire Conservative Association.[108] This ensured that the Tories made considerable gains at the following revision, on which the 1841 election was held.

By 1841, therefore, the Bedford interest had become severely weakened, but without it being obvious. The issue of protection, however, brought matters to a head. According to the steward, many of the Bedford tenants threw themselves 'into the arms of the Tory squire and parson and for the occasion were wonderfully caressed by them'.[109] Fearing for his seat, Lord Charles Russell, the Bedford nominee, decided to reject the official Whig 'fixed duty' line in favour of the graduated scale.[110] However, the public split which this threatened with his prominent half-brother Lord John, coupled with the risk of a humiliating defeat, forced him to withdraw at the last minute. Two Tory protectionists were returned instead, without opposition.[111] As the *Bedford Mercury* explained, 'having had the misfortune to differ from his noble relative on the subject of the corn laws he [Lord Charles] refused to revoke his opinions and he consequently lost his seat'.[112]

Although the Bedford interest avoided public humiliation in an actual contest, the 1841 election was still decisive in undermining the family's personal power and the estate's political pre-eminence. This worked in two ways. First, the Bedford tenants openly challenged the estates's authority by signing and submitting a petition against a 'fixed duty'.[113] As the steward later remarked, this issue seriously 'damaged the political influence of the duke more than all the acts of the squires and parsons'.[114] Secondly, Bedfordshire's Liberals openly rejected the family's political leadership by deciding that their inept management of registration must end. Tory objections in the registration courts could no longer go unchallenged as a result of the duke's, or his successor's, personal predilections. Thus, as the *Bedford Mercury* explained, 'immediately after the county election, a numerous and highly respectable meeting of the Liberals was held for the purpose of forming an association to attend to the county registration'.[115] Vice-presidents and committees were appointed by the local agents in each polling district, and a

107 Diary of Burgoyne, Tory agent for Biggleswade, 13 Jan. 1835, 1 Aug. 1837, BRO, CRT 190/171(i).
108 *Bedford Mercury*, 13 June 1840.
109 Bennet to C. Haedy, 1843, BRO, Russell MSS R3/4707.
110 John Morley, *The life of Richard Cobden*, London 1908, i. 297; VCH, *Bedfordshire*, London 1908, ii. 65.
111 Viscount Alford and William Astell.
112 *Bedford Mercury*, 10 July 1841.
113 Cottingham, 'Bedford estates', 37.
114 Bennet to Haedy, 1843, BRO, Russell MSS R3/4707.
115 *Bedford Mercury*, 10 July 1841.

new and completely independent registration fund was started. As a result, Liberal electoral organisation effectively shifted from inside to outside the estate.[116] Viewed from the perspective of electoral control and preponderant political influence, the power of the Bedford estates had clearly been marginalised and outmanœuvred by 1841. The steward's prediction of 1832, that 'elections will not be what they have been', had proved both poignant and prophetic.[117]

West Somerset

In counties where a variegated pattern of landownership prevented any single proprietor from having a predominant influence, attitudes to the new registration machinery were especially important. This was particularly true of Somerset where contested elections tended to be the norm rather than the exception. In 1832 two Reformers, Edward Ayshford Sanford and Charles Kemeys Tynte, had been elected with ease for the newly created Western division.[118] By the time of the 1835 contest, however, increasing agricultural distress had started to erode both of their large majorities over their Tory opponent, Bickam Escott.[119] As one of Sanford's agents remarked, 'the malt duty question is continually thrown out to me when I have canvassed' and the Tories 'appear to have gained nearly as much as Mr Sanford has lost'.[120] With support for the Conservative and Liberal parties becoming more evenly matched, organised registration activity now became decisive in influencing the outcome of West Somerset's next contest.

The establishment of a West Somerset Reform Association in July 1835, following the public appeal of the Reform Association in London, initially augured extremely well for the Liberals' registration prospects.[121] Its new chairman, Sir Thomas Lethbridge,[122] described by Sydney Smith as 'the most reforming reformer we have in these parts', lost no time in creating a special registration committee with Edward W. Cox as its secretary.[123] Their efforts at the annual revision, however, were to be severely compromised by disagreements within the Liberal camp over legitimate and illegitimate registration

---

116 Cottingham, 'Bedford estates', 34–5.
117 Bennet to Adam, 8 July 1832, BRO, Russell MSS R3/3731.
118 The 1832 results were Sanford 4,815, Tynte 4,299 and Escott 1,449.
119 Sanford MSS DD/SF/4547, fos 47–8.
120 A. P. Browne to S. T. Lucas, 22 Dec. 1834, ibid. fo. 42.
121 Sir T. B. Lethbridge to Sanford, 28 June 1835, ibid. fo. 87; Morning Chronicle, 10 July 1835.
122 Sir Thomas Buckler Lethbridge (1778–1849), of Sandhill Park, Taunton, MP for Somerset 1806–12, 1820–30.
123 Nowell C. Smith (ed.), The letters of Sydney Smith, Oxford 1953, ii. 564; Cox to Sanford, 12 Sept. 1835, Sanford MSS DD/SF/4551, fo. 50.

tactics. Shortly before the highly charged revision of 1835 Lethbridge wrote
to Sanford to ask if he would

> as one of the members for the Western division of the county, authorize some
> efficient professional men to go round and attend the courts of the revising
> barristers, for the purpose of defending such voters as may have been objected
> to who are favourable to you and Mr Tynte, and for sustaining the objections
> to other voters who may *not* be in yours and Mr Tynte's favor.

Sanford, however, expressed 'considerable doubt as to the propriety of the
professional adviser of a sitting member endeavouring to substantiate objections to the claims of voters' and declined to help.[124] Undeterred, the Reform
association pressed ahead with a series of resolutions aimed at encouraging a
'full attention to the registration'.[125] To these, however, Sanford was firmly
opposed. As he informed his principal agent:

> I send you a copy of the resolutions which have been forwarded to me by Mr
> Cox as secretary of the registration committee. I do not entirely understand
> them, unless they are intended as a censure of Tynte and myself for not being
> sufficiently active in defending votes and making objections . . . on no account
> whatsoever will I allow a single vote to be objected to; substantiate as many
> votes as you can.[126]

This Liberal reluctance to press home objections against Tory voters had
important consequences at the 1835 revision. Although both parties lodged
over a thousand new claims, the Tories successfully struck off almost twice as
many voters as the Liberals, giving them a clear gain of 403 on that year's
electoral roll.[127] The Tories' advantage, explained one of the Liberal agents,
'arises from their having a profesional agent in every district' who 'personally
examined into the title of our friends to vote' and 'made all their objections
far more effectively'.[128] Underpinning their compromised Liberal registration
strategy lay a fundamental lack of unity and common purpose among the
Reformers as a whole. Sanford, for example, had refused to openly coalesce
with the more radical Tynte during the 1835 election, even though they
shared at least one election agent.[129] Where their names did become united,
as one observer noted, 'the style of address with which Mr Sanford's name is
associated would not be much to his tastes, nor the matter quite in unison
with his sentiments'.[130] More significantly, Sanford rejected the Reform asso-

124 Lethbridge to Sanford, with reply, 31 Aug. 1835, Sanford MSS DD/SF/4551, fo. 49.
Sanford's reservations showed a strong similarity to those of the duke of Bedford, with whom
he frequently corresponded.
125 Cox to Sanford, 12 Sept. 1835, ibid. fo. 50.
126 Sanford to Thomas, 15 Sept. 1835, ibid. fo. 51.
127 *The Times*, 13 Oct. 1835.
128 White to Sanford, 27 Sept. 1835, Sanford MSS DD/SF/4551, fo. 52.
129 Thomas Hawkes, ibid. fo. 62.
130 F. Falkener to Sanford, 24 Dec. 1834, ibid. fo. 45.

ciation's request that he would share registration expenses with Tynte, and would 'countenance nothing either directly or indirectly in the shape of coalition'.[131] After the Conservatives had made even further inroads into Liberal support at the 1836 revision, however, his attitude softened enough to contemplate both MPs 'placing the same sum at the disposal of the registration committee'.[132] Further co-operation followed, eased along by Tynte's purchase of Sanford's lands at Durleigh, and by the time of the 1837 general election both men were being billed together as Reformers in a rather belated formal union.[133]

Two years of compromised registration activity, however, had made Tory gains in a future election inevitable. On the strength of their performance at the 1836 registration, on which the 1837 election was held, the Conservatives brought forward two fresh candidates, Thomas Dyke Acland and Francis Dickinson. The very close partisan nature of the 1837 contest, compared with that of 1835, was striking. In 1835 just over a third of the electorate (35 per cent) had shown a distinct Tory preference by plumping for their only candidate, Escott, and just over half (51 per cent) had cast a clear Liberal vote by polling for both the Reformers.[134] Two years later, however, support for the parties had become far more evenly matched, with 46 per cent of the electors voting for both Conservative candidates, and 44 per cent polling for both the Liberals. In these circumstances it was the 213 voters who split their votes between Acland and Sanford, and their slight advantage in plumpers, which proved decisive in putting Acland in first place, on 3,883 votes, and Sanford in second, with 3,556, just thirty-two ahead of the other Tory candidate Dickinson.[135]

These extremely disappointing results inevitably brought about a fundamental reappraisal of strategy among the Reformers. The loss of Tynte's seat, in particular, engendered a great deal of bitterness. As he himself told Sanford, 'never will I *offer* myself again'.[136] Sanford, sobered by his tiny majority, now set about placing the forthcoming registration revision of 1837 on a much firmer footing. His plans, however, did not meet with much approval. James Waldron, the local Whig agent, offered this incisive critique of his proposals to step up electoral recruitment in the registration courts:

> I do not quite agree with your quotation from Sir Robert Peel 'Register, Register, Register!' I think it well for him, but bad for us, for I believe we have done injury to our cause by calculating that an elector who does not value the right of voting sufficiently to take care of his own interest would be for us and not against us. . . . I should rather say *disregister* all you can of your opponents and

131 Sanford to Thomas, 15 Sept. 1835, ibid. fo. 51.
132 Tynte to Sanford, 14 Oct. 1836, ibid. fo. 66.
133 Tynte to Sanford, 17 Oct. 1836, ibid. fo. 67; 1837 election posters, ibid. DD/SF/2617.
134 Breakdown of 1835 West Somerset poll, ibid. DD/SF/4548 fo. 26.
135 Breakdown of 1837 West Somerset poll, Dickinson MSS DD/DN/293.
136 Tynte to Sanford, 8 Oct. 1837, Sanford MSS DD/SF/4551, fo. 99.

leave others to seek their rights unless it be in cases where there can be no doubt whatever entertained.[137]

This notion of a fundamental Tory predisposition among those with unclaimed electoral rights is extremely significant.[138] The registration activity of both parties had helped to place almost 1,200 'new' electors on West Somerset's electoral roll for 1835, but the vast majority of them appear to have voted for the Tories.[139] While the number of firm Liberal partisans at both elections had remained fairly fixed (3,254 voters had split their votes between the two Liberals in 1835 and 3,410 in 1837), the number of firm Tory supporters had increased by 1,189, from 2,221 voters who had plumped for Escott in 1835, to 3,410 who voted for both the Tories in 1837. Even after allowing for the Tories' superior record at sustaining objections, Waldron's figures suggest that newly enfranchised Tory supporters outnumbered new Liberal recruits by a factor of at least three to one.[140]

After the 1837 election, and with the Whig agent's remarks clearly in mind, Sanford ditched his scruples and lent his full support to objecting to Tory voters in the registration courts. The results they achieved at the 1837 revision were impressive, and also indicative of the extent to which the Liberals' performance had been compromised in previous years. The Reformers lodged 811 objections, compared with the Tories' 534. This resulted in a net gain of 224 more Liberal voters on the 1837–8 registers by comparison with that of 1836–7.[141] Surprisingly, however, these gains were not followed up in subsequent years and the West Somerset Reform Association appears to have fallen into decline. This may have had more to do with personalities than politics. Lethbridge, who was the driving force behind the association, had suffered an extremely humiliating and completely unexpected defeat at Bridgwater in 1837, which he took very badly. Despite the considerable influence possessed by the Tynte family, and the fact that Bridgwater had returned two Liberals in 1835, Lethbridge only polled a total of five votes from an electorate of 558. Although the revision of 1837 proved what the Reformers might have been capable of in an uncompromised county registration campaign, without the active support and enthusiasm of Lethbridge they were unable to sustain the momentum necessary for further successes in subsequent years. In 1841 Sanford chose to follow Tynte into political retirement and the two Conservative candidates, Acland and Dickinson, were returned without opposition.

---

137 James Waldron to Sanford, 12 Aug. 1837, ibid. fo. 93.
138 See ch. 2 above for a more detailed discussion of the newly enfranchised.
139 1834–7 West Somerset electoral registers, SoRO, Luttrell MSS DD/L160/18, box 111.
140 Based upon figures in Sanford MSS DD/SF/4551, fos 52, 102.
141 Ibid.

North Wiltshire

Like Somerset, Wiltshire also had a variegated pattern of landownership which tended to prevent any single proprietor from being dominant. Unlike Somerset, however, small pockets of proprietorial control still existed. After 1835 these were again disturbed by a series of intense registration campaigns, which not only brought a large number of new voters on to the registers, undermining the electoral basis of local parish loyalties, but also helped to polarise the electorate along far more pronounced and predictable party lines. Registration activity increasingly decided the outcome of North Wiltshire's elections, and by 1841 it had become the main electoral determinant. This had important consequences for the career of Walter Long, one of the division's MPs from 1835.[142] At the 1832 general election two Reformers, Paul Methuen[143] and Sir John Astley,[144] had been returned for North Wiltshire with large majorities. Astley's retirement in 1835, however, opened a vacancy that the Reformers, under the leadership of the advanced Whig Lord Radnor,[145] were eager to fill. Although Long solicited their support 'as a friend to Reform both in Church and State', in the ensuing negotiations he refused to attach himself to any party line.[146] 'Unless I can go into the House of Commons as what I profess to be a free, liberal and independent man', he declared, 'I have no desire to go there at all'.[147] Like Heathcote in South Lincolnshire, Long's declared aim 'was to keep aloof from party as much as possible' and in both 1835 and 1837 he solicited the support of 'numerous electors, holding opposite opinions in politics'.[148] He made his non-party stance clear during his canvass in 1834:

> totally uninfluenced by Party motives I intend if elected to judge of each measure according to its own merits and circumstances. On these grounds I have received the most flattering promises of support from both Whigs and Tories in every part of this division.[149]

Lord Radnor's rather half-hearted attempt to find an alternative Whig candidate met with little success, and in the 1835 election both Long and Methuen

---

142 Walter Long (1793–1867), of Rood Ashton, MP for North Wiltshire 1835–65.
143 Paul Methuen, 1st baron Methuen (1779–1849), of Ashcombe, MP for Wiltshire 1812–19, and North Wiltshire 1832–7.
144 Sir John Dugdale Astley (1778–1842), of Everley, MP for Wiltshire 1820–32, and North Wiltshire 1832–4.
145 William Pleydell-Bouverie, 3rd earl of Radnor (1779–1869), MP for Dowton 1801–2, and Salisbury 1802–28.
146 Long to Radnor, 19 Dec. 1834, WRO, Pleydell-Bouverie MSS 490/1383.
147 Long to Radnor, 24 Dec. 1834, ibid.
148 Crosby, *Parliamentary record*, 145.
149 Election address, 31 Dec. 1834, Long MSS 947/1840; Long to Radnor, 26 Dec. 1834, WRO, Pleydell-Bouverie MSS 490/1383.

Table 11
Proprietors and voting in twenty-one North Wiltshire parishes, 1837

Name of parish	Politics of proprietor(s) [Whig or Tory]	No. of voters	Split votes for			Plumpers for			Total vote for		
			LM	LB	BM	L	B	M	L	B	M
Alderton	Mr Neeld [Tory]	7	–	–	–	–	7	–	–	7	–
Ashley	Mr Estcourt [Tory]	1	–	–	–	–	1	–	–	1	–
Brinkworth	Lord Suffolk [Whig]	51	18	5	16	1	8	3	24	29	37
Brokenboro'	Lord Suffolk [Whig]	11	4	–	1	–	3	3	4	4	8
Chippenham	Mixed [8 Whig 6 Tory]	59	23	13	8	–	6	9	36	27	40
Crudwell	Pitt [Tory] and de Grey [Whig]	8	1	2	–	–	4	1	3	6	2
Grittleton	Mr Neeld [Tory]	11	–	5	–	–	6	–	5	11	–
Hullavington	Mr Neeld [Tory]	25	–	3	1	–	21	–	3	25	1
Lea and Cleverton	Lord Pembroke [Whig]	13	8	3	2	–	–	–	11	5	10
Leigh Delamere	Mr Neeld [Tory]	5	–	3	–	–	2	–	3	5	–
Littleton Drew	Mr Neeld [Tory]	17	1	3	1	–	12	–	4	16	2
Long Newnton	Mr Estcourt [Tory]	2	–	–	–	–	2	–	–	2	–
Luckington	Lord Beaufort [Tory]	19	1	3	–	–	15	–	4	18	1
Nettleton	Mr Neeld [Tory]	29	3	3	3	–	20	–	6	26	6
Oaksey	Mr Pitt [Tory]	17	1	2	–	–	13	1	3	15	2
Ramsbury	Mixed [1 Whig 3 Tory]	72	6	12	4	–	49	1	18	65	11
Sherston Magna	Lord Beaufort [Tory]	56	1	9	–	–	46	–	10	55	1

Name of parish	Politics of proprietor(s) [Whig or Tory]	No. of voters	Split votes for			Plumpers for			Total vote for		
			LM	LB	BM	L	B	M	L	B	M
Somerford Magna	Demainbray [Whig]	23	1	11	4	–	5	2	12	20	7
Sopworth	Lord Beaufort [Tory]	12	1	–	–	–	11	–	1	11	1
Stanton St Quintin	Lord Radnor [Whig]	19	13	1	1	1	1	2	15	3	16
Wootton Bassett	Mixed [8 Whig 2 Tory]	73	8	13	12	–	36	4	21	61	24
Totals		530	90	91	53	2	268	26	183	412	169

Source: Long MSS 947/1841.

were returned unopposed.[150] By the time of the 1837 dissolution, however, extensive Conservative registration activity, which included payment of the elector's 1s. registration fee,[151] had helped to place over 1,500 new voters on the North Wiltshire register, many of whom had signed the large requisition to the new Tory candidate, the well known former advanced Whig, Sir Francis Burdett.[152] Whatever influence could be mustered, both by Tories and Reformers, was called into play and used extensively during the extremely fierce contest that followed. The Tories in particular spent voluminously, though the *Examiner's* estimate of their expenses at £20,000 seems rather excessive.[153] Long, as the only 'independent' candidate, took an acute interest in both the degree of proprietorial control and the pull of party in the 1837 contest, and his surviving canvassing returns offer a rare insight into both.[154] On the basis of their local expertise his agents identified seventeen parishes out of a total of 209 that were under the direct influence of a single proprietor, and a further four with mixed proprietorship. Together these isolated pockets of proprietorial control contained 530 voters, or one-eighth (12.6 per cent) of the entire electorate who went to the poll in 1837. The voting that occurred in these parishes is reproduced in table 11. The three candidates, Walter Long, Sir Francis Burdett (Tory) and Paul Methuen (Whig), are denoted by the letter L, B and M respectively.

One striking feature of this analysis is that although the five parishes owned by a Whig together would have returned Methuen and Long, while all

150 Radnor's requisition to Sir John Cam Hobhouse was declined: Methuen to Radnor, 31 Dec. 1834, WRO, Pleydell-Bouverie MSS 490/1383.
151 Messrs Keary, Stokes and White, box 415/432; *Devizes and Wiltshire Gazette*, 27 July, 3 Aug. 1837.
152 Sir Francis Burdett (1779–1844), of Ramsbury, MP for Boroughbridge 1796–1802, Middlesex 1802–6, Westminster 1807–37, and North Wiltshire 1837–44.
153 *The Examiner*, 13 Aug. 1837.
154 Annotated 1836–7 North Wiltshire electoral register, 21–128, Long MSS 947/1841.

of the twelve Tory parishes would have returned Burdett and Long, the degree of partisan polling within Tory and Whig parishes was very different. Of the 201 electors living in parishes owned exclusively by a Tory proprietor, for example, 156 (or 78 per cent) behaved in a distinctly Tory way by plumping for the only Conservative candidate, Burdett. A further 15 per cent split their votes between Long and Burdett. In total, therefore, some 93 per cent of the electors in the Tory-owned parishes cast what amounted to an 'anti-Whig' vote. By contrast, the 117 electors living under a Whig proprietor failed to behave in such a clearly defined partisan way. Only ten (9 per cent) plumped for the only Whig candidate, Methuen, while forty-four (38 per cent) split their votes between Methuen and Long. Most notable of all, however, is the fact that a further thirty-nine (33 per cent) actually voted anti-Whig, either by splitting Long–Burdett, or by plumping for a non-Whig. Moreover, another twenty-four (21 per cent) cast one vote for Methuen, but then gave their second to Burdett, rather than to Long. This is very significant. Taken together, over half the electors (54 per cent) in Whig-controlled parishes failed to cast a clear Whig vote. By contrast, only 7 per cent of electors in Tory parishes failed to support the Tory candidate.[155]

This important difference needs to be explained. One obvious answer is that Tory proprietors such as John Neeld,[156] whose heavy-handed approach to canvassing at Cricklade was ridiculed by the local Liberal press, simply exercised more influence than their Whig counterparts.[157] Free from any ideological restrictions regarding the pure and unfettered operation of the reformed franchise, they either expected or forced their tenants to comply with their wishes to a greater extent than Whig landlords. The problem here, however, is that there is not much evidence to suggest that Whig proprietors were any more lax or liberal in their control. Lord Radnor, who owned the parish of Stanton St Quintin, exercised a notoriously firm hold over all of his estates.[158] His attitude was summed up by his son, who deemed it 'bad taste for a tenant to . . . oppos[e] the known wishes and feelings of his landlord'.[159] Whatever their private attitudes, however, in public landowners on both sides would have been governed by customary conventions restricting both the circumstances in which pressure might be applied, and its effectiveness. Neeld's canvassing tactics at Cricklade were singled out by the local press precisely because they were considered irregular rather than routine. The

---

[155] In the Tory-owned parishes, nine voters split for Long and Methuen, two plumped for Methuen, and five gave a non-partisan split, making a total of sixteen voters out of 201 (or 8%).

[156] John Neeld, MP for Cricklade 1835–59, and Chippenham 1865–8.

[157] *Wiltshire Independent*, 20 July 1837.

[158] In the following year, for example, he became involved in a bitter public feud with Archdeacon Croft of Canterbury, the leader of East Kent's Tories, who accused him of using his influence at Folkestone to intimidate and coerce the electors of Hythe: *Kent Herald*, 4 Oct. 1838; Croft to Radnor, 18 July 1838, BeRO, Pleydell-Bouverie MSS D/EPb O14, fo. 22.

[159] E. P. Bouverie to John Banks, 4 July 1837, BeRO, Pleydell-Bouverie MSS D/EPb O14, fo. 12.

detailed canvassing returns of Messrs Creswick and Co., who acted as agents for Long, also show that although many tenants gave one vote to their landlord, they usually regarded their second vote as their own.[160] Attempts to influence the second vote, even if this rather inauspiciously took place on the actual rent day itself, met with very limited success. In the parish of Hilmarton, for example, nearly a third of a Mr Poynder's twenty-three tenants failed to vote in the way he desired (for Long and Burdett), despite the comment that 'his rent day is on Monday and it will be then determined how they will dispose of their second vote'.[161] In short, the idea that Whig proprietors put less pressure on their tenants, and the notion that heavy-handed influence actually translated into votes, are both unsatisfactory. They cannot explain why the degree of partisan voting in Tory and Whig controlled parishes was so markedly different.

An alternative explanation is that the Conservative registration campaigns had helped to place many 'new' Tory voters on the register, even in those parishes that were owned by a Whig proprietor. The possible extent of this is revealed by the fact that Conservative agents not only paid the 1s. on behalf of new claimants, but also charged for extensive 'horsehire' in travelling around, 'obtaining the signatures of claimants for registration'.[162] This, combined with the Tories' superior efforts at disfranchising their opponents in the registration courts, meant that the electoral composition of some parishes had changed considerably between 1835 and 1837. In a private report sent to Peel about Wiltshire, it was the Conservatives' 'exertions and expenses with respect to the registration in previous years' that were singled out by the election manager Granville Somerset as major factors 'during the late contest'.[163] Thomas Bucknall-Estcourt, the Tory MP for Devizes, also had no doubts about the impact of such work.[164] He later recalled that

> In 1836 a certain number of gentlemen met at Neeld's in London and agreed to attend to the registration and we put down our names for sums from £50 downwards. The result of that attention was the Conservative triumph at the election in 1837, for we added at the registration of 1836 a much larger majority to the list than Burdett's majority.[165]

As well as ensuring an unexpected defeat for Methuen who, as the *Wiltshire Independent* remarked, was 'an old and tried representative' with the weight of 5,500 acres behind him, Tory registration activity also began to threaten Long's independence, despite his prominent position as the owner of about

---

160 Canvass books, Messrs Creswick and Co (Faulkner MSS) 137/97/18–19.
161 Ibid.
162 'Expenses 1830–44', Messrs Keary, Stokes and White box 415/432.
163 Granville Somerset to Peel, 19 Aug. 1837, Peel MS Add. 40424, fo. 85.
164 Thomas H. S. Bucknall-Estcourt [later Sotheron], (1801–76), of Devizes, MP for Marlborough 1829–32, Devizes 1835–44, and North Wiltshire 1844–65.
165 T. H. S. Sotheron to Long, 1 Nov. 1841, Long MSS 947/1842/3.

13,500 acres in the division.[166] During the 1837 election he was forced to spell out, on more than one occasion, that he had not 'entered nor will enter into any coalition whatsoever', and that he 'stood quite unconnected with either of the two other candidates'.[167] Unlike Heathcote in South Lincolnshire, however, faced with an increasingly partisan electorate, Long preferred to sacrifice his neutrality rather than his seat. By 1839, after carefully assessing the results of a canvass made necessary by the prospect of an imminent dissolution, he decided to declare in favour of the Conservatives. His attempt 'to keep aloof from party as much as possible' had failed. As he explained in a public statement of his conversion, which appeared in the *Devizes and Wiltshire Gazette*:

> the time is now arrived when every man who has at heart the best interest of his country must either take his stand as a Conservative or as a Radical: with this choice before me, I must choose the former.[168]

Although he cited the Irish and colonial policies of the Melbourne administration as important reasons for his declaration, the difficulties of maintaining an independent position and the increasing dominance of the Tories through their superior registration activity were also decisive factors. Most symbolically, after he and Burdett were both returned unopposed for the division in 1841, Long was presented with a bill for one-third of all the Conservative registration expenses going back to 1836. These amounted to a staggering £1,695 19s. 9d., of which Long duly agreed to pay £565 6s. 7d., but not all at once.[169] The message here was clear: it was registration that had secured North Wiltshire for the Conservatives and, as a prime beneficiary, Long was obliged to pay.

West Riding

The West Riding of Yorkshire was by far the largest parliamentary constituency in the United Kingdom. By 1839 it had in excess of 30,000 electors, making it over one and a half times the size of its nearest rival, the metropolis of London.[170] As in Middlesex, South Lancashire, Kent and Surrey, urban freeholders made up a large part of the electorate. Almost a quarter of them qualified in respect of a 40s. freehold property within a parliamentary borough, the vast majority in the newly enfranchised industrial towns of Bradford, Leeds and Sheffield, while a further 45 per cent resided in the

---

166 *Wiltshire Independent*, 20, 27 July 1837, cited in VCH, *Wiltshire*, Oxford 1957, v. 302.
167 Election poster, 26 July 1837, Messrs Creswick and Co (Faulkner MSS) 137/97/81.
168 Long to J. L. Phillips, 27 May 1839, in Crosby, *Parliamentary record*, 145.
169 A further £123 6s. 2d. was added for election expenses: Sotheron to Long, 1 Nov. 1841, Long MSS 947/1842/3.
170 See appendix 3.

densely populated non-parliamentary boroughs of the Aire and Calder valleys, making a combined urban electorate of about 21,000, or 70 per cent of the total.[171] This marked degree of urban penetration was counterbalanced by the considerable influence of a highly active political peerage, which included earl Fitzwilliam and earl de Grey, the duke of Norfolk and the duke of Devonshire, and Lord Wharncliffe.[172] The resulting colourful interplay of commercial, industrial and landed interests, in which no one group was ever predominant, helped to focus particular attention on party organisation and registration activity as the key factors governing electoral developments within this new parliamentary division. In this respect at least, the failures of the Reformers were to prove just as important as the successes of the Tories in securing the return of two Conservatives for the West Riding by 1841.

As with many other county divisions, the Tories did not contest the return of two Reformers in either 1832 or 1835, but they gained considerable confidence and encouragement from other elections. The loss of one Liberal seat in Leeds was especially instructive. At the previous revision of 1834, on which the 1835 contest was held, the town's Tories had successfully objected to all the Liberal compound rate-payers.[173] Although the newly established Leeds Reform Association had lodged many counter-objections, the net gain for the Tories was still 274 votes.[174] This victory, and the subsequent return of Sir John Beckett at the top of the poll with a majority of 138, sent a clear message to Tories throughout the West Riding.[175] As the *Leeds Intelligencer* commented:

> its influence upon the Conservative cause generally will be beneficial; for if such a battle can be successfully waged in Leeds wherein Dissent so abounds where is the county or borough in which victory might not follow similar energy or spirit?[176]

The unexpected 1835 general election was to prove decisive in stimulating the emergence of far more permanent organisations on both sides throughout the West Riding. In the following month, for example, the Leeds Operative Conservative Society was established under the patronage of Beckett and three other leading Conservatives.[177] Their declared aim, according to the

---

171 Based on PP 1837–8 (329) xliv. 574; PP 1840 (579) xxxix. 187–90; PP 1847 (751) xlvi. 336; PP 1857–8 (108) xlvi. 577; Thompson, 'West Riding', 215–17. Residents of parliamentary boroughs could vote in counties if their qualification was sufficient for a 40s. freehold vote but insufficient for the £10 household franchise, or as qualified borough voters with a separate freehold property: 2 Will. IV c. 45, 728, clause 24. See ch. 4 above for more details.
172 Thompson, 'West Riding', 215; *Dod's electoral facts*, 359.
173 Fraser, *Urban politics*, 187; Thompson, 'West Riding', 220.
174 *The Times*, 16 Oct. 1834.
175 Sir John Beckett (1775–1847), of Somerby Park, Lincolnshire, MP for Cockermouth 1818–21, Haslemere 1826–32, and Leeds 1835–7.
176 *Leeds Intelligencer*, 10 Jan. 1835.
177 Ibid. 5 Mar. 1836. The other three were Robert Hall, Thomas Blayds and Mr Perring.

secretary William Paul, was 'making it their constant business to watch the registrations', in this 'noble object' being 'found the essence of Operative Conservative Societies'.[178] Like many ostensibly urban organisations, this society's activities extended well beyond the borough's boundaries into outlying villages, such as Pudsey, Horsforth, Idle and Batley, and into neighbouring unrepresented townships such as Dewsbury, which were all part of the county constituency.[179] In the following month a Conservative Loyal and Constitutional Association was established at Bradford, under the chairmanship of Matthew Thompson, which again concentrated much of its energy on the county electorate.[180] This was closely followed by the establishment of the West Riding Conservative Association in April 1835, for co-ordinating the work of all the various district committees that had sprung up throughout the division.[181] According to its secretary Robert Baxter, a Doncaster solicitor, it was essentially an umbrella organisation, entirely

> dependent upon the local efforts of agents in the different polling places to manage the registration; the West Riding being so extensive that it could not be managed by three individuals, and those agents were again dependent upon local parties.[182]

In response, the Reformers improved existing organisations and established new ones. Prior to 1835 Lord Fitzwilliam's principal agent, J. C. Gotch, had been responsible for ensuring that 'someone in our interest would look after the new claimants in their respective villages', and collect 'all the information we can both to support our friends and sustain the objections we may make'.[183] This activity, however, had been on a relatively small scale. The total amount spent by Gotch on the 1833 revision, for example, was a mere £95 17s. 8d.[184] One month after the formation of the West Riding Conservative Association, therefore, Fitzwilliam helped to establish the West Riding Reform and Registration Society under the chairmanship of a prominent Whig landowner, F. H. Fawkes, to co-ordinate the efforts of the various Reform societies which were now emerging throughout the Riding.[185] These included the Bradford Reform Society, established on 27 February 1835 'to give the utmost efficiency to the provisions of the Reform Act by carefully watching the formation of the official lists of voters at the revising barrister's

---

[178] Paul, *Operative Conservative societies*, 13–15; 'Declaration of Leeds Operative Society', Peel MS Add. 40418, fo. 174.

[179] Paul, *Operative Conservative societies*, 32.

[180] Wright, 'Bradford', 154.

[181] *Spectator*, 14 Apr., 12 Sept. 1835 cited in Raymond, 'English political parties', 273.

[182] The 'three individuals' were Baxter and the two solicitors responsible for Conservative registration activity, Mr Alexander and Mr Allcock: PP 1846 (451) viii. 467, minute 4361.

[183] J. C. Gotch to Fitzwilliam, 14 July 1834, Wentworth Woodhouse MSS WWM.G83/206.

[184] Ibid.

[185] 'Bradford Reform Society minute book', WYAS, DB4 no. 2, fo. 14r–v.

court', and the new Leeds Reform Registration Association, which super-seded the old Leeds Reform Association founded by Edward Baines.[186] Like their Tory counterparts, the work of these town societies extended into the surrounding countryside through a system of district subcommittees, and concentrated almost entirely on registration. This was especially true of the Bradford society, which lost no time in employing a professional registration agent on a salary of 30s. a week, and launching a special Bradford Reform Registration Society 'for securing an effectual registration of electors for the West Riding throughout the whole of the Bradford District'.[187]

Tory organisation received a further boost from the experience of Peel's first ministry. As news of Peel's impending resignation spread, small commit-tees were formed, initially just to draw up and solicit support for testimonial addresses to the king. The following address, compiled by a hastily formed Doncaster Conservative Committee, was typical:

> We venture humbly to avow our conviction that Sir Robert Peel and his col-leagues, by their measures and conduct, have gained the confidence of the nation, and would receive, in case of appeal to the country, a decided and pre-ponderating support.[188]

The potential to capitalise on these testimonials played an important part in the Tories' decision to contest the West Riding by-election of May 1835, necessitated by viscount Morpeth's acceptance of ministerial office.[189] Many of these new committees undertook election work on behalf of the Tory candidate John Stuart Wortley, and became assimilated into the electoral machinery of the new divisional Conservative association.[190] Although Morpeth's 9,066 votes eventually gave him a clear majority of 2,807 over Wortley, the contest was described by the Liberals as 'a hard struggle'.[191] The lessons drawn by both sides focused even further attention on the importance of co-ordinated registration activity in determining the outcome of any future election.

The 1835 West Riding registration revision was, even by that years' stan-dards, bitterly contested. Over a third of the county's electorate were objected to, yet the total number of electors still rose by an astonishing 11,395 (63 per cent).[192] This was the largest increase to occur in any constituency after South Staffordshire, and reflected enormous efforts on both sides to bring

---

186 Ibid. fo. 4v; Fraser, 'Leeds politics', 99, and *Urban politics*, 190.
187 'Bradford Reform Society minute book', DB4 no. 3, fos 11r–14r.
188 'Address of Doncaster Conservative Committee to the King', 7 Apr. 1835, SRO, MD 3734/6.
189 Morpeth was appointed chief secretary to Ireland.
190 John Stuart Wortley, 2nd baron Wharncliffe (1801–55), MP for Bossiney 1823–32, and the West Riding of Yorkshire 1841–5.
191 Edward Romilly to Edward Strutt, 27 Apr. 1835, Belper of Kingston MSS DD/BK/7/7, fo. 223.
192 *Leeds Intelligencer*, 24 Oct. 1835; appendix 3.

'new' voters on to the register. Some tactics were even suggestive of the sophisticated registration campaign waged by the Anti-Corn Law League in the 1840s. Faggot votes, for example, were created on both sides, either by splitting property up or by conveying rent-charges. Baxter, the secretary of the West Riding Conservative Association, subsequently admitted that 'the sending in of claims has been abused nearly to as great an extent as of objections'.[193] Similar tactics were again employed at the 1836 revision, which may even have been the object of a special campaign by the Conservative central party managers. The *Leeds Mercury*, for example, alleged that the solicitors attending to the registration that year had been hired directly by the Carlton.[194] At this revision, on which the 1837 general election was held, the Tories successfully 'struck out' almost three times as many voters as their opponents, adding a further '726 votes' to their alleged gain of '2,000 votes on the registry of last year'.[195] The combined impact of these registration revisions was clearly demonstrated at the 1837 general election. Whereas Wortley had lost by 2,807 in the May 1835 by-election, he was now only 403 votes behind his nearest rival.

The Reformers' electoral performance was also affected by a number of specific issues which undermined the Whig–Liberal alliance. In Bradford, for example, moderate Whigs and Dissenters split over the issue of Church disestablishment, allowing the Tories to raise the spectre of spoliation among a property owning electorate.[196] Opposition to the New Poor Law, especially among the Radicals of the larger parliamentary boroughs such as Bradford and Sheffield, fuelled further Liberal disunity, despite the fact that anti-poor law frenzy itself tended to be most widespread among non-electors.[197] Condemnation of the New Poor Law by local Tories proved a powerful vehicle for the spread of Conservative operative societies into the non-parliamentary boroughs of the West Riding. Widespread hostility to the formation of the Keighley Poor Law Union, for example, helped ensure the successful establishment of the Bingley Operative Conservative Association, at the Brown Cow Inn, on 26 January 1836.[198] The formation of Bradford's Conservative Operative Society, whose activities again covered both the borough and the surrounding districts of the Riding, also benefited from a fierce anti-poor law campaign.[199] During the 1837 election the Tories exploited the 'excitement caused by the New Poor Law' and Whig–Liberal divisions to the

---

[193] PP 1846 (451) viii. 467, 510–13, minutes 4346, 4995, 5044–5.
[194] Close, 'The elections of 1835 and 1837', 432.
[195] *The Times*, 29 Nov. 1836.
[196] Wright, 'Bradford', 140–1.
[197] M. E. Rose, 'The Anti-Poor Law movement in the north of England', *Northern History* i (1966), 70–91.
[198] WYAS, Busfeild-Ferrand MSS 51 D79/1/3.
[199] 'Bradford Operative Conservative Society minute book', DB4 no. 3, fo. 2.

full, condemning the absurdity of a measure upon which even the Reformers could not agree.[200]

The Reformers were not only politically more divided than their opponents, they also lacked their organisational unity. The advent of the urban Conservative operative society, for example, did not mark the emergence of any Tory–Radical alliance. On the contrary, the Leeds Conservative Operative Society was distinctly anti-Radical with its declared 'deference and respect to all who are in high stations' and regard for 'the ALTAR, the THRONE, and the COTTAGE'.[201] Membership of the Bradford Operative Conservative Society was similarly only open to those who professed distinctly Tory rather than just anti-Whig principles.[202] Both societies remained indifferent to the kind of demagogical campaign waged by Richard Oastler over factory reform and the New Poor Law.[203] Instead, with the patronage and financial backing of local Conservative dignitaries, their declared purpose was to see 'the peer, the tradesman and the operative firmly united in the bonds of union and good fellowship'.[204] Unlike Liberal and Radical organisations, Tory operative societies never developed a distinct autonomy or political agenda of their own, but instead remained almost entirely dependent upon the instructions and subscriptions of an upper-class Tory leadership.[205]

Above all, it is clear that the Reformers experienced increasing problems of co-ordination and control. Because of the extremely large number of urban freeholders in the division, responsibility for the routine but essential work of voter registration mainly rested with the organisations of the larger towns. Although leading landed Whigs, such as F. H. Fawkes and Fitzwilliam, played an important role in presiding over the West Riding Reform and Registration Association, everyday management and control increasingly fell into the hands of urban Liberal activists in the parliamentary boroughs, who acquired considerable power of their own.[206] Differences of style and substance soon emerged over strategy, including candidate selection. In Huddersfield, for example, the Whig–Liberal alliance split in two after failing to agree on the choice of a candidate for the May 1837 by-election.[207] The previous year the Holbeck division of the Leeds Reform Registration Association had nominated the Radical aristocrat Sir William Molesworth as a future candidate for the borough of Leeds after he had been de-selected by the Whigs in East Cornwall. This completely reversed the standard procedure whereby candidates were chosen by the party leaders for subsequent approval by such ward committees. The Whig leaders were horrified, especially since Molesworth

200 Election address of J. S. Wortley, 3 July 1837, Wharncliffe MSS WhM/530.
201 Paul, *Operative Conservative societies*, 8.
202 'Bradford Operative Conservative Society minute book', DB4 no. 3, fo. 3.
203 Fraser, 'Leeds politics', 101.
204 Hill, *Toryism*, 47.
205 For a more general discussion see ch. 2 above.
206 Thompson, 'West Riding', 221–3; Fraser, 'Leeds politics', 102.
207 *The Times*, 1 May 1837.

had categorically refused to pledge support for the Melbourne ministry, and responded with a series of measures designed to tighten their control.[208] Local troubleshooters were recruited by the West Riding Reform and Registration Association, most of them Fitzwilliam's own trusted solicitors, in a bid to stem any further erosion of their authority.[209] Their efforts were to have little effect, however, especially in countering other highly divisive forces, such as Chartism and the Anti-Corn Law League. Fraser's conclusion that 'the later eighteen-thirties were characterised by growing disillusion with the Whigs, increased tension within the Liberal alliance and a plethora of movements which fragmented political opinion' applied as much to the county as it did to the boroughs.[210] In the face of these developments, the landed Whigs increasingly declined to take the lead, leaving the free-traders of the towns to seize the initiative. By 1839 it was clear that the Whig–Liberal alliance was effectively at an end.

The Tories, by contrast, remained united and continued to pay an unrelenting attention to the county and borough registrations. On the strength of their performance at the 1839 and 1840 revisions, they decided to bring forward a second candidate, who was adopted at a meeting of their central committee held at the Strafford's Arms Hotel in Wakefield on 31 May 1841.[211] In the contest which followed the issue of protection undoubtedly played a part in some of the rural districts, but it was not a significant factor across the county as a whole.[212] Instead it was superior registration activity which enabled the Tories to win both West Riding seats, and to re-capture one at Leeds and another at Bradford, in what was a broad-based victory throughout the division.[213] As Dundas explained to Le Marchant, 'it was not the rural voters only, but the Leedsmen, the men of Bradford and many other large towns who did the business'.[214] Significantly, the number of electors who voted for both Liberal candidates in 1841 (11,834) was almost identical to that of 1837 (11,878). The Conservative vote, by contrast, had increased by 1,780 (16 per cent), from 10,940 in 1837 to 12,720 in 1841. During the

---

208 Fraser, 'Leeds politics', 103–4, and Urban politics, 193.
209 Some minor confusion remains over who exactly was appointed and when: cf. Fraser, 'Leeds politics', 102; Thompson, 'West Riding', 220–3. In 1843 Edward Newman, Fitzwilliam's Barnsley solicitor, described his position as 'legal secretary' to the association, a post he had held for 'ten years': PP 1846 (451) viii. 506, minute 4905. Other local Whig troubleshooters included T. W. Tottie, who was appointed to look after Leeds in 1836, Thomas Wilson, who later became chairman of the Barnsley Reform Association, and J. A. Ikin, who had responsibility for 'arrangements' in the Bradford district: Thomas Wilson to Sir F. L. Wood, 4 Nov. 1841, LDA, Wilson MSS DB178/33.
210 Fraser, 'Leeds politics', 104.
211 Edmund Denison: 1841 West Riding pollbook, 7.
212 Thompson, 'West Riding', 224.
213 Raymond, 'English political parties', 150.
214 David Dundas to Denis Le Marchant, 27 July 1841, House of Lords Record Office, Le Marchant MSS.

same period, the division's registered electorate had also grown by 1,652.[215] This apparent correlation between electoral expansion and Conservative gains was not lost on the West Riding's leading Reformers. After their defeat the chairman of the Barnsley District Reform Association, Thomas Wilson, became especially active in 'considering how the system of registration might be improved'.[216] In a series of recommendations sent to the chairman of the West Riding Reform and Registration Association, he identified a number of factors that had allowed the Tories to gain the upper hand at the annual registration revisions. By far the most important was his belief that those with unclaimed electoral rights were more likely to vote Tory than Whig in the event of their being brought on to the registers. Thus although the Reformers had been extremely active in searching out and submitting new claims, this had not necessarily been to their advantage. A superficial analysis of the 1830s suggests how this might have worked.[217] Between the elections of 1835 and 1841, the number of registered voters in the West Riding had increased from 18,061 to 30,998 (or 72 per cent). Over the same period, however, the number of firm Tory partisans had grown by over 100 per cent, from 6,259 in the May 1835 by-election to 12,720 in the 1841 general election, while support for the Whigs had only climbed by 31 per cent, from 9,066 to 11,834.[218] The Tories' repeated assertions that 'new claims' were 'nearly three to one' in their favour, appears to have been no idle boast.[219] Other factors may have contributed to this shift in partisan behaviour, including switches in party allegiance.[220] Wilson, however, was also convinced that wholesale electoral recruitment had tended to benefit the Tories much more than the Whigs. Commenting on 'the causes of the recent defeat of the Liberal candidates' he advised Fitzwilliam that

> It does not seem to be generally borne in mind that the Reform Bill has shown the electoral franchise to parties that have no idea of political duties or political principles, and that these feelings must be created or awakened in them, if they are to be enlisted in the ranks of Reform.[221]

Wilson accordingly outlined a series of plans aimed at greatly extending Liberal party activity throughout the Riding. New organisations, such as the Penistone Reform Association, had already started to form in the aftermath

---

215 1837 and 1841 West Riding pollbooks.
216 Wilson to Fawkes, 10 Aug. 1841, LDA, Wilson MSS DB 178/33.
217 Only an individual-level analysis of voting behaviour, such as that undertaken in ch. 2 above, could quantify the extent of this Tory bias among 'new' electoral participants. The very large size of this constituency, however, makes such an investigation extremely difficult.
218 Appendix 3; 1835 and 1841 West Riding pollbooks.
219 *The Times*, 27 Sept., 17 Oct. 1838.
220 Beverley's voters, for example, demonstrated a relatively high propensity to switch sides in successive contests during this period: Phillips, *Boroughs*, 220–1.
221 Wilson to Fitzwilliam, 12 Aug. 1841, LDA, Wilson MSS DB178/33.

of defeat, and Wilson was keen to capitalise on these developments 'while the feeling arising out of late events is still strong'.[222] His new plans for 'extending' the work of the West Riding Reform and Registration Association contained another proviso that was again an important censure on past practice:

> It is necessary, however, that all ranks should deliberately take part in the work, otherwise there would be a danger of the association tending to too democratic a character. It is on this account that I have pointed out the necessity of the aristocracy of the party being seen at the various meetings and taking an interest in them.[223]

During the 1830s many landed Whigs had clearly found the constantly recurring process of registration tedious, preferring to leave this routine aspect of electioneering firmly in the hands of Liberal activists. This had contributed substantially to a shift of power within the Whig–Liberal alliance in favour of the urban element, which had helped to gradually erode the authority of the Whig leadership. Significantly, the chairman of the West Riding Reform and Registration Association dismissed Wilson's plans to establish a 'most complete organisation' not only as too expensive, but also as politically too ambitious. His less than sanguine view of the Whig–Liberal alliance in the West Riding was incisive and conclusive:

> Unfortunately there is no bond of union among us or we should not be now as we are *prostrate* before a *powerful* antagonist. And I am very sorry to hear that Reform Associations are now forming under the spur of defeat on the principles, which have in being so very prematurely pushed, tended in dividing to weaken our forces. As long as Ballot and the Millocracy doctrines form the bond of union locally, our union generally cannot fail to be but . . . hollow and impotent.[224]

---

222 Penistone Reform Assocation rules, 4 Nov. 1841; Wilson to Fawkes, 10 Aug. 1841, ibid.
223 Wilson to Fitzwilliam, 12 Aug. 1841, ibid.
224 Fawkes to Wilson, 31 Aug. 1841, ibid.

PART III
THE BOROUGHS

6

No Representation Without Taxation:
Rates and Votes

Most accounts of the Reform Act see its impact primarily in terms of parliamentary elections and party organisation. Political life in these areas, as the previous two parts of this study have shown, was profoundly altered after 1832, mainly as a result of the practical but largely unintended effects of voter registration. One of the Reform Act's most dramatic long-term consequences, however, has yet to be explored. In the third part of this book, its politicising effects are examined not only from an electoral perspective, but also from a bureaucratic one. Numerous studies have observed that after 1832, 'political attitudes became hardened and most local institutions, from the Court-Leet, Corporation, Vestry, Improvement and Police Commissions to the election of Church Wardens and Poor Law Officials, became politicized'.[1] As Eastwood has recently noted, 'the period after 1832 saw the emergence of a local political culture which was more formally, even structurally, partisan'.[2]

A crucial factor behind this widely noted process of politicisation was the way in which the 'small print' of the Reform Act created constitutional links to other institutions of nineteenth-century government, most notably the parish vestry and the poor law system. As was noted in chapter 1, it was the much criticised parish overseers who were given the responsibility for drawing up the new lists of electors before each year's revision. But by far the most significant interconnection between parliamentary elections and local administration was provided by clause 27, which made possession of the new £10 household franchise entirely dependent upon the prompt payment of all local rates and assessed taxes.[3] This not only added a significant electoral dimension to the whole business of setting and levying the local rates, but also gave the overseers, collectors and churchwardens responsible for their collection considerable powers of disfranchisement. Some urban parish vestries, of course, were already becoming highly politicised before 1832, especially in areas lacking other types of local administration.[4] Under the rate-paying clause, however, many of their decisions, such as whether to 'compound' the rates of poorer householders or when to set a new rate, would

---

[1] Walsh, 'Working class political integration', 148.
[2] David Eastwood, *Government and community in the English provinces, 1700–1870*, London 1997, 165.
[3] 2 Will. IV c. 45, 729, clause 27.
[4] Fraser, *Urban politics*, 26–30.

now have far-reaching electoral implications.[5] This chapter shows how this formal link between voting and taxation after 1832 helped to bring about what has been called 'one of the defining features of early Victorian politics', namely the 'politicising of minor institutions'.[6]

The origins of the rate-paying clause

Given its subsequent role in nineteenth-century political development, one of the most surprising features of the rate-paying clause was the casual way in which its details were drafted. Rather than being included in the original bill of March 1831, the specific terms and conditions attached to the £10 franchise were part of the last-minute changes made by the Whig ministry in order to secure the support of Lord Wharncliffe and the so-called 'waverers'.[7] To guarantee its 'respectability', Grey and Wharncliffe agreed that 'it might be so loaded with conditions as to be equal to a £20 or £30 qualification'.[8] The resulting clause, as the Radical MP Thomas Duncombe later put it, 'required not only that a man should be taxed, but that he should absolutely have paid his taxes' before he registered for the vote.[9] Although critics like the Whig MP Sir John Hobhouse warned that it would disfranchise nearly a quarter of all £10 householders, and Colonel De Lacy Evans, another Radical, estimated that it would deprive 'at least two-thirds of those entitled to their franchise', there was remarkably little discussion of its implications.[10] As the anti-Reformer Charles Williams Wynn complained to the Commons in August 1832, 'that degree of publicity was not given to the discussion of the details which was desirable'.[11]

Why were Whig ministers apparently so indifferent to the potential impact of this clause? The first and most obvious reason was that to most politicians the idea of a link between taxation and voting appeared quite normal. In the unreformed electoral system, for example, there were thirty-seven 'scot and lot' boroughs in England with an inhabitant rate-payer franchise, twelve boroughs where the freemen also had to pay rates, and three more 'burgage' boroughs where the rate-paying tenants of certain properties possessed the

---

5 'Compound' householders had their rates paid directly by their landlords, or 'compounded' in their rents, in order to save on the costs of collection. This meant that it was the landlord's name, rather than the householder's, which appeared in the list of rate-payers used to compile the electoral registers. Estimates vary, but the practice of compounding probably disfranchised about one-sixth of the potential household electorate: PP 1867 (136, 305) lvi. 449–69.

6 Stewart, *Party and politics*, 39.

7 For the original and far less specific requirements see *Hansard*, 3rd ser. iv. 5–6, clause 21.

8 Lord Sandon to Lord Wharncliffe, 23 Nov. 1831, Harrowby MSS xix, fo. 188.

9 *Hansard*, 3rd ser. xxxii. 1170.

10 Ibid. xiv. 1231, 1329.

11 Ibid. 1288.

vote.[12] What made clause 27 so different, however, was the new requirement that electors had to qualify and register for the franchise *every* year. Rather than voters being able to fall behind with their rates and then settle their accounts at election time, as was so often the case before 1832, under the Reform Act all the new £10 householders had to pay all rates due on 6 April by the 20 July of each year, or else face exclusion from that year's electoral register.[13] This far more stringent relationship between 'a man's right of voting' and 'the day and hour of his paying the King's taxes', which, of course, was now completely independent of an actual election taking place, greatly increased the scope for disfranchisement and the electoral importance of local taxation.[14] Abuses of the rating system at election time had already become common in frequently contested 'scot and lot' constituencies, such as Westminster.[15] The payment of rates on behalf of impoverished electors was also an established form of 'treating' in some pre-Reform contests. With the introduction of annual voter registration, however, the whole business of rating was likely to become far more politicised, as practices previously confined to the excitement of an election now had an impact upon the composition of the electorate in each and every year.

A second reason why ministers failed to pick up on these issues was because of the rather confusing and politically loaded advice they received from various election experts and Reform activists. When Joseph Parkes, for example, was asked by Lord Althorp for his views on the clause, he focused primarily on the problem of 'compounding', pointing out that 'in such a town as Birmingham', where there were 'thousands of £10 rent houses where land-lords pay rates', it would 'have little practical effect'. 'If you ask me whether if with that addition to the franchise, of *rating* as necessary, I should consider the bill sacrificed in any essential point by the concession', he declared, 'of course I reply certainly not.'[16] Indeed, for Parkes and many other Radical activists it was not so much the issue of 'rating', as the £10 qualification itself which was the 'most unfortunate, unconstitutional and ill-advised' part of the government's plans.[17] Like his friend the Liberal MP Charles Tennyson, who with his support had proposed a modified 'scot and lot' franchise for Birmingham in a bill of 1828, Parkes believed that restricting the borough franchise to rate-payers of above £10 annual house rental was fundamentally flawed and would exclude 'the mass of intelligence . . . found to reside in the class of artisans . . . particularly the younger and more energetic portion'. Moreover, not only would 'variations in the value of money continually alter the relation of such a franchise to the state of society', but the '*rate makers*

---

[12] Thorne, *The House of Commons, 1790–1820*, i. 29.
[13] 2 Will. IV c. 45, 729, clause 27.
[14] *Hansard*, 3rd ser. xxxii. 1170.
[15] *Mirror of Parliament*, London 1831, ii. 486.
[16] Parkes to Lord Althorp, 13 Nov. 1831, Althorp House, Spencer MSS box 6.
[17] Ibid.

prior to an election would be frequently acted upon by party feeling, unduly to admit or exclude members who approached the line on either side'.[18]

Bolstered by the additional pressure of Reform riots in places like Nottingham and Bristol, Parkes and Tennyson believed that the chances of the £10 qualification being dropped were high enough for them to concentrate all their energies on trying to persuade the cabinet to adopt a 'simple constitutional franchise of scot and lot', rather than one 'founded upon a *pecuniary* rateable value'.[19] In the event, however, the £10 qualification remained unaltered, and although Althorp later tried to reduce the severity of the rate-paying requirements, even suggesting that an offer of payment should be deemed equivalent to actual settlement, these and other safeguards against abuses were not included in the revised bill, which was hurriedly introduced by Lord John Russell on 12 December 1831.[20] Indeed, the only relaxation of the conditions was the clause giving all 'compound' householders an option to pay their taxes themselves, which would then enable them to be named in the rate book.[21] Not only was this totally impractical since application had to be made each time a new rate was made (usually four, but sometimes six, times a year), but the 'compound' householder also had to pay the full rate, not the reduced sum which the overseers usually accepted from landlords in return for their collection of the money. The result for the 'compound' householder, as Professor Seymour suggested, was effective disfranchisement and exclusion from the political process.[22] The result for the parish could hardly have been more dramatic. It was effectively forced to participate in the national political system – a development most symbolically confirmed by the stipulation requiring the annual 1s. registration fee to be included and collected as part of the parish poor rate.[23]

Rates and votes: the electoral dimension

The first and most conspicuous use of rates in the reformed electoral system was as a means of either prompting or preventing the disfranchisement of known opponents and supporters, examples of which are provided in Monmouth. At the first registration of 1832 the duke of Beaufort's Conservative agents, Messrs Powles and Tyler, purchased copies of Monmouth's poor rate books and objected to all the Liberal voters who were behind with their payments.[24] These electors should automatically have been

18 Tennyson to Althorp, 21 Oct. 1831, ibid.
19 Parkes to Althorp, 13 Nov. 1831, ibid.
20 Brock, *Great Reform Act*, 264–5; Bryan Keith-Lucas, *The English local government franchise: a short history*, Oxford 1952, 46–7.
21 2 Will. IV c. 45, 729, clause 30.
22 Seymour, *Electoral reform*, 150.
23 2 Will. IV c. 45, 738, clause 56.
24 Registration accounts, Leonard Twiston Davis MSS 4371, 4609.

disqualified, but many overseers clearly failed to fulfil the duties immediately required of them under the new system. Moreover, a separate objection was also worthwhile because of the trouble it caused the claimant. Despite the provisions of the Reform Act which specifically allowed for the inspection of the rate books by the revising barrister, in practice both proof of rental value and rate payment were often required in the registration court.[25] On the eve of a typical revision, therefore, it was not uncommon for parish officers and rent collectors to receive frantic letters, such as this one from a Swansea elector, demanding 'receipts for rental and the poor rate to be sent by post *without fail . . .* or the votes will be stuck off'.[26]

With so many Liberal supporters facing possible disfranchisement, Benjamin Hall, Monmouth's Liberal candidate, undertook a personal scrutiny of the rate books before paying up arrears during a special three-day tour of the town.[27] Usually it was not the candidate but his agent who performed such activities. According to an Essex activist it was common practice for them to 'pay the rates and taxes to qualify particular persons . . . to be inserted on the register'.[28] Original election accounts testify to the prevalence of these payments in the run up to many revisions. In Newark, for example, the Tory agents acting for W. E. Gladstone and Lord John Manners spent £5 8s. on 'poor rates paid for various electors to prevent loss of qualification' at the 1840 revision.[29] This aided the return of both candidates in the general election of the following year. Similarly in Cardigan, a Liberal agent claimed for expenses 'of poor rates paid by William Williams for voters' prior to the revision of 1841.[30]

What Sir Thomas Fremantle's agent euphemistically termed 'perusing poor rates' was clearly a common but clandestine practice, requiring ingenuity and discretion.[31] The registration expert, William Manning, cited the case of a Greenwich elector who was disqualified in 1833 after his rates had been paid by his employers, and like him most revising barristers appear to have demanded payment 'in person'.[32] Ipswich's barristers, for example, struck off voters when it emerged that their rates had been settled by others on their behalf.[33] The growing corpus of electoral registers, however, allowed local parties to identify and target their recipients with an unprecedented

[25] 2 Will. IV c. 45, 737, clause 51.

[26] David Griffiths to J. C. Wolridge, 29 Sept. 1840, Dowlais Iron Company records D/D G, vol. 1840 (1) fo. 244. The votes referred to were his and a Mr Bedlington's.

[27] Thomas Jones Phillips to Messrs Powles and Tyler, 10, 21 July 1832, Leonard Twiston Davis MSS 5997, 6003.

[28] PP 1835 (547) viii. 35, minute 531.

[29] 'Account of the expenses of Mr Gladstone and Lord John Manners at the election for the borough of Newark, June 1841', Messrs Hodgkinson and Beevor DDH/51/25.

[30] 1841 election expenses, NLW, Goderddan Estate MSS box 72.

[31] 1837 registration bill of John King, Fremantle MSS D/FR/144/1/1/6a.

[32] Manning, *Courts of revision*, 204.

[33] *Ipswich Express*, 22 Sept., 13 Oct. 1840.

level of precision and privacy. The most effective agents employed an 'abstract of the poor rate', like the one compiled by the chairman of the Barnsley District Reform Association in his effort to improve their registration performance in the West Riding boroughs.[34] Where a large amount of arrears precluded wholesale rate payments, a system of loans was sometimes introduced instead. This was used extensively by the Conservatives in Ipswich, as part of a registration campaign which resulted in the defeat of two Liberal members at the 1835 election.[35] Hopeful rate-payers might even make application for these loans directly to an MP himself. The following note, for example, was received by Pryse Pryse [sic], Liberal MP for Cardigan, on the eve of the 1841 revision: 'Dear Sir, I have just been informed that without I pay the Poor Rate this evening I shall be disqualified from voting . . . I shall feel greatly obliged by your lending me the necessary.'[36] Such practices, according to the Liberal election activist Parkes, were especially common in boroughs where all the electors, including the ancient-right voters, were rate- payers. Giving evidence before an 1835 select committee he related how 'all agents (the first step in a scot and lot borough) ascertain the non-payment of rates, and in many instances we go and pay persons whom we know to be in our own interest . . . in order to secure their votes'.[37]

A second aspect of the rate which directly affected the composition of the parliamentary electorate was the level at which it was set. Where the cost of poor relief increased and drove up the rates, it had the 'knock-on' effect of increasing the cost of electoral participation, making it more difficult for poorer householders to avoid debt and disfranchisement. Lower rates, by the same token, eased the cost of electoral participation and reduced the number of disqualifications for non-payment. Depending on the level of the rate, therefore, access to the franchise might be either restricted or facilitated. In places where the vestry was 'closed', new political power was accordingly gained by the small oligarchy of parishioners who controlled the rate. In Bristol, for example, where it was alleged that the select vestries had long acted as 'Tory electioneering clubs', the Tory White Lion Club and the Bristol Conservative Operative Society were given exclusive use of the local rate books for registration purposes.[38] In places where the vestry was, by contrast, relatively 'open', new life was injected into parish politics. In his study of Salford, for example, Derek Fraser concluded that 'the most obvious manifestation of this "new vigour" was the election in 1833 of a Whig–Radical select vestry, whose immediate achievement was to reduce poor rates from 5s. in

---

34 'West Riding registration table', 1841, LDA, Wilson MSS DB/178/33.
35 PP 1835 (547) viii. 82–4, minutes 1417–21, 1448–57.
36 1841 election expenses, Goderddan Estate MSS box 72.
37 PP 1835 (547) viii. 94, minute 1612.
38 Sidney Webb and Beatrice Webb, *English local government from the revolution to the Municipal Corporations Act: the parish and the county*, London 1906, 242 n. 3; Bush to Vyvyan, 19 Sept. 1833; William Betty to Vyvyan, 30 Jan. 1834, Vyvyan MSS DDV/BO/61/55–9.

1832 to 1s. in 1834'. This, in turn, acted as a spur for the formation of the Salford Operative Conservative Association in 1835, whose declared aim was 'to regain the management of parochial and town affairs'.[39]

The new electoral importance of the body responsible for setting and levying rates inevitably focused extra attention on the twin institutions of the poor law and the parish vestry. Poor relief, of course, was already under serious review prior to the passing of the Reform Act, but the link between rates and registration added an extra political dynamic to economic and utilitarian arguments for its complete overhaul. The resulting Poor Law Amendment Act of 1834 represented a radical departure from previous reforms, such as the Sturges Bourne Acts, which had reinforced rather than restricted the administrative province of the parish unit.[40] By transferring control of poor relief from the parish vestry to an extra-parochial board of guardians, and by attempting to establish a much more uniform and economic system, the New Poor Law was of great electoral significance in many parliamentary boroughs.[41] By 1837 351 unions had been formed, amounting to 65 per cent of the rateable value of England and Wales.[42] Moreover, in the financial year beginning 25 March 1834, there was a 13 per cent reduction in the amount of money spent on the poor; average expenditure falling from 9s. 1d. to 7s. 11d. per head. In the next year it went down by 25 per cent and by 1837 expenditure was an astounding 36 per cent lower than it had been in 1834.[43] This rapid decrease led to a reciprocal decline in the level of the poor rates. In 1834 the total amount of poor rates levied in England and Wales was £8,338,071. By 1835, it had declined to £7,373,807 (a decrease of almost 12 per cent) and in the following year a further reduction of 24 per cent was achieved. In 1837, for the first time, the drop in the rates finally caught up with the reduction in expenditure, with both amounts over a third lower than they had been in 1834.[44]

These figures suggest that the cost of electoral participation must have fallen considerably in many parliamentary boroughs after 1834, which helps to account, at least in part, for subsequent increases in the number of householders on the parliamentary registers. The dramatic 10 per cent increase in the size of the borough electorate in 1835 was initiated by local party activity in the registration courts, but was then intensified and accelerated by the additional impetus of municipal reform. Easing the cost of electoral participation, however, facilitated both. Falling rates meant that fewer voters were

39 Fraser, *Urban politics*, 62–3.
40 David Eastwood, *Governing rural England: tradition and transformation in local government, 1780–1840*, Oxford 1994, 181.
41 4 and 5 Will. IV c. 76.
42 V. D. Lipman, *Local government areas, 1834–1945*, Oxford 1949, 42–3.
43 PP 1841 (33) xxi. 89.
44 PP 1839 (562) xliv. 4–7.

disfranchised for being in arrears, and that some poorer householders were encouraged into the electoral process for the first time as 'new' voters. The New Poor Law also helped to standardise (as well as to reduce) the cost of enfranchisement. Before 1834 no uniform method of assessing and levying rates existed. Each parish worked its own formulae, and it was even possible for households of the same rental value within the same parish to pay different amounts.[45] Although parishes were not automatically re-rated after being unionised, the New Poor Law encouraged the adoption of far more uniform rating procedures by directing the guardians 'to make a fair and just assessment'.[46] This process was further confirmed and consolidated by the Parochial Assessments Act of 1836, which established a standard structure of rating for the first time, allowing new surveys and valuations to be made on direct application to the poor law commissioners.[47]

The extent to which the new system was adopted by parishes in parliamentary boroughs was impressive. A list of English boroughs, and the date at which their constituent parishes became part of a union, is given in appendix 4. By 1841 nearly three-quarters of the 188 English boroughs contained parishes acting under the direct orders of the commissioners.[48] In the remaining fifty-two, measures to reduce the burden of the poor rates had already been introduced before 1834, usually by forming a self-governing union under a local act of incorporation or under Gilbert's Act of 1782.[49] Although effectively exempt from the provisions of the New Poor Law, these parishes were nevertheless often singled out by the commissioners as models of administrative efficiency.[50] Except, therefore, for a very small number of single parishes which were 'stranded' in the middle of local act unions and unable to combine with neighbouring parishes, the administration of poor relief had been substantially remodelled and the cost of poor relief and the parliamentary vote significantly reduced across a broad spectrum of English

---

45 On inequitable rating see Edwin Cannan, A history of local rates in England, London 1912, 79.

46 4 and 5 Will. IV c. 76, 712, clause 35.

47 6 and 7 Will. IV c. 96.

48 In 1841, 52 borough constituencies contained parishes still operating under local acts, known as incorporations of the poor. For the parochial composition of each borough constituency, and the dates of parochial assimilation to a poor law union, see Frederic A. Youngs, Jr, Guide to the local administrative units of England, I: Southern England, London 1979; II: Northern England, London 1991. For details of incorporations and Gilbert's Act unions see PP 1844 (578) xl. 333–4; PP 1842 (156) xxxv. 40–3; PP 1841 (211) xxi. 17–22.

49 By 1834 there were only 67 Gilbert Act unions: Keith-Lucas, Local government franchise, 21 n. 5. A decade later there were just 17. Only one, Arundel, was in a parliamentary borough – the rest were in county constituencies, most notably the West Riding of Yorkshire and North Hampshire: PP 1844 (578) xl. 333–4.

50 The system adopted at Manchester, for instance, received praise: E. C. Midwinter, Social administration in Lancashire, 1830–1860: poor law, public health and police, Manchester 1969, 13.

boroughs by 1841. This alone suggests an important electoral dimension to the nineteenth-century reform of poor law administration, which has not received the attention it deserves.

Capturing control of the rates

The poor law has emerged as a central political institution in many studies of local party development during this period, most notably in the strangely unsung work of Derek Fraser.[51] All the evidence suggests that poor law and parish vestry elections became quickly integrated into broader battles for political control, helping to intensify and stabilise partisan patterns of political behaviour at constituency level. Preston's new Operative Conservative Association, for example, attached almost as much weight to 'gaining a majority on the local board of guardians' as they did to their municipal and parliamentary activities.[52] The Bradford Operative Conservative Society, which had been established in August 1837, played a major role in securing the election of exclusively Tory guardians until 1844. The importance they attached to these positions is clearly revealed by their surviving minute book. On the eve of a typical election, 'the president, treasurer and secretary impressed upon the meeting the necessity of every member using his influence in the ensuing election of poor law guardians to secure the return of fit and proper persons of Conservative principles'.[53]

Winning seats on the new and highly publicised unions served as an important preliminary goal for a minority party anxious to improve its partisan profile. It was a particularly effective way of undermining any local political ascendancy, especially in constituencies where the prospect of parliamentary or municipal successes seemed remote. In Clitheroe, for example, the parliamentary and municipal dominance of the Liberal party was seriously disturbed by the Tories' capture of the union in 1837. Building on their new authority and partisan presence, the town's Tories launched a successful election petition against the return of the Liberal MP, Matthew Wilson, at the 1841 general election.[54] Once in charge, a local party could also reward its friends and followers with the paid positions of clerk, treasurer and relieving officer.[55] There was a lot more attached to these positions than patronage and public profile alone. Manchester's voters had an early taste of the electoral influence possessed by their poor law administrators in 1833, when 245 of them were disfranchised after 'a new poor rate was made a few

---

[51] D. Fraser, 'The poor law as a political institution', in Fraser, New Poor Law, 111–27, and Urban politics, 25–90.
[52] See Walsh, 'Working class political integration', 413.
[53] 'Bradford Operative Conservative Society minute book', DB4 no. 3, fos 2, 40.
[54] See Walsh, 'Working class political integration', 294–5.
[55] First annual report of the poor law commissioners, London 1835, 81.

weeks before 5 April, and many persons had not paid it at the time the lists were made out'.[56] In neighbouring Salford, almost a decade later, a Liberal board of guardians repeatedly delayed the levy of a rate in order to prevent the disfranchisement of their own supporters.[57] Similar activities occurred at the Leicester Union, where it was reported that 'not a single question was mooted which was not made a political one', and the Tories, who had quickly captured control, were 'able until 1845 to use its authority to partisan ends'.[58]

The most advantageous electoral function of the poor law, however, remained under the control of the parish, thus helping to prolong its administrative significance beyond 1834. This was the business of rate collection, which on the whole continued to be performed by parish officers serving as assistant overseers, rate collectors or churchwardens.[59] Their most straightforward tactics involved failing to collect the full amount and creating small arrears. This occurred at Cheltenham in 1841, when an assistant overseer, who was also the brother of the Liberal party agent, collected the rates so as to favour Liberal voters.[60] A more sophisticated ruse was employed by the Conservatives at Bristol, where it emerged that the 'churchwardens, who are the chairmen of the Tory committee, appoint the collectors, and the collectors have immense power in influencing the registration. They may receive [the poor rate] without the shilling and disfranchise by that means'.[61] Disfranchised voters might become wise to certain tactics and take suitable precautions, but as the *Manchester Guardian* observed, by 'a hundred tricks of the tax collectors the payment might be most innocently and unavoidably . . . delayed'.[62] Salford's assistant overseer, for example, was discovered to have pre-dated the receipt of rates in order to prevent the disqualification of many Tories, while ensuring that Liberal voters in the same position were struck off, an abuse which led to his dismissal by the poor law commissioners for 'fraud upon the franchise of the duly qualified rate payers'.[63]

---

56 *Manchester Herald*, 2 Oct. 1833.

57 Fraser, *Urban politics*, 88, and 'The poor law as a political institution', 125.

58 *Leicester Chronicle*, 18 May 1839, cited in A. Temple Patterson, *Radical Leicester: a history of Leicester, 1780–1850*, Leicester 1954, 226; Radice, 'Identification, interests and influence', 254.

59 The guardians could appoint their own collectors directly on application to the commissioners: W. Cunningham Glen, *The general consolidated and other orders of the poor law commissioners*, London 1871, 207, 448. This happened at the Bolton Union in Lancashire, for example, but in most places, including the neighbouring unions of Clitheroe, Burnley, Blackburn, Haslingden and Bury, assistant overseers continued to be appointed by the magistrates on the recommendation of the parish vestry: R. Boyson, 'The history of poor law administration in north east Lancashire, 1834–1871', unpubl. MA diss. Manchester 1960, 132–5. Fraser *Urban politics*, 65–9, provides some interesting accounts of conflicts between unions and vestries over the appointment of rival rate collectors.

60 *Cheltenham Examiner*, 20 Oct. 1841, cited in Courtenay, 'Cheltenham', 106.

61 PP 1835 (547) viii. 395, minute 6553. The 'shilling' refers to the registration fee.

62 *Manchester Guardian*, 18 Oct. 1834; *The Times*, 16 Oct. 1834.

63 Fraser, *Urban politics*, 66, 86–8.

The most celebrated case, which was brought before the Commons by Duncombe, involved the rate collectors of the metropolitan boroughs, who were accused of repeatedly tricking their opponents into not paying their taxes in order to disfranchise them.[64] At the City revision of 1833, for example, it transpired that the officers of St Bride had deliberately failed to collect the full rate from certain persons.[65] The following year 'very many solvent persons were disqualified' in Westminster and Lambeth owing to 'the collectors not calling, and the matter escaping the notice of the persons rated'.[66] The potential for abuse was particularly rife in the metropolis because of its traditional use of 'antedated receipts for rates', whereby 'a nominal instead of a legal title to the franchise was created'.[67] As Francis Place explained to Brougham:

> It has not been a regular custom to collect the rates due 5 April before 20 July in any year, and as the rate and tax collectors may or may not collect the whole of the rates and taxes due before the 20 July, they may disfranchise whom they please. They may also put down whom they please as qualified as £10 house-holders, or as scot and lot voters, and they have done so to a great extent.[68]

What Charles Tennyson had failed to foresee in 1831 was soon brought home to him during his preliminary canvass of Lambeth at the general election of 1835. Responding to Tennyson's request for support, one disgruntled elector spoke for many when he complained 'that my servant and next door neighbour Henry Sarcel, have lost the right of voting owing to the neglect of the collector of poor taxes, which as I have been informed, has been the case with many other persons'.[69]

The politicisation of the parish

With parish officers possessing so much potential influence over the borough franchise, it is not surprising that their election or appointment often became contested and highly partisan. The vibrancy and dynamism of parish politics is well attested in this period, and of course many urban vestries created their own peculiar conflicts and disputes. The problem for the psephologist lies in distinguishing between contests generated by parish pump or poor law issues, and those reflecting a broader partisan perspective, triggered by an intrusion of parliamentary electioneering activity at the parochial level. With rate

---

64 *Hansard*, 3rd ser. xxxii. 1170; *The Times*, 7, 22 Oct. 1834.
65 *The Times*, 5 Oct. 1833.
66 Ibid. 7, 22 Oct. 1834. The metropolitan borough of Lambeth comprised the parishes of Lambeth, Camberwell and Newington.
67 Ibid. 25 Sept. 1835.
68 Place to Brougham, 5 Apr. 1837, Place MS Add. 35150, fo. 252r.
69 Slade to Tennyson, 29 Dec. 1834, LAD iv/3/66.

collection having such a large bearing upon the parliamentary franchise, it must be wondered to what extent parish polls became infected by an increasingly parliamentary, rather than local, partisan perspective. Contemporary press reports readily projected party labels on to parochial candidates, but how accurately did this partisanship reflect and correspond with the type of party-based attachments being exhibited in national contests?

One of the most intriguing discoveries to emerge from 'longitudinal' studies of elections held in the 1830s has been the extent to which voters began to exhibit the same partisan choices in both national and local contests. Recent research on municipal polls in particular, has revealed that in direct contrast to the experience of other periods, the nationally-oriented voting behaviour elicited in the election of MPs was quickly reproduced at a local level in the selection of new town councillors.[70] Contrary to most expectations, voters behaved almost identically at both types of election. Unfortunately, official pollbooks for parish and vestry contests simply do not exist, at least not in the same way as those compiled for parliamentary and municipal purposes. Solicitors' polling records, however, can provide a tantalising glimpse into the way voters responded in parish and parliamentary contests.

At Lichfield, for example, the polling returns of Messrs Hinckley, Birch and Exham, who acted as Conservative agents for the Dyott family, reveal a very strong correlation between the partisanship exhibited at a poll for an assistant overseer, held in the parish of St Chad on 18 and 19 May 1843, and voting at the 1841 general election. Of the 154 voters who participated in both these contests, an impressive 140 (91 per cent) polled at the parish level precisely as they had done in the parliamentary election, by reproducing their previous partisan allegiance.[71] Looking at the persistence of support separately, sixty-nine voters out of a possible seventy-seven (90 per cent) followed up a partisan 'plump' for the single Tory parliamentary candidate, Richard Dyott, by voting for the Tory assistant overseer, Hitchins. On the Liberal side, seventy-one electors out of a possible seventy-seven (92 per cent) repeated their partisan preference for two Liberal MPs by voting for Gorton, the Liberal poor law candidate. Although the 154 'experienced' parliamentary voters only accounted for two-fifths (42 per cent) of the entire parochial

70 Salmon, 'Local politics and partisanship', 357–76; John A. Phillips, 'Unintended consequences: parliamentary blueprints in the hands of provincial builders', in David Dean and Clyve Jones (eds), *Parliament and locality, 1660–1939*, Edinburgh 1998, 92–105; John A. Phillips and Charles Wetherell, 'Parliamentary parties and municipal politics: 1835 and the party system', in John A. Phillips (ed.), *Computing parliamentary history: George III to Victoria*, Edinburgh 1994, 48–85.
71 This analysis is based upon the polling returns for 'Booth No. 3 St. Chad and the Close, 1 July 1841', and 'Assistant Overseer's Poll, St. Chad, 18–19 May 1843', Lichfield Joint RO, Messrs Hinckley, Birch and Exham D15/4/11/6, 9. A more detailed account of the methodology used to calculate the persistence of partisanship across these types of election can be found in Salmon, 'Local politics and partisanship', 359–62. See also ch. 7 below.

turnout of 371 electors, the Sturges Bourne multiple voting system boosted their electoral power by a further 20 per cent, giving them 'actual' control of 184 votes.[72] Their near dominance at this poor law contest was only prevented by the presence of twenty-five wealthy female electors, such as Grace Brown of Sandford Street, who possessed four votes. Without these women, whose allegiance was split pretty evenly between the parties, almost half the votes cast at this parish poll would simply have amounted to a repeat performance of an earlier parliamentary preference. Viewed from the perspective of this overseer's contest, which is one of a very limited number where a direct comparison between parochial and parliamentary voting behaviour can be made, parish elections appear to have been no less immune to the intrusion of nationally-oriented partisanship than other types of provincial poll during this period.

The voting system adopted for the election of guardians introduced yet another dynamic into the politicisation of parish affairs. By extending the system of plural voting already in use in some of the larger parishes under Sturges Bourne's Act of 1818 and introducing a special scale for owners, even if they were non-resident, these elections acted as an important catalyst in the process of parochial politicisation.[73] Their complex electoral procedures meant that parish polling became inherently more formal and intrinsically more political, if only because a simple show of hands at a vestry meeting no longer sufficed. Contemporary critics like Joshua Toulmin Smith even argued that the proper discussion of parochial affairs declined as the formal mechanism of the poll and the party campaign took over.[74] The potential for abuse of the system was considerable and acted as an open invitation to many local political activists, especially in the larger towns. The irony here was that the electoral procedures of the New Poor Law actually encouraged the very scenario they were intended to prevent:

> for the purpose of enabling each rate payer to vote in the most free and deliberate manner, and, as far as may be, without solicitations or canvassing, and without the loss of his time, or the obstruction of his business . . . the voting paper is directed to be left at the voter's place of abode . . . and collected.[75]

These instructions made fraud and forgery easy. At Bodicote, for example, in the Banbury Poor Law Union, guardians' elections were described by one embittered candidate as 'a complete farce', with the use of fraudulent voting

---

[72] The 1818 Sturges Bourne Act gave additional votes to wealthy ratepayers for each extra £25 of rateable value up to a maximum of 6 votes: Eastwood, *Governing rural England*, 130–1; K. B. Smellie, *A history of local government*, London 1963, 13.

[73] Owners acquired an extra vote for each additional £25 of rateable value above £50, up to a maximum of 6 votes. Rate-payers assessed above £200 gained a second vote, and above £400 a third: 4 and 5 Will. IV c. 76, 714, clause 40; PP 1841 (33) xxi. 61.

[74] Joshua Toulmin Smith, *The parish: its obligations and powers: its officers and their duties*, London 1854, 50–1.

[75] PP 1841 (33) xxi. 59.

papers and the wholesale manipulation of the multiple voting system by the Tory candidate and partisan poor law officials.[76] In Honley, in Huddersfield Union, the magistrates convicted the parish overseers for receiving and rejecting votes 'without any legal grounds for the same', during the guardians' elections of 1838. Similar practices at Kensington left the union 'without any elected guardians for two or three weeks, owing to the length of time required to examine into the validity of the very numerous disputed votes'.[77] Voting by proxy, for owners and rate-payers, broadened the scope for chicanery still further.[78] False proxies were notoriously difficult to detect and might even swing an election.[79] Considerable political power was transferred to those entrusted with their exercise, usually local rent collectors and land agents. Duncombe, for example, asserted that in Gravesend 'the proxies held by two rent-collectors alone decided the election of the majority of Poor Law Guardians'.[80] In Chelsea, it was reported that one agent possessed no fewer than 833.[81]

The full extent of electoral malpractice, however, is difficult to assess because the poor law commissioners had a vested interest in protecting the system from criticism. Edwin Chadwick, the commission's secretary, was also its chief architect and a firm advocate of its extension to parliamentary elections. The *First annual report of the poor law commissioners* lavished praise on the system and no serious examination took place until the poor law board replaced the commission.[82] Its investigations painted a rather different picture. In Leeds, for example, an 1852 inquiry discovered that 'voting papers had been partially distributed; they had been altered; they had been destroyed; they had been filled up by Tory party agents'.[83] At a Nottingham election, it was observed that 100 voting papers were stolen and then returned, all completed, in the same handwriting.[84] The clerk's role, in particular, in running the election of the guardians, who were his direct employers and paymasters, was criticised as 'pregnant with mischief and jobbing of the very worst kind'.[85] As Toulmin Smith put it:

> The whole thing is but a hollow sham . . . the entire control of the whole elections . . . is put in the hands of the clerk, who admits or rejects what votes he thinks proper . . . and has every other facility given him for falsifying the

76 John Wilson, An account of . . . the election of a guardian for the township of Boddicot [Bodicote], Banbury 1840, 8–17, 20. See also PP 1835 (547) viii. 430 for similar practices.
77 Wilson, Election of a guardian, 17, 25.
78 4 and 5 Will. IV c. 76, 714, clause 40; PP 1841 (33) xxi. 61.
79 See, for example, Patterson, Radical Leicester, 226.
80 Hansard, 3rd ser. lxxvi. 444.
81 Report of commissioners on continuance of the commission, London 1840, 42.
82 First annual report, passim.
83 Fraser, Urban politics, 59.
84 PP 1878 (297) xvii. 344, minute 1019.
85 Wilson, Election of a guardian, 27.

so-called elections. The votes are given by voting papers, sent round by him, collected by him, and examined and allowed by him; and he alone declares the poll.[86]

Of course not all guardians were elected. Roughly one-fifth of each board was composed of local magistrates serving as unelected *ex-officio* guardians.[87] This too, however, tended to amplify rather than to restrict the potential for conflict at the parochial level.[88] Their appointment by the lord lieutenant was important because, as the premier Lord Melbourne himself put it, 'in some counties he has election interests to serve and nominates none but persons of his own interest'.[89] Potential partisan divisions were therefore endemic within many boards of guardians, especially since criticism of over-worked local magistrates had featured heavily in the campaign to reform the system of poor relief in the first place. Tensions between elected and unelected guardians were common. Magistrates were viewed as representatives of the landed class and the Established Church, from whom they were largely drawn.[90] This often contrasted strongly with the social background, politics and religious denomination of many urban elected guardians in the boroughs. As Nassau Senior suggested, after 1834 magistrates were 'either excluded from influence in the management of their own parishes, or forced to accept a seat in the board of guardians and to debate and vote among shop-keepers and farmers'.[91]

The electoral dynamics of the New Poor Law not only helped to fuel political tensions at the local administrative level and infuse parish affairs with an increasingly sophisticated partisan agenda, but the extra-parochial structure of the new unions also physically broadened their psephological impact. Political conflicts, which had previously been confined to a single parish or town, now expanded into surrounding areas. The average number of parishes in each of the unions formed in 1835 and 1836 was eighteen.[92] Many of these were situated around the nucleus of a local market town, this being consid-

---

[86] Smith, *Parish*, 143–6.

[87] See 4 and 5 Will. IV c. 76, 713, clause 39.

[88] In rural areas, however, it has been suggested that the magistracy's role as *ex-officio* guardians bolstered the political authority of traditional landed elites, encouraging cohesion rather than conflict: Anthony Brundage, 'The landed interest and the New Poor Law: a reappraisal of the revolution in government', *EHR* lxxxvii (1972), 27–48, and *The making of the New Poor Law: the politics of inquiry, enactment and implementation, 1832–39*, London 1978, 105–79. This view has not been without its critics: P. Dunkley, 'The landed interest and the New Poor Law: a critical note', *EHR* lxxxviii (1973), 836–41; David Eastwood, 'The making of the New Poor Law redivivus: debate', *Past and Present* cxxvii (1990), 184–94.

[89] Torrens, *Memoirs of Viscount Melbourne*, i. 177.

[90] On public perception of the magistracy during this period see Eastwood, *Governing rural England*, 46–55, 76–95.

[91] M. C. M. Simpson (ed.), *Correspondence and conversations of Alexis de Tocqueville with Nassau William Senior from 1834 to 1859*, London 1872, i. 204.

[92] Lipman, *Local government areas*, 42–3.

ered the ideal type of union by the commissioners.[93] The vestry politics of the larger towns, in particular, were therefore extended as opponents sought to win control of the guardians' elections in neighbouring parishes. Only four of the twenty parishes in the Bradford Union, for example, were within the boundaries of the parliamentary borough.[94] The remaining sixteen parishes were part of the West Riding constituency, but their capture was equally important in terms of winning control over rating and gaining influence over the borough's registration. During the guardians' elections of 1839, the Bradford Conservative Society took their electioneering activities well beyond the borough boundaries into the surrounding parishes of the union, establishing 'a canvassing committee of Operatives to act . . . in conjunction with the Conservative Society'.[95] The physical parameters of local party conflict were thus enlarged; poor law and parish elections became an integral part of a distinctly reformed political culture, and the board of guardians a highly political institution. As Edward Littleton noted in his diary: 'attended the board of guardians . . . we could not keep off politics'.[96]

Rates, registration and ancient-rights

After 1832 the electoral influence of poor law and parish officers was not just confined to the rate-dependent franchises. Control over finance and the provision of poor relief also provided them with a more general form of electoral power. In Banbury, for example, the guardians refused to supply cheap coal from the 'coal fund' to their political opponents.[97] Even more crucially, however, these officers legally determined who was in receipt of 'parochial relief or other alms', which under clause 36 of the Reform Act automatically prevented an elector from voting.[98] Relief covered a wide range of assistance. Overseers, for example, were advised that voters became 'disqualified when the parish surgeon attended them whilst sick', or visited 'their wife during her confinement'. Others lost their votes for 'employment by the parish in labour, at an inferior rate of wages to what would be given by individuals'.[99] At Newport one George Wills was 'expunged' from the 1832 register because 'his son was employed in the house of industry (poor house) shaving a hundred men a week'.[100] The relief clause was particularly significant in towns where there were a large number of freemen and other ancient-right voters, whose electoral rights were not dependent upon prompt rate payment or the 1s.

93 See Anne Digby, 'The rural poor law', in Fraser, New Poor Law, 149.
94 See Youngs, Local administrative units, ii. 775, 848.
95 'Bradford Operative Conservative Society minute book', DB4 no. 3, fos 38v, 40r.
96 Diary entry, 7 Aug. 1837, Hatherton MSS D1178/1.
97 See Wilson, Election of a guardian, 9.
98 2 Will. IV c. 45, 731, clause 36.
99 Cooke, Plain instructions for overseers, 41–2.
100 Manning, Courts of revision, 69.

registration fee. It was generally this group of electors who were the most willing to sell their votes to the highest bidder. But it was also this group, rather than the more prosperous £10 householders, who were more likely to apply for parish relief. The scale of potential disfranchisement was often large. In 1833, for example, Sir Richard Vyvyan's agent at Bristol reported that the Liberals were planning to object to 'nearly two hundred freemen receiving parish relief' who had supported the Tories at the previous election.[101] Boroughs like Preston, where there was an inhabitants-at-large qualification, were peculiarly susceptible to large-scale voter impoverishment. In 1832, for example, only 11 per cent (675) of its 6,291 ancient-right voters were rated at £10 annual value or above.[102]

Local party agents and activists eagerly sought information about who was in receipt of relief. After the 1835 Peterborough election, for instance, the firm of Messrs Atkinson and Lawrence was engaged to 'superintend the business of registration' on behalf of the two successful Whig candidates. According to their surviving committee book, they were immediately 'instructed to obtain the names of all scot and lot voters who have received parish relief with a view of objecting to the claims of such as are not likely to vote in the Liberal interest'.[103] It was equally important to ensure that the claims of any supporters who had been disqualified were properly renewed the following year. Because disqualification was for relief received during a twelve-month period before the last day of July – which then disfranchised the voter for a whole year from the ensuing November – over two years could elapse before a voter might realise that he had been excluded from the next electoral register.[104] Under these circumstances, and in the inevitable lull between elections, the perspicuity of a local party agent was often crucial in ensuring that a fresh claim was made on the voter's behalf, at the correct time. In a typical case at Cirencester, the Conservative agents Messrs Mulling and Ellett took it upon themselves to claim on behalf of a disqualified voter who, as their notes remarked, had been

> sent to North Leach House of Correction on the 5th July 1837, remained there until the 19th (14 days). Children lived in the House during his absence and once or twice received relief from the parish. Has not had relief within 12 calendar months proceeding [sic.] the last day of July 1838.[105]

Ancient-right voters were therefore not immune from the control exercised by poor law administrators. Neither were they unaffected by the rate-paying clauses. The costs associated with a household vote had a significant

101 Bush to Vyvyan, 19 Sept. 1833, Vyvyan MSS DDV/BO/61/55.
102 1832 Preston pollbook, LRO, PO4/AO2.
103 'Minute book of Whig committee for Sir Robert Heron and J. N. Fazakerley', Fitzwilliam MSS Fitz. misc. vol. 503, entry for 'Tues., October 1835'.
104 2 Will. IV c. 45, 731, clause 33.
105 GRO, Messrs Mulling, Ellett and Co. D1388/box 107.

'knock-on' effect on the popularity of the pre-Reform voting qualifications, whose continuance after 1832 has been one of the most misunderstood provisions of the Reform Act. The number of ancient-right voters did not decline steadily after Reform. On the contrary, in some boroughs their numbers dramatically increased. In Taunton, for example, 361 potwallers and 588 £10 householders were registered in 1832.[106] Two years later, however, the number of potwallers had jumped to 574 (a rise of 59 per cent), while the number of householders remained almost unchanged at 619 (an increase of 5 per cent).[107] This was no isolated incident. Two distinct factors helped to prolong and even proliferate pre-Reform voting qualifications after 1832.

First, many of those who qualified both as £10 householders and as ancient-right voters increasingly opted for the latter, especially where this avoided prompt payment of rates in addition to the unpopular registration fee.[108] In the more prosperous ancient boroughs, large numbers of electors were often able to choose between these different types of qualification. In Durham, for example, 31 per cent of the electorate had multiple votes in 1832.[109] Early electoral registers were often riddled with doubly or even triply qualified voters, especially in boroughs with their own county status and an additional 40s. freeholder qualification, such as Tewkesbury.[110] These multiple qualifications inflated the size of initial electorates by an estimated 10 to 20 per cent, and caused all sorts of problems for the overseers and town clerks charged with drawing up the lists.[111] A particularly vexed question arose over the liability for the registration fee of those ancient-right voters who were also assessed to the poor rate, with which the 1s. was now included. Lord John Russell, responding to a query from a bemused overseer at Stafford, considered that 'overseers ought to collect from every freeman rated to the relief of the poor, but they cannot collect from those who are not rated'.[112] As with so much of the Reform Act, however, the intention of the legislators did not translate into electoral reality. In practice, many revising barristers agreed with the freemen's notion that 'they need not pay their registration fee'.[113] In one typical dispute over this issue in Exeter, the assistant overseer of the

---

106 A potwaller or potwalloper was the occupier of a room with a fireplace suitable for cooking, and in practice included all inhabitant residents, householders or lodgers, who boiled their own pots.
107 Taunton electoral registers, SoRO, DD/SAS/TN 14, C/795.
108 An elector, of course, could only vote once in any particular contest, irrespective of how many times he was qualified.
109 Radice, 'Identification, interests and influence', 31. See also Taylor, 'Interests, parties and the state', 58–9, for incidents of multiple votes in other boroughs.
110 PP 1837–8 (329) xliv. 639.
111 See ch. 1 above and also the comments of the returning officers in PP 1833 (189) xxvii. 111–249; PP 1837–8 (329) xliv. 553–858.
112 Russell to Thomas Frith, 28 Oct. 1833, Staffordshire Mercury, 2 Nov. 1833.
113 Manchester Guardian, 10 Oct. 1835.

parish of Heavitree threatened to disqualify an ancient-right voter for refusing to pay the 1s. Atypically, the elector's reply has survived:

> I have been registered as an occupier of a house in the circus and been assessed one shilling to the poor rate and paid it. I have also been registered as a freeman. The magistrates have determined, that no freemen can be called upon for the shilling. If you look at the Reform Act you will see that the overseers can *only* call upon *occupiers* in *their parish* for the shilling, and that the only mode of recovering it, is by inserting it in the *poor rate*, and no person but an occupier can be assessed in a poor rate. If I was obliged to pay for unnecessary registering in every parish in which I had property, my vote would be rather a dear one.[114]

Freedom from rating requirements and the registration fee not only encouraged many voters to seize and maintain their ancient-right qualifications. Second, and far more important, it enhanced the popularity of qualifying for the first time as a freeman voter *after* 1832. One of the most common misreadings of the Reform Act has been that it curtailed the freeman franchise to the existing holders only. One recent account, for example, following many previous writers, has stated 'that only those freemen who possessed the vote in 1832 could continue to exercise the vote during their lifetime'.[115] But the Reform Act itself deliberately exempted resident freemen made 'in respect of birth and servitude' from its provisions, and only abolished the voting rights of all non-resident freemen, and 'future honorary freemen' or 'freemen by marriage'.[116] As an 1835 overseer's manual explained, all freemen 'must have been entitled to vote on the 1st March 1831, or have acquired their right since, by birth or servitude, derived from or through a party entitled on the 1st March'.[117] It was this that allowed for subsequent increases in the number of freemen in many boroughs, and created the widely remarked upon long-term stability of this franchise.[118] In Durham, for example, the freeman vote grew from a registered total of 492 in 1832 to 558 in 1837.[119] Grimsby's 'freemen continued to be a force to be reckoned with until well beyond the middle of the century'.[120] Canterbury's corporation records, in line with many others, reveal a substantial number of freeman admissions

---

114 R. C. Campion to John Kew, 1835, DRO, Heavitree (Exeter) parish records, 3004A/PD4.
115 Taylor, 'Interests, parties and the state', 55.
116 2 Will. IV c. 45, 730, clause 32; 5 and 6 Will. IV c. 76, 1014, clauses 4, 5; Russell, *A treatise on the Reform Act*, 43; Rogers, *Parliamentary Reform Act*, 39; Price, *Complete election guide*, pp. xxi–xxiii; Seymour, *Electoral reform*, 28–9.
117 Cooke, *Plain instructions for overseers*, 70–1.
118 See Taylor, 'Interests, parties and the state', 58.
119 1832 Durham pollbook, DuRO, D/X 212/5; PP 1837–8 (329) xliv. 835.
120 Cooper, 'Electoral politics in Grimsby', 269.

after 1832.[121] An analysis of individual registers confirms that increases in the electorate during the 1830s, including the dramatic rise of 1835, were rarely confined to the householders alone. Where electoral recruitment occurred, it tended to embrace all qualifications. In Shrewsbury, for example, the electorate increased as a whole in 1835, and not just in one of its constituent parts. In 1833, 691 (45 per cent) of the 1,539 electors were registered as freemen. Despite a massive 16 per cent increase in the size of Shrewsbury's electorate at the 1835 revision, their proportion remained identical with 797 freemen (45 per cent) on the 1835–6 register of 1,786 electors.[122]

The Municipal Corporations Act of 1835 actually facilitated this expansion of the freeman franchise by sweeping away the old corporations, many of which had kept a tight rein on their freeman admissions for party or religious purposes. The Tory corporations of Evesham, Worcester, Northampton and Leicester, for example, had deliberately excluded Dissenters from their freeman rolls.[123] Municipal reform transferred responsibility both for the present freemen, and all those who 'might hereafter have acquired, in respect of birth or servitude . . . the right of voting', to the new elected town councils, releasing this franchise from the earlier restrictions that had been imposed by the old corporations.[124] And although freemen were charged for their admission, fees being fixed by 55 Geo. III. c. 184 at a minimum of £1, this was often far cheaper and more convenient than the combined burden of prompt rate payment and the 1s. registration fee required for the new household franchise.[125] There were other potential financial dividends too. In Leicester, for example, where the cost of admission was £1 9s., keeping 'descriptions of houses' below £10 annual value avoided assessment for the local window and house tax.[126] Moreover, candidates and their agents frequently offered to pay the costs of admission on the freeman's behalf, in the hope of creating votes in their favour. At Maldon, for example, the Liberal agent reported 'it to be the constant practice for the candidate, or his agent, to pay the expense of the admission'.[127] In Kingston-upon-Hull, the secretary of the Conservative Association, Samuel Brown, 'paid for the freedoms to be taken up on behalf of the Blues in 1839 and 1840'.[128] A successful campaign to create freemen votes might even prove to be of decisive importance at the annual registration contest. In an 1838 report sent to Bonham, for instance, Sir James Graham reported that:

---

[121] See Stella Corpe and Anne Oakley (eds), *The freemen of Canterbury, 1800–35, compiled from Canterbury city archives*, Canterbury 1990.
[122] Shrewsbury Local Studies Library, D55–7, Acc. 295.
[123] PP 1835 (116) xxiii. 190–1, 289–91; Owen Chadwick, *The Victorian Church*, London 1966, i. 108.
[124] 5 and 6 Will. IV c. 76, 1014, clause 4.
[125] Cooke, *Plain instructions to overseers*, 72.
[126] PP 1835 (547) viii. 129–37, minutes 2207, 2381–4.
[127] Ibid. 35, minute 514.
[128] PP 1854 (1703) xxii. 8.

in East Cumberland we shall have gained about 50, and at Carlisle about 20: but we were not able to make 75 Freemen at the latter place in time to come on the register of this year: but they are ripe and sure for next year; and when they shall have been made, they will almost turn the scale and place the 2 seats for Carlisle within our reach.[129]

The practice of paying for admission was in general carried out far more systematically by the Tories than by the Liberals, but these payments provided no guarantee of a freeman's electoral loyalty. The type of partisanship engendered by payment alone was unstable, impermanent and could easily backfire. In April 1835, for example, Coventry's Conservatives launched a special campaign 'to assist those friends, of Conservative principles, who have not the means to take up the freedom of the city'. Some of the freemen they created, however, then offered their support to the Liberals, on condition of further payment.[130] Any automatic presumption of a freeman's compliance was also liable to incur hostility, and generate even greater expense. In Durham, for example, Lord Londonderry's influence relied heavily on the support of those freeman voters whose admissions he had funded. In 1841, however, he forced a second Conservative candidate, Sheppard, to retire and as a result the Radical candidate was returned unopposed, alongside Londonderry's Tory nominee and nephew, Captain Fitzroy. Londonderry's actions provoked outrage, forcing his agent to spend over £1,500, which was 'absolutely necessary in order to counteract the strong feeling excited against your lordship and Captain Fitzroy amongst the freemen'.[131]

Partisan payment of admission costs was clearly an imperfect mechanism of local electoral control. Where it operated, however, it made access to the freeman franchise even easier and cheaper. Given the choice, most electors opted for less expensive forms of political participation, some even preferring to sell their vote rather than pay for their electoral independence. The frequently misunderstood continuity of ancient-right qualifications after 1832 had two important consequences for the operation of the reformed electoral system as a whole. First, it meant that the politics of venality and financial negotiation traditionally associated with the freeman voters remained a central feature of some borough contests, undermining purely partisan, issue-based patterns of electoral behaviour. Second, the sustained numerical significance of the freeman franchise meant that any collective shift in partisanship among the freemen voters was likely to have an important, even decisive, electoral impact. It was in this context that the original municipal

---

129 Graham to Bonham, 16 Oct. 1838, Peel MS Add. 40616, fos 17v–18r.
130 See PP 1835 (547) viii. 64–5, minutes 1075–80.
131 Thomas Maynard to Londonderry, 24 June, 5 Aug. 1841, Londonderry MSS D/Lo/C132 (2) fos 9, 12. For an alternative account of this election see Radice, 'Interests, influence and independence', 366–8.

reform bill, with its attempt to abolish the freeman franchise, was to prove so disastrous for the Liberals, alienating an entire group of electors and encouraging them to become firm Tory partisans.[132]

Rates and religion

One final political link between rating and voting needs to be considered. As well as lowering the cost of electoral participation for many householders, the rating provisions of the New Poor Law inflamed sectarian tensions between the Established Church and the Nonconformist community, which were already being exacerbated at a local level through the mechanics of partisan registration activity.[133] Under the New Poor Law, church rates were prevented from being included or 'compounded' with the poor rates – a common practice which had lent a highly inflammatory dimension to the acquisition of voting rights in the initial years of registration. This not only affected parishes in borough constituencies, where possession of the parliamentary franchise was dependent upon the prompt payment of all poor rates, but applied to all parishes equally. As the National, Municipal and Parochial Register of July 1835 explained, 'when a union is formed for making one common rate for the relief of the poor, it becomes a rate distinct from all other local assessments'.[134] The implications of this reform were spelt out in 1839 in an official return on local taxation:

> the sum requisite for church rate expenditure was usually paid over from the poor rate to the church-wardens; thereby avoiding the useless difficulty of assessment of a fraction of a penny on the pound, and the labour of collecting sums too small for regular accompt; but since the Poor Law Amendment Act ... this convenient practice cannot be permitted; and a church rate more than sufficient for one year must be imposed, and the surplus carried to accompt.[135]

Church rates were thus a far more obvious and visible tax after 1834. The rating requirements of the New Poor Law lent prominence and practical fiscal substance to what has recently been described as 'the greatest Dissenting grievance'.[136] In many towns, such as Leeds, Manchester, Birmingham, Nottingham and Leicester, the issue of church rates was already highly controversial. The annual elections for the positions of churchwarden, for instance, had become heavily politicised as Dissenters sought to capture control and obstruct the levy of a church rate.[137] On the Anglican side,

---

132 See ch. 7 below, and Salmon, 'Local politics and partisanship', 372–4.
133 See ch. 1 above.
134 The National, Municipal and Parochial Register i (July 1835), 89.
135 PP 1839 (562) xliv. 48.
136 Ellens, Church rate conflict, 1.
137 See Fraser, Urban politics, 31–54.

reliance on church rate income was also considerable, accounting 'for as much as 12 per cent of the total revenues of the Church'.[138] Compounding had helped obscure and minimise the financial burden of the church rate. On the eve of the 1832 Reform Act, for example, some 10 per cent (£41,489) of all church rate income was being quietly 'paid over' in this way.[139] The collection of a separate and 'sufficient' rate, however, created an extra, and in some places, an entirely new local tax, injecting an unprecedented urgency and dynamism into Dissenting voluntaryism. After 1834, the tone and agenda of Nonconformist campaigns against church rates became increasingly militant and insistent, fuelling Anglican suspicions that abolition would prove an irrevocable step towards disestablishment.[140] The issue of church rates even began to dominate some county contests, such as the Rutland election of 1837.[141] Viewed from a national political perspective, the Church-in-Danger cry of the Tories, and the Irish appropriation proposals of the Whigs obviously played an important role in exacerbating religious divisions between the Nonconformists and the Established Church during the 1830s. At a local level, however, the payment of an 'extra' tax was also fundamental. It was certainly much less remote, and much more intrusive, than the rhetoric of Westminster.

The rate-paying clauses of the Reform Act had a massive psephological impact upon the borough constituencies of England and Wales. Payment of local taxes became a prerequisite for inclusion in the electoral process, making possession of the franchise a positive financial outlay. This 'crabbed and obtrusive intermixture of fiscal obligations with political functions' had two important consequences.[142] First, by associating enfranchisement with expense, electoral participation became less attractive and less accessible. Some simply spurned the franchise, as was shown in chapter 1. Others, such as the 'compound' householders and those in arrears, were excluded from the electoral rolls. The extent of disfranchisement is difficult to assess, but Duncombe reckoned that his bill of 1837 to abolish those provisions of the Reform Act that made 'registration in cities and boroughs conditional upon payment of poor's rates and assessed taxes', would enfranchise 'about half a million persons'.[143] With so many would-be voters excluded from the franchise on purely pecuniary grounds, enormous opportunities were opened up for local party activists to recruit new followers and to prevent the disfranchisement of known friends, by providing assistance with their rates. This

---

138 Ellens, *Church rate conflict*, 16.
139 PP 1839 (562) xliv. 48.
140 Ellens, *Church rate conflict*, 60–9.
141 *Lincolnshire Chronicle*, 4 Aug. 1837. For the electoral role of this issue see Richard Brent, 'The Whigs and Protestant dissent in the decade of reform: the case of church rates, 1833–1841', *EHR* cii (1987), 887–910; Coohill, 'Ideas of the Liberal party', 163–96.
142 *Manchester Guardian*, 18 Oct. 1834.
143 PP 1837 (105) iii. 183–5; *Hansard*, 3rd ser. xxxii. 1170.

type of activity, at a local level, helped inject an important personal dimension into partisanship, tightening a party's hold over the individual voter and intensifying the politicisation process.

A second consequence of the rate-paying requirements was the acquisition of new political power by those responsible for controlling and collecting local taxes. By providing poor law officials and the administrative bodies to which they were responsible with influence over electoral registration, political transactions at the parochial level were transformed. Local political parties, whose main interest was parliamentary elections, were irresistibly drawn into the parochial arena, as they competed to capture control of rating for registration purposes. Parish politics quickly became an integral part of the politicisation process, helping to reinforce nationally-oriented perceptions of party at a local level. This link between the poor law and the franchise was best symbolised by the fact that the annual 1s. registration fee had to be collected and included as part of the poor rate, full and prompt payment of which was an essential prerequisite of electoral enfranchisement.[144] Much has been written about the nineteenth-century poor law, but the importance of this formal link with the reformed electoral system has not received the attention it deserves.[145]

After the Reform Act, the overhaul of poor law administration assumed an even greater urgency. The two were inextricably linked, the one, as the *Annual Register* put it, 'having paved the way for the passing of the other'.[146] The 1834 Poor Law Amendment Act, of course, generated its own intense political conflicts and concerns and even led to the emergence of an Anti-Poor Law Movement.[147] But from a purely partisan perspective, these controversies were far less important in hardening partisanship at a parochial level than conflicts over local rates. Attitudes towards the New Poor Law were separate and distinct from partisanship, and frequently cut across, rather than reinforced, party lines. Indeed, as Atton found in his study of Ipswich, 'there was little to choose between the parties' attitudes to the Poor Law' at a local level, since they both became associated with the administration of the workhouse system in practice. Thus in Banbury, for example, opposition to the New Poor Law was used heavily by the Liberals in their 1837 general election campaign against the Conservatives, who controlled the local union.[148] Moreover, anti-poor law frenzy itself tended to be most widespread among non-electors and of limited electoral significance.[149] Rating and registration probably contributed far more to the politicisation of local administration than the blurred party lines of local poor law policy. Even resistance to the

---

144 2 Will. IV c. 45, 738, clause 61.
145 An obvious exception here is the work of Derek Fraser.
146 *Annual Register*, London 1837, 128.
147 Fraser, 'The poor law as a political institution', 117–22.
148 Eastwood, *Governing rural England*, 185.
149 Rose, 'The Anti-Poor Law movement', 70–91.

New Poor Law, as Derek Fraser demonstrated in his study of Salford, could be inspired by the fear of losing control over registration.[150]

Not all voters were directly affected by the rate-paying clauses. Almost 40 per cent of the 1832 borough electorate claimed the franchise as ancient-right voters – qualifications which far from being 'grand fathered' and dying out, as has been widely stated, actually received an indirect boost in popularity. This was especially true of the freemen voters who, contrary to what has previously been stated, continued to be admitted to their ancient rights in considerable numbers after 1832. There were also substantial numbers of rate-payers whose houses were assessed at less than £10 annual rental value.[151] This group was excluded from the parliamentary franchise, but included in that which was introduced in 1835 for municipal elections, the reform of which is explored in chapter 7. Because possession of this local government franchise also depended upon the prompt payment of all assessed taxes and rates, the electoral power of parish poor law administrators was extended even further.[152] In both the reformed parliamentary and municipal franchises, rating became an essential prerequisite of enfranchisement and a powerful mechanism of electoral control. Thus at both the national and local governmental level, there was effectively 'no representation without taxation' for the borough householder. As a result, the politics of the parish ceased to be merely parochial and became an essential part of the broader battle for political control – a shift neatly captured in Disraeli's *Sybil*:

'Shall you stand for Birmingham, Ormsby, if there be a dissolution?' said Lord Fitz-Heron.
'I have been asked,' said Mr Ormsby; 'but the House of Commons is not the House of Commons of my time, and I have no wish to re-enter it. If I had a taste for business, I might be a member of the Marylebone vestry.'[153]

---

[150] Fraser, *Urban politics*, 64–8.
[151] Keith-Lucas, *Local government franchise*, 60–3.
[152] 5 and 6 Will. IV c. 76, 1015, clause 9. In municipal boroughs with no separate court of quarter sessions, the board of guardians also took over responsibility for collection of the county rates.
[153] Benjamin Disraeli, *Sybil, or the two nations*, London 1845, bk 4, ch. xi.

7

The Electoral Politics of Municipal Reform

The Great Reform Act of 1832 continues to hog much of the limelight in accounts of Britain's political development during the nineteenth century and to fuel an ongoing historical debate. The electoral impact of the Municipal Corporations Act of 1835, with its creation of new town councils and annual municipal elections across England and Wales, is by contrast often overlooked. Existing accounts tend to view it either in terms of the political development of local government in rapidly expanding towns,[1] or as a parliamentary postscript to 1832, which reinforced the attack on old political corruption by abolishing the unreformed 'closed' corporations.[2] Relatively little comparative work, however, highlighting the structural and technical relationship that existed between the new municipal and parliamentary electoral systems has been done.[3] Indeed, in many ways it seems to have been assumed that the new councils, unlike their notorious unreformed predecessors, had no immediate connection with the parliamentary franchise. In particular, the crucial link between the municipal and parliamentary voter registration process and its merger of constituency and council politics has not received the attention it deserves. This chapter explores the nature of this important interconnection, and emphasises its electoral consequences at both the local and national political level.

The parliamentary background

The electoral impact of municipal reform must be seen within the context of the aims of its sponsors and the fears of its opponents at Westminster. After parliamentary reform, reform of the corporations became a high priority. The two were closely linked. The precedent of Scottish municipal reform in 1833, the need to address key issues of urban governance and the problem of unin-

---

1 For example E. P. Hennock, *Fit and proper persons: ideal and reality in nineteenth-century urban government*, London 1973; Graham Bush, *Bristol and its municipal government, 1820–51*, Bristol 1976; D. Fraser (ed.), *Municipal reform and the industrial city*, Leicester 1982, and *Urban politics*.
2 For example G. B. A. M. Finlayson, 'The municipal corporation commission and the report, 1833–35', *BIHR* xxxvi (1963), 36–52, and 'The politics of municipal reform, 1835', *EHR* lxxxi (1966), 673–92.
3 Exceptions include Keith-Lucas, *Local government franchise*, and two memorable articles by the late John Phillips, whose contribution is discussed in more detail below.

corporated boroughs, also provided urgent and essentially non-partisan reasons for re-modelling the system of local government.[4] Abolition of the ancient 'closed' corporations was bound to affect the Tories more adversely than the Whigs, but both parties nevertheless recognised and embraced the necessity for reform. During his brief premiership, for example, Peel made no attempt to undermine the work of the municipal corporations commission and even accepted its initial recommendations. In the localities, there was also a popular demand for the abolition of oligarchical corporations, sometimes even from their own self-elected mayors and aldermen.[5] As the duke of Wellington publicly admitted soon after William IV's dismissal of Melbourne, 'no minister can now conduct the affairs of this country without immediately proceeding to the reform of both the English and Irish Churches, and also of the corporations'.[6]

But while the necessity for municipal reform was admitted across a broad political spectrum, its details were to prove extremely controversial. The commission's report and the ensuing legislation introduced by the Whigs in the middle of 1835 were considered highly partisan. Indeed, its 'far-reaching political and party implications' prompted a bitter conflict between the Tory-dominated House of Lords and the government's supporters.[7] Yet, to the astonishment of most observers, the Conservatives led by Peel in the Commons overruled the Lords' objections and assisted their political opponents in passing what appeared to many to be a very unsatisfactory compromise.

The resulting system of local government affected 178 boroughs, 135 of which returned MPs to parliament,[8] and provided a permissive legislative framework within which further incorporations might take place.[9] What the bill's framers had originally intended to achieve, and how it subsequently turned out both on paper and in practice, are questions of fundamental importance for understanding the political origins of a system of local government that was to survive – albeit with modifications – for the next 140 years.[10] If the bill's legislative progress is viewed from the standpoint of the

---

[4] Useful summaries include G. B. A. M. Finlayson, *England in the eighteen thirties, decade of reform*, London 1981, 23–31; Elie Halévy, *A history of the English people, 1830–1841*, London 1927, 217–22; Keith-Lucas, *Local government franchise*, 48, 186.
[5] Preston's mayor, for example, welcomed the municipal reform bill: Walsh, 'Working class political integration', 368.
[6] *The Times*, 26 Nov. 1834.
[7] Finlayson, 'The politics of municipal reform', 673.
[8] Forty-seven of these boroughs adopted existing municipal boundaries, while the remainder utilised the parliamentary boundaries associated with the 1832 Reform Act: 5 and 6 Will. IV c. 76, 1014, 1047–52, clause 7, schedules A, B.
[9] Birmingham and Manchester, for example, were not mentioned in the original act but assumed corporate status in 1838.
[10] For a summary of its subsequent development see Bryan Keith-Lucas, *English local government in the nineteenth and twentieth centuries* (Historical Association pamphlet, 90), London 1977, 5–40.

electoral strategies being pursued by the party managers, it becomes clear why the debates over municipal reform were so heavily politicised, only then to result in what Melbourne later described as 'a deliberate compromise between the parties in parliament'.[11]

The municipal 'compromise': the electoral dimension

Peel's description of registration as 'a perfectly new element of political power' which would increasingly 'determine the policy of party attacks' has been quoted extensively since it was first published, but without its central premiss ever having been explored.[12] Municipal reform was probably the first major piece of legislation that was directly influenced by 'the registration'. After the general election of January 1835, with its resulting balance of parties in the Commons, the potential impact of the next revision began to influence tactical decisions in parliament. Peel, in particular, became increasingly anxious to prevent any dissolution taking place upon the existing registers. As he explained to his close friend and confidant Henry Goulburn early in May:

> the main point now to consider is this. Will the near future registry or the present be most favourable to the Conservative interest? My notion is that we shall have [an] early dissolution, and that if the present registry be more favourable to the government than the new one, the pretext for dissolution will be sought accordingly. Now we ought to act on the same principles, and if the future registry will be more favourable (as I conclude it will be) for the Conservative cause, we ought to be very careful not to force a dissolution until that cause can have that advantage.[13]

Next day his convictions were confirmed by Bonham's advice 'that in nineteen cases out of twenty it is desirable for us that no dissolution should take place till the next registry comes into play'.[14] The desire to avoid a dissolution helps to explain Peel's neutrality over municipal reform during the second half of 1835. Indeed, he even informed Hardinge that he had 'not read the corporation report, at least not read it with proper attention', but had resolved to be 'as free as air on the corporation question'.[15]

Peel's determination not to oppose the Whig bill eventually produced an

---

11 Melbourne to Clarendon, 23 Jan. 1844, Bodl. Lib., MS Clar. dep. c. 525/1.
12 Since the letter's first printing in Parker, *Peel*, ii. 368, it has been used by Ostrogorski, *Democracy*, i. 150; Seymour, *Electoral reform*, 124; Hill, *Toryism and the people*, 51; A. Aspinall (ed.), *The correspondence of Charles Arbuthnot*, London 1941, 210, and *Diaries*, p. lvii; Gash, *Politics in the age of Peel*, 117–18; Prest, *Politics in the age of Cobden*, 130–1; Evans, *Great Reform Act*, 62; T. A. Jenkins, *Sir Robert Peel*, London 1999, 94.
13 Peel to Goulburn, 5 May 1835, Goulburn MSS Acc. 319, box 40.
14 Bonham to Peel, 6 May 1835, Peel MS Add. 40420, fo. 138.
15 Peel to Henry Hardinge, 24 Apr. 1835, Peel MS Add. 40314, fo. 89r.

open rift between him and the Tory peers in the Lords, led by the duke of Wellington. As Charles Arbuthnot later recounted, 'what passed on the municipal bill did for a moment put Peel and the duke at cross purposes, and for a time there certainly was want of communication between them'.[16] Although Wellington had initially concurred with Peel about the need for restraint, at meetings at the former's residence, Apsley House, the Tory peers had resolved to go into committee, against Peel's wishes, to hear evidence from the threatened corporations at the bar of their chamber.[17] Peel's response was to absent himself from London for most of August, while the Lords proceeded to amend the original bill out of all recognition.[18]

Peel disagreed with the Tory peers on two counts. The first related to the substance of many of their amendments, which were clearly designed to wreck the reforming principles of the bill. When Lord Lyndhurst, the bill's chief opponent, attempted to establish aldermen for life, for example, Peel complained to Goulburn that

> it will ensure a worse election and take nothing in return but a powerless minority fastened on the council for life by that very act of parliament which destroyed the principle of self-election, and yet preserved enough of it, to irritate and not control. . . . I do not concur in the course taken by the Lords.[19]

More important, however, Peel was concerned with the broader consequences of their actions. As Gash noted, they risked giving the Whigs 'a gratuitous justification for resigning; and Peel was not sure they would resist the temptation'.[20] This helps to explain why Peel returned so unexpectedly to London at the end of August and, to everyone's surprise, supported the Whig government in their refusal to accept many of the Lords' changes. As Greville observed, he 'threw over the Lords. . . . Nothing could exceed the dismay and rage (though suppressed) of the Conservatives at his speech'.[21] According to Joseph Parkes, the secretary of the municipal corporations commission, Peel 'burked his party, declared for the Commons and his own exclusive amendments, and recommended conciliation! The coup was fatal to the Lords'.[22] Lyndhurst's proposal to establish aldermen for life was thus rejected, although in return the government conceded the principle of aldermen serving for a period of six years and a number of other modifications, including protection of freemen's property and preservation of their voting rights, the division of

---

[16] Arbuthnot to Hardinge, 11 Jan. 1836, ibid. fo. 128r.
[17] Parkes to Durham and Ellice, 14 Aug. 1835, Lambton MSS.
[18] Fuller accounts of this important episode can be found in Gash, Sir Robert Peel, 131–40; George Kitson Clark, Peel and the Conservative party, London 1929, 269–99.
[19] Peel to Goulburn, 23 August 1835, Goulburn MSS Acc. 319, box 40.
[20] Gash, Sir Robert Peel, 136.
[21] Greville memoirs, iii. 304.
[22] Parkes to Durham and Ellice, 6 Sept. 1835, Lambton MSS.

the larger boroughs into wards and a minimum property qualification for councillors.[23]

This willingness on the part of the government to compromise on what were fundamental issues, rather than mere technicalities, also requires explanation. Liberal tactics were similarly influenced by the forthcoming registration contest. This was particularly evident during the bitter struggle in the Lords in August 1835, when Liberal party managers decided that either some form of deal, or a temporary delay, would be necessary in order to avert a clash between the two Houses. As Parkes explained to Lord Brougham, municipal reform's chief advocate in the Lords:

> I agree with you about the danger of *present* collision. On no account, if avoidable, must we risk a Tory dissolution before November; after that the Devil dissolving will not injure but serve the popular cause.[24]

Even when the Lords unexpectedly backed down, under intense pressure from Peel, and allowed the new compromise bill to pass, the need to avoid a dissolution still remained a prime objective. At the beginning of September, only a month before the new registers came into play, Parkes's recommendations were clear. As he put them to E. J. Stanley, 'if we get over the month of November and into a new electoral register, with such a degree of municipal reform, we may defy Peel and any union of Tories or *coalitions* he may erect'.[25]

Intended and unintended consequences

The municipal compromise of 1835 not only had significant electoral causes, but it also had far-reaching electoral consequences. Two aspects of the original bill's proposals, in particular, related directly to parliamentary elections and were highly partisan in conception and intent. Both, however, were to be substantially altered, with largely unanticipated results. The first concerned corporate control over local patronage and spending. In the 1835 general election, the loss of fifty-seven borough seats to the Tories was attributed by Liberal party managers almost exclusively to the continuing influence of the unreformed corporations, most of which were considered to be strongholds of Anglicanism and Toryism.[26] Their distribution of charitable bequests and dispensation of local appointments had provided ample opportunity to gain what most Reformers regarded as an unfair electoral advantage. Parkes, in particular, was acutely aware of this. He later alleged that the corporations had possessed '£150,000 a year to prostitute in electioneering influence in 140 boroughs, most of them parliamentary, besides patronage to alms-houses,

---

23 For a summary of the concessions see Finlayson, 'The politics of municipal reform', 686.
24 Parkes to Brougham, 18 Aug. 1835, Brougham MSS.
25 Parkes to Stanley, 6 Sept. 1835, Parkes MSS.
26 See Finlayson, 'The politics of municipal reform', 674 n. 5.

loans and the administration of the estate and trusts and all the resulting power of various species'. Municipal reform, he believed, would 'not only neutralize but transfer most of this great political annual fund to the Liberals', and thereby effect 'a *great* action on the elections'.[27] Similar perceptions were also shared by many Tories, anxious over the likely consequences of municipal reform. One Tory MP, for example, predicted to the House that it would lead to the loss of fifty-eight Conservative seats.[28] Lord Falmouth privately warned Peel that 'without their influence, working naturally though silently, hardly a single Conservative could have been returned' in Cornwall.[29] Both sides, therefore, believed that municipal reform would destroy what in many places had amounted to a Tory monopoly over local patronage.

The hope of Liberal activists like Parkes, that the act would 'break to pieces the Tory cliques of the old corporators, and in the article of patronage alone make a great dent in the influence over the *parliamentary* elections' was, however, both naïve and over-optimistic.[30] In theory, the changes would enable the Liberals to build an effective patronage system, as Parkes reminded Brougham:

> it is a fact that the Liberals are naturally looking to the municipal patronage, county attorneys to town clerkships, Liberal bankers to treasurerships, etc. etc. . . . our supporters have a right to indulge these influences, it is human nature.[31]

However, as *The Times* observed, few of the new reformed councils had either the power or the means to emulate the activities of their predecessors.[32] As the successor institutions to the unreformed corporations, they not only took over their property and sources of income but also inherited liability for often considerable debts. Many corporations during the 1820s had spent vast sums in defending their actions and constitutional status against attacks from reforming lawyers in the courts. Stafford corporation, for example, had incurred 'debts and liabilities' of £8,500 and by 1833 the interest on its mortgage alone accounted for almost half its total annual expenditure. Not surprisingly, one of the first actions of the new Stafford council was to sell off property.[33] Moreover, in the parliamentary compromise between the parties those clauses giving the greatest potential electoral influence to the new councils had either been successfully struck out, or at least delayed in their implementation. Their power to grant licences, for example, was dropped,

[27] Parkes to Durham, 29 Aug. 1836, Lambton MSS.
[28] *Hansard*, 3rd ser. xxix. 767.
[29] Falmouth to Peel, 9 June 1835, Peel MS Add. 40420, fo. 207.
[30] Parkes to Durham, 23 Oct. 1835, Lambton MSS.
[31] Parkes to Brougham, 18 Aug. 1835, Brougham MSS.
[32] *The Times*, 29 Dec. 1835.
[33] William White, *Directory of Staffordshire*, Sheffield 1834, 140; VCH, *Staffordshire*, vi, Oxford 1979, 226.

while a moratorium was effectively placed on their control over charitable trusts.[34] All by-laws, as one astute pamphleteer complained, had to be submitted to the government for approval or veto within forty days.[35] Beyond their control over local policing and lighting, set out in the original act, the new councils therefore had relatively little local autonomy and patronage at their disposal.[36] It was only through subsequent legislation that they assumed the administrative and civic roles traditionally associated with modern urban governance.

Second, and far more important, the original municipal corporations bill had proposed a total abolition of the parliamentary freeman franchise after the death of the existing holders.[37] This threatened to alter the settlement achieved by the 1832 Reform Act which, as the previous chapter noted, had deliberately allowed for the creation of new 'birth and servitude' freemen voters after 1832, and had only disfranchised the existing non-resident freemen and all future honorary freemen and 'freemen by marriage'.[38] Although subsequently dropped, it was the proposal to abolish the freeman franchise completely, combined with the attack on Tory municipal oligarchies, which lent the original bill its overwhelmingly partisan character.[39] Parkes, for example, had predicted in June 1835 that

> The corporation bill will be poison to Toryism. It is really good and efficacious. . . . We *burke* the freemen, and by a clause which will be a subject of great conflict close the doors for ever against all inchoate rights and future perpetuation of the freedom for the *parliamentary* franchise.[40]

Parkes's assumption that freemen tended to vote Tory, however, requires some qualification. Seymour found to his surprise that 'in sixteen boroughs where, during the period between the Reform Acts, the ancient-right voters formed at least half the electorate, the Liberals carried one hundred and ninety-five seats to one hundred and forty-eight won by their rivals'. Individual polls also suggest that the Tories derived no 'great electoral advantage' from the freemen.[41] In Canterbury, for example, where they formed more than half of the city's parliamentary electorate, 47 per cent of the freemen voted for the Liberals and 42 per cent for the Tories at the 1835 general election. It was

---

34 Finlayson, 'The politics of municipal reform', 680. The transfer of municipal charitable trusts was delayed until 1 Aug. 1836 to allow time for the charity commission, with Brougham at its head, to investigate.

35 Weasal Wideawake, *King versus people . . . certain provisions of the municipal corporations bill*, London 1835, 13–14.

36 See 5 and 6 Will. IV c. 76, 1024–39, clauses 58, 76–88, 90–1, 100, 111.

37 Finlayson, 'The politics of municipal reform', 680–3; Keith-Lucas, *Local government franchise*, 52–4.

38 2 Will. IV c. 45, 730, clause 32; Russell, *A treatise on the Reform Act*, 43.

39 See Finlayson, 'The politics of municipal reform', 680–1.

40 Parkes to Durham, 1 June 1835, Lambton MSS.

41 Seymour, *Electoral reform*, 87; Raymond, 'English political parties', 189.

only in 1837, after the attempt to abolish their franchise, that support among the freemen for the Tories soared by 10 per cent. The behaviour of the £10 householders, by contrast, remained almost identical, with approximately a third of the £10 householders voting Tory, and just over half voting Liberal at both elections.[42]

Work by local political historians suggests a similar shift. In Newcastle-upon-Tyne, St Albans and York, for example, Conservative support among the freemen increased substantially after municipal reform.[43] In her analysis of Durham's reformed elections, Radice identified a 'new tension between freemen and £10 voters following the debates over municipal reform', and found that in the 1837 contest freemen were twice as likely to plump Conservative than were £10 householders.[44] At Bristol, on the eve of the first municipal elections, the principal Tory agent estimated that there would be a 'majority of freemen in our favour [of] about one thousand'.[45] The Whigs' so-called 'abuse' of the freemen was also cleverly exploited by Conservative central managers in their 1837 election campaign. The Carlton Club distributed 'for general use' an article by William Mackworth Praed on 'the doings of the Whigs with the freemen', which had originally been addressed to his Yarmouth constituents.[46] Municipal reform, at least in the short term, seems to have turned grateful freemen voters into the very partisans that popular perception had widely held them to be. As Parkes subsequently admitted to Brougham:

> We committed a great mistake in the bill. It was absurdly foolish, impolitic and hopeless to attack the freemen *parliamentarily*. I always remonstrated against it . . . nor was it exactly fair to attempt it thro' the *municipal* bill. I pressed its abandonment even after the first Commons majority. We were clearly fighting a windmill, and causing unpopularity among a large class of the people. These were my *private* opinions. Campbell aggravated the harm by blagguarding [sic.] the freemen as a class; *that* was not necessary.[47]

Yet despite such obvious disappointment over the bill's original intentions many Reformers remained convinced that the municipal revolution 'must be a smasher of local Toryism'.[48] After all, Peel's electoral strategy had overridden the truculence of the Lords and allowed a compromise, but still recognisably 'Liberal', measure to pass. And, if nothing else, the newly-elected town councils would now assume responsibility for all future freeman admissions, releasing this part of the parliamentary franchise from the restrictions

---

42 1835 and 1837 Canterbury parliamentary pollbooks.
43 Brett, 'Liberal middle classes', 250–1, 326.
44 Radice, 'Identification, interests and influence', 325–30.
45 Bush to Vyvyan, 29 Oct. 1835, Vyvyan MSS DDV/BO/62/62.
46 Praed to Twiss, 14 July 1837, Bodl. Lib., MS Don. d. 95, fos 99–100. The article first appeared in the *Norfolk Chronicle* of 13 Aug. 1836.
47 Parkes to Brougham, 18 Aug. 1835, Brougham MSS.
48 Parkes to Stanley, 11 Oct. 1835, Parkes MSS.

that had often been placed on the acquisition of freeman voting rights by the old Tory and Protestant corporations.[49] Activists like Parkes jubilantly predicted that the resulting act would seal 'the fate of Toryism',[50] describing it as *'quantum suff'*.[51] At the municipal level, however, the compromise of 1835 was to have electoral consequences that neither its supporters nor its opponents could have foreseen at the time. Affecting both council and parliamentary contests, these unintended technical side effects, many of which have only recently come to light, were to have a profound impact on local politics and party performance in this period and beyond. The remaining sections of this chapter examine why this was the case.

The similarity of the municipal and parliamentary electorates

One immediately surprising feature of municipal reform was that the newly-created municipal electorate often turned out to be much smaller than the parliamentary one. Bryan Keith-Lucas alerted historians to this some fifty years ago by demonstrating how, contrary to most expectations, 'the total parliamentary franchise was greater than the municipal by about 15 per cent' in the thirty-nine boroughs for which comparable statistics were compiled by the Home Office. Shena Simon's earlier work on Birmingham, Leeds, Liverpool, Manchester and Sheffield also revealed that 'in three out of the five towns the municipal list was less than the parliamentary by about 2,000 voters'.[52] Surviving municipal pollbooks present a similar picture.[53] Bristol's first municipal electorate, for example, was less than half the size of its parliamentary constituency.[54] In Canterbury a mere 869 voters were registered for the first council contest, compared with a parliamentary electorate of 1,467.[55] At Poole the municipal list stood at 383, but the parliamentary at 460, while

---

49 5 and 6 Will. IV c. 76, 1014, clause 4. See ch. 6 above for more details.

50 Parkes to Durham, 5 Jan. 1836, Lambton MSS.

51 'Quantum sufficit', meaning as much as suffices: Parkes to Stanley, 11 Oct. 1835, Parkes MSS. In a misreading of the same letter Finlayson, 'The politics of municipal reform', 688, and Phillips and Wetherell, 'Parliamentary parties and municipal politics', 59, both have 'quantum stuff'.

52 Keith-Lucas, *Local government franchise*, 61; Shena D. Simon, *A century of city government: Manchester, 1838–1938*, Manchester 1938, 429.

53 Municipal pollbooks, unlike their more prestigious parliamentary counterparts, are rare and were probably never intended for publication: Phillips, 'Unintended consequences', 92–6.

54 Phillips and Wetherell, 'Parliamentary parties and municipal politics', 61; Bush, *Bristol*, 118–21.

55 1835 Canterbury parliamentary pollbook; 1835 Canterbury municipal pollbook, Canterbury City Library, U802. 781.

Norwich's first municipal roll of 2,401 was dwarfed by its parliamentary register of 4,240.[56]

The reasons for this shortfall, as *The Times* observed, arose 'from the required three years continued rating'.[57] As Colonel Leslie Grove Jones explained to Francis Place:

> In the English municipal bill if I am not mistaken, a *three years residence is exacted* as a qualification beyond the assessment to poor and borough rates, this is monstrous and I believe causes the number of municipal electors to be less numerous than the parliamentary ones.[58]

Thus although there was no minimum property qualification for the municipal franchise, this was more than negated by a very significant extension of the rate-paying and residency requirements already in force in the parliamentary franchise.[59] Under the terms of the final act, all municipal voters had to have been resident rate-payers for three years (though not necessarily at the same property), and to have paid all but the previous six months' taxes.[60] By contrast, £10 householders only needed to have 'occupied' their property for one year and to have paid all but the last three and a half months' taxes.[61] Putting these extra burdens on council voters had been vigorously opposed by Radicals such as John Roebuck and Place, who was responsible for the wholesale attack on them which appeared in the first issue of the *Municipal Corporation Reformer*, launched on 13 June 1835:

> the greatest disadvantage under which this proposed sound franchise labours, and one which ought never to be allowed to incumber it, is the vexatious and useless *rate-paying* clause, which cannot fail of producing extensive litigation and disfranchisement.[62]

In a far-reaching development, however, these Radical objections were skilfully played down by those who had done the most to get an extremely reluctant cabinet to adopt an inhabitant householder franchise in the first place. As Parkes suggested to Durham, it was 'a grand point to get a household suffrage. . . . I never thought when we began with the cabinet that we should spoon them with it', and although he privately condemned the 'three years term of rate paying', he believed that it was far more important to maintain a 'united party' in order to 'carry the essentials of the bill' through the

---

[56] PP 1836 (128) xxi. 554–63; 1835 Poole parliamentary pollbook; 1835 Norwich municipal pollbook, BL, 10361 c. 50 (2); 1835 Norwich parliamentary pollbook.
[57] *The Times*, 17 Sept. 1835.
[58] Jones to Place, 4 July 1837, Place MS Add. 35150, fo. 262v.
[59] See ch. 6 above.
[60] 5 and 6 Will. IV c. 76, 1015, clause 9.
[61] Occupiers were only required to have been resident for six months: 2 Will. IV c. 45, 729, clause 27.
[62] *Municipal Corporation Reformer*, 13 June 1835.

Commons.[63] 'Far from perfect as the Corporation Act was', he later admitted to Place, 'and reduced as was its original degree of perfection, yet it has done or will in its effects *do the business*'.[64] More than a year later this issue was still proving a major source of disagreement between Parkes, who had insisted on pushing the measure through, and Place, who maintained that the municipal bill 'should have been rejected'.[65]

The disfranchisement caused by these extra rate-paying and residency requirements not only reduced the size of the municipal franchise well below the parliamentary one in many boroughs. Far more significantly, it meant that those who met such stringent criteria were usually fairly wealthy and were often able to qualify as £10 householders as well. Keith-Lucas's analysis of the Home Office returns revealed that nearly 73 per cent of the municipal electorate also possessed a parliamentary vote.[66] Municipal pollbooks confirm an important overlap between the two franchises. In Bristol, Beverley, Shrewsbury and Preston, for example, approximately two-thirds of the municipal electors qualified for the parliamentary franchise.[67] At Canterbury 72 per cent of those who polled in the first town council elections were also registered as parliamentary electors. At Norwich 65 per cent were on the parliamentary lists, while at Poole the figure was 77 per cent. This structural similarity between the two franchises was further enhanced by the fact that many of the remaining municipal electors, despite lacking any other voting qualification, closely resembled their parliamentary counterparts in socio-economic composition.[68] Poorer householders were generally excluded from the municipal lists because small properties, especially those under £6 annual value, were usually not assessed to the rates. In Norwich, for example, where the lowest rated house was about £7 yearly rental value, nearly 1,500 poorer householders were excluded from the municipal register because they paid no rates at all.[69] At Manchester only about a quarter of the householders actually paid the poor rate.[70] In Berwick-on-Tweed, only forty-five per cent of the houses were rated and in Bridgwater only half.[71] Other householders were

63 Parkes to Durham, 1 June 1835, Lambton MSS; Parkes to Tennyson, 20 June 1835, Tennyson d'Eyncourt MSS TdE H 31/14.
64 Parkes to Place, 2 Jan. 1836, Place MS Add. 35150, fo. 99.
65 Parkes to Place (with annotations in Place's hand), 8 Jan. 1837, ibid. fo. 218v.
66 Keith-Lucas, *Local government franchise*, 61.
67 Phillips and Wetherell, 'Parliamentary parties and municipal politics', 61–2; Phillips, *Boroughs*, 225–34; Walsh, 'Working class political integration', 372.
68 For an important discussion of this point see Phillips and Wetherell, 'Parliamentary parties and municipal politics', 63–5.
69 PP 1835 (547) viii. 135, minutes 2447–50.
70 Ellens, *Church rate conflict*, 11.
71 Anon, *What should the Lords do with the corporation reform bill? With tables showing the extent of its proposed constituency in comparison with the parliamentary franchise*, London 1835, 43.

disfranchised because they 'compounded' their rates with their landlords, and so did not appear in the official ratebooks.[72]

Contrary to studies that have assumed both a quantitative and qualitative gulf between the municipal and parliamentary electorate, therefore, the former franchise was a microcosm of the latter.[73] A very substantial overlap existed between the two electorates. This physical connection was to have a dramatic impact on council politics. It ensured that any attention to the municipal registers would have an important 'knock-on' effect on the parliamentary registers, and *vice versa*. In the lead-up to Bristol's parliamentary revision of 1836, for instance, the local Conservative agent reported that

> there is a considerable number of new voters, about one thousand. The Radical party, to qualify for the Municipal, have paid their taxes much better than last year and will have the majority of the new householders.[74]

Because of the way in which the two franchises were constructed party gains and losses on one set of electoral registers would correlate closely with those on the other. Not only were the potential sources of disfranchisement in practice the same – receipt of poor relief, arrears of rates, residential mobility – but the adversarial process of claims and objections employed in compiling both types of register was almost identical and occurred at the same time each year.[75] Parliamentary lists were revised by the barristers at any time between 15 September and 25 October.[76] After the anomaly of the first municipal registrations of 1835, which were conducted by specially appointed revising barristers, subsequent municipal lists were revised by the mayor and two annually-elected assessors during the first fortnight of October.[77] Both types of electoral register were completed by the end of that month, and both were then valid for a year from 1 November.[78] Unwittingly, municipal reform transferred the very same registration system that was to have such an impact on English parliamentary elections to the new town council elections as well. No one seems to have noticed this at the time, but then it was only *after* the municipal reform bill had passed in September 1835 that the dramatic struggle over the parliamentary registers of that year took place.

This curiously neglected link between the municipal and parliamentary electoral systems encouraged local political parties, whose main concern was winning parliamentary elections, to participate directly in the municipal

---

[72] See ch. 6 above.
[73] See, for example, Vernon, *Politics and the people*, 27.
[74] Bush to Vyvyan, 14 Aug. 1836, Vyvyan MSS DDV/BO/62/75.
[75] 5 and 6 Will. IV c. 76, 1015–7, clauses 9, 15–18. On the disfranchisement caused by residential mobility see Phillips and Wetherell, 'Parliamentary parties and municipal politics', 64–5.
[76] 2 Will. IV c. 45, 736, clause 49.
[77] 5 and 6 Will. IV c. 76, 1016, clause 18.
[78] 2 Will. IV c. 45, 737–9, clause 54; 5 and 6 Will. IV c. 76, 1018, clause 22.

political arena. By objecting to the votes of their known political opponents, and by enlisting and defending as many supporters as possible, parties were able to use the annual revision of municipal burgesses to influence the parliamentary registration as well. In Canterbury, for example, it was 'admitted on all hands' that the first municipal revision of 1835 would 'materially affect the prospects of party at the succeeding parliamentary contests'.[79] According to the local Liberal paper:

> In the early stages of the registration under the Municipal Corporations Act, the Tories, maddened by the anticipation of defeat, employed every means to reduce the Liberal interest to a minority [and] served objections upon nearly two hundred and fifty of the Liberals, nearly a third of the whole constituency![80]

The 'greater part' of these objections, it soon transpired, were 'frivolous and vexatious' and carried out 'under the direction of the secretary to the Conservative Club'.[81]

As this example suggests, in some boroughs the extra work of fighting the municipal registrations was quickly taken up by the political bodies already engaged in the annual parliamentary revisions. In other constituencies, however, entirely new organisations were set up, specifically geared towards municipal matters. In Ipswich, Colchester, Leicester, Nottingham, Lancaster and Leeds, for example, special branch associations were established in each of the new municipal wards.[82] At Preston an Operative Conservative Association for 'paying a careful and vigilant attention to the parliamentary and municipal registrations' was started.[83] In Beverley 'both parties set up ward committees to supervise local registration' and to 'plan for parliamentary as well as council elections'.[84] The importance of municipal reform in stimulating this type of local party activity was clearly evident in Bristol, where the Tories established a 'new society' exclusively dedicated to the management of council contests in 1836.[85] Even in Hertford, where the electoral activities of Lord Mahon and Lord Salisbury had obviated the need for a formal Conservative organisation, the new council elections prompted the town's leading Tories to act. As they explained to Mahon:

> we have entered into a subscription amongst ourselves which has become annual to us owing to the operation of the Whig Corporation Act. The candi-

[79] *Kent Herald*, 5 Nov. 1835.
[80] Ibid. 19 Nov. 1835.
[81] Ibid. 3 Dec. 1835.
[82] Atton, 'Municipal and parliamentary politics', 335–8; M. E. Speight, 'Politics in the borough of Colchester, 1812–1847', unpubl. PhD diss. London 1969, 182; Walsh, 'Working class political integration', 228, 306; Paul, *Operative Conservative societies*, 13–14.
[83] *Preston Pilot*, 16 July 1836.
[84] Phillips, *Boroughs*, 233.
[85] Vyvyan MSS DDV/BO/62/78–9.

dates have paid £10 each and perhaps your lordship will do as you did last year. The excuse for the application to you is that by our exertions we keep the party together which has considerable influence upon the parliamentary elections.[86]

Not every party association plunged headlong into municipal affairs. Some initially rejected involvement with council elections. Two months after its formation in 1837, for example, the Banbury Conservative Association resolved not to 'interfere with the elections of Town Councillors for the ensuing year'. But with so many of the borough's municipal voters (86 per cent) also registered as parliamentary electors, party performance in the annual municipal registration revisions could not simply be ignored. By 1839, electoral reality had forced this association, like so many others, to attend to the annual revision of burgesses as well.[87]

MPs and local activists were quick to recognise the important connection between council contests and parliamentary polls. Because of the overlap between the two franchises, municipal elections became an increasingly important annual indicator of partisan support in a parliamentary contest, allowing local constituency associations to monitor opinion and to make bold, even over-optimistic, electoral predictions. 'Impenetrably dull must be the cranium who for one moment can cherish a hope ever again to return Radical members for the borough of Poole', boasted one contributor to *The Times* after the Conservatives had won all three council seats in the south ward, 'the stronghold of the Radicals', in 1836.[88] On the strength of their municipal gains in 1839 the Conservatives of Bury St Edmunds resolved to run a second Tory candidate at the next parliamentary election, despite the expensive contest that this would provoke.[89] Lichfield's municipal contests were also considered to be 'of great consequence as to the parliamentary election', the results of 1840 apparently having 'settled the parliamentary contest'.[90]

In some boroughs local MPs took an acute interest, and even were actively involved, in the municipal registrations and council contests. In Bridgnorth, for example, the Conservative Thomas Whitmore spent far more on fighting the borough's municipal revision than the parliamentary one, subscribing £52 12s. 4d. in 1837 and £81 5s. 6d. in 1838.[91] At Shrewsbury, the Liberal representative Robert Slaney helped to organise the council campaigns and, on the eve of an election, would personally address the assembled municipal

86 Longmore to Mahon, 16 Nov. [no year], Stanhope MSS U1590, C382.
87 'Banbury Conservative Association minute book', BCA I/1, Acc. 1259, fos 10, 66; PP 1837–8 (329) xliv. 827.
88 *The Times*, 9 Nov. 1836.
89 Macintyre to Fremantle, 23 Jan. 1840, Fremantle MSS D/FR/80/14.
90 *Dyott's diary*, ii. 376; *The Times*, 4 Nov. 1840.
91 ShRO, Apley MSS 5586/3–4.

electors.[92] Until his retirement in 1837, Sir Richard Vyvyan and his principal agent Henry Bush played a major role in directing the municipal campaigns of Bristol's Tories.[93] New councils openly courted and cultivated connections with their MPs, both sitting and prospective. George Dashwood, for example, regularly attended the dinners of High Wycombe's Liberal council, held in the *Red Lion*, before being returned unopposed for the borough in 1837.[94] Even where an MP abstained from personal involvement in municipal affairs, it was not uncommon for him publicly to acknowledge the services of the leading party activists on the council. After important municipal gains at Hertford in 1838, for example, Mahon held a dinner for the town clerk in 'honour of his services to the Conservative cause'.[95] Two years later, after the defeat of the only Radical candidate in the council elections, 'the return of a second Conservative' in the event of a parliamentary contest was said to be 'certain'.[96]

The importance of these local council contests and their link with national party performance was ultimately reflected in the election correspondence received by the central party managers and their deputies. In 1838, for instance, one campaigner confidently predicted to Bonham that 'the effect of our majority in the Town Council will tell at last; and I find our friends clearly of opinion, that it was wise to begin with the *municipal* majority, which in turn the Parliamentary cannot fail to follow'.[97] In a similar vein, Mahon informed Bonham that in Dover

> the new Mayor to be chosen this autumn is Mr Thompson, a warm Conservative, and that the other vacancies in the Municipal body will in like manner be supplied from the Conservative party so that there may be reason to expect a corresponding improvement in the Parliamentary franchise.[98]

Municipal polls and parliamentary parties

The interconnection between the municipal and parliamentary electoral systems was to have a dramatic impact on England's first town council elections. The rise of partisanship in parliamentary contests after 1832 is now well attested.[99] What psephologists are only just beginning to discover, however, is the extent to which local municipal contests also became polar-

---

92 Shrewsbury Local Studies Library, Morris-Eyton MSS box 3, fo. 292.
93 Bush to Vyvyan, 14 Aug., 2 Dec. 1836, Vyvyan MSS DDV/BO/62/75, 78.
94 G. Tatern to Dashwood, 19 Jan. 1836, Bodl. Lib., MS D. D. Dashwood c. 22, G1/7/11.
95 *County Press*, 6 Apr. 1839.
96 *The Times*, 5 Nov. 1840.
97 [?] to Bonham, 27 Dec. 1838, Peel MS Add. 40616, fo. 39.
98 Mahon to Bonham, 23 Oct. 1838, Stanhope MSS U1590, C330/1.
99 Phillips and Wetherell, 'The Great Reform Act of 1832'; Phillips, *Boroughs*.

ised along clear national party lines during this period. Recent studies of municipal pollbooks have revealed two remarkable features.

First, the degree of voter partisanship exhibited in town council elections was often extremely high, and sometimes even surpassed that of a parliamentary poll. At Poole, for example, 85 per cent of the electors cast a clear party vote in the first council contest of 1835, compared with 70 per cent at that year's general election.[100] In Shrewsbury, Colchester, Canterbury and Beverley more than two-thirds of the municipal voters demonstrated a decidedly partisan preference by selecting councillors who were all from the same party.[101] Bristol's first municipal electors 'overwhelmingly voted for a single party rather than spreading their support'.[102] In Norwich an impressive 1,795 of the 2,207 burgesses (81 per cent) cast all six of their council votes for either all the Tory or all the Liberal candidates.[103]

Some degree of party voting, of course, was to be expected, especially given the partisan passions and expectations aroused by Reform, and the legacy of party contests in many of the 'open' unreformed corporations.[104] But the circumstances of earlier polls were entirely different to these 1835 elections. What made the level of straight party voting in the first council contests so remarkable was the vast and confusing array of possibilities confronting each elector at the poll.[105] Unlike most parliamentary constituencies, where electors possessed two votes, municipal electors had up to a maximum of either twelve, nine or six votes to dispose of, depending on the number of councillors to be chosen in each ward.[106] With split voting between the parties still proving a feature of parliamentary elections, how likely was it that council voters would use all their multiple votes to support

100 PP 1836 (128) xxi. 554–63; 1835 Poole parliamentary pollbook, 33–44.

101 Phillips and Wetherell, 'Parliamentary parties and municipal politics', 70; Phillips, 'Unintended consequences', 101, and *Boroughs*, 233.

102 Bush, *Bristol*, 121.

103 1835 Norwich municipal pollbook, 1–68.

104 Elections to the unreformed corporations of Norwich and Maidstone, for example, had been unusually 'open' and partisan: Hayes, 'Politics in Norfolk', 63–97; John A. Phillips, 'From municipal matters to parliamentary principles: eighteenth-century borough politics in Maidstone', *JBS* xxvii (1988), 327–51.

105 With two candidates usually standing for each council seat, and with every elector's ability to use as many of his votes as he pleased, the number of voting permutations (at least in theory) was vast. Phillips calculated that in six seat wards contested by twelve candidates, each voter 'faced 5,664 possible choices'. By the same token, nine seat wards with eighteen candidates 'raised an even more daunting 88,939 possibilities'. In reality, of course, far fewer permutations were actually recorded on the day: Phillips and Wetherell, 'Parliamentary parties and municipal politics', 74–5, 83–5; Phillips, 'Unintended consequences', 100.

106 Of the 178 councils created in England and Wales, eighty-nine (50%) had warding arrangements that gave each elector twelve votes, thirty (17%) that gave each elector nine votes and fifty-six (31%) that gave each six votes. Only three boroughs were different. In Leeds each elector had four votes, in Liverpool three, while in Bristol the number of votes varied according to ward: 5 and 6 Will. IV c. 76, 1047–51; Bush, *Bristol*, 118–21.

just one party in what was, after all, a local poll?[107] Caricatures and satires of prospective councillors, such as those produced at Norwich's first contest, lampooned their subjects as well-known community figures rather than creatures of party.[108] Why then should so many council voters have eschewed provincial prejudices in favour of purely party-based political alignments? And how, when it came to the poll itself, did so many manage to negotiate their way through the lengthy lists of candidates so effectively?

The new 'mode of voting' adopted for the election of councillors played a crucial role in promoting these remarkable levels of municipal partisanship. As with the New Poor Law guardians' elections of the previous year, a system of ticket voting was introduced, although very few appear to have noticed this at the time.[109] Unlike those elections, however, and in a manner far more reminiscent of a parliamentary poll, each municipal elector was required to attend the polling booth in person and, if necessary, to affirm their entitlement to a returning officer, before 'delivering' in a 'voting paper'.[110] Thus at Poole, for example, a ballot paper which was 'sent' by a burgess who was 'ill' and 'could not personally come to the polling booth' was 'not recorded', but one submitted by a voter who had made it as far as the 'hall entrance' was received.[111] The extent to which this system was intended to create some form of 'secret ballot' is debatable.[112] Papers could be folded or even 'sealed in a envelope', as happened at Poole, where there were early abuses of the system.[113] But each set of ballot papers could also be scrutinised by any elector for at least six months afterwards, on the 'payment of one shilling for every search'.[114] Indeed, it was precisely this entitlement which appeared to sanction the publication of municipal pollbooks. Moreover, as an observer of Norwich's first council election pointed out, 'although there was no casting up of books, similar to that which takes place for parliamentary elections, yet the state of the poll was ascertained on both sides'.[115]

This was possible because the introduction of the paper ballot for municipal elections encouraged a special type of activity by local political parties, which previous accounts have failed to recognise.[116] An elector not only

---

107 On split voting in parliamentary elections see Cox, *Efficient secret*, 103; Nossiter, *Influence*, 178–81, and ch. 1 above.

108 Anon., *Municipal characters or waggeries to the Whigs*, Norwich 1836.

109 See ch. 6 above.

110 5 and 6 Will. IV c. 76, 1019–20, clauses 32–4. This important difference was overlooked by Vernon, *Politics and the people*, 155.

111 PP 1836 (128) xxi. 561–3.

112 Phillips, 'Unintended consequences', 93–5.

113 PP 1836 (128) xxi. 554, 559. Poole's mayor and clerk were charged with 'the abstraction of 4 voting papers, the introduction of 9 duplicate papers, and the mutilation of 2 other papers': ibid. 310.

114 5 and 6 Will. IV. c. 76, 1020, clause 35.

115 *Norfolk Chronicle*, 2 Jan. 1836.

116 According to Vernon, *Politics and the people*, 155, for example, there was 'little reaction to the introduction of this system in any of the constituencies'.

faced a vast and confusing range of voting possibilities in the first council contests, but, under the new voting system, every year he was also required to submit a list of candidates

> not exceeding the number of councillors then to be chosen . . . containing the Christian names and surnames of the persons for whom he votes, with their respective places of abode and descriptions, such paper being previously signed with the name of the burgess voting, and with the name of the street, lane, or other place in which the property for which he appears on the burgess roll is situated.[117]

The very same difficulties of 'sufficient' descriptions encountered in voter registration were therefore transferred to the municipal polling process as well.[118] And just as local parties were drawn into assisting their supporters in the annual revision courts, they now helped to shepherd them through the complex council voting system by issuing pre-printed ballot papers, rather like those already in use in some states in America, which the voter only had to sign. In the week before Canterbury's first council contest, for example, the Liberal committee sat daily 'for the purpose of supplying the burgesses with voting papers, and all information respecting the elections'. 'Let no one throw away a single vote', was their much publicised watchword.[119] Posters for Birmingham's first elections 'respectfully requested' voters to contact their ward committees, 'who will supply them with voting cards'.[120] Similar activities occurred at Shrewsbury, where the Liberal committee urged supporters to call 'for their voting papers, to prevent any inaccuracy of description or otherwise taking place'.[121] To assist municipal electors even further, each party's official list of council candidates was usually printed on different coloured paper. At Poole, for example, the 'Conservative list' was white, and the 'Radical list' blue, making each slate easily distinguishable.[122] Shrewsbury's parties left nothing to chance and produced differently coloured party-strips for use in each ward.[123] Electors, of course, were not compelled to use these printed ballot papers. They were perfectly free to prepare their own, or even to modify a party list as they saw fit. But the evidence of surviving polls suggests that few voters availed themselves of such opportunities, and that when they did, they often bungled it. In the south-east ward at Poole, for instance, only 22 of the 159 voters (14 per cent) chose not to use a party list, and five of these submitted invalid papers.[124]

The second impressive feature of municipal polls was the extent to which

---

[117] 5 and 6 Will. IV c. 76, 1019, clause 32.
[118] See ch. 1 above.
[119] *Kent Herald*, 24 Dec. 1835.
[120] Birmingham municipal election poster, 24 Dec. 1838, BL, 1850 d. 26. (64).
[121] Morris-Eyton MSS box 3, fo. 1564; Phillips, *Boroughs*, 234.
[122] PP 1836 (128) xxi. 558.
[123] ShRO, SRO/4365/IV/1–7.
[124] PP 1836 (128) xxi. 554.

Figure 4
Extract from Canterbury's 1835 municipal pollbook (copied from page 9)

The six Tory candidates (in the left-hand columns) were Halford, Partridge, Curteis, Wootton, Sankey and Bennett. The six Liberals (on the right) were Brent, Plummer, Philpot, Cooper, Weeks and Miette.

	H	P	C	W	S	B	Br	Pl	Ph	Co	We	M
Northgate Ward												
Abram, John	—	—	—	—	—	—						
Ash, Benjamin							—	—	—	—	—	—
Abbott, John	—						—	—	—	—	—	
Aiano, Charles							—	—	—	—	—	—
Abrahams, Jacob							—	—	—	—	—	—
Apps, John							—	—	—	—	—	—
Baker, Henry							—	—	—	—	—	—
Baker, Thomas							—	—	—	—	—	—
Beard, Samuel							—	—	—	—	—	—
Beard, John							—	—	—	—	—	—
Beard, Richard	—	—					—				—	—
Bing, William	—	—	—	—	—	—						
Bing, Thomas	—	—	—	—	—	—						
Bing, Daniel	—	—	—	—	—							
Bligh, William	—	—	—	—			—					—
Brent, John							—	—	—	—	—	—
Brockwell, Charles	—	—	—	—	—	—						
Bullbrook, Henry							—	—	—	—	—	—
Beckford, William							—	—	—	—	—	—
Baldock, John							—	—	—	—	—	—
Buckton, John	—	—	—	—		—	—					
Bean, Clement							—	—	—	—	—	—
Bourn, John				—		—	—					
Bentham, George	—	—	—									
Bourne, John	—	—	—	—	—	—						
Boorman, John	—	—	—	—	—	—						
Beer, William							—	—	—	—	—	—
Bird, Henry	—	—	—		—					—		
Brice, William							—	—	—	—	—	—
Baylay, William Frederick	—	—	—	—	—	—						
Bennett, William	—	—	—	—	—	—						
Braham, Wm. Spencer							—	—			—	—

Source: 1835 Canterbury municipal pollbook, 9.

they became infused with exactly the same type of persistent or 'fixed' forms of partisanship that were fast becoming the norm in parliamentary contests. It was here that the link between the parliamentary and municipal electoral systems was to have its most dramatic impact. Recent work by Phillips and Wetherell, centred around a 'longitudinal' analysis of contests held in Shrewsbury, found that 'voters in the council elections behaved much as they did in parliamentary elections', and that 'electorates viewed both parliamentary and municipal political choices in essentially national terms'. Phillips's similar analysis of the Bristol electorate revealed that 'if someone voted for the whigs nationally, that person voted for the whigs locally', and that 'the same rule applied for tory voters'. 'The Municipal Corporations Act', he concluded, 'managed to create partisans who responded to the national political world even at local elections.'[125] This is a very important discovery. Possession of a local vote, and a parliamentary vote, does not mean that they have to be used in the same way. Electing a body to administer local affairs is not the same as electing a national government, and the issues and criteria involved in local polls are frequently far removed from the political agenda and importance attached to a general election. The results of local and national elections in the latter half of the twentieth century demonstrate this quite clearly.[126]

An analysis of other municipal polls from the 1830s reveals the same surprising level of national-oriented partisanship. Figure 4 reproduces part of the voting that occurred at Canterbury's first council contest in the Northgate ward, as it appears in the surviving pollbook. The first elector listed, John Abram, can clearly be seen to have cast all his votes for the six Tory candidates, who were arranged by the pollbook's publisher in the left-hand columns. Benjamin Ash, by contrast, voted for all six Liberal candidates on the right-hand side. From observation of one typical page such as this, the high level of straight party votes is immediately apparent.[127] However, it is the correlation between voting behaviour in this contest and other elections that provides the real measure of the strength and solidity of these party-based attachments. John Abram may have submitted a Tory ballot paper in this council contest, but was this party preference a persistent phenomenon or simply an isolated incident? Looking at the surviving parliamentary pollbook shows that he also 'plumped' for the single Tory candidate, S. R. Lushington, at the 1835 general election. With similar consistency, Benjamin Ash voted for the two Liberal parliamentary candidates, Lord

125 Phillips and Wetherell, 'Parliamentary parties and municipal politics', 82–3; Phillips, 'Unintended consequences', 104.
126 Colin Rallings and Michael Thrasher (eds), *Local elections handbook*, Plymouth, 1985–.
127 Of the 749 voters who polled, 494 (66%) cast all six votes for one party: 1835 Canterbury municipal pollbook, 3–19.

Albert Conyngham and Frederick Villiers.[128] Contrary to the experience of other periods, both of these electors behaved at a local poll precisely as they had done at a recent national one.

The voting of John Abbott, however, is more difficult to assess. Although he cast five of his votes for Liberal councillors, he gave his sixth to a Tory (*see* figure 4). Richard Beard was even less partisan, voting for two Tory and four Liberal candidates, while Daniel Bing, George Bentham and William Braham all failed to cast their full quota of six votes, in what amounted to a form of 'plumping'.[129] In order to determine the proportion of municipal electors who were effectively repeating their parliamentary partisanship, therefore, party-based voting in these council contests has been defined in the following way. Either: a) the voter cast all his six votes for one party, b) the voter cast five votes for one party and one vote for the other, or c) the voter 'plumped' for four or more candidates from one party. Thus Richard Beard is not considered to have repeated his parliamentary vote for the Liberals at this council contest because, by choosing two Tory and four Liberal councillors, he did not show a firm enough Liberal bias (*see* figure 4).[130] Similarly, George Bentham's mere three 'plumps' for the Tories are considered insufficient for him to be viewed as a partisan, whereas Henry Bird's selection of five Tory councillors are deemed to have outweighed his single vote for a Liberal candidate. Setting the criteria for party voting so strictly allows for a very tough assessment of the relationship between parliamentary and municipal polling.

Processing all of Canterbury's council electors in this way reveals that 400 (or 82 per cent) of the voters out of a possible 487 simply reproduced their previous parliamentary partisan allegiance. Put into context, over half (53 per cent) of Canterbury's first municipal turnout of 749 voters were not just 'experienced', but also 'persistent' political partisans, who polled at a local level precisely as they had done nationally.[131] Applying the same methods to Norwich, where there was already a legacy of nationally-oriented partisanship in the city's 'open' corporation contests, the proportion of electors effectively repeating their parliamentary preference in the first council elections was even higher. A voter-by-voter analysis of this constituency shows that 1,287 council electors out of a possible 1,456 (90 per cent) chose to reproduce their previous parliamentary allegiance. Again, this solid phalanx of persistent partisans accounted for over half (58 per cent) of the total munic-

---

128 1835 Canterbury parliamentary pollbook, 24, 33.

129 Phillips and Wetherell, 'Parliamentary parties and municipal politics', 85, calculated that there were 120 such ways in which voters could 'plump' in these elections, but in fact there were many more than this. If an elector chose to use just one of his six votes, for example, he could use that vote in twelve different ways. Using two votes, to select any two of the twelve candidates, the elector had sixty-six possible ways of voting. Using three votes, to select any three of the twelve candidates, the permutations increased to 220, and so on.

130 1835 Canterbury parliamentary pollbook, 30.

131 Ibid. 13–42; 1835 Canterbury municipal pollbook, 3–19.

ipal turnout of 2,207 voters.[132] Repeat partisanship was also the dominant form of electoral behaviour at Poole's first council contest, despite the fact that almost a third of the parliamentary electorate had given a non-party vote at the earlier 1835 general election. Of the 217 voters who participated in both polls, no less than 123 (57 per cent) were firm and fixed partisans, who cast all nine of their council votes for exactly the same party that they had backed at the national level.[133]

The other obvious way of assessing the partisan persistence of these municipal electors is to test the durability of their behaviour in subsequent contests. John Abram may have voted for six Tory councillors in 1835 (see figure 4), but how did he then poll at the ensuing council election of 1836, or at the next general election? And what of those electors, like John Abbott or John Apps, who had not polled in the previous parliamentary contest, but who went on to do so in 1837? Did their propensity to maintain party loyalties in subsequent contests differ from the 'experienced' parliamentary voters, either locally or nationally? Again the evidence of constituencies where complete polling records permit such an analysis, such as Bristol and Shrewsbury, is compelling. Not only did most municipal electors vote the same way in the next set of council elections, but they also transferred their municipal partisanship to subsequent parliamentary contests.[134] This was clearly evident at Canterbury where 418 of the 494 voters (85 per cent) who cast all six of their votes for one party in 1835 then used *all* of their available votes to support the same party in the ensuing 1836 council by-election, which was held to fill the vacancies created by the appointment of councillors as aldermen.[135] Looking further ahead, 352 voters from this same group (71 per cent) then reaffirmed this marked party preference in the 1837 general election, by voting for either both Liberal or both Tory candidates. Moreover, this high level of persistent partisanship was not just confined to the majority who were already 'experienced' at the national level. Of the sixty-three 'inexperienced' council voters who cast a straight party vote in 1835 and subsequently participated at the next parliamentary election, all but four went on to support exactly the same party nationally that they had done locally.[136]

Viewed from the perspective of these municipal elections, the increasingly fixed forms of voter choice evinced in the parliamentary elections of the

---

[132] 1835 Norwich parliamentary pollbook, 1–105; 1835 Norwich municipal pollbook, 1–68.

[133] 1835 Poole parliamentary pollbook, 33–44; PP 1836 (128) xxi. 554–63.

[134] See Phillips and Wetherell, 'Parliamentary parties and municipal politics', 74; Phillips, 'Unintended consequences', 103.

[135] In Dane John and Westgate wards two seats became vacant, and at Northgate one.

[136] Analysis based upon 1835 municipal and parliamentary pollbooks; 1836 Canterbury municipal pollbook, Canterbury City Lib., U802. 781, 3–16; 1837 Canterbury parliamentary pollbook.

1830s were quickly transferred to provincial polls as well. England's first council contests produced remarkably high levels of partisanship, and an extremely high incidence of repeat voting among the majority of voters who were also 'experienced' at the parliamentary level. Moreover, this occurred in spite of the vast and complex array of voting possibilities open to them, and the far more localised factor of personality. Even more surprisingly, however, the municipal minority who lacked any previous parliamentary experience also exhibited similar patterns of partisanship. They not only sustained their behaviour at subsequent council contests, but also transferred it to national polls when the opportunity arose. In marked contrast to the habits of later generations, the vast majority of England's first council voters appear to have invested the choice of local councillors with a nationally-oriented partisan perspective right from the start. This was to have an important effect on party performance, as the final section of this chapter makes clear.

Municipal reform and party performance

The first municipal elections were held at the end of December 1835. At face value the results justified the worst fears of the Tories and the confident boasting of the Reformers. The vast majority of the new councils were overwhelmingly Whig or Radical. Tory victories only occurred in a small number of towns, like Nottingham, where the Liberals had been in control of the old corporation.[137] These first election results, however, were coloured by a spirit of reaction and confusion, and many Reformers were lulled into a false sense of security. The Tories, by contrast, were galvanised into furious activity and in 1836 *The Times* gave details of twenty-five boroughs where they had made substantial municipal gains.[138] In Shrewsbury, as Phillips demonstrated, 'the Conservatives fought back quickly', eventually winning complete control of the council in 1839.[139] Kent's Conservatives quickly regained control of Maidstone, Rochester and Dover.[140] An initial Liberal triumph in Warwick also proved ephemeral, with the Tories regaining 'political control in one of the two wards as early as 1837'.[141] At Leeds the Operative Conservative

137 Keith-Lucas, *Local government franchise*, 57–8.
138 Beverley, Bridport, Colchester, Coventry, Dover, Durham, Grantham, Guildford, Ipswich, Leeds, Liverpool, Macclesfield, Monmouth, Newark, Norwich, Nottingham, Poole, Preston, Reading, St Albans, Stamford, Tewkesbury, Windsor, Worcester and York: *The Times*, 3–5 Nov. 1836.
139 Phillips and Wetherell, 'Parliamentary parties and municipal politics', 77.
140 Andrews, 'Political issues in the county of Kent', 105.
141 David Paterson, *A Victorian election: Warwick, 1868* (University of Warwick Open Studies: Coventry Historical Association pamphlet, 12) Coventry 1982, 10.

Society claimed the credit for an important Tory victory in the council election of 1838.[142]

In many boroughs it is clear that the problems that had already started to
undermine the Liberals' parliamentary registration campaigns were simply
reproduced at the municipal level.[143] In Bristol, for instance, internal divisions and lack of finance had already compromised their attention to the
parliamentary registers.[144] Additional attention to the municipal registers
stretched their resources to breaking point.[145] The problem, as one of Bristol's
exhausted agents suggested, was that, 'the revision will be no sooner finished,
than the corporation election will begin, so that election matters will occupy
about half the year'.[146]

The need for a clear and unified party platform in municipal polls also
tended to benefit the Conservatives much more than the Liberals. At the
municipal level, the union of Radicals and Whigs seems to have proved even
less workable than it was in parliamentary elections, and it was frequently
Radicals who won the first municipal contests at the expense of Whig candidates. As Hardinge informed Peel:

> the Whigs I hear are very busy . . . they admit municipal reform has and will do
> little for them. In several places such as Calne and Doncaster the Whig corpo-
> rations have been displaced by Radicals . . . Liverpool and four or five more
> large towns will in all probability become Radical for the next election.[147]

The practical link between the municipal and parliamentary electoral
systems also encouraged the politicisation of yet another set of council polls,
which are often overlooked. On 1 March every year each borough had to
elect two auditors, to oversee finance, and, more important, two assessors, to
act with the mayor as revising barristers and returning officers.[148] Control of
these positions could yield considerable partisan advantage. With the support
of his assessors, for instance, it was possible for the mayor to influence the
whole municipal registration process. Early abuses, such as the case of York's
Liberal mayor who attempted to manipulate the 1836 revision, led to the
enactment of a special but ineffective provision in 1837, allowing King's
Bench to amend municipal registers through a writ of *mandamus* and, where
necessary, supervise their compilation directly.[149] Although the act prevented

---

[142] The Tories took ten of the available sixteen seats: Paul, *Operative Conservative societies*,
14.
[143] See ch. 2 above.
[144] Bush to Vyvyan, 21 Dec. 1834, Vyvyan MSS DDV/BO/62/9.
[145] Bush to Vyvyan, 14 Aug. 1836, ibid. 62/75.
[146] Bush to Vyvyan, 10 Oct. 1835, ibid. 62/63.
[147] Hardinge to Peel, 7 Jan. 1836, Peel MS Add. 40314, fo. 117r.
[148] 5 and 6 Will. IV c. 76, 1020, clause 37.
[149] *The Times*, 4 Nov. 1836; 7 Will. IV and 1 Vict. c. 78, 620–1, clauses 24, 26.

questions about the legitimacy of the presiding officers being used to challenge a return, in practice it seems to have done little to curtail corruption.[150] Liberal gains in the Ipswich council elections of 1837, for example, were attributed by the *Ipswich Journal* to the partisan bias of the mayor and the two assessors in conducting the municipal registration.[151] In Bristol the Tory mayor, J. K. Haberfield, created delays at the 1838 revision and prevented the burgess roll from being finished in time for the election. Bristol's 1838 municipal contest was therefore fought on the basis of the 1837 registers, which proved 'triumphantly advantageous to the Conservatives'.[152] A more blatant example of mayoral manipulation of the registers was committed by George Hudson, the railway tycoon, in his capacity as the new Tory mayor of York. In 1839 Hudson 'set both law and reason at defiance' when he quashed 100 Liberal objections against Tory burgesses on the grounds that the city did not have a 'burgess' list because its inhabitants were 'citizens'.[153] This helped the Tories gain an even larger majority on York's council in 1839. Because of the link between the two registration systems, any municipal advantage was certainly worth pursuing. As Sir James Graham reminded Bonham during one particularly bitter contest, 'the municipal election is already ours and this ascendancy will ultimately operate on the parliamentary return'.[154]

Municipal gains, however, did not translate into immediate control of the new councils. The methods adopted for determining their composition meant that it was some time before electoral successes affected the majority party in the council chamber. After the anomaly of 1835, when the first councils had to be chosen in their entirety, only a third of the council seats came up for election in each year, meaning that a third of those elected in 1835 remained in office until 1838.[155] In addition, a quarter of the council served as aldermen nominated by the councillors in 1835: half of them appointed for three years, the other half for six. Although the most popular councillors to be elected in 1835 stepped down from office in 1838, half of those selected as aldermen in 1835 would not have retired until 1841.[156] The tendency of councillors to appoint their defeated friends as aldermen helped to prolong these earlier partisan orientations even further, turning the aldermanic bench into a sort of 'haven for defeated councillors'.[157] Put simply,

---

[150] Atton, 'Municipal and parliamentary politics', 53.

[151] Ibid. 285.

[152] *The Times*, 6 Nov. 1838.

[153] Brett, 'Liberal middle classes', 332–5.

[154] Graham to Bonham, 22 Sept. 1839, Peel MS Add. 40616, fo. 93.

[155] The choice of councillors who had to make way in 1836 and 1837 was based upon the number of votes they had received in 1835, those with the highest serving the longest. Thereafter every councillor served a three-year term: 5 and 6 Will. IV c. 76, 1019, clause 31.

[156] Ibid. 1018, clause 25.

[157] Atton, 'Municipal and parliamentary politics', 56.

those who were elected into office in 1835 would still have composed exactly half the council on the eve of the 1838 elections. 1839 was therefore the first year in which the composition of town councils was not directly, or indirectly, influenced by the anomaly of the first municipal contests. Significantly, the election results of that year gave the Tories a further seventy-eight council seats, allowing them to take control of twenty-four more town councils.[158] One year later Bonham informed the Conservative leader Peel that he was

> just winding up a rather extensive correspondence as to the registrations and the ensuing municipal elections, of which some three or four will be most important in their results, and I may add that this year is likely to prove more strongly than any previous one the truth of my conviction that, in England at least, the municipal reform bill has done hardly any, if any mischief.[159]

Contrary to popular perception, municipal reform did not produce significant electoral dividends for the Liberals. In fact, in terms of parliamentary election results it proved a bitter disappointment. In the 135 parliamentary boroughs initially affected by the measure, which together returned 235 MPs, the Tories won 114 parliamentary seats, and the Liberals 121, at the general election of 1835. These Tory successes, it was believed, were largely attributable to the corrupt influence of the unreformed corporations. Yet in the 1837 election, after the passage of municipal reform, the Tories did even better in these boroughs, winning a further five seats from the Liberals. By 1841 the Tories were in a position to take well over half these seats. In other words, in those boroughs where the Liberals believed that elected councils would be most efficacious, they won 121 seats before the reforms, and 107 seats six years after.[160] Viewed from the perspective of its Radical proponents like Parkes, the abolition of the ancient 'closed' corporations clearly failed in many of its primary partisan objectives. It did not create an expanded householder franchise, it antagonised the freemen voters but was unable to curtail their electoral rights, and it was never able to provide a heterogeneous Liberal party with an effective system of local partisan patronage. As Keith Atton concluded in his analysis of parliamentary and municipal politics in Ipswich, 'the hopes of those who had organized the reform were not fulfilled'.[161]

---

158 *Oxford Herald*, 9 Nov. 1839. The boroughs cited were Andover, Bristol, Bury, Cambridge, Chichester, Dover, Exeter, Eye, Hertford, Hull, Kidderminster, Leeds, Lichfield, Liverpool, Macclesfield, Oxford, Salisbury, Shrewsbury, Southampton, Stafford, Stockport, Warwick, Weymouth and York.
159 Bonham to Peel, 27 Oct. 1840, Peel MS Add. 40428, fo. 342.
160 The 135 parliamentary boroughs affected by municipal reform are listed in 5 and 6 Will. IV c. 76, 1047–51, schedules A and B. Using *Dod's electoral facts* and Crosby, *Parliamentary record* to determine partisan affiliation, the later division of the 235 seats was as follows: 1837 election, Tories 119, Liberals 116; 1841 election, Tories 128, Liberals 107.
161 Atton, 'Municipal and parliamentary politics', 91.

It was at the municipal level, however, that the unintended consequences of the act were to prove most striking. The frequency and intensity of national contests during the 1830s provides some explanation for the emergence of clear party platforms in the new council elections, as does the partisan furore stirred up by the whole issue of corporation reform. But it does not explain why, contrary to the experience of later periods, the type of voting behaviour and response elicited in national contests was so clearly reproduced at a local level in the selection of town councillors. Why, as we saw earlier, did party triumph over provincialism, and the kind of electoral behaviour involved in the selection of MPs increasingly dominate the election of local town councillors as well? And how were the dynamics of nationally-oriented partisanship so quickly and effectively transferred to the local political arena?

Here the contested nature of registration politics in the first decade of reform and the introduction of the paper ballot for council elections assume a central significance. The rate-paying and residency provisions of the Municipal Corporations Act ensured a strong overlap between parliamentary and municipal electorates, but it was the unforeseen link between the municipal and parliamentary registration processes that attracted local party organisations, whose main focus was parliamentary, to participate in the municipal political arena. Because the outcome of municipal registrations had a direct bearing upon the composition of the parliamentary electorate, the kind of local party activity increasingly associated with the election of MPs in this period quickly became the norm in council contests as well.

This curiously neglected link between the two electoral systems helped to ensure the wholesale politicisation of municipal contests, along clear national party lines. The new 'mode of voting' played a crucial role in this, enabling local parties to issue pre-printed ballot papers and guide their supporters through the complexities of the first council polls in novel and highly effective ways. As a result, the first municipal elections produced remarkably high levels of straight party voting, and much the same forms of persistent partisanship that were increasingly characteristic of parliamentary contests. The impact of municipal reform, in these circumstances, was to help to bring the politics of Westminster much closer to the urban electorate and to infuse local affairs with an increasingly national partisan perspective. The intensity of these developments, especially in terms of projecting a coherent electoral platform, clearly favoured the more homogeneous of the parties. It was in this context that the Conservatives recovered so quickly, destroying the hopes of Radical activists like Parkes that the municipal revolution would 'be a smasher of local Toryism'.[162] Even at Launceston, a notoriously corrupt corporate borough where the Reformers had everything to gain and the

---

[162] Parkes to Stanley, 11 Oct. 1835, Parkes MSS.

Tories much to lose, the bill failed to live up to its expectations.[163] As one disillusioned Liberal supporter put it:

> I observe the influence of party has a much stronger effect . . . than formerly, a lamentable result. . . . I conceived that the municipal reform bill must have been of great service at Launceston, the regular sweep of the old fraternity was a great point gained, and the qualification clause would be of more advantage to our party as the most respectable than to the other, but I now acknowledge it to be a *vitiated principle*.[164]

---

[163] For political activity in Launceston see PP 1835 (116) xxiii. 653–7.
[164] Mounson to Howell, 6 Nov. 1836, CRO, Howell of Trebursye MSS DDHL/2/300.

Conclusion

This study set out to fill an obvious gap in the historiography of the Great Reform Act of 1832, by examining the practical consequences of its curiously neglected provisions concerning voter registration, rate payments and other such 'small print'. But in tracing these developments, it has also helped to clear up much of the confusion surrounding the Reform Act's broader impact and meaning, especially with regard to its dramatic modernising effects on the ground. In particular, it has been able to relate the widely-noted emergence of more modern types of voting behaviour after 1832 to the new ways in which the franchise was actually being acquired, adding a further layer of sophistication to the ideological and sociological explanations of politics provided in more conventional accounts. Put simply, it has demonstrated that the circumstances in which the vote was obtained during the 1830s had a powerful influence on how it was employed in that decade's spate of general elections. This does not deny the importance of issues and ideology in shaping electoral behaviour – it simply brings to prominence the role also played by the operation of the representative system, which was subject to far less regional variation and local interpretation. Perhaps most significantly, however, this book has shown that the politicising 'knock-on' effects of the Reform Act's provisions concerning registration and the payment of rates were not just confined to the electorate, where most attention has traditionally been focused, but that they also affected local administration and bureaucracy.[1] By charting their constitutional interaction with other types of reform legislation, most notably the Poor Law Amendment Act of 1834 and the Municipal Corporations Act of 1835, this study has provided a much needed exposition of what has been hailed as 'one of the defining features of early Victorian politics', namely the 'politicising of minor institutions' along clear national party lines.[2]

The structure of politics in the post-Reform decade

If this book can be said to have been informed by a single overarching theme, it is that seemingly minor provisions of the Reform Act concerning the payment of rates and the registration of votes had a dramatic impact upon the political life of the nation. The first reason to be identified for this was the

---

[1] An obvious exception here is the strangely unsung work of Derek Fraser.
[2] Stewart, *Party and politics*, 39.

cautionary construction of the annual registration system, outlined in chapter 1, which made the preliminary stage of electoral participation complicated and costly for the individual voter, producing an unexpectedly high level of voter indifference in the immediate aftermath of Reform. As one concerned MP observed on the eve of the first revision, 'it was the duty of this House to induce every one qualified to place his name on the register; though it was extremely difficult to induce many to do so, and rather than take any trouble they would give up their right to the franchise'.[3] This slack take-up of the vote allowed ample space and opportunity for one of the key developments of the 1830s – the emergence of permanent local party associations for attending to the annual routines of registration. The drive to maximise support in the constituencies became acute after the unexpected general election of January 1835, with its resulting balance of parties in the Commons, and at the subsequent revision of that year the electorate increased by a dramatic 17 per cent, which was the largest single expansion in the nineteenth century to occur in a year in which there was no measure broadening the franchise.[4] Alongside the quantitative significance of 1835, there were also important qualitative implications for the process of enfranchisement itself. Aided by the ambiguities of the Reform Act, local parties turned the annual revision process into a complex legal drama which, as well as 'reminding the people of their political rights, and preparing them for the discharge of their political duties', affected them in a highly personal way.[5] At any revision they might be forced to defend their entitlement against a partisan objection, at considerable inconvenience and financial expense. On the other hand, they could leave such business to a local association, as its acknowledged adherent. Both responses helped to polarise the electorate, by encouraging voters either to confront or to identify with a local party well in advance of any election that might take place.

This leads to the first major conclusion of this study, which has been that the contentious nature of registration politics was a key component in the widely-noted process of electoral politicisation that occurred during the post-Reform decade. The practical operation of the registration system lessened the space for the individual voter and heightened the importance of party attachments at the preliminary stage of electoral participation. Confrontation in the registration courts, intensified by the adversarial process of claims and objections, provided an annual public platform for party conflict. Indeed as The Times noted in 1839, 'a general registration resembles a general election in most points'.[6] Viewed from the perspective of the 1830s, the patterns of behaviour of the unreformed and reformed electorates were markedly different. In the post-Reform decade voters not only became more

---

3   *Hansard*, 3rd ser. xiv. 1288.
4   Craig, *British electoral facts*, 79, and *British parliamentary election results*, 623.
5   *The Times*, 3 Oct. 1833.
6   Ibid. 5 Nov. 1839.

party-orientated – the increase in the level of partisanship in 1837 was the largest for any general election held between 1831 and 1910[7] – but also far more likely to maintain their partisanship in successive elections.[8] The activity and apparatus of the annual registration system were essential to this development.

A related theme, developed in chapter 2, was the primacy of local rather than central organisational developments in determining how each party fared in the registration courts and general elections of this period. Despite the advent of the Carlton and Reform clubs, party leaders on both sides remained cautious about extra-parliamentary activity and declined to place their electoral organisations on any centralised or systematic footing. It was in the constituencies, rather than at the centre, that significant structural and stylistic differences emerged between the parties, and where the real genesis for party political performance in this period lay. For a variety of reasons, which go far beyond a simple affirmation of the dictum that all politics is local, the activities of the Conservatives proved more progressive and popular than those of the Reformers. Their newly established Conservative associations, in particular, demonstrated an early awareness of the crucial role played by social functions in sustaining the partisan enthusiasm necessary for registration activity in the long lulls between elections. In terms of their broad appeal, their active recruitment of working-class and female supporters, and their assimilation of local political interests and influences, local Tories came to terms with the post-1832 franchise far more rapidly than their opponents, adopting organisational techniques that were not taken up by the central party managers until the 1870s.

The tendency of political historians to equate modernisation with 'liberalism' therefore does not hold true for the development of parties during the post-Reform decade. Contrary to accounts which have assumed that 'the new system created a environment favourable to the whig-liberals', chapter 2 also revealed that the Conservatives enjoyed a natural electoral advantage after 1832, in that previously unregistered electors tended to exhibit a Tory preference once brought on to the registers.[9] This political partiality, among a small but significant group of voters, ensured that where wholesale recruitment occurred, the Tories benefited much more than the Liberals. The rapidly expanding electorate of the 1830s therefore made future Conservative gains almost inevitable. The boast of the Tories that 'the entire working of the system is in favour of the Conservative party' corresponded closely with the complaints of leading Reformers.[10] As Joseph Parkes put it to the Liberal chief whip in 1837, 'the *representative system*, as at present constituted,

---

7 Cox, *Efficient secret*, 103–4; Phillips and Wetherell, 'Great Reform Act of 1832', 416–24.
8 Phillips and Wetherell, 'Great Reform Act of 1832', 425–32; Phillips, *Boroughs*; Radice, 'Identification, interests and influence', 441–8, 452, 459.
9 Austin Mitchell, *The Whigs in opposition, 1815–1830*, Oxford 1967, 252.
10 *Surrey Standard*, 10 Oct. 1835, cited in Prest, *Politics in the age of Cobden*, 50.

cannot but pass annually more and more into the hands of the Tories. I have long foreseen it'.[11]

Studying how the registration system functioned in the constituencies not only helps to explain each party's national performance, but it also provides new perspectives on how county politics operated after 1832. Too often downgraded as the simple product of interactions between landed influences, the vibrancy and vitality of rural electoral life has been obscured in many accounts and the study of county electorates has even been dismissed as otiose.[12] In the analysis undertaken in chapters 4 and 5, however, it has been argued that county politics cannot be explained by the simple expedients of deference and dependence alone, and that rural elections were often just as complex and genuinely participatory events as their borough counterparts and are thus worthy of serious attention. Quantitative investigations of electoral behaviour by parish, type of qualification and location of residence indicate very clear limits to proprietorial control, and increasingly high levels of voter independence within a rapidly expanding rural electorate. A close correlation between the behaviour of resident voters and outvoters, in particular, exposes the inadequacy of landed influence as a mechanism for exploring and explaining rural politics. Reinforcing these points, chapter 5 has charted the declining power of landed control, the enhanced importance of party affiliation and the impact of registration upon county electioneering within six separate county constituencies. Contrary to what has often been assumed, these case studies show that registration politics was often just as critical in the counties as it was in the boroughs, and that owing to its ability to settle electoral outcomes in advance it provides a far more plausible explanation than 'deference politics' for many of the so-called 'missing contests' of the early Victorian period.[13]

A second major contention of this study has been the decisive role played by registration politics in the politicisation of local administration. The emergence of a distinctively 'reformed' local political culture after 1832 is now well attested. Numerous studies have observed how, in the aftermath of the Reform Act, 'political attitudes became hardened and most local institutions, from the Court-Leet, Corporation, Vestry, Improvement and Police Commissions to the election of Church Wardens and Poor Law Officials, became politicized'.[14] As Eastwood's recent survey of English provincial government has noted, 'where before local politics had been given a partisan edge by custom, tradition, and the prerogatives of status, the period after 1832 saw the emergence of a local political culture which was more formally, even structurally, partisan'.[15]

---

11 Parkes to Stanley, 3 Aug. 1837, Parkes MSS.
12 Phillips, *Boroughs*, 39–40.
13 Stewart, *Party and politics*, 38; Evans, *Great Reform Act*, 62; Moore, 'The matter of the missing contests'.
14 Walsh, 'Working class political integration', 148.
15 Eastwood, *Government and community*, 165.

A crucial explanation for this process of politicisation, explored in chapter 6, was the Reform Act's interconnection of voting with local rates. After 1832, voter registration in the boroughs became entirely dependent upon the prompt payment of all assessed taxes. Indeed, in both the reformed parliamentary and municipal franchises there was effectively 'no representation without taxation' for the borough householder. This link between voting and taxation transformed local politics by providing poor law officials and local rate collectors, as well as the various administrative bodies to whom they were responsible, with a powerful influence over the franchise. 'Tax collectors', as Place complained, were able to 'disfranchise whom they please, by simply omitting to call for the rates and taxes due'.[16] Local political parties, whose main interest was parliamentary, were therefore increasingly drawn into the parochial arena, as they competed to capture control of the rates and poor law appointments for electoral purposes. Poor law and parish elections became integrated into the overall battle for political control, helping to intensify and stabilise nationally-oriented patterns of partisanship at a local level.

The formal link between taxation and the franchise also heightened the institutional prominence of the poor rate, adding a practical political dynamic to economic and utilitarian arguments for a more centralised, extra-parochial system of relieving the poor. And the New Poor Law of 1834 itself had an important psephological impact, in that where the level of poor rates fell the cost of electoral participation was reduced, fewer voters were disfranchised for being in arrears and some poorer householders were even encouraged into the electoral process as 'new' voters. At the same time, church rates became a far more conspicuous tax, because they could no longer be 'compounded' or integrated with the poor rates. This inflamed local sectarian tensions, which were already being exacerbated through the mechanics of partisan registration activity, and helps to account for the increasing political urgency of Dissenting voluntaryism after 1832.[17] By replacing the administrative unit of the parish with the much larger poor law union, party conflicts over local rates were extended beyond existing borough boundaries into the surrounding areas. Coupled with the adoption of a formal paper ballot for the election of poor law guardians, which was easily exploited by local officials, this neglected aspect of the Reform Act helps to explain why the spread of local party conflict was so rapid and pervasive in this period, both in institutional and geographical terms.

Connections between local rates and registration proved especially germane in the new town council elections introduced by the Municipal Corporations Act of 1835. Chapter 7 revealed that there was a strong structural similarity between the parliamentary and municipal electorate, as a result of the latter's stringent rating and residence requirements, and that

---

16 Place to Duncombe, 8 Apr. 1837, Place MS Add. 35150, fo. 257r.
17 See Ellens, *Religious routes to Gladstonian Liberalism*, 19–69.

roughly two-thirds of those who qualified for the municipal franchise also possessed the parliamentary vote as £10 householders. This overlap was crucial. It meant that loss of the municipal suffrage on the basis of a technicality could easily translate into loss of the parliamentary vote, especially as the annual municipal registration process occurred simultaneously with the parliamentary one and adopted a similarly adversarial procedure. Any attention to the municipal registers was likely to have a direct impact upon the parliamentary registers, and *vice versa*. 'Municipal elections', as Graham reminded Bonham, 'ultimately operate on the parliamentary return.'[18] Local party organisations, whose primary focus was parliamentary elections, were therefore increasingly drawn into municipal affairs. In marked contrast to the experience of other periods, the type of voting behaviour exhibited in the election of MPs quickly became the norm for town councillors as well.[19] Aided by the introduction of the paper ballot, which was barely commented on at the time, council contests became infused with exactly the same type of persistent partisan behaviour increasingly associated with parliamentary elections. This reinforced normative concepts of partisan behaviour at constituency level, and helped contribute to the rapid politicisation of reformed local government along national party lines.

Of course, not all the changes described in this study were quite so tidy and clear-cut. Registration and rating revolutionised the nature and structure of electoral activity, but there were other aspects of electioneering where the post-1832 system closely resembled its predecessor.[20] Herein lies much of the apparent 'continuity' commented on at the time and by historians ever since. Coupled with an ongoing scholastic tendency to evaluate whether the Reform Act was 'Great', this has schematised our judgement of 1832 in ultimately unhelpful ways.[21] Many features of electoral life were not so much 'changed' or allowed to 'continue' after 1832, as rearranged within a more complex electoral infrastructure. The business of claiming the vote, for instance, became distinct from the business of casting it, impromptu preliminaries at the poll were replaced by permanent political procedures, and the essential rhythms and routines of electoral activity on the ground were recast in familiar but more recognisably 'modern' forms.

Two components of electioneering, in particular, might be said to have shifted their function and acquired new meaning. The first was the mechanism of the canvass, explored in chapter 3, which became more concerned with mobilising support in those constituencies where registration had already performed the task of assessing and recruiting it. Divested of its status

---

[18] Graham to Bonham, 22 Sept. 1839, Peel MS Add. 40616, fo. 93v.

[19] Phillips, 'Unintended consequences', 98–105; Salmon, 'Local politics and partisanship', 359–76.

[20] See O'Gorman, *Voters, patrons, and parties*, 386–93, and 'The electorate before and after 1832', 181–3.

[21] Cannon, *Parliamentary reform*, 254–5.

as a primary electoral determinant, the canvass offered plenty of alternative space for theatre, ritual and ceremonial reciprocation between candidate and constituent. Thus although 1832 restricted the length of the poll to two days, and this was further reduced to a single day in boroughs in 1835, it did little to diminish the community culture and costs traditionally associated with a lengthy pre-Reform contest. A second and more important restructuring of electoral activity occurred in terms of local party organisation. After 1832 the frequency and volume of work associated with successful electioneering dramatically increased. Larger electorates and annual voter registration necessitated more permanent and elaborate forms of party organisation, which had to be active between elections when interest and enthusiasm were much less easy to muster. And although the constituency associations of the 1830s relied heavily upon the patronage and financial support of traditional political elites, as was shown in chapters 2 and 4, their status was far from servile or subservient. The more successful bodies instead represented a genuine juncture of old and new electioneering influences, under the collective umbrella of party, and were dependent upon attracting large numbers of activists, through popular festivities and social functions, in order for them to perform the dull routines of registration on a regular basis. The services of these unpaid minions were essential, providing local parties with what one agent termed 'the means of obtaining perfect local knowledge and of exercising universal local influence'.[22] Electioneering, at least in this sense, became less an aristocratic preserve and more a collective community operation after 1832, requiring the involvement of a wider body of personnel in a much broader range of activities on an annual basis. As the *Leeds Mercury* observed, 'a plodding shopkeeper on a committee who sees that the registration is attended to does more good than a dozen wealthy squires who reserve all their energy for the election itself'.[23]

Electoral performance during the 1830s also became increasingly dependent upon the work of election agents and firms of local solicitors, especially at the annual registration court. Again this was an area of electoral activity in which traditional political elites played little or no direct part. Although the importance of election agents was already growing in the unreformed electoral system, 1832 broadened their power much further.[24] The registration system gave all those with legal competence and local knowledge much greater potential control over the composition of the electorate and the likely outcome of an election, on an annual basis. Within the complex legal framework of the annual revision, outlined in chapter 1, the seasoned election attorney effectively reigned supreme. After 1832, agents and registration activists became an increasingly influential force, not only in the day-to-day running of the new constituency associations, but also in provin-

22 'West Riding of Yorks registration', 1841, LDA, Wilson MSS DB178/33.
23 *Leeds Mercury*, 26 Nov. 1836, cited in Fraser, 'Leeds politics', 102.
24 O'Gorman, *Voters, patrons, and parties*, 81–9.

cial politics generally. This professionalisation of local political life goes some way towards resolving the apparent dichotomy in the recent literature between interpretations which have stressed the 'party participatory' nature of the Reform Act, and those which have argued that it was an 'individually restrictive' measure which 'limited popular representation'.[25] As the lawyer Chambers predicted in his *Errors and anomalies in the principles and detail of the registration clauses*, published in the immediate aftermath of Reform:

> In every district will the retained agent, or solicitor, be yearly employing his emissaries in looking after the lists, qualifying and arranging his partisans, in raking up every objection against others: perhaps against a poor man who is unable to defend himself, and keeping alive an eternal war of litigation, in which few peaceable citizens will wish to involve themselves.[26]

The post-Reform decade in context

The developments outlined in this book brought Britain far closer to a modern type of two-party electoral system during the early nineteenth century than has previously been supposed. Much the same forms of constituency association and local political activity traditionally associated with the rise of the caucus or even the advent of the Primrose League in the second half of the century could, in effect, all be found operating after 1835. But what of their longer-term significance? Some of the party developments, in particular, appear to have been rather short-lived. By the late 1840s, and certainly by the early 1850s, the highly organised party struggles and nationally-oriented forms of voter partisanship that had increasingly dominated constituency politics in the post-Reform decade were far less evident. Indeed, as Phillips noted, they 'did not persist even in some places where they might have been most expected to survive'.[27] Pockets of intense local activity remained, and municipal politics in particular enjoyed a new dynamism from the early 1850s, but there is no denying that a smooth and sustained transformation of British politics failed to unfold over the next few decades.[28] Combined with the widely observed electoral continuities before and after Reform, it is easy to see why some historians have cautioned so strongly against 'hailing a new start to party politics in the 1830s'.[29]

This view of the 1830s, however, is problematic, not least because it assumes that political developments should follow a linear and progressive course. The evidence presented in this study has suggested a far more complex pattern of change than the teleological one usually associated with

25 Cf. Phillips, *Boroughs*, and Vernon, *Politics and the people*.
26 Chambers, *Errors and anomalies*, 30.
27 Phillips, *Boroughs*, 301.
28 Taylor, 'Interests, parties and the state', 61.
29 O'Gorman, *The emergence of the British two-party system*, 119–20.

the concept of political 'modernisation'. Crucially, it appears that the rapid development of two-party politics was far more pronounced in the constituencies than in the House of Commons, where recent studies of 'high' politics have even identified the emergence of an 'unofficial alliance' between the two front benches during the 1830s, which amounted to a 'Victorian consensus'.[30] Along with the previously noted reluctance of party leaders to embrace more modern forms of central electoral organisation, this suggests that political change may not have been the same at all levels during this period.[31] Parliamentary and constituency politics diverged. Fuelled by the highly adversarial annual registration system and the mobilisation of the electorate at four general elections in less than a decade, politics became far more polarised in the provinces where, as Phillips suggested, men 'accustomed to using the very broadest brushes available, either whitewashed or blackened with tar the parties in local debates'.[32] During the 1830s voters appear to have approached their electoral choices with a far more monolithic view of the two national parties than was in reality the case at Westminster, blissfully unaware of 'the nuances that make the parliamentary history of this period so complicated'.[33]

Recognising that the development and perception of party politics at constituency level was different from that within parliament goes a long way towards explaining the gulf that had emerged between the Conservative party and its leadership by 1841, which was to make itself so conspicuously apparent in the crisis over the repeal of the corn laws in 1846.[34] Without the registration system, the Conservatives' rush to engage in new forms of political activism in the constituencies during the 1830s and their ability to engineer such a dramatic electoral recovery would not have been possible, perhaps allowing more room for the type of 'consensus' politics identified in recent studies of 'high' politics to develop further. As the The League newspaper later pointed out, it was the Conservatives' attention to this 'vulnerable point of the Reform Bill' that had allowed for the rapid 'reconstruction of a great political party, even by the means of the very measure which was the monument of its defeat'.[35] Without the 'knock-on' effects of registration,

---

30 The aim of such co-operation, according to the view's main proponent, was to 'reduce the influence of each front bench's ultra supporters' and to enable the government 'to legislate in a moderate manner': Newbould, Whiggery and Reform, 9, 315. The character and composition of the parliamentary parties during this period have, of course, been subject to intense debate: Hilton, The age of atonement; Brent, Liberal Anglican politics; Coohill, 'Ideas of the Liberal party'; Mandler, Aristocratic government; Ellis A. Wasson, Whig renaissance: Lord Althorp and the Whig party, 1782–1845, New York 1987.

31 See ch. 2 above.

32 Phillips, 'Great Reform Act of 1832', 427.

33 Ibid.

34 I. D. C. Newbould, 'Sir Robert Peel and the Conservative party: a study in failure?', EHR xcviii (1983), 529–57; Evans, Sir Robert Peel, 41–61; Jenkins, Sir Robert Peel, 89–95.

35 The League, 10 Feb. 1844, cited in Prest, Politics in the age of Cobden, 81.

perhaps even a re-alignment of parties would have taken place, based around a centre-party coalition of moderate Whigs and Peelite Conservatives? These moderate groups, after all, had more in common with each other than with the extreme wings of their respective parties, by whom the initiative in electoral organisation had effectively been seized.[36] In the event, the electoral dynamics of the 1830s forced both parties to maintain what were essentially false alliances – the moderate Whigs with the advanced Reformers and the Peelite Conservatives with the Tory Ultras. Redress came for the Whigs in 1839 when they were no longer able to govern, and for the Conservatives in 1846, when their party split in two.

Looked at in this way, the dramatic political developments of the 1830s appear much less exceptional and unrelated to subsequent events. The manner in which the intense partisanship of the post-Reform decade was created by itself offers some explanation for why it proved unsustainable in the longer term, while the extent to which the 1840s and 1850s actually witnessed a 'decline of party politics'[37] has in recent years come under increasing scrutiny.[38] It is surely significant that the methods and perceptions of party organisation associated with the later Victorian period never had to be re-invented or re-legitimised, having become firmly embedded in the political consciousness by 1841. The Liberals, in particular, were able to build continuously on the developments of the 1830s and 1840s with the support of local Dissent. As one recent reappraisal of the Liberal party in this period has suggested, 'the new structures, habits and expectations necessary for the highly organised, professionally run and ideologically coherent parties of later decades' were already 'in place'.[39]

Then there are the far more obvious links in terms of the franchise mechanics detailed in this study and the new forms of political activism and electioneering that the Reform Act introduced. Prest, for instance, has written powerfully of how 'the entire period between 1832 and 1847 can be interpreted as one continuous registration battle'.[40] Taking its cue from the party activities of the 1830s, and drawing heavily on the expertise of disaffected agents like Joseph Parkes, the Anti-Corn Law League launched a highly effective registration campaign in 1843 which has been seen as an important contributory factor in Peel's fateful decision to abandon agricultural protection, and which provided much needed stimulus and local personnel for the emerging Liberal constituency associations of the mid-Victorian period.[41] Further work clearly needs to be done on the tech-

---

36 See ch. 2 above.
37 Norman Gash, *Aristocracy and people: Britain, 1815–65*, London 1979, 250–82.
38 For a useful synthesis of criticisms made against the 'decline of party' view see Jenkins, *Parliament, party and politics*, 28–58.
39 Coohill, 'Ideas of the Liberal party', 273.
40 Prest, *Politics in the age of Cobden*, 133.
41 Ibid. 81–99; Miles Taylor, *The decline of British Radicalism, 1847–1860*, Oxford 1995, 72. As with the party developments of the 1830s, legislative 'small print' was again to have a

nical electoral processes and modifications to the voting system that were to affect every elector, in every constituency, in subsequent decades. But the message of this detailed study of the 1830s is unequivocal. As more is learnt about the constitutional context in which all local parties operated and the act of voting actually took place, the easier it will be to move our understanding of electoral politics beyond the regional diversity of case studies, and to begin to construct a model of the Victorian electoral system appropriate to the nation as a whole.

Over half a century ago, a call was made by J. Alun Thomas for the 'historian and political scientist' to have far more 'regard for the working constitution of the county'.[42] On the basis of just such an approach, this book has been able to affirm the truly innovative character of the Reform Act of 1832, on three broad counts. First, the practical operation of the registration system introduced a powerful new form of highly personal contact between elector and party, and not only at election times, which provided a permanent mechanism for conducting the heat of national politics down into the electorate, irrespective of whether or not there was an actual poll. In the post-Reform decade the 'knock-on' effects of rating and registration led to the establishment of permanent party organisations for attending to the annual revision, and to the rise of electoral behaviour which was substantially more partisan and far more likely to be sustained at subsequent polls. Second, these developments initiated a decisive shift in the balance of electoral forces at constituency level, in which older political idioms and influences began to be outmoded by party-based attachments and more modern and professional forms of political activity. Registration, as Peel acknowledged, provided 'a perfectly new element of political power' and even began to 'determine the policy of party attacks'.[43] Third, and most significantly, the Reform Act's long overlooked technical interconnection with other institutions of nineteenth-century government transformed the structure and substance of politics in the provinces, by encouraging nationally-oriented party organisation to become a permanent feature of parochial and municipal life. It was on the basis of this profoundly altered constitutional relationship between local politics and national parties that Britain's modern representative democracy was to be erected.

---

significant impact on events in the constituencies. Without the provisions of the 1843 Registration Act, which abolished the county registration fee and allowed freeholders to cast their votes at the nearest polling station, for instance, it is doubtful that Cobden's crusade to swamp the county electoral registers with urban 40s. freeholders and the owners of borough rent-charges would have proved quite so effective: 6 and 7 Vict. c. 18, 644–9, clauses 36, 58.

42 Thomas, *The system of registration*, 81.
43 Parker, *Sir Robert Peel*, ii. 368.

APPENDICES

APPENDIX 1

The Re-distribution of English and Welsh Seats in 1832

After many confusing alterations, the final scheme was as follows:

Disfranchisement

Schedule A: fifty-five English 'rotten' boroughs[1] returning two MPs and another (Higham Ferrers) with a single MP lost their own representation = 111 spare seats.

Schedule B: thirty smaller English boroughs[2] lost one of their two MPs = 30 spare seats.

Clause 6: The four MPs for Weymouth and Melcombe Regis were halved = 2 spare seats.

Total number of available seats for re-distribution= 143.

Enfranchisement

Schedule C: twenty-two new boroughs[3] to elect two MPs = 44 seats.

Schedule D: twenty-one new boroughs[4] to elect a single MP = 21 seats.

Clause 12: Yorkshire increased from four to six MPs (two for each Riding) = 2 seats.

---

[1] Aldborough, Aldeburgh, Amersham, Appleby, Beeralston, Bishop's Castle, Boroughbridge, Bossiney, Bletchingley, Brackley, Bramber, Callington, Camelford, Castle Rising, Corfe Castle, Downton, Dunwich, East Grinstead, East Looe, Fowey, Gatton, Great Bedwyn, Haslemere, Hedon, Heytesbury, Hindon, Ilchester, Lostwithiel, Ludgershall, Milborne Port, Minehead, Newport, New Romney, Newton, Newtown, Okehampton, Old Sarum, Orford, Plympton, Queenborough, St Germans, St Mawes, St Michael's (also known as Mitchell and Midshall), Saltash, Seaford, Steyning, Stockbridge, Tregony, Wendover, Weobley, West Looe, Whitchurch, Winchelsea, Wootton Bassett, Yarmouth.

[2] Arundel, Ashburton, Calne, Christchurch, Clitheroe, Dartmouth, Droitwich, Eye, Great Grimsby, Helston, Horsham, Hythe, Launceston, Liskeard, Lyme Regis, Malmesbury, Midhurst, Morpeth, North Allerton, Petersfield, Reigate, Rye, St Ives, Shaftesbury, Thirsk, Wallingford, Wareham, Westbury, Wilton, Woodstock.

[3] Birmingham, Blackburn, Bolton, Bradford, Brighton, Devonport, Finsbury, Greenwich, Halifax, Lambeth, Leeds, Macclesfield, Manchester, Marylebone, Oldham, Sheffield, Stockport, Stoke-upon-Trent, Stroud, Sunderland, Tower Hamlets, Wolverhampton.

[4] Ashton-under-Lyne, Bury, Chatham, Cheltenham, Dudley, Frome, Gateshead, Huddersfield, Kidderminster, Kendal, Merthyr Tydvil, Rochdale, Salford, South Shields, Swansea, Tynemouth, Wakefield, Walsall, Warrington, Whitby, Whitehaven.

Clause 13–14: twenty-six English counties[5] divided and increased from two to four MPs = 52 seats.

Clause 15: seven English counties[6] given a third MP = 7 seats.

Clause 15: counties of Carmarthen, Denbigh and Glamorgan given a second MP = 3 seats.

Clause 16: Isle of Wight made a single Member county = 1 seat.

Total new English and Welsh seats = 130

Of the thirteen seats which were left over, eight were allocated to Scotland and five to Ireland.

[5] Cheshire, Cornwall, Cumberland, Derbyshire, Devon, Durham, Essex, Gloucestershire, Kent, Hampshire, Lancashire, Leicestershire, Lincolnshire, Norfolk, Northamptonshire, Northumberland, Nottinghamshire, Shropshire, Somersetshire, Staffordshire, Suffolk, Surrey, Sussex, Warwickshire, Wiltshire, Worcestershire.

[6] Berkshire, Buckinghamshire, Cambridgeshire, Dorsetshire, Herefordshire, Hertfordshire, Oxfordshire.

APPENDIX 2

Voting Qualifications after 1832 (England and Wales)

The county franchise

Unlike borough voters, county electors did not have to be resident (except where indicated below). Neither did they have to be assessed to the land tax or to have paid their taxes – a requirement which had been exacted intermittently in the century before 1832. Property had to have been held for at least six months before a man could register for the freehold or copyhold franchise and for at least twelve months in the case of leaseholders and occupiers, but any property which had been acquired by inheritance, marriage or promotion to a benefice or office was exempt from these conditions. Besides land, houses and buildings, there was a vast range of other types of property which might confer the vote, including tithes, rent charges, annuities and emoluments derived from land, mortgages, shares with an interest in the soil (such as shares in mines, rivers, gasworks and cemeteries), tolls of bridges or markets and purchases of redeemed land tax. In 1846 a select committee investigation discovered that there were 1,276 different types of electoral qualification in the counties, 576 for freehold, 400 for copyhold, 250 for leasehold and fifty for occupiers (PP 1846 (451) viii. 378). The four main categories were:

Freeholders
1. Adult males in possession of a freehold property worth at least 40s. per year (i.e. in terms of the rent or income which could be derived from it).
2. Adult males with a lifetime interest in a 40s. freehold property under any one of the following conditions:
　(a) if the freehold was acquired before the passing of the Reform Act (7 June 1832)
　(b) if it had been acquired since through inheritance, marriage or promotion to any benefice or office
　(c) if the freeholder was resident and in 'bona fide' occupation of the property.
3. Adult males with a lifetime interest in a freehold property worth at least £10 per year.

Copyholders
Adult males with property worth at least £10 per year which was held by ancient custom (e.g. copy of court-roll) or by any form of tenure other than freehold.

Leaseholders
1. Adult males in possession of a leasehold property worth at least £10 per year provided that the original term of the lease was for sixty years or more.
2. Adult males in possession of leasehold property worth at least £50 per year provided that the original term of the lease was for twenty years or more.
3. The sub-lessees of the above, but only if they were resident and in actual occupation of the leasehold premises.

Occupiers or tenants-at-will
Adult males occupying property and paying rent of at least £50 per year .

N.B. A person could not qualify for the county franchise in respect of property which would give them a borough vote. However, property in a borough which was worth less than £10 per year, or which was occupied by a tenant, could confer a county vote (*see* chapter 4).

The borough franchise

At the commencement of each year's registration (31 July) all borough voters must have been resident for six calendar months within seven miles of the borough's main polling place and not received parish poor relief or alms during the previous year. Boroughs which had returned MPs before 1832 retained their ancient-right franchises (unless, of course, the borough had been disfranchised) subject to the conditions set out below. In the boroughs which were enfranchised in 1832, there was only a £10 household franchise.

£10 householders
Adult males owning or renting any house, warehouse, counting-house, shop or other building, being held either separately or jointly with any land, which had a yearly rental value of at least £10 provided:
    (a) that at the commencement of each year's registration (31 July) they had been in possession of the property for at least one year and
    (b) that during that time the property had been rated to the parish poor rate (if there was one) and that all taxes due by 6 April had been paid before 20 July.

Freemen (in the surviving freeman boroughs)
All non-resident freemen were disqualified, along with all 'honorary' freemen and freemen 'by marriage' created after 1 March 1831, leaving:
1. Resident freemen who were entitled to vote on or before 1 March 1831.
2. Resident freemen who qualified subsequently by birth or by seven years' servitude.
A freeman permanently lost his entitlement to the vote, however, if his name was omitted from the electoral register for two successive years.

Other types of ancient-right voter

The following categories of voter who had qualified for the franchise requirements of their particular borough before 1832 could continue to vote during their lifetime, provided that at the commencement of each year's registration (31 July) they retained their original entitlement and their names had not been omitted from the electoral register for two successive years:

1. Scot and lot voters (inhabitant rate-payers).
2. Potwallers (householders who boiled their own pots).

Provided that their qualification had existed before 1 March 1831 or, in the case of property which had been acquired by inheritance, marriage or promotion to a benefice or office, before 7 June 1832, the following types of elector were also entitled to vote:

3. Resident burgage tenants (the occupiers of certain burgage properties conferring the vote).
4. Resident freeholders.

N.B. In boroughs (with a freehold or burgage franchise) which had a county status, resident freeholders and burgage tenants could continue to qualify after 1832 .

APPENDIX 3

Registration and Polling Returns by Borough and County, 1832–1839

Note on presentation and sources

The registration returns for each borough and county in England and Wales are arranged by the date of each revision, rather than the year in which the electoral registers were mostly in force. The 1835 return, for example, gives the number of registered electors entitled to vote at a parliamentary election held between 1 November 1835 and 1 November 1836. The columns also provide the number of electors who polled in the 1832, 1835 and 1837 general elections. These are also arranged chronologically. The January 1835 election figures, for example, appear before the October 1835 registration return. Uncontested elections are indicated by n/c and blank entries indicate a lack of reliable information. There are no figures for 1838 as these returns are missing from the data compiled by the Home Office.

The *Parliamentary papers* (*see* bibliography) upon which these registration figures are based suffer from a number of imperfections, the most common being confusion over dates. When in November 1837 the Home Office clerks wrote to each constituency requesting a return of the number of electors registered for 1836 and 1837, for example, it was unclear whether they were referring to the registers in force for the greater part of those two years (i.e. the registers compiled in 1835 and 1836), or those which had been revised in October 1836 and October 1837. As William Pearson, the returning officer of Thirsk, explained in his reply, 'the numbers are set forth on three registrations instead of two, because I do not clearly understand whether the return is required according to the registers of 1836 and 1837, or of 1835 and 1836' (PP 1837–8 (329) xliv. 628). Where possible, therefore, the entries have been cross-checked with surviving electoral registers.

Table 1
Registration and polling returns by borough, 1832–9

Boroughs	Number of electors 1832	Number who polled 1832	Number of electors 1833	Number of electors 1834	Number who polled 1835	Number of electors 1835	Number of electors 1836	Number who polled 1837	Number of electors 1837	Number of electors 1839
Abingdon	300	201	276	292	n/c	301	306	n/c	324	323
Andover	246	n/c	261	240	209	229	260	n/c	257	242
Arundel	351	n/c	373	360	n/c	336	322	281	312	261
Ashburton	198	n/c	197	190	160	193	226	185	236	269
Ashton under Lyne	433	362	460	515	380	566	603	457	617	671
Aylesbury	1,654	1,268	1,616	1,544	1,210	1,528	1,414	1,188	1,416	1,652
Banbury	329	n/c	345	368	250	332	353	256	371	386
Barnstaple	720	684	778	790	748	813	794	676	805	811
Bath	2,853	2,329	2,705	2,764	1,766	2,829	2,994	2,051	3,095	3,119
Beaumaris District	329	n/c	292	218	n/c	328	323	n/c	336	295
Bedford	1,573	960	1,235	1,252	834	862	1,192	815	1,182	878
Berwick on Tweed	705	635	722	787	627	722	706	625	725	755
Beverley	1,011	971	1,020	1,042	994	1,061	1,062	975		1,053
Bewdley	337	n/c	426	414	n/c	414	414	n/c	400	420
Birmingham	4,309	n/c	4,146	3,681	2,561	4,847	5,236	3,123	5,555	4,619
Blackburn	626	604	626	761	618	786	842	589	842	912
Bodmin	252	222	270	313	234	327	333	249	332	339
Bolton	1,040	935	1,052	1,020	927	1,227	1,340	1,079	1,405	1,471
Boston	869	788	850	938	813	1,074	711	623	749	1,086
Bradford	1,139	967	1,166	1,225	1,013	1,300	1,347	1,060	1,348	1,465
Brecknock	242	224	262	309	n/c	312	312	258	339	335
Bridgnorth	755	n/c	796	791	698	745	790	727	810	778
Bridgwater	484	n/c	484	430	399	497	558	280	567	573
Bridport	426	400	419	420	394	436	505	445	533	558
Brighton	1,649	1,434	1,568	1,535	1,382	1,998	1,968	1,646	2,091	2,533
Bristol	10,309	6,634	10,133	10,100	5,873	10,347	9,992	6,376	9,856	10,878
Buckingham	300	269	311	351	n/c	344	341	299		391
Bury	539	459	411	526	n/c	619	637	425	678	790
Bury St Edmunds	590	521	619	633	580	654	654	551	655	695
Calne	191	n/c	187	178	n/c	178	186	n/c	178	179
Cambridge City	1,499	1,274	1,456	1,582	1,341	1,720	1,368	1,298	1,698	1,857
Cambridge University	2,269	n/c			n/c			n/c		
Canterbury	1,511	1,203	1,494	1,467	1,307	1,630	1,835	1,505		1,774
Cardiff District	687	533	672	672	533	648	635	n/c	590	765
Cardigan District	1,030	n/c	904	899	n/c	947	920	n/c	980	863
Carlisle	977	646	925	946	n/c	465	1,012	n/c	1,013	953
Carmarthen District	684	597	690	773	572	886	786	623	868	977
Carnarvon District	855	773	1,223	1,217	728	1,154	1,099	790		1,037
Chatham	677	572	676	672	621	783	785	n/c	777	877
Cheltenham	919	n/c	1,069	960	437	1,249	1,324	930	1,573	1,713
Chester	2,028	1,574	2,107	2,053	n/c	1,985	2,298	1,457	2,388	2,170

257

Boroughs	Number of electors 1832	Number who polled 1832	Number of electors 1833	Number of electors 1834	Number who polled 1835	Number of electors 1835	Number of electors 1836	Number who polled 1837	Number of electors 1837	Number of electors 1839
Chichester	852	771	849	958	558	826	885	631	884	829
Chippenham	208	183	220	217	n/c	228	239	n/c	240	265
Christchurch	206	n/c	206	354	n/c	239	271	221	239	269
Cirencester	604	n/c	629	615	498	602	585	n/c	586	552
Clitheroe	306	281	359	351	n/c	366	375	321	374	386
Cockermouth	305	255	307	328	257	292	297	229		288
Colchester	1,099	991	1,161	1,152	1,040	1,164	1,175	739	1,276	1,206
Coventry	3,285	1,989	3,580	3,577	3,206	3,681	3,662	3,323	3,659	3,810
Cricklade	1,534	n/c	1,627	1,633	n/c	1,761	1,687	1,389	1,636	1,646
Dartmouth	243	n/c	234	240	n/c	255	257	n/c	262	261
Denbigh District	1,131	n/c	1,066	987	732	915	909	749	928	914
Derby	1,384	1,136	1,509	1,478	1,254	1,707	1,751	1,318	1,731	1,820
Devizes	315	276	277	311	260	343	341	n/c	266	375
Devonport	1,777	1,473	1,882	1,870	1,626	2,083	2,145	n/c	2,101	2,121
Dorchester	322	n/c	302	318	n/c	398	397	n/c		339
Dover	1,651	1,396	1,620	1,564	1,347	1,846	1,677	1,511	1,800	1,681
Droitwich	243	n/c	226	285	247	357	341	n/c	326	298
Dudley	670	547	715	727	577	776	844	674		937
Durham	806	765	921	892	829	923	949	857		1,031
Evesham	359	332	355	338	n/c	345	354	307	359	370
Exeter	2,952	2,055	3,223	3,239	2,242	3,448	3,488	n/c	3,433	3,669
Eye	253	n/c	256	282	n/c	278	301	n/c	252	332
Finsbury	10,309	7,344	9,294	10,299	7,180	12,523	12,264	7,489	13,300	12,974
Flint District	1,359	n/c	1,239	1,067	n/c	1,169	1,169	984		1,053
Frome	322	263	295	285	250	307	291	244	310	339
Gateshead	454	n/c	508	506	n/c	481	534	372		522
Gloucester	1,527	1,198	1,572	1,523	1,257	1,644	1,644	1,284	1,674	1,872
Grantham	698	650	672	667	559	633	669	585	678	691
Great Grimsby	656	456	613	592	487	519	590	n/c	581	515
Greenwich	2,714	2,391	2,464	2,516	2,210	2,912	3,107	2,434	3,155	3,610
Great Grimsby	656	456	613	592	487	519	590	n/c	581	515
Guildford	342	303	370	537	338	430	425	250		495
Halifax	536	492	630	648	601	648	970	793		873
Harwich	214	186	179	156	123	138	162	146	167	181
Hastings	574	473	678	673	559	810	924	696	953	958
Haverfordwest	723	n/c	635	538	366	699	706	409	718	726
Helston	241	n/c	368	356	n/c	356	366	286		406
Hereford	920	610	874	891	813	1,066	909	816		1,123
Hertford	700	670	692	633	616	681	631	580	619	614
Honiton	511	492	474	471	401	518	460	435	455	447
Horsham	257	191	270	280	251	297	319	292	338	366
Huddersfield	608	415	604	671	350	778	800	630	826	865
Huntingdon	384	287	335	294	n/c	391	356	n/c	389	386
Hythe	469	415	494	477	n/c	492	476	379	503	509
Ipswich	1,219	951	1,195	1,209	1,090	1,418	1,418	1,202		1,619
Kendal	327	n/c	362	362	n/c	354	321	n/c	348	351

Boroughs	Number of electors 1832	Number who polled 1832	Number of electors 1833	Number of electors 1834	Number who polled 1835	Number of electors 1835	Number of electors 1836	Number who polled 1837	Number of electors 1837	Number of electors 1839
Kidderminster	390	332	368	368	321	407	440	355	441	469
King's Lynn	836	n/c	774	865	662	862	885	752	930	1,144
Kingston Upon Hull	3,863	3,305	3,980	4,244	3,108	4,275	4,222	2,990		4,767
Knaresborough	278	260	260	264	239	262	271	236	227	240
Lambeth	4,768	3,225	4,212	4,435	2,890	7,154	7,040	4,497		6,647
Lancaster	1,109	n/c	1,212	1,207	n/c	1,207	1,161	989	1,228	1,311
Launceston	243	223	312	323	247	360	353	n/c		393
Leeds	4,171	3,519	5,062	4,774	3,633	5,052	5,579	3,719	5,894	6,182
Leicester	3,063	2,795	3,253	3,049	2,830	3,311	3,569	3,266	3,581	3,687
Leominster	779	n/c	741	694	n/c	692	671	579	664	624
Lewes	878	n/c	779	761	715	832	842	792	890	900
Lichfield	861	563	930	695	625	914	901	n/c	878	876
Lincoln	1,043	878	1,124	1,124	885	1,028	1,041	864	1,023	1,041
Liskeard	218	n/c	226	216	178	229	260	208	271	285
Liverpool	11,283	8,551	12,346	12,492	8,100	12,981	13,449	9,091	13,890	14,970
London	18,584	11,500	18,306	18,288	10,712	19,456	19,456	11,577	19,678	19,064
Ludlow	359	339	372	360	350	402	375	353	367	422
Lyme Regis	212	183	239	250	n/c	245	243	208	256	277
Lymington	249	219	265	294	n/c	285	285	227	296	305
Macclesfield	718	588	755	895	687	895	975	764		908
Maidstone	1,108	873	1,341	1,385	905	1,482	1,566	1,241	1,655	1,687
Maldon	716	671	776	789	721	800	876	749		844
Malmesbury	291	n/c	286	292	n/c	238	260	207	257	280
Malton	667	n/c	631	616	n/c	623	603	n/c		558
Manchester	6,726	5,267	7,187	8,432	5,595	10,123	10,123	6,146	11,185	12,150
Marlborough	240	198	250	254	n/c	263	280	n/c		291
Marlow (Great)	457	n/c	357	373	240	378	259	n/c	280	373
Marylebone	8,901	6,076	7,583	7,752	4,787	10,952	10,843	7,036	11,799	11,625
Merthyr-Tydvil	502	n/c	438	561	n/c	534	582	485		
Midhurst	252	n/c	252		n/c	246	248	n/c	261	273
Monmouth District	899	748	1,031	1,088	852	1,138	1,169	826	1,226	1,304
Montgomery District	723	656	807	899	n/c	961	1,037	915	1,002	1,021
Morpeth	321	n/c	330	336	n/c	354	360	n/c	368	363
Newark on Trent	1,575	1,518	1,149	1,273	n/c	1,288	1,221	n/c		1,130
Newcastle under Lyme	973	941	958	987	922	1,003	991	881	990	1,031
Newcastle upon Tyne	3,905	2,850	4,097	4,054	3,107	4,110	4,572	3,161	4,582	4,530
Newport, I of W	425	365	480	522	463	603	603	506	633	669
Northallerton	232	209	243	261	n/c	270	278	n/c	271	281
Northampton	2,497	2,406	2,325	2,178	2,058	2,133	2,079	1,922	2,103	2,057
Norwich	4,238	3,817	4,123	4,240	3,484	4,242	4,242	3,697	4,390	4,334
Nottingham	5,220	3,322	5,166	5,294	n/c	5,398	5,398	3,454	5,475	5,436
Oldham	1,131	848	1,064	1,029	n/c	1,285	1,372	835		1,402
Oxford City	2,312	2,139	2,340	2,436	2,203	2,498	2,424	2,151	2,563	2,773

Boroughs	Number of electors 1832	Number who polled 1832	Number of electors 1833	Number of electors 1834	Number who polled 1835	Number of electors 1835	Number of electors 1836	Number who polled 1837	Number of electors 1837	Number of electors 1839
Oxford University	2,496	n/c	2,533		n/c			n/c		
Pembroke District	1,208	n/c	1,126	1,168	n/c	1,182	1,152	n/c		1,179
Penryn and Falmouth	875	717	818	811	736	835	888	761	903	885
Peterborough	773	n/c	740	685	591	578	552	494	558	569
Petersfield	234	210	244		190	287	320	249		343
Plymouth	1,461	n/c	1,459	1,571	1,290	1,776	1,811	1,309	1,898	1,907
Pontefract	956	n/c	918	862	828	815	795	681		722
Poole	412	360	436	450	311	574	645	504	624	543
Portsmouth	1,295	983	1,193	1,340	1,143	1,439	1,439	1,116	1,561	1,837
Preston	6,352	5,528	4,165	4,056	3,350	4,204	3,656	3,265	3,782	3,633
Radnor District	529	n/c	504	517	n/c	522	551	n/c	578	500
Reading	1,001	n/c	930	1,002	840	972	1,035	880	1,032	1,141
Reigate	152	n/c	163	165	99	195	205	n/c	207	198
Retford (East)	2,312	1,980	2,434	2,459	2,190	2,835	2,680	2,256	2,822	2,785
Richmond	273	n/c	250	278	n/c	287	272	n/c	284	289
Ripon	341	330	373	383	360	414	424	n/c	405	383
Rochdale	687	632	747	746	695	832	857	723	942	965
Rochester	973	694	972	967	873	1,002	1,015	913	1,041	1,124
Rye	422	290	454	471	312	522	523	n/c	593	524
Saint Albans	657	637	650	544	518	595	613	561	630	585
Saint Ives	584	509	614	599	n/c	608	579	495	566	598
Salford	1,497	1,220	1,347	2,336	1,367	2,335	2,628	1,778	2,437	2,519
Salisbury	576	531	638	650	n/c	721	707	n/c		698
Sandwich	916	847	913	934	840	894	911	769		977
Scarborough	432	384	418	412	267		488	423	514	559
Shaftesbury	634	528	576	554	380	524	469	443	505	491
Sheffield	3,508	2,726	3,464	3,587	2,986	3,903	4,028	2,700		4,451
Shoreham	1,925	1,154	1,882	1,910	n/c	1,945	1,940	1,330	1,982	1,988
Shrewsbury	1,714	1,314	1,539	1,248	1,163	1,786	1,473	1,312	1,538	1,865
Southampton	1,403	1,046	1,202	1,172	911	1,226	1,433	1,107	1,500	1,463
Southwark	4,775	2,810	4,731	5,249	n/c	5,388	5,477	2,898	5,641	5,047
South Shields	475	419	529	518	401	625	644	n/c		686
Stafford	1,176	1,049	1,343	1,117	940	1,271	1,246	980		1,265
Stamford	851	766	781	755	n/c	755	724	201	701	679
Stockport	1,012	955	944	936	873	1,137	1,192	881	1,278	1,279
Stoke upon Trent	1,349	1,235	1,121	1,266	n/c	1,445	1,475	1,161	1,667	1,623
Stroud	1,247	1,156	1,302	1,305	938	1,295	1,340	992	1,293	1,202
Sudbury	509	474	547	554	527	578	599	502	602	594
Sunderland	1,378	1,132	1,357	1,359	1,107	1,484	1,532	1,176	1,581	1,657
Swansea District	1,307	n/c	1,352	1,303	n/c	1,371	1,349	n/c	1,354	1,247
Tamworth	586	n/c	520	505	n/c	531	497	444	491	501
Taunton	949	n/c	1,233	1,193	n/c	1,165	943	798	1,165	1,024
Tavistock	247	193	259	289	177	291	291	n/c	329	347
Tewkesbury	386	364	384	396	379	396	522	370	505	409

Boroughs	Number of electors 1832	Number who polled 1832	Number of electors 1833	Number of electors 1834	Number who polled 1835	Number of electors 1835	Number of electors 1836	Number who polled 1837	Number of electors 1837	Number of electors 1839
Thetford	146	n/c	158	160	n/c	156	161	n/c	155	160
Thirsk	254	n/c	282	267	n/c/	292	283	n/c	302	327
Tiverton	462	402	492	473	402	492	498	425	496	496
Totnes	217	179	277	259	n/c	312	318	280	297	341
Tower Hamlets	9,906	7,320	9,179	9,462	3,208	13,189	13,318	n/c		13,551
Truro	405	386	458	510	456	556	579	488	609	644
Tynemouth	760	590	511	660	n/c	639	704	522	551	764
Wakefield	722	n/c	720	617	499	672	713	588	733	809
Wallingford	453	367	384	366	n/c	354	332	277	360	368
Walsall	597	535	592	578	n/c	679	746	612	878	837
Wareham	387	315	358	339	n/c	372	368	325		428
Warrington	456	379	413	447	278	557	635	532		633
Warwick	1,340	1,248	1,265	971	930	1,046	1,046	909	1,013	977
Wells	358	318	356	377	n/c	388	402	n/c		414
Wenlock	691	635	775	809	746	950	906	n/c		949
Westbury	185	n/c	194	192	n/c	211	213	194		291
Westminster	11,576	4,453	14,588	13,268	4,254	15,695	15,262	6,350	15,745	14,254
Weymouth	475	431	531	518	398	617	589	481	629	660
Whitby	422	356	400	432	n/c	431	458	n/c	464	445
Whitehaven	458	384	476	460	n/c	475	476	n/c	463	508
Wigan	423	287	470	495	457	497	498	469	513	565
Wilton	214	n/c	200	203	n/c	228	210	n/c		205
Winchester	537	430	577	515	407	576	614	458	599	618
Windsor	507	461	479	504	453	628	703	511	678	667
Wolverhampton	1,700	1,463	1,827	1,839	1,522		2,155	1,675	2,170	2,643
Woodstock	317	n/c	314	306	n/c	304	330	243	385	369
Worcester	2,366	n/c	2,924	2,936	2,217	2,579	3,238	n/c	3,196	2,561
Wycombe (High)	298	264	325	309	293	383	387	n/c	383	399
Yarmouth (Great)	1,683	1,555	1,708	1,615	1,432	1,719	1,740	1,474	1,719	1,904
York	2,873	2,645	2,890	2,890	2,545	2,928	2,829	2,456	2,864	3,326

Table 2
Registration and polling returns by county, 1832–9

Counties	Number of electors 1832	Number who polled 1832	Number of electors 1833	Number of electors 1834	Number who polled 1835	Number of electors 1835	Number of electors 1836	Number who polled 1837	Number of electors 1837	Number of electors 1839
Anglesey	1,187	n/c	1,156	1,155	n/c	1,439	1,450	1,279	2,373	2,448
Bedfordshire	3,966	3,471	4,015	4,015	n/c	4,152	4,134	n/c		4,323
Berkshire	5,582	4,749	5,632	5,632	n/c	5,843	5,599	3,707	5,755	5,708
Brecknockshire	1,668	n/c	1,797	1,897	n/c	2,255	2,255	1,790	2,295	2,799
Buckinghamshire	5,306	4,189	4,775	5,371	3,946	5,689	5,760	4,457		6,025
Cambridgeshire	6,435	5,923		7,032	6,469	7,391		n/c	4,040	4,089
Cardiganshire	1,184	n/c	1,048	1,352	n/c	1,778	1,790	n/c	1,829	2,040
Carmarthenshire	3,887	3,502	4,301	4,227	3,659	5,210	5,210	4,315	5,125	5,535
Carnarvonshire	1,688	n/c	1,454	1,642	n/c	1,803	1,791	n/c	2,050	2,247
Cheshire North	5,103	4,341	5,124	5,045	n/c	5,900	6,029	n/c	5,839	5,923
Cheshire South	5,130	4,756	6,265	6,343	n/c	6,852	7,084	5,712	6,672	7,439
Cornwall East	4,462	n/c	4,446	4,392	n/c	5,518	5,469	4,648		5,957
Cornwall West	3,353	n/c	3,504	3,612	n/c	5,013	4,928	n/c		4,911
Cumberland East	4,035	n/c	8,084	3,992	n/c	4,623	4,638	3,699		4,842
Cumberland West	3,848	3,266		4,149	3,237	4,406	4,437	n/c		4,332
Denbighshire	3,401	3,050	3,248	3,395	2,843	3,538		n/c	3,689	3,947
Derbyshire North	4,370	3,657	4,328	4,175	n/c	5,410	5,527	4,481		5,722
Derbyshire South	5,541	4,771	5,398	5,359	4,548	6,630	6,575	n/c		6,675
Devon North	5,368	n/c		6,236	n/c	7,889	7,757	n/c	7,871	10,895
Devon South	7,453	6,658	8,160	8,213	n/c	10,946	10,775	8,449	10,561	8,760
Dorset	5,632	n/c	5,771	5,679	n/c	6,320	6,263	n/c	6,366	6,702
Durham North	4,267	3,841	4,759	4,772	n/c	5,208	5,197	4,282	5,423	5,622
Durham South	4,336	3,994	4,466	4,454	n/c	4,864	4,843	n/c	4,882	4,904
Essex North	5,163	4,513	5,425	5,351	n/c	5,833	5,899	n/c		5,816
Essex South	4,488	3,593	4,649	4,655	3,156	5,286	5,547	3,933		5,670
Flintshire	1,271	n/c	1,280	1,344	n/c	2,151	2,189	1,847	2,221	2,861
Glamorganshire	3,680	n/c	3,609	3,611	n/c	4,370	4,373	3,601	4,494	5,054
Gloucestershire East	6,437	5,753	6,569	6,521	n/c	7,584	7,598	n/c	7,683	7,930
Gloucestershire West	6,521	5,940	6,493	6,473	n/c	6,859	6,936	n/c	7,004	7,743
Hampshire North	2,424	1,859	2,633	2,694	n/c	3,508	9,133	n/c	9,214	3,668
Hampshire South	3,143	2,770	3,692	3,785	3,260	5,475		4,468		5,794
Herefordshire	5,013?	n/c	4,940	4,970	4,306	7,175	7,226	n/c	7,232	7,289
Hertfordshire	4,245	3,810	4,531	4,520	n/c	5,098	5,137	n/c	5,245	5,349
Huntingdonshire	2,647?	n/c	2,595	2,653	n/c	2,677	2,806	2,275		2,824
Kent East	7,026	6,138	7,164	7,087	n/c	7,228	7,293	5,466		7,344
Kent West	6,678	5,562	6,836	6,850	4,549	8,322	8,432	6,641		8,661
Lancashire North	6,593	n/c	6,576	6,581	n/c	9,943	9,922	n/c	9,691	9,648
Lancashire South	10,039	8,297	11,213	11,519	9,850	17,800	17,576	13,967	17,754	18,148
Leicestershire North	3,658	3,063	3,714	3,806	n/c	4,144	4,166	n/c	4,299	4,179

Counties	Number of electors 1832	Number who polled 1832	Number of electors 1833	Number of electors 1834	Number who polled 1835	Number of electors 1835	Number of electors 1836	Number who polled 1837	Number of electors 1837	Number of electors 1839
Leicestershire South	4,125	n/c	4,150	4,244	n/c	4,590	4,143	n/c	4,600	4,854
Lincolnshire North	9,134	8,338	9,040	8,872	7,827	10,165	10,063	n/c	10,141	10,147
Lincolnshire South	7,956	n/c	7,890	7,784	n/c	8,215	8,215	n/c	8,100	8,729
Merionethshire	580	n/c	713	698	n/c	785		n/c	1,336	1,329
Middlesex	6,939	5,132	7,796	8,005	5,927	12,431	12,817	9,214		13,919
Monmouthshire	3,738	n/c	3,755	3,714	n/c	4,360		n/c	4,347	4,447
Montgomeryshire	2,523	n/c	2,770	2,737	n/c	2,846	2,845	n/c	2,819	2,842
Norfolk East	7,041	6,229	7,072	7,281	6,385	8,098	8,138	6,744	8,343	8,474
Norfolk West	4,396	n/c	4,548	4,633	3,944	6,980	7,170	5,900	7,258	7,559
Northamptonshire North	3,363	3,063	3,533	3,552	n/c	3,627	3,757	3,164	3,857	4,127
Northamptonshire South	4,425	n/c	4,501	4,463	n/c	4,478	4,626	n/c	4,600	4,607
Northumberland North	2,322	n/c	2,359	2,367	n/c	2,703	2,705	n/c	2,786	2,742
Northumberland South	5,192	4,606	5,243	5,042	n/c	5,121	5,121	n/c	5,070	5,270
Nottinghamshire North	2,889	2,548	3,084	3,379	n/c		3,410	2,913	3,608	3,746
Nottinghamshire South	3,170	n/c	3,220	3,432	n/c		3,389	n/c	3,621	3,614
Oxfordshire	4,721	n/c	4,748	4,716	n/c	5,055	5,253	4,125		5,721
Pembrokeshire	3,700	n/c	2,891	3,664	n/c	3,866	3,706	n/c	3,710	3,697
Radnorshire	1,046	n/c	974	1,074	939	1,857	1,944	n/c	1,945	2,034
Rutland	1,296	n/c	1,317	1,264	n/c	1,391	1,325	n/c	1,337	1,373
Shropshire North	4,682	4,297	4,757	4,653	n/c	5,016	4,971	n/c	8,414	5,039
Shropshire South	2,791	661	2,851	2,837	n/c	3,566	3,537	n/c		3,776
Somersetshire East	8,996	7,694	9,211	9,107	n/c	8,504	9,561	n/c		9,759
Somersetshire West	7,884	5,812	7,849	7,658	6,323	8,854		7,349		9,024
Staffordshire North	8,756	7,886	8,717	8,717	n/c	9,611		7,182	9,540	10,020
Staffordshire South	3,107	n/c	3,990	3,990	n/c	7,534		6,269	7,871	8,469
Suffolk East	4,265	3,826	4,787	5,034	4,345	6,147	6,278	n/c		6,404
Suffolk West	3,326	2,920	3,610	3,731	3,256	4,952	4,959	3,810		5,091
Surrey East	3,150	2,211	3,436	3,537	2,753	5,308	5,531	3,937		
Surrey West	2,912	2,527	2,981	2,967	2,550	3,681	3,688	2,970		
Sussex East	3,382	2,753	3,750	3,811	n/c	4,824	4,687	3,869		5,316
Sussex West	2,365	n/c	2,279	2,408	n/c	3,122	3,152	2,202		3,538
Warwickshire North	3,730	3,357	4,621	4,779	4,105	6,505	6,632	5,099		6,786
Warwickshire South	2,550	2,272	2,625	2,901	n/c	3,997	4,304	n/c		4,253
Westmorland	4,392	3,584	4,658	4,644	n/c	4,846	4,775	n/c	4,683	4,480
Wight, Isle of	1,167	824	1,192		820			1,188		
Wiltshire North	3,614	2,296	3,592	3,560	n/c	5,059	5,068	4,183		5,259

263

Counties	Number of electors 1832	Number who polled 1832	Number of electors 1833	Number of electors 1834	Number who polled 1835	Number of electors 1835	Number of electors 1836	Number who polled 1837	Number of electors 1837	Number of electors 1839
Wiltshire South	2,540	n/c	2,490	2,448	n/c	3,059	2,962	n/c		2,913
Worcestershire East	5,161	4,349	3,436	5,164	4,261	5,867	5,995	4,771		6,328
Worcestershire West	3,122	n/c	4,079	4,127	3,619	4,612	4,654	n/c		4,589
Yorks. East Riding	5,559	n/c	5,086	5,140	n/c	7,965		6,182	7,180	7,496
Yorks. North Riding	9,539	8,580	9,607	9,545	8,396	11,768	11,738	n/c	11,716	11,911
Yorks. West Riding	18,056	n/c	18,087	18,061	n/c	29,456	29,346	23,774	29,076	30,122

Additional notes:
All the Cambridgeshire registration figures, except those for 1837 and 1839, include the Isle of Ely.
The 1833 Cumberland East figure is for both divisions.
The 1836 and 1837 Hampshire North registration figures include both divisions.
In the absence of pollbooks for Hampshire South, the number of electors polling in 1837 is an estimate based on the election results.
The 1837 Shropshire North registration figure includes both divisions.

The Assimilation of English Boroughs to the New Poor Law

The column marked PLU shows the date at which either a majority or all of the parishes within a parliamentary borough became part of a Poor Law Union. In addition:

Gilbt   denotes that parishes within the borough were part of a Gilbert Union

inc   denotes that relief was administered by an Incorporation of the Poor

nd   indicates that no date has been found

Borough	PLU	Borough	PLU	Borough	PLU
Abingdon	1835	Chatham	1835	Guildford	1836
Andover	1894	Cheltenham	1885	Halifax	1837
Arundel	Gilbt	Chester	inc	Harwich	1838
Ashburton	1836	Chichester	inc	Hastings	1835
Ashton u Lyne	1837	Chippenham	1835	Helston	1894
Aylesbury	1835	Christchurch	1835	Hereford	1836
Banbury	nd	Cirencester	nd	Hertford	1835
Barnstaple	1835	Clitheroe	1858	Honiton	1894
Bath	1836	Cockermouth	1838	Horsham	1869
Bedford	1858	Colchester	1835	Huddersfield	1837
Berwick on Tweed	1836	Coventry	inc	Huntingdon	1836
Beverley	1836	Cricklade	1835	Hythe	1835
Bewdley	1836	Dartmouth	1836	Ipswich	1835
Birmingham	inc	Derby	1837	Kendal	1836
Blackburn	1837	Devizes	1835	Kidderminster	1836
Bodmin	1837	Devonport	inc	King's Lynn	nd
Bolton	1837	Dorchester	1836	Kingston u Hull	inc
Boston	1862	Dover	1835	Knaresborough	1854
Bradford	1837	Droitwich	1836	Lambeth	inc
Bridgnorth	1836	Dudley	1867	Lancaster	1839
Bridgwater	1836	Durham	1837	Launceston	1837
Bridport	1894	Evesham	1836	Leeds	1844
Brighton	inc	Exeter	inc	Leicester	1836
Bristol	inc	Eye	1835	Leominster	1858
Buckingham	1858	Finsbury	inc	Lewes	1835
Bury	1837	Frome	1836	Lichfield	1836
Bury St Edmunds	1835	Gateshead	1836	Lincoln	1836
Calne	1835	Gloucester	nd	Liskeard	1894
Cambridge	1900	Grantham	1836	Liverpool	1837
Canterbury	inc	Great Grimsby	1836	London	1837
Carlisle	1838	Greenwich	1836	Ludlow	1836

Borough	PLU	Borough	PLU	Borough	PLU
Lyme Regis	1836	Reading	1835	Thetford	1835
Lymington	1835	Reigate	1836	Thirsk	1837
Macclesfield	1836	Retford (East)	1836	Tiverton	1835
Maidstone	1866	Richmond	1837	Totnes	1836
Maldon	1883	Ripon	1852	Tower Hamlets	inc
Malmesbury	1835	Rochdale	1837	Truro	1837
Malton	1837	Rochester	1835	Tynemouth	1836
Manchester	1841	Rye	1895	Wakefield	1837
Marlborough	1835	Saint Albans	1835	Wallingford	1835
Marlow (Great)	1835	Saint-Ives	1858	Walsall	1836
Marylebone	inc	Salford	1838	Wareham	1836
Midhurst	1835	Salisbury	inc	Warrington	1836
Monmouth	nd	Sandwich	1836	Warwick	1836
Morpeth	1836	Scarborough	1837	Wells	1836
Newark on Trent	1836	Shaftesbury	1835	Wenlock	1836
Newcastle u Lyme	1838	Sheffield	1837	Westbury	1894
Newcastle u Tyne	1836	Shoreham	inc	Westminster	inc
Newport, I of W	inc	Shrewsbury	inc	Weymouth	1836
Northallerton	1837	Southampton	inc	Whitby	1837
Northampton	1835	Southwark	inc	Whitehaven	1838
Norwich	inc	South Shields	1836	Wigan	1837
Nottingham	1836	Stafford	1836	Wilton	1835
Oldham	1837	Stamford	1835	Winchester	1835
Oxford	inc	Stockport	1837	Windsor	1835
Penryn	1837	Stoke u Trent	1836	Wolverhampton	1894
Peterborough	1835	Stroud	1836	Woodstock	1835
Petersfield	1869	Sudbury	1835	Worcester	1836
Plymouth	inc	Sunderland	1836	Wycombe (High)	1835
Pontefract	1862	Tamworth	1865	Yarmouth (Great)	nd
Poole	1835	Taunton	1836	York	1837
Portsmouth	1836	Tavistock	1898		
Preston	1837	Tewkesbury	nd		

Sources: Youngs, *Local administrative units*, passim; PP 1841 (211) xxi. 17–22; PP 1842 (156) xxxv. 40–3; PP 1844 (578) xl. 333–4

Bibliography

Unpublished primary sources

Aberystwyth, National Library of Wales (NLW)
Aston Hall MSS
Bettisfield MSS
Cefnbryntalch MSS
Chirk Castle MSS
Leonard Twiston Davis MSS
Dolaucothi MSS
Messrs Eaton, Evans and Williams solicitor's papers
Edwinsford MSS
Goderddan Estate MSS
Harpton Court MSS
Lucas MSS
Mayberry MSS
Tredegar Park MSS
Wynnstay MSS

Aylesbury, Buckinghamshire Record Office (BuRO)
Archdeacon MSS
Fremantle MSS

Bakewell, Chatsworth House
Devonshire MSS

Bedford, Bedfordshire Record Office (BRO)
Burgoyne diary (typescript) CRT 190/171 (i)
Election papers Misc. Acc. 4002, Z231/7/1–4
Lucas (De Grey) MSS
Russell MSS

Bradford, West Yorkshire Archive Service (WYAS)
Busfeild-Ferrand MSS
'Bradford Operative Conservative Society minute book', DB4 no. 3
'Bradford Reform Society minute book', DB4 no. 2

Bury St Edmunds, Suffolk Record Office (SufRO)
Conservative election expenses Acc. 2396/56
Election posters Acc. Misc. 5188, HD 534/4–5
Hervey MSS

Canterbury, City Library
Municipal pollbooks

Cardiff, Glamorgan County Record Office (GCRO)
Dowlais Iron Company records

Carlisle, Cumbria Record Office (CuRO)
Messrs Bleaymire and Shephard solicitor's papers
Lonsdale MSS
Quarter session records Q RP/3/25–42

Chelmsford, Essex Record Office (ERO)
Lennard MSS

Chichester, West Sussex Record Office (WSRO)
Cobden MSS
Goodwood MSS
Smith MSS

Durham, Durham County Record Office (DuRO)
Londonderry MSS
Strathmore MSS

Durham, University Department of Palaeography and Diplomatic
Grey of Howick MSS

Exeter, Devon Record Office (DRO)
Acland of BroadClyst MSS
Bedford (London) MSS
Buller of Crediton MSS
Election papers 59/7/4
Heavitree (Exeter) parish records 3004 A/PD 4
Ilbert of West Alvington MSS
Political letters 58/3/6
Totnes borough records 1579 A/12

Gloucester, Gloucestershire County Record Office (GRO)
Messrs Brookes and Badham solicitor's papers
Hyett MSS
Messrs Mulling, Ellett and Co. solicitor's papers
Messrs Ticehurst Wyatt solicitor's papers

Hertford, Hertfordshire Record Office (HeRO)
Bulwer Lytton MSS
Messrs Crawters of Hertford solicitor's papers

Messrs Longmore and Sworder solicitor's papers
Wilshere MSS

Huntingdon, Huntingdonshire Record Office (HuntRO)
Hinchingbrooke MSS

Kingston-upon-Thames, Surrey Record Office (SuRO)
Conservative election expenses Acc. 3033
Election papers SC38/1/5–12
Electoral lists and claim forms 2516/5/2
'First annual report of the East Surrey Conservative Association for the hundred
    of Brixton, 1836', Acc. 766
Goulburn MSS

Lambeth, Lambeth Archives Department (LAD)
Lambeth election papers iv/3/3–122

Leeds, Leeds District Archives (LDA)
Battie-Wrightson MSS
Harwood-Clanricarde MSS
Wilson MSS

Lewes, East Sussex Record Office
Ashburnham MSS

Lichfield, Lichfield Joint Record Office
Messrs Hinckley, Birch and Exham solicitor's papers

Lincoln, Lincolnshire Archives Service (LAS)
Ancaster MSS
Brownlow MSS
Messrs Sharpe and Wade solicitor's papers
Tennyson D'Eyncourt MSS

Liverpool, Liverpool Record Office
Derby MSS
Wainewright MSS

London, British Library (BL)
Aberdeen MSS
Herries MSS
Peel MSS
Place MSS
Election posters 1850 d. 26. (64)
Municipal pollbooks

London, House of Lords Record Office
Le Marchant MSS (transcripts kindly provided by J. T. Coohill)

London, Public Record Office, Kew (PRO)
Russell MSS

London, Reform Club, 104 Pall Mall (RCA)
Reform Club archives

Maidstone, Centre for Kentish Studies (CKS)
Filmer MSS
Knatchbull MSS
Stanhope of Chevening MSS

Manchester, Manchester Central Library
Smith MSS
Wilson MSS

Newcastle-upon-Tyne, Northumberland Record Office
Blackett-Ord (Whitfield) MSS
Middleton (Belsay) MSS
Ridley (Blagdon) MSS

Northampton, Northamptonshire Record Office (NRO)
Cartwright (Aynho) MSS
Fitzwilliam (Milton) MSS
'Whig election committee minute book', Misc. Acc. ZB 43

Nottingham, Nottinghamshire Archives Office (NAO)
Belper of Kingston MSS
Craven-Smith-Milnes of Hockerton (Winkburn) MSS
Glynne-Gladstone MSS
Edward Smith Godfrey papers, QA CP 5/4
Messrs Hodgkinson and Beevor solicitor's papers

Oxford, Bodleian Library (Bodl. Lib.)
Dep. e.155
Election cuttings and posters G. A. Oxon b.129
MS Clar. Dep.
MS D.D. Dashwood
MS Don. d. 94–5
MS Eng. lett. c. 56
MS Phillipps-Robinson

Oxford, Oxfordshire County Archives Service
'Banbury Conservative Association minute book', Acc. 1259, BCA I/1

Preston, Lancashire Record Office (LRO)
Election papers DD. Pr 131/24–27
Garnett of Quernmore MSS
Knowsley MSS
Quarter session orders QSO/2/35

Reading, Berkshire Record Office (BeRO)
Bouverie-Pusey MSS
Election addresses Misc Acc 1749, D/EX 424
Pleydell-Bouverie MSS
Walter MSS

Sandon Hall, Stafffordshire
Harrowby MSS [transcripts consulted at the *History of Parliament*, University of London]

Sheffield, Sheffield Record Office (SRO)
Address of Doncaster Conservatives MD/3734/6
Bagshawe MSS
Liberal election papers MD/2695/39–46
Oakes of Norton MSS
Wentworth Woodhouse MSS
Wharncliffe MSS

Shrewsbury, Shrewsbury Local Studies Library
Bridgnorth elections LSD 055.7
Morris-Eyton MSS
Shrewsbury elections D55.7 Acc 295

Shrewsbury, Shropshire Record Office (ShRO)
Apley MSS
Bridgnorth elections 4001/Admin/7/box 50
Election papers SRO/4365/1–7
Shropshire electoral registers QE/6/2/2–3

Southampton, University Library
Wellington MSS [online database]

Stafford, Staffordshire Record Office (StRO)
Anson MSS
Bill MSS
Hatherton MSS
Sutherland MSS

Stafford, William Salt Library
Election posters D1798/319–21

Taunton, Somerset Record Office (SoRO)
Dickinson MSS
Hylton MSS
Luttrell MSS
Sanford MSS
Taunton elections DD/SAS/TN 14 C/795

Trowbridge, Wiltshire and Swindon Record Office (WRO)
Messrs Creswick and Co (Faulkner) solicitor's papers
Messrs Keary, Stokes and White solicitor's papers
Long MSS
Pleydell-Bouverie MSS

Truro, Cornwall Record Office (CRO)
Adams of Laneast and Egloskerry MSS
Cornwall county registration map FS 3/595
Election addresses FS 3/200
Howell of Trebursye MSS
Messrs Rogers and Son solicitor's papers
Tremayne of Heligan MSS
Vyvyan of Trelowarren MSS

Winchester, Hampshire Record Office (HRO)
Compton MSS
Winchester elections W/B9/1/1–3

Typescripts of the following collections were kindly provided by William Thomas:

Brougham MSS, University College, London
Ellice MSS, National Library of Scotland, Edinburgh
Kent MSS, Library of Congress, Washington, D.C.
Parkes MSS, University College, London
Pencarrow MSS, Pencarrow, Bodmin
Lambton MSS, Lambton Estate Office, Chester-le-Street
Melbourne MSS, Royal Archives, Windsor Castle
Spencer MSS, Althorp House, Althorp

Published primary sources

Electoral registers
Bedford 1832–3
Bedfordshire 1832–3, 1835–7, 1838–9
Bridgnorth 1832–3, 1837–8, 1840–1
Buckingham 1836–7, 1837–8, 1840–1
Buckinghamshire 1838–9
Bury St Edmunds 1837–8, 1838–9, 1840–1
Durham South 1840–1
Essex North 1832–3, 1838–9
Essex South 1832–3, 1839–40
Kent West 1834–5, 1836–7
Lichfield 1832–3
Monmouth 1832–3, 1834–5, 1835–6
Monmouthshire 1840–1
Norfolk East 1832–3, 1834–5, 1840–1
Norfolk West 1834–5
Preston 1832–41
Shrewsbury 1833–4, 1834–5, 1835–6, 1840–1
Shropshire South 1833–4, 1836–7
Somerset West 1834–5
Suffolk West 1832–3, 1836–7
Sussex East 1832–3, 1836–7
Taunton 1832–3, 1834–5, 1837–8, 1840–1
Westmorland 1832–3, 1837–8, 1839–40
Winchester 1833–42

Municipal pollbooks
Canterbury 1835, 1836
Colchester 1835, 1836
Liverpool 1835, 1840
Norwich 1835
Poole 1835
Sandwich 1840
Stratford-upon-Avon 1838

Parliamentary pollbooks
Bedford 1835, 1837
Bradford 1841
Brighton 1835, 1837
Bury St Edmunds 1835, 1837, 1841
Canterbury 1835, 1837
Cambridge 1837
Cambridgeshire 1826, 1830, 1831, 1832

Cheltenham 1841
Cumberland East 1832
Durham 1832, 1835, 1837
Durham North 1832, 1837
Essex North 1832
Essex South 1832, 1841
Huntingdonshire 1826, 1830, 1831, 1837
Kent West 1835, 1837
Kingston-upon-Hull 1835
Leicester 1832, 1835, 1837
Lichfield 1835, 1841
Lincolnshire North 1832, 1835, 1841
Lincolnshire South 1841
Montgomery 1841
Newcastle-upon-Tyne 1832, 1835, 1836 by-election, 1837
Norfolk East 1832, 1835, 1837, 1841
Norfolk West 1835, 1837
Northamptonshire 1831
Northamptonshire North 1832, 1837
Norwich 1835
Poole 1835
Preston 1835, 1837, 1841
Radnorshire 1835
Rutland 1841
Shrewsbury 1835
Somerset West 1835, 1837
Staffordshire North 1832, 1837
Sussex East 1832, 1837
Tewkesbury 1832, 1835
Totnes 1837
Westmorland 1837
Winchester 1837
Yorkshire East Riding 1837,
Yorkshire West Riding 1835 by-election, 1837, 1841

Newspapers and periodicals

Albion
Annual Register
Bedford Mercury
Blackburn Gazette
Blackwoods' Edinburgh Magazine
Bradford Observer
Bristol Gazette
Bristol Mercury
Champion

Chartist Circular
Cheltenham Examiner
The Conservative
County Press: for Hertfordshire, Bedfordshire, Buckinghamshire, Huntingdonshire, Cambridgeshire, Essex and Middlesex
Derby and Chesterfield Reporter
Devizes and Wiltshire Gazette
Dover Telegraph
Durham Advertiser
Durham Chronicle
Edinburgh Review
Essex Independent
Essex Standard and Colchester and County Standard
Examiner
The Globe
Gloucester Journal
Hereford Times
Ipswich Express
Ipswich Journal
Kent Gazette
Kent Herald
Kentish Chronicle
Lancaster Gazette
Leeds Intelligencer
Leeds Mercury
Leicester Chronicle
Leicester Herald
Lincoln, Boston, Gainsborough and Newark Gazette
Lincoln Gazette
Lincoln, Rutland and Stamford Mercury
Lincolnshire Chronicle and General Advertiser
Liverpool Mercury
Maidstone Gazette
Manchester Courier
Manchester Guardian
Manchester Herald
Manchester and Salford Advertiser
Metropolitan Conservative Journal
Monmouthshire Beacon
Morning Chronicle
Morning Herald
Municipal Corporation Reformer
The National, Municipal and Parochial Register
Norfolk Chronicle
Oxford Conservative

Oxford Herald
Preston Pilot
Quarterly Review
Reformed Parliament
Salisbury and Wiltshire Herald
Spectator
Staffordshire Advertiser
Staffordshire Mercury
Stamford Mercury
Standard
Surrey Standard
The Times
West Devon Standard
Westminster and Foreign Quarterly Review
Whig Dresser
Wiltshire Independent
Worcester Guardian

Official publications (in date order)
Hansard's parliamentary debates, 3rd series
Mirror of Parliament
First annual report of the poor law commissioners, London 1835
Second annual report of the poor law commissioners, London 1836
Report of the commissioners on the continuance of the commission, London 1840

Parliamentary papers
Return of inhabitant householders of Birmingham, PP 1828 (59) xxi. 1–4
Number of justices . . . distinguishing clergy and laymen, PP 1831–2 (39) xxxv. 231–72.
Electors registered, PP 1833 (189) xxvii. 21–249; PP 1834 (591) ix. 602–8; PP 1836 (190, 199, 248) xliii. 363–467; PP 1837–8 (329) xliv. 553–858; PP 1840 (272, 579) xxxix. 187–225; PP 1844 (11) xxxviii. 428–43; PP 1847 (751) xlvi. 335–44
Report on election expenses, PP 1834 (591) ix. 263–646
Reports on bribery at elections, PP 1835 (547) viii. 1–828; PP 1844 (538) xviii. 6–557; PP 1852 (1431) xxvii. 1–507; PP 1852–3 (382) viii. 73–190; PP 1854 (1703) xxii. 1–1160; PP 1870 [c.11] xxx. 9–1240
Report on Orange Institutions, PP 1835 (605), xvii. 1–459.
First report of commissioners appointed to inquire into municipal corporations of England and Wales, PP 1835 (116) xxiii. 1–798
Report from select committee on Poole borough municipal election, PP 1836 (128) xxi. 307–563
A return relating to revising barristers, PP 1836 (240) xliii. 361–2
Returns relating to Friendly Societies, PP 1837 (71) li. 91–125; PP 1842 (73) xxvi. 275–321

Second report on railways, PP 1839 (517) x. 127–745

Minutes of evidence on London and Birmingham Railway bill, PP 1839 (242) xiii. 331–458

Local taxation: returns relative to poor rates, PP 1839 (562) xliv. 1–50

Fifth report on railway communication, PP 1840 (474) xiii. 189–729

Poor law amendment act: accounts, PP 1841 (33) xxi. 53–89

Return of unions governed by local acts, PP 1841 (211, 292) xxi. 17–23

Report from select committee on election proceedings, PP 1842 (458) v. 75–262

Returns relating to unions under Gilbert's act, PP 1842 (156) xxxv. 37–44; PP 1844 (578) xl. 331–4

Report from select committee on votes of electors, PP 1846 (451) viii. 175–615

Abstract returns of the number of houses of the value of £10 . . . and the number of persons omitted from the lists of voters in 1846 for non-payment of assessed taxes, PP 1847 (243) xlvi. 333

Returns relating to electors for counties, PP 1852 (4) xlii. 303–7; PP 1857–8 (108) xlvi. 511–80; PP 1864 (203) x. 403–604; PP 1870 (360) vi. 191–370

Return relative to the condition of the people, PP 1865 (195) xlvii. 447–9

Returns relating to parliamentary boroughs, PP 1867 (136, 305) lvi. 449–69

Report from the select committee on parliamentary and municipal elections, PP 1868–9 (352) viii. 1–626

Report from the select committee on poor law guardians, PP 1878 (297) xvii. 263–692

Bills

Bills for the more effectual registration of persons entitled to vote, PP 1834 (368) ii. 163–203; PP 1835 (36, 577) ii. 583–667; PP 1836 (9, 17, 287, 310, 385) iii. 385–683; PP 1837 (14) iii. 115–70; PP 1837–8 (487, 706) iii. 633–76

A bill to render the register of electors final, PP 1836 (10) iii. 685–9; PP 1837 (320, 362) iii. 171–81

A bill to legalize certain lists of voters, PP 1836 (563) iii. 755–6

A bill to repeal so much of an act . . . as makes the right to registration in cities and boroughs conditional upon payment of poor rates and assessed taxes, PP 1837 (105) iii. 183–5

Bills to regulate the payment of rates and taxes by parliamentary electors, PP 1837 (311) iii. 187; PP 1837–8 (29) iii. 457–8

A bill to prevent persons from losing their votes at election, PP 1839 (265) iii. 355–6

A bill for establishing a court of appeal from revising barristers, PP 1839 (310) iii. 281–9

A bill for the registration of parliamentary electors, PP 1840 (321) ii. 403–48; PP 1841 (16) iii. 277–322

A bill to make further provision as to certain rights of voting, PP 1840 (322) ii. 449–50; PP 1841 (95) iii. 417–19

Statutes

An act to amend the representation of the people in England and Wales, 1832, 2 William IV c. 45

An act to settle and describe the divisions of counties and the limits of cities and boroughs, 1832, 2 and 3 William IV c. 64

An act for the amendment and better administration of the laws relating to the poor in England and Wales', 1834, 4 and 5 William IV c. 76

An act to limit the time of taking the poll in boroughs, 1835, 5 and 6 William IV c. 36

An act to provide for the regulation of municipal corporations in England and Wales, 1835, 5 and 6 William IV c. 76

An act to regulate parochial assessments, 1836, 6 and 7 William IV c. 96

An act to legalize certain lists of voters, 1836, 6 and 7 William IV c. 101

An act for rendering more easy the taking the poll at county elections, 1836, 6 and 7 William IV c. 102

An act to make temporary provision for the boundaries of certain boroughs, 1836, 6 and 7 William IV c. 103

An act to amend an act for the regulation of municipal corporations in England and Wales, 1837, 7 William IV and 1 Victoria c. 78

An act to amend the jurisdiction for the trial of election petitions, 1839, 2 and 3 Victoria c. 38

An act to define the notice of elections, 1840, 3 and 4 Victoria c. 81

An act for the prevention of bribery at elections, 1841, 4 and 5 Victoria c. 57

An act to amend the law for the trial of controverted elections, 1841, 4 and 5 Victoria c. 58

An act for the better discovery and prevention of bribery and treating in the election of members of parliament, 1842, 5 and 6 Victoria c. 102

An act to amend the law for the registration of persons entitled to vote, 1843, 6 and 7 Victoria c. 18

An act to regulate times of payment of rates and taxes by parliamentary electors, 1848, 11 and 12 Victoria c. 90

An act to consolidate and amend the laws relating to bribery, treating, and undue influence at elections, 1854, 17 and 18 Victoria c. 102

Contemporary books and articles

A Conservative elector, *Fruits of Whig legislation as already ripened in the new poor law and marriage acts*, London 1837

Anon, *Municipal characters or waggeries to the Whigs*, Norwich 1836

Anon, *North Derbyshire electors' manual*, 1839

Anon, *The assembled Commons or parliamentary biographer with an abstract of the law of election . . . by a member of the Middle Temple*, London 1838

Anon, *The county voters' manual; or a practical guide for the annual registration of voters in counties by a barrister of the temple*, London 1842

Anon, *The parliamentary indicator: containing a list of the members returned to the Commons' House of Parliament*, London 1835

Anon, *The Reform Act with explanatory notes and an analysis by a barrister*, London 1832

Anon, *The Reform Bill rendered plain, being the substance of every clause . . . by a barrister at law*, London 1832

Anon, *What should the Lords do with the corporation reform bill? With tables showing the extent of its proposed constituency in comparison with the parliamentary franchise*, London 1835

Aspinall, A. (ed.), *The correspondence of Charles Arbuthnot*, London 1941

——— (ed.), *Three early nineteenth century diaries*, London 1952

Bagehot, Walter, *Essays on parliamentary reform*, London 1896

Baines, Sir E., *The life of Edward Baines*, London 1859

Battye, Thomas, *A disclosure of parochial abuse*, Manchester 1796

Boase, W. M., *Hints on the exercise of the elective franchise addressed to the electors of the united borough of Penryn and Falmouth*, Falmouth 1835

Bourne, Kenneth (ed.), *The letters of the third viscount Palmerston to Laurence and Elizabeth Sulivan, 1804–1863*, London 1979

Campbell, Lord, *Lives of the chancellors and keepers of the great seal of England*, London 1869

Carpenter, William, *The elector's manual*, London 1832

Chambers, J. D., *An examination into certain errors and anomalies in the principles and detail of the registration clauses of the Reform Act with suggestions for their amendment*, London 1832

——— *The new bills for the registration of electors critically examined*, London 1836

——— *A complete dictionary of the law and practice of elections*, London 1837

Cockburn, A. E., *Questions on election law arising from the Reform Act with the decisions of the revising barristers*, London 1834

Cooke, W. H., *Plain instructions for overseers*, London 1835

Coppock, James, *The electors' manual; or plain directions by which every man may know his own rights, and preserve them*, London 1835

Cox, Edward W., *The law and practice of registration and elections*, London 1847

Deacon, Edward E., *A letter to the rt. hon. Sir James Graham bt. MP on the bill now pending before the House of Commons for the more effectual registration of voters in the election of members of parliament in England and Wales*, London 1837

Delane, W. F. A., *A collection of decisions in the courts for revising the lists of electors*, London 1834, 1836

Dillon, Sir John Joseph, *Horae icenae: being the lucubrations of a winter's evening on the result of the general election of 1835*, London 1835

Disraeli, Benjamin, *Coningsby, or the new generation*, London 1844, rev. edn, Harmondsworth 1983

——— *Sybil, or the two nations*, London 1845, rev. edn, Harmondsworth 1980

——— *Lord George Bentinck, a political biography*, London 1852, rev. edn, London 1905

——— and Sarah Disraeli, *A year at Hartlebury or the election*, London 1834, rev. edn, London 1983

Dod, Charles R., *Dod's parliamentary companion*, London 1833–

Elliott, George Percy, *A practical treatise on the qualifications and registration of parliamentary electors in England and Wales*, London 1839

Fagan, Louis Alexander, *The Reform Club: its founders and architect, 1836–86*, London 1887

Glen, W. Cunningham, *The general consolidated and other orders of the poor law commissioners*, London 1871

Gore, John (ed.), *Creevey selected and re-edited*, London 1948

Grant, James, *The great metropolis, by the author of 'random recollections of the Lords and Commons'*, London 1837

Jeffery, R. W. (ed.), *Dyott's diary, 1781–1845*, London 1907

Jennings, Louis J. (ed.), *The Croker papers*, London 1884

Kriegel, Abraham D. (ed.), *The Holland House diaries, 1831–1840*, London 1977

Macaulay, T. B., *The complete works of Lord Macaulay*, London 1898

Mackay, Alexander, *Electoral districts or the appointment of the representation of the country on the basis of its population, being an enquiry into the working of the Reform Bill*, London 1848

Manning, William M., *Proceedings in courts of revision in the Isle of Wight before James Manning Esq. revising barrister: to which are added cases decided in South Hants in 1835*, London 1836

Martin, Sir Theodore, *A life of Lord Lyndhurst from letters and papers in possession of his family*, London 1883

Marx, Karl, 'The elections in England, Tories and Whigs', in *Karl Marx and Frederick Engels on Britain*, Moscow 1953, 349–55

———— 'Lord John Russell', in *Marx and Engels on Britain*, 426–45

Molesworth, W. N., *The history of the Reform Bill of 1832*, London 1865, rev. edn, Clifton, NJ 1972

Montagu, Basil and W. J. Neale, *The law of parliamentary elections*, London 1839

Oldfield, T. H. B., *Representative history of Great Britain and Ireland*, London 1816

Osborne, S. G., *Hints to the charitable, being practical observations on the proper regulation of private charity*, London 1838

Parker, C. S. (ed.), *The life of Sir Robert Peel from his private papers*, London 1899

Paul, William, *A history of the origin and progress of operative Conservative societies*, Leeds 1839

Paynter, T., *The practice at elections being plain instructions*, London 1837

Peel, Sir Robert, *Speeches . . . during his administration, 1834–1835*, London 1835

———— *Address . . . to the electors of the borough of Tamworth on the close of the poll, July 25 1837*, Tamworth 1837

———— *A correct report of the addresses . . . to the electors of Tamworth, July 24 1837, and August 7 1837*, Tamworth 1837

Price, George, *Complete election guide*, London 1832

Prideaux, Charles Greville, *An act to amend the law for the registration of voters*, London 1843

Reeve, Henry (ed.), *The Greville memoirs*, London 1874–87

Reid, Stuart J., *Life and letters of the first earl of Durham, 1792–1840*, London 1906

Rogers, F. J. N., *Parliamentary Reform Act with notes*, London 1832

———— *The law and practice of elections and election committees*, London 1837, 1841

Rowe, William, *The act for the amendment of the representation of the people in England and Wales*, London 1832

Russell, William, *A treatise on the Reform Act with practical directions to overseers and town-clerks*, London 1832

Sanders, Lloyd C. (ed.), *Lord Melbourne's papers*, London 1890

Sheppard, H. I., *The law and practice relative to the elections of members of parliament*, London 1836

Simpson, M. C. M. (ed.), *Correspondence and conversations of Alexis de Tocqueville with Nassau William Senior from 1834 to 1859*, London 1872

Smith, Nowell C. (ed.), *The letters of Sydney Smith*, Oxford 1953

Stephens, A. J., *A practical treatise on the law of elections, with directions for candidates, electors, agents, returning officers, overseers, claimants, and objectors*, London 1840

Timbs, John, *Club life of London*, London 1886

Torrens, W. T. McCullagh (ed.), *Memoirs of the rt. hon. William second viscount Melbourne*, London 1878

Toulmin Smith, Joshua, *The parish: its obligations and powers: its officers and their duties*, London 1854

Wade, John, *Appendix to the black book: an exposition of the principles and practices of the reform ministry and parliament*, London 1835

Walmsley, Hugh M., *The life of Sir Joshua Walmsley*, London 1879

Walpole, Spencer, *The life of Lord John Russell*, London 1889

Warren, Samuel (ed.), *Select extracts from Blackstone's commentaries*, London 1837

Wideawake, Weasal, *King versus people . . . certain provisions of the municipal corporations bill*, London 1835

Wilson, John, *An account of the extraordinary and unlawful proceedings resorted to in the election of a guardian for the township of Boddicot*, Banbury 1840

Wilson, Philip Whitwell (ed.), *The Greville diary*, New York 1927

Wordsworth, Charles, *The law and practice of elections (for England and Wales) as altered by the Reform Act, including the practice on election petitions*, London 1832

Works of reference

Acworth, W. M., *The railways of England*, London 1889

Anon, *The clerical guide or ecclesiastical directory*, London 1822

Aspinall, A. and E. A. Smith (eds), *English historical documents*, XI: *1783–1832*, London 1971

Bateman, J., *Great landowners of Great Britain and Ireland*, London 1883

Camps, Anthony J., *Poll books: a list of those in the library of the Society of Genealogists*, London 1961

Cheffins, R. H. A., *Parliamentary constituencies and their registers since 1832*, London 1998

Corpe, Stella and Ann Oakley (eds), *The freemen of Canterbury, 1800–35, compiled from Canterbury city archives*, Canterbury 1990

Cox, *The clergy list for 1844*, London 1844

Craig, F. W. S (ed.), *British parliamentary election results, 1832–1885*, London 1977

—— *British electoral facts, 1832–1980*, Chichester 1981

Crosby, George, *Crosby's parliamentary record*, York 1841

Dod, Charles R., *Dod's electoral facts from 1832 to 1853*, ed. H. J. Hanham, Brighton 1972

Foster, John, *Index ecclesiasticus, 1800–1840*, Oxford 1890

Gibson, Jeremy and Colin Rogers, *Electoral registers since 1832; and burgess rolls*, Birmingham 1990

—— *Poll books, 1696–1872: a directory to holdings in Great Britain*, Birmingham 1990

Gross, Charles, *A bibliography of British municipal history*, Leicester 1966

HMC, *Papers of British cabinet ministers, 1782–1900* (Guides to sources for British history, 1), London 1982

—— *Papers of British politicians, 1782–1900* (Guides to sources for British history 7), London 1989

McCalmont, F. H., *The parliamentary poll book: British election results, 1832–1918*, ed. J. Vincent and M. Stenton, Brighton 1971

Rallings, Colin and Michael Thrasher (eds), *Local elections handbook*, Plymouth 1985–

Sims, John (ed.), *A handlist of British parliamentary poll books*, Leicester 1984

Thorne, R. G. (ed.), *The House of Commons, 1790–1820*, London 1986

VCH, *Bedfordshire*, London 1908

VCH, *Wiltshire*, Oxford 1957

VCH, *Staffordshire*, Oxford 1979

White, William, *Directory of Staffordshire*, Sheffield 1834

Youngs, Frederick A. Jr, *Guide to the local administrative units of England*, I: *Southern England*, London 1979

—— *Guide to the local administrative units of England*, II: *Northern England*, London 1991

Secondary sources

Alington, Cyril, *Twenty years: being a study in the development of the party system between 1815 and 1835*, Oxford 1921

Aspinall, A., 'English party organisation in the early nineteenth century', *EHR* xli (1926), 389–411

—— *Lord Brougham and the Whig party*, Manchester 1939

—— *Politics and the press, c. 1780–1850*, London 1949

Aydelotte, W. O. (ed.), *The history of parliamentary behavior*, Princeton, NJ 1977

Baskerville, S., P. Adman and K. Beedham, 'Manuscript poll books and English county elections in the first age of party: a reconsideration of their provenance and purpose', *Archives* xix (1991), 384–403

Beales, D. E. D., 'Parliamentary parties and the "independent" member, 1810–1860', in Robson, *Ideas and institutions of Victorian Britain*, 1–19
—— *The political parties of nineteenth century Britain*, London 1971
—— 'Peel, Russell and Reform', *HJ* iv (1974), 873–82
—— 'The electorate before and after 1832: the right to vote, and the opportunity', *PH* xi (1992), 139–50
Best, G. F. A., 'The Whigs and the church establishment in the age of Grey and Holland', *History* xlv (1960), 103–18
Black, E. C., *The association: British extra-parliamentary political organization*, Cambridge, Mass. 1963
Blake, Robert, *Disraeli*, London 1966
—— *The Conservative party from Peel to Churchill*, London 1970
Blondel, Jean, *Voters, parties and leaders*, Harmondsworth 1963
Bourne, J. M., *Patronage and society in nineteenth century England*, London 1986
Bowle, John, *Politics and opinion in the nineteenth-century*, London 1963
Bradfield, B. T., 'Sir Richard Vyvyan and the country gentlemen, 1830–1834', *EHR* lxxxiii (1968), 729–43
Brent, Richard, *Liberal Anglican politics: Whiggery, religion, and Reform, 1830–1841*, Oxford 1987
—— 'The Whigs and Protestant dissent in the decade of reform: the case of church rates, 1833–1841', *EHR* cii (1987), 887–910
—— 'New Whigs in old bottles', *PH* xi (1992), 151–6
Brett, Peter, 'Political dinners in early nineteenth-century Britain: platform, meeting place and battleground', *History* lxxxi (1996), 527–52
Brightfield M. F., *John Wilson Croker*, London 1940
Brock, Michael, *The Great Reform Act*, London 1973
Brose, Olive J., *Church and parliament: the reshaping of the Church of England, 1828–1860*, London 1959
Brundage, Anthony, 'The landed interest and the New Poor Law: a reappraisal of the revolution in government', *EHR* lxxxvii (1972), 27–48
—— *The making of the New Poor Law: the politics of inquiry, enactment and implementation, 1832–39*, London 1978
—— *England's 'Prussian minister': Edwin Chadwick and the politics of government growth, 1832–1854*, University Park, Penn. 1988
Buckley, Jessie K., *Joseph Parkes of Birmingham*, London 1926
Bulmer-Thomas, I., *The growth of the British party system*, London 1965
Bush, Graham, *Bristol and its municipal government, 1820–51*, Bristol 1976
Butler, D. E., *The electoral system in Britain since 1918*, Oxford 1963
—— *British general elections since 1945*, Oxford 1989
Butler, J. R. M., *The passing of the Reform Bill*, London 1914
Cannadine, David, *Lords and landlords: the aristocracy and the towns, 1774–1967*, Leicester 1980
—— (ed.), *Patricians, power and politics in nineteenth-century towns*, Leicester 1982
Cannan, Edwin, *A history of local rates in England*, London 1912

Cannon, John, *Parliamentary reform, 1640–1832*, Cambridge 1973

Chadwick, Owen, *The Victorian Church*, London 1966

Christie, Ian R., *British 'non-elite' MPs, 1715–1820*, Oxford 1995

Christie, O. J., *The transition from aristocracy, 1832–1867*, London 1927

Clark, George Kitson, *Peel and the Conservative party*, London 1929

────── *The making of Victorian England*, London 1962

────── *Churchmen and the condition of England, 1832–1885*, London 1973

Clark, J. C. D., *English society, 1688–1832*, Cambridge 1985

Close, D. H., 'The formation of a two-party alignment in the House of Commons', *EHR* lxxxiv (1969), 257–77

────── 'The rise of the Conservatives in the age of reform', *BIHR* xlv (1972), 89–103

Clive, John, *Scotch reviewers*, London 1957

Coleman, Bruce, *Conservatism and the Conservative party in the nineteenth century*, London 1988

Conacher, J. B., *The Peelites and the party system*, London 1972

────── (ed.), *The emergence of British parliamentary democracy in the nineteenth-century*, New York 1971

Condon, Mary, 'The Irish Church and the reform ministries', *JBS* iv (1964), 120–42

Cooper, Leonard, *Radical Jack: the life of the first earl of Durham*, London 1959

Cowherd, Raymond G., *The politics of English dissent*, New York 1956

Cox, Gary W., *The efficient secret: the cabinet and the development of political parties in Victorian England*, Cambridge 1987

Cragoe, Matthew, *An Anglican aristocracy: the moral economy of the landed estate in Carmarthenshire, 1832–1895*, Oxford 1996

Crosby, T. L., *English farmers and the politics of protection, 1815–52*, Hassocks 1977

Davis, Richard, W., *Political change and continuity, 1760–1885: a Buckinghamshire study*, Newton Abbot 1972

────── 'The Whigs and the idea of electoral deference: some further thoughts on the Great Reform Act', *Durham University Journal* xxxvi (1974), 79–91

────── 'The mid-nineteenth century electoral structure', *Albion* viii (1976), 142–53

────── 'Toryism to Tamworth: the triumph of reform, 1827–1835', *Albion* xii (1980), 132–46

Dean, David and Clyve Jones (eds), *Parliament and locality, 1660–1939*, Edinburgh 1998

Digby, Anne, 'The rural poor law', in Fraser, *New Poor Law*, 149–70

Doyle, Patrick J., 'The general election of 1841: the representation of south Staffordshire', *Transactions of the South Staffordshire Archaeological and Historical Society* xii (1970–1), 57–61

Drake, Michael, 'The mid-Victorian voter', *Journal of Interdisciplinary History* i (1971), 473–90

Dunkley, P, 'The landed interest and the New Poor Law: a critical note', *EHR* lxxxviii (1973), 836–41

Eastwood, David, 'Toryism, Reform, and political culture in Oxfordshire, 1826–1837', *PH* vii (1988), 98–121

——— 'The making of the New Poor Law redivivus: debate', *Past and Present* cxxvii (1990), 184–94.

——— 'Peel and the Tory party reconsidered', *History Today* (Mar. 1992), 27–33

——— *Governing rural England: tradition and transformation in local government, 1780–1840*, Oxford 1994

——— 'Contesting the politics of deference: the rural electorate, 1820–60', in Lawrence and Taylor, *Party, state and society*, 27–49

——— *Government and community in the English provinces, 1700–1870*, London 1997

——— 'The age of uncertainty: Britain in the early-nineteenth-century', *Transactions of the Royal Historical Society* viii (1998), 91–115

——— 'Parliament and locality: representation and responsibility in late-Hanoverian England', in Dean and Jones, *Parliament and locality*, 68–81

Edsall, N. C., *The anti-poor law movement, 1833–44*, Manchester 1971

Ellens, J. P., *Religious routes to Gladstonian Liberalism: the church rate conflict in England and Wales, 1832–1868*, University Park, Penn. 1994

Erickson, A. B., *The public career of Sir James Graham*, Oxford 1952

Escott, Henry Sweet, *Club makers and club members*, London 1914

Evans, Eric J., *Sir Robert Peel: statesmanship, power and party*, London 1991

——— *The Great Reform Act of 1832*, London 1994

Feiling, Keith Grahame, *The second Tory party, 1714–1832*, London 1959

Finlayson, G. B. A. M., 'The municipal corporation commission and the report, 1833–35', *BIHR* xxxvi (1963), 36–52

——— 'The politics of municipal reform, 1835', *EHR* lxxxi (1966), 673–92

——— 'Joseph Parkes of Birmingham, 1796–1865: a study in philosophic radicalism', *BIHR* xlvi (1973), 186–201

——— *England in the eighteen thirties, decade of reform*, London 1981

Fisher, J. R., 'Issues and influence: two by-elections in south Nottinghamshire in the mid-nineteenth century', *HJ* xxiv (1981), 155–65

——— 'The limits of deference: agricultural communities in a mid-nineteenth century election campaign', *JBS* xxi (1981), 90–105

——— 'The Tory revival of the 1830s: an uncontested election in south Nottinghamshire', *Midland History* vi (1981), 95–108

Flick, Carlos, *The Birmingham Political Union and the movements for reform in Britain, 1830–1839*, Hamden, Conn. 1978

Foster, D., 'The politics of uncontested elections: north Lancashire 1832–1865', *Northern History* xiii (1977), 232–47

Foster, R. E., 'Peel, Disraeli and the 1835 Taunton by-election', *Transactions of the Somerset Archaeological and Natural History Society* cxxvi (1982), 111–18

Francis, John, *A history of the English railway: its social relations and revelations, 1820–1845*, London 1851

Fraser, D., 'The fruits of reform: Leeds politics in the eighteen-thirties', *Northern History* vii (1972), 89–111

——— The evolution of the British welfare state: a history of social policy since the industrial revolution, London 1973

——— 'The poor law as a political institution', in Fraser, New Poor Law, 111–27.

——— Urban politics in Victorian England: the structure of politics in Victorian cities, Leicester 1976

——— (ed.), The New Poor Law in the nineteenth century, London 1976

——— (ed.), Municipal reform and the industrial city, Leicester 1982

Gash, Norman, 'F. R. Bonham: Conservative "political secretary", 1832–47', EHR lxiii (1948), 502–22

——— Politics in the age of Peel: a study in the technique of parliamentary representation, 1830–1850, London 1953

——— Mr secretary Peel: the life of Sir Robert Peel to 1830, London 1961

——— Reaction and reconstruction in English politics, 1832–1852, Oxford 1965

——— Sir Robert Peel: the life of Sir Robert Peel after 1830, London 1972

——— Aristocracy and people: Britain, 1815–65, London 1979

——— 'The organization of the Conservative party, 1832–1846, part I: the parliamentary organization', PH i (1982), 137–59

——— 'The organization of the Conservative Party, 1832–1846, part II: the electoral organization', PH ii (1983), 131–52

Gattrell, V. A. C., 'Incorporation and the pursuit of Liberal hegemony in Manchester, 1790–1839', in Fraser, Municipal reform, 16–60

Golby, John, 'A great electioneer and his motives: the 4th duke of Newcastle', HJ viii (1965), 201–18

Graham, A. H., 'The Lichfield House compact, 1835', Irish Historical Studies xii (1961), 209–25

Grego, Joseph, A history of parliamentary elections and electioneering in the old days, London 1886

Gwyn, William B., Democracy and the cost of politics, London 1962

Halévy, Elie, A history of the English people, 1830–1841, London 1927

Hamer, D. A., The politics of electoral pressure: a study in the history of Victorian reform agitations, Brighton 1977

Hanham, H. J., Elections and party management: politics in the time of Disraeli and Gladstone, London 1959

——— The reformed electoral system in Great Britain, 1832–1914 (Historical Association pamphlet, 69), London 1968

Hart, Jenifer, Proportional representation: critics of the British electoral system, 1820–1945, Oxford 1992

Hawkins, Angus, Parliament, party and the art of politics in Britain, 1855–59, Stanford 1987

——— ' "Parliamentary government" and Victorian political parties, c. 1830–c. 1880', EHR civ (1989), 638–69

Heesom, Alan, ' "Legitimate" versus "illegitimate" influences: aristocratic electioneering in mid-Victorian Britain', PH vii (1988), 282–305

Hennock, E. P., Fit and proper persons: ideal and reality in nineteenth-century urban government, London 1973

Hill, B.W., *British parliamentary parties, 1742–1832*, London 1985

Hill, R. L., *Toryism and the people, 1832–1846*, London 1929

Hilton, Boyd, 'Peel: a reappraisal', *HJ* xxii (1979), 585–614

—— *The age of atonement: the influence of evangelicalism on social and economic thought, 1795–1865*, Oxford 1988

Hogarth, C. E., 'The Derbyshire parliamentary elections of 1832', *Derbyshire Archaeological Journal* lxxxix (1969), 68–85

—— 'The 1835 elections in Derbyshire', *Derbyshire Archaeological Journal* xciv (1974), 45–59

—— 'Derby and Derbyshire elections, 1837–47', *Derbyshire Archaeological Journal* xcv (1975), 48–58

Hoppen, K. Theodore, *Elections, politics, and society in Ireland, 1832–1885*, Oxford 1984

—— 'The franchise and electoral politics in England and Ireland, 1832–1885', *History* lxx (1985), 202–17

—— 'Roads to democracy: electioneering and corruption in nineteenth-century England and Ireland', *History* lxxxi (1996), 553–71

Hunt, J. W., *Reaction and Reform, 1815–1841*, London 1972

Jaggard, Edwin, 'Cornwall politics, 1826–1832: another face of reform?', *JBS* xxii (1983), 80–97

—— *Cornwall politics in the age of reform, 1790–1885*, Woodbridge 1999

Jenkins, Brian, *Henry Goulburn, 1784–1856: a political biography*, Montreal 1996

Jenkins, T. A., *The Liberal ascendancy, 1830–1886*, London 1994

—— *Parliament, party and politics in Victorian Britain*, Manchester 1996

—— *Sir Robert Peel*, London 1999

—— 'The whips in the early-Victorian House of Commons', *PH* xix (2000), 259–86

Jennings, W. Ivor, *Party politics*, I: *Appeal to the people*; II: *The growth of parties*; III: *The stuff of politics*, Cambridge 1962

Jephson, H., *The platform: its rise and progress*, London 1892

Johnson, D. W. J., 'Sir James Graham and the "Derby Dilly" ', *University of Birmingham Historical Journal* iv (1953–4), 66–80

Jowitt, J. A., 'Parliamentary politics in Halifax, 1832–47', *Northern History* xii (1976), 172–201

Kebbel, T. E., *A history of Toryism from 1783 to 1881*, London 1886

Keith-Lucas, Bryan, *The English local government franchise: a short history*, Oxford 1952

—— *English local government in the nineteenth and twentieth centuries* (Historical Association pamphlet, 90), London 1977

Kemp, Betty, 'The general election of 1841', *History* xxxviii (1952), 146–57

Kent, G. B., 'The beginnings of party political organization in Staffordshire, 1832–1841', *North Staffordshire Journal of Field Studies* i (1961), 86–100

Kerr, D. A., *Peel, priests, and politics*, Oxford 1982

Kriegel, Abraham D., 'The politics of the Whigs in opposition, 1834–1835', *JBS* vii (1968), 65–91

Lambert, John, 'Parliamentary franchises, past and present', *Nineteenth Century* xxvi (1889), 942–62

Large, D., 'The decline of "the party of the Crown" and the rise of parties in the House of Lords, 1783–1837', *EHR* lxxviii (1963), 669–95

Lawrence, Jon, *Speaking for the people: party, language and popular politics in England, 1867–1914*, Cambridge 1998

—— and Miles Taylor (eds), *Party, state and society: electoral behaviour in Britain since 1820*, Aldershot 1997

Le May, G. H. L., *The Victorian constitution: conventions, usages and contingencies*, London 1979

Lipman, V. D., *Local government areas, 1834–1945*, Oxford 1949

Lopatin, Nancy, 'Political unions and the Great Reform Act', *PH* x (1991), 105–23

—— *Political unions, popular politics and the Great Reform Act of 1832*, London 1999

Lubenow, William C., *The politics of government growth: early Victorian attitudes toward state intervention, 1833–1848*, Newton Abbot 1971

McCarthy, Justin, *A history of our own times*, London 1912

Maccoby, S., *English radicalism, 1832–52*, London 1935

McCord, Norman, 'Gateshead politics in the age of reform', *Northern History* iv (1969), 167–83

—— 'Some aspects of north-east England in the nineteenth century', *Northern History* vii (1972), 73–88

MacDonagh, Oliver, *Early Victorian government, 1830–1870*, London 1977

McDowell, R. B., *British Conservatism, 1832–1914*, London 1959

McNulty, D., 'Class and politics in Bath, 1832–48', *Southern History* viii (1986), 112–29

Machin, G. I. T., *The Catholic question in English politics, 1820–1830*, Oxford 1964

—— *Politics and the Churches in Great Britain, 1832 to 1868*, Oxford 1977

Mandler, Peter, *Aristocratic government in the age of Reform: Whigs and Liberals, 1830–1852*, Oxford 1990

Mendilow, Jonathon, *The romantic tradition in British political thought*, London 1986

Midwinter, E. C., *Social administration in Lancashire, 1830–1860: poor law, public health and police*, Manchester 1969

Mitchell, Austin, *The Whigs in opposition, 1815–1830*, Oxford 1967

Mitchell, Jeremy C. and James Cornford, 'The political demography of Cambridge', *Albion* ix (1977), 242–72

Mitchell, Leslie, *Holland House*, London 1980

Mitchell, L. G., 'Foxite politics and the Great Reform Bill', *EHR* cviii (1993), 338–64

Moneypenny, W. F. and G. E. Buckle, *The life of Benjamin Disraeli, earl of Beaconsfield*, London 1910–20

Moore, D. C., 'The other face of reform', *Victorian Studies* v (1961–2), 7–34

—————— 'Concession or cure: the sociological premises of the first Reform Act', *HJ* ix (1966), 39–59

—————— 'Social structure, political structure, and public opinion in mid-Victorian England', in Robson, *Ideas and institutions of Victorian Britain*, 20–57

—————— 'Political morality in mid-nineteenth century England: concepts, norms, and violations', *Victorian Studies* xiii (1969–70), 5–36

—————— 'The matter of the missing contests: towards a theory of the mid-19th century British political system', *Albion* vi (1974), 93–119

—————— *The politics of deference: a study of the mid-nineteenth century English political system*, Hassocks 1976

Morley, John, *The life of William Ewart Gladstone*, London 1903

—————— *The life of Richard Cobden*, London 1908

Munford, W. A., *William Ewart MP, 1789–1869: portrait of a Radical*, London 1960

Newbould, Ian D. C., 'William IV and the dismissal of the Whigs, 1834', *Canadian Journal of History* xi (1976), 311–30

—————— 'Sir Robert Peel and the Conservative party: a study in failure?', *EHR* xcviii (1983), 529–57

—————— 'The emergence of a two-party system in England from 1830 to 1841: roll call and reconsideration', *Parliaments, Estates and Representation* v (1985), 25–31

—————— 'Whiggery and the growth of party 1830–1841: organization and the challenge of reform', *PH* iv (1985), 137–56

—————— *Whiggery and Reform, 1830–1841: the politics of government*, London 1990

Nicholas, H. G. (ed.), *To the hustings: election scenes from English fiction*, London 1956

Nicholls, Sir George, *A history of the English poor law*, London 1904

Nossiter, T. J., *Influence, opinion, and political idioms in reformed England: case studies from the north-east, 1832–1874*, Hassocks 1975

O'Gorman, Frank, *The emergence of the British two-party system, 1760–1832*, London 1982

—————— 'Electoral deference in "unreformed" England: 1760–1832', *Journal of Modern History* lvi (1984), 391–429

—————— 'The unreformed electorate of Hanoverian England: the mid-eighteenth century to the Reform Act of 1832', *Social History* xl (1986), 33–52

—————— 'Party politics in the early nineteenth century', *EHR* cii (1987), 63–84

—————— *Voters, patrons, and parties: the unreformed electorate of Hanoverian England, 1734–1832*, Oxford 1989

—————— 'The electorate before and after 1832: a reply', *PH* xii (1993), 171–83

Olney, Richard J., *Lincolnshire politics, 1832–1885*, Oxford 1973

Osborne, Bertram, *Justices of the peace, 1361–1848*, Shaftesbury 1960

Ostrogorski, M., *Democracy and the organisation of political parties*, London 1902

Palmer, Roy, *The sound of history: songs and social comment*, Oxford 1988

Paterson, David, *A Victorian election: Warwick 1868* (University of Warwick

Open Studies: Coventry Historical Association pamphlet, 12), Coventry 1982

Patterson, A. Temple, 'Electoral corruption in early Victorian Leicester', *History* xxxi (1946), 113–24

―――― *Radical Leicester: a history of Leicester, 1780–1850*, Leicester 1954

Patterson, M. W., *Sir Francis Burdett and his times, 1770–1844*, London 1931

Philbin, J. Holladay, *Parliamentary representation, 1832 England and Wales*, New Haven, Conn. 1965

Phillips, John A., *Electoral behaviour in unreformed England: plumpers, splitters and straights*, Princeton, NJ 1982

―――― 'The many faces of reform: the Reform Bill and the electorate', *PH* i (1982), 115–35

―――― 'Poll books and English electoral behaviour', in Sims, *A handlist of British parliamentary poll books*, pp. v–xviii

―――― 'Partisan behaviour in adversity: voters in Lewes during the reform era', *PH* vi (1987), 262–79

―――― 'From municipal matters to parliamentary principles: eighteenth-century borough politics in Maidstone', *JBS* xxvii (1988), 327–51

―――― *The Great Reform Bill in the boroughs: English electoral behaviour, 1818–1841*, Oxford 1992

―――― and Charles Wetherell, 'The Great Reform Bill of 1832 and the rise of partisanship', *Journal of Modern History* lxiii (1991), 621–46

―――― and Charles Wetherell, 'Parliamentary parties and municipal politics: 1835 and the party system', in Phillips, *Computing parliamentary history*, 48–85

―――― and Charles Wetherell, 'The Great Reform Act of 1832 and the political modernization of England', *American Historical Review* c (1995), 411–36

―――― 'Unintended consequences: parliamentary blueprints in the hands of provincial builders', in Dean and Jones, *Parliament and locality*, 92–105

―――― (ed.), *Computing parliamentary history: George III to Victoria*, Edinburgh 1994

Pinto-Duschinsky, Michael, *British political finance, 1830–1980*, Washington 1981

―――― and Shelley Pinto-Duschinsky, *Voter registration: problems and solutions*, London 1987

Porritt, Edward, 'Barriers against British democracy', *Political Science Quarterly* xxvi (1911), 1–31

―――― and Anne Porritt, *The unreformed House of Commons*, Cambridge 1909

Prest, John, *Lord John Russell*, London 1972

―――― *Politics in the age of Cobden*, London 1977

―――― *Liberty and locality: parliament, permissive legislation and ratepayers' democracies in the nineteenth century*, Oxford 1990

―――― 'The promulgation of the statutes', in Dean and Jones, *Parliament and locality*, 106–12

Prothero, Iorwerth, *Artisans and politics in early nineteenth-century London: John Gast and his times*, Folkestone 1979

Pugh, Martin, *The Tories and the people, 1880–1935*, Oxford 1985

————— *The evolution of the British electoral system, 1832–1987* (Historical Association pamphlet, 15), London 1990

Pulzer, Peter G. P., *Political representation and elections: parties and voting in Great Britain*, London 1967

Rae, W. Fraser, 'Political clubs and party organisation', *Nineteenth Century* iii (1878), 908–32

Read, Donald, *Press and people, 1790–1850: opinion in three English cities*, London 1961

————— *Peel and the Victorians*, Oxford 1987

Rees, R. D., 'Electioneering ideals current in south Wales, 1790–1832', *Welsh History Review* ii (1965), 233–50

Robbins, Keith, *Nineteenth-century Britain: integration and diversity*, Oxford 1988

Roberts, David, *Paternalism in early Victorian England*, London 1979

Robson, Robert (ed.), *Ideas and institutions of Victorian Britain*, London 1967

Rogers, Nicholas, *Whigs and cities*, Oxford 1989

Rose, M. E., 'The Anti-Poor Law movement in the north of England', *Northern History* i (1966), 70–91

Rowe, Violet, 'The Hertford borough bill of 1834', *PH* xi (1992), 88–107

Rydz, D. L., *The parliamentary agents: a history*, London 1979

Sainty, John and Gary W. Cox, 'The identification of government whips in the House of Commons, 1830–1905', *PH* xvi (1997), 339–58

Salmon, Philip, 'Local politics and partisanship: the electoral impact of municipal reform, 1835', *PH* xix (2000), 357–76

Schonhardt-Bailey, Cheryl, 'Linking constituency interests to legislative voting behaviour: the role of district economic and electoral composition in the repeal of the corn laws', in Phillips, *Computing parliamentary history*, 86–118

Seymour, Charles, *Electoral reform in England and Wales: the development and operation of the parliamentary franchise*, New Haven, Conn. 1915

Shattock, Joanne, *Politics and reviewers: the* Edinburgh *and the* Quarterly *in the early Victorian age*, Leicester 1989

Simmons, Jack, *The railways of Britain*, New York 1968

Simon, Shena D., *A century of city government: Manchester, 1838–1938*, London 1938

Sims, John (ed.), *A handlist of British parliamentary poll books*, Leicester 1984

Smellie, K. B., *A history of local government*, London 1963

Smith, E. A., 'The election agent in English politics, 1734–1832', *EHR* lxxxiv (1969), 12–35

————— *Lord Grey, 1764–1845*, Oxford 1990

————— *Reform or revolution? A diary of reform in England, 1830–32*, Stroud 1992

————— *Wellington and the Arbuthnots*, Stroud 1994

Smith, John Milton, 'Earl Grey's cabinet and the objectives of parliamentary reform', *HJ* xv (1972), 55–74

Southgate, Donald, *The passing of the Whigs, 1832–1886*, London 1962

————— (ed.), *The Conservative leadership, 1832–1932*, London 1974

Speck, W. A., *Tory and Whig: the struggle in the constituencies, 1710–1915*, London 1970

Stewart, Robert, *The foundation of the Conservative party, 1830–1867*, London 1978

——— *Henry Brougham, 1778–1868: his public career*, London 1986

——— *Party and politics, 1830–1852*, London 1989

Taylor, Miles, *The decline of British Radicalism, 1847–1860*, Oxford 1995

——— 'Interests, parties and the state: the urban electorate in England, c. 1820–72', in Lawrence and Taylor, *Party, state and society*, 50–78

——— 'The six points: Chartism and the reform of parliament', in O. Ashton, R. Fyson and S. Roberts (eds), *The Chartist legacy*, Rendlesham 1999, 1–23

Thomas, John A., *The House of Commons, 1832–1901: a study of its economic and functional character*, Cardiff 1939

——— 'The system of registration and the development of party organisation, 1832–1870', *History* xxxv (1950), 81–98

Thomas, William, *The philosophic radicals*, Oxford 1979

Thompson, Dorothy, *The Chartists: popular politics in the industrial revolution*, Aldershot 1984

Thompson, F. M. L., 'Whigs and Liberals in the West Riding, 1830–1860', *EHR* lxxiv (1959), 214–39

Tilby, A. Wyatt, *Lord John Russell: a study in civil and religious liberty*, London 1930

The Times, *The history of the Times*, I: *The thunderer in the making, 1785–1841*, London 1935

Trevelyan, G. M., *Lord Grey of the Reform Bill*, London 1920

Turberville, A. S., 'The House of Lords and the advent of democracy', *History* xxix (1944), 152–83

——— *The House of Lords in the age of reform, 1784–1837*, London 1958

Veitch, G. S., *The genesis of parliamentary reform*, London 1913, repr. 1964

Vernon, James, *Politics and the people: a study in English political culture, c. 1815–1867*, Cambridge 1993

Vincent, J. R., 'The electoral sociology of Rochdale', *Economic History Review* xvi (1963), 76–90

——— *Pollbooks: how Victorians voted*, Cambridge 1967

Wald, Kenneth, *Crosses on the ballot*, Princeton 1983

Wallas, Graham, *The life of Francis Place, 1771–1854*, London 1925

Ward, J.T., *Sir James Graham*, London 1967

Wasson, Ellis A., *Whig renaissance: Lord Althorp and the Whig party, 1782–1845*, New York 1987

Webb, Sidney and Beatrice Webb, *English local government from the revolution to the Municipal Corporations Act: the parish and the county*, London 1906

——— *English local government from the revolution to the Municipal Corporations Act: the manor and the borough*, London 1908

White, R. J. (ed.), *The Conservative tradition*, London 1964

Witmer, Helen Elizabeth, *The property qualification of members of parliament*, New York 1943

Wolffe, John, *The Protestant crusade in Great Britain, 1829–1860*, Oxford 1991

Woods, M., *A history of the Tory party*, London 1924

Wright, D. G., 'A radical borough: parliamentary politics in Bradford, 1832–41', *Northern History* iv (1969), 132–66

—— *Popular Radicalism: the working-class experience, 1780–1880*, London 1988

Wroughton, John (ed.), *Bath in the age of reform, 1830–1841*, Bath 1972

Young, Ken and Patricia Garside, *Metropolitan London: politics and urban change, 1837–1981*, London 1982

Unpublished theses

Aldridge, James, 'The parliamentary franchise at Preston and the Reform Act of 1832', BA diss. Manchester 1948

Andrews, Julia H., 'Political issues in the county of Kent, 1820–1846', MPhil. diss. London 1967

Atton, Keith, 'Municipal and parliamentary politics in Ipswich, 1818–1847', PhD diss. London 1979

Boyson, R., 'The history of poor law administration in north east Lancashire, 1834–1871', MA diss. Manchester 1960

Brett, Peter, 'The Liberal middle classes and politics in three provincial towns – Newcastle, Bristol, and York – c. 1812–1841', PhD diss. Durham 1991

Close, D. H., The elections of 1835 and 1837 in England and Wales', DPhil. diss. Oxford 1967

Coohill, Joseph, 'Ideas of the Liberal party: perceptions, agendas, and Liberal politics in the House of Commons', DPhil. diss. Oxford 1998

Cooper, Christopher J., 'Electoral politics in Grimsby, 1818–35', PhD diss. Open University 1987

Cottingham, Eve, 'The Bedford estates and agricultural politics in early Victorian England', BA diss. Oxford 1981

Courtenay, Adrian, 'Parliamentary representation and general elections in Cheltenham Spa between 1832 and 1848: a study of a pocket borough', MPhil. diss. Open University 1990

Finlayson, G. B. A. M., 'The Municipal Corporations Act, 1835', BLitt. diss. Oxford 1959

Hayes, B. D., 'Politics in Norfolk, 1750–1832', PhD diss. Cambridge 1957

Kent, G. B., 'Party politics in the county of Staffordshire during the years 1830 to 1847', MA diss. Birmingham 1959

Oxley, Geoffrey W., 'The administration of the old poor law in the west Derby hundred of Lancashire, 1601–1837', MA diss. Liverpool 1966

Radice, Paula Kim Vandersluys, 'Identification, interests and influence: voting behaviour in four English constituencies in the decade after the Great Reform Act', PhD diss. Durham 1992

Raymond, Harold Bradford, 'English political parties and electoral organization, 1832–1867', PhD diss. Harvard 1952

Richardson, Sarah, 'Independence and deference: a study of the West Riding electorate, 1832–1841', PhD diss. Leeds 1995

Salmon, Philip, 'Electoral reform at work: local politics and national parties, 1832–41', DPhil. diss. Oxford 1997

Speight, M. E., 'Politics in the borough of Colchester, 1812–1847', PhD diss. London 1969

Vernon, James, 'Politics and the people: a study in English political culture and communication, 1808–68', PhD diss. Manchester 1991

Walmsley, Philip M., 'Political, religious and social aspects of Stroud parliamentary borough, 1832–52', MLitt. diss. Bristol 1990

Walsh, David, 'Working class political integration and the Conservative party: a study of class relations and party political development in the north-west, 1800–1870', PhD diss. Salford 1991

Zimmeck, Meta, 'Chartered rights and vested interests: Reform era politics in three Sussex boroughs: Rye, Arundel and Lewes', MA diss. Sussex 1972

Index